C++

FOR DUMMIES

A Wiley Brand

7th Edition

by Stephen R. Davis

FOR DUMMIES

A Wiley Brand

C++ For Dummies®, 7th Edition

Published by: **John Wiley & Sons, Inc.,** 111 River Street, Hoboken, NJ 07030-5774, www.wiley.com

Copyright © 2014 by John Wiley & Sons, Inc., Hoboken, New Jersey

Media and software compilation copyright © 2014 by John Wiley & Sons, Inc. All rights reserved.

Published simultaneously in Canada

No part of this publication may be reproduced, stored in a retrieval system or transmitted in any form or by any means, electronic, mechanical, photocopying, recording, scanning or otherwise, except as permitted under Sections 107 or 108 of the 1976 United States Copyright Act, without the prior written permission of the Publisher. Requests to the Publisher for permission should be addressed to the Permissions Department, John Wiley & Sons, Inc., 111 River Street, Hoboken, NJ 07030, (201) 748-6011, fax (201) 748-6008, or online at http://www.wiley.com/go/permissions.

Trademarks: Wiley, For Dummies, the Dummies Man logo, Dummies.com, Making Everything Easier, and related trade dress are trademarks or registered trademarks of John Wiley & Sons, Inc. and may not be used without written permission. All other trademarks are the property of their respective owners. John Wiley & Sons, Inc. is not associated with any product or vendor mentioned in this book.

For general information on our other products and services, please contact our Customer Care Department within the U.S. at 877-762-2974, outside the U.S. at 317-572-3993, or fax 317-572-4002. For technical support, please visit www.wiley.com/techsupport.

Wiley publishes in a variety of print and electronic formats and by print-on-demand. Some material included with standard print versions of this book may not be included in e-books or in print-on-demand. If this book refers to media such as a CD or DVD that is not included in the version you purchased, you may download this material at http://booksupport.wiley.com. For more information about Wiley products, visit www.wiley.com.

Library of Congress Control Number: 2013958400

ISBN 978-1-118-82377-4 (pbk); ISBN 978-1-118-82382-8 (ebk); ISBN 978-1-118-82383-5 (ebk)

Manufactured in the United States of America

10 9 8 7 6 5 4 3 2 1

Contents at a Glance

Introduction **1**

Part I: Getting Started with C++ Programming **7**

Chapter 1: Writing Your First C++ Program..9
Chapter 2: Declaring Variables Constantly...33
Chapter 3: Performing Mathematical Operations...47
Chapter 4: Performing Logical Operations 53
Chapter 5: Controlling Program Flow..69

Part II: Becoming a Functional C++ Programmer **87**

Chapter 6: Creating Functions...89
Chapter 7: Storing Sequences in Arrays 105
Chapter 8: Taking a First Look at C++ Pointers..121
Chapter 9: Taking a Second Look at C++ Pointers 135
Chapter 10: The C++ Preprocessor...153

Part III: Introduction to Classes **167**

Chapter 11: Examining Object-Oriented Programming................................169
Chapter 12: Adding Class to C++...175
Chapter 13: Point and Stare at Objects 191
Chapter 14: Protecting Members: Do Not Disturb.......................................207
Chapter 15: "Why Do You Build Me Up, Just to Tear Me Down, Baby?"..................215
Chapter 16: Making Constructive Arguments 225
Chapter 17: The Copy/Move Constructor 247
Chapter 18: Static Members: Can Fabric Softener Help? 261

Part IV: Inheritance **271**

Chapter 19: Inheriting a Class 273
Chapter 20: Examining Virtual Member Functions: Are They for Real? 281
Chapter 21: Factoring Classes..291

Part V: Security **301**

Chapter 22: A New Assignment Operator, Should You Decide to Accept It 303
Chapter 23: Using Stream I/O 315
Chapter 24: Handling Errors — Exceptions..337

Chapter 25: Inheriting Multiple Inheritance 347
Chapter 26: Tempting C++ Templates 359
Chapter 27: Standardizing on the Standard Template Library 369
Chapter 28: Writing Hacker-Proof Code 381

Part VI: The Part of Tens 407

Chapter 29: Ten Ways to Avoid Adding Bugs to Your Program 409
Chapter 30: Ten Ways to Protect Your Programs from Hackers 417

Index 431

Table of Contents

Introduction *1*

   About This Book 1
   Icons Used in This Book 4
   Beyond the Book 4
   Where to Go from Here 5

Part I: Getting Started with C++ Programming *7*

   Chapter 1: Writing Your First C++ Program **9**

      Grasping C++ Concepts 9
      Installing Code::Blocks 11
         Windows 11
         Ubuntu Linux 13
         Macintosh 15
      Creating Your First C++ Program 19
         Creating a project 19
         Entering the C++ code 21
         Cheating 23
         Building your program 24
      Executing Your Program 25
      Reviewing the Annotated Program 26
         Examining the framework for all C++ programs 27
         Clarifying source code with comments 27
         Basing programs on C++ statements 28
         Writing declarations 29
         Generating output 30
      Calculating Expressions 30
         Storing the results of an expression 30
         Examining the remainder of Conversion 31

   Chapter 2: Declaring Variables Constantly **33**

      Declaring Variables 33
      Declaring Different Types of Variables 34
         Reviewing the limitations of integers in C++ 35
         Solving the truncation problem 36
         Looking at the limits of floating point numbers 37

Declaring Variable Types 38
    Types of constants 40
    Range of Numeric Types..41
    Special characters 42
Wide Loads on Char Highway..43
Are These Calculations Really Logical?.............................44
Mixed Mode Expressions..44
Automatic Declarations 46

Chapter 3: Performing Mathematical Operations 47

Performing Simple Binary Arithmetic................................47
Decomposing Expressions 48
Determining the Order of Operations...............................49
Performing Unary Operations..50
Using Assignment Operators 51

Chapter 4: Performing Logical Operations 53

Why Mess with Logical Operations?..................................53
Using the Simple Logical Operators..................................54
    Storing logical values 55
    Using logical int variables...57
    Be careful performing logical operations
        on floating-point variables 57
Expressing Binary Numbers..59
    The decimal number system 59
    Other number systems..60
    The binary number system 60
Performing Bitwise Logical Operations.............................62
    The single-bit operators...63
    Using the bitwise operators 64
    A simple test..65

Chapter 5: Controlling Program Flow 69

Controlling Program Flow with the Branch Commands..........69
Executing Loops in a Program 71
    Looping while a condition is true 72
    Using the autoincrement/autodecrement feature 74
    Using the for loop 75
    Avoiding the dreaded infinite loop..............................78
    For each his own..79
    Applying special loop controls 80
Nesting Control Commands 82
Switching to a Different Subject?.......................................84

Part II: Becoming a Functional C++ Programmer 87

Chapter 6: Creating Functions 89

Writing and Using a Function 89
  Defining our first function 92
  Defining the sumSequence() function 92
  Calling the function sumSequence() 92
  Divide and conquer 93
Understanding the Details of Functions 93
  Understanding simple functions 94
  Understanding functions with arguments 94
Overloading Function Names 98
Defining Function Prototypes 99
Defaulting Arguments 101
Passing by Value and Passing by Reference 102
Variable Storage Types 104

Chapter 7: Storing Sequences in Arrays 105

Arraying the Arguments for Arrays 105
  Using an array 107
  Initializing an array 110
  Accessing too far into an array 110
  Arraying range-based for loops 111
  Defining and using arrays of arrays 112
Using Arrays of Characters 112
  Creating an array of characters 112
  Creating a string of characters 114
Manipulating Strings with Character 115
Adding Some Library Functions 117
Making Room for Wide Strings 118

Chapter 8: Taking a First Look at C++ Pointers 121

Variable Size 121
What's in an Address? 122
Address Operators 123
Using Pointer Variables 125
  Using different types of pointers 126
Passing Pointers to Functions 126
  Passing by value 127
  Passing pointer values 127
  Passing by reference 128
Constant const Irritation 129

Making Use of a Block of Memory Called the Heap...............................130
Limited scope..131
Examining the scope problem...132
Providing a solution using the heap...................................133

Chapter 9: Taking a Second Look at C++ Pointers **135**

Defining Operations on Pointer Variables................................135
Reexamining arrays in light of pointer variables...........................136
Applying operators to the address of an array...........................138
Expanding pointer operations to a string................................139
Justifying pointer-based string manipulation 141
Applying operators to pointer types other than char 142
Contrasting a pointer with an array...142
When Is a Pointer Not?...144
Declaring and Using Arrays of Pointers...................................145
Utilizing arrays of character strings...146
Accessing the arguments to main()..148

Chapter 10: The C++ Preprocessor. **153**

What Is a Preprocessor?...153
Including Files 154
#Defining Things 157
Okay, how about not #defining things?..................................160
Enumerating other options...161
Including Things #if I Say So 162
Intrinsically Defined Objects..164
Typedef..166

Part III: Introduction to Classes...............................**167**

Chapter 11: Examining Object-Oriented Programming **169**

Abstracting Microwave Ovens..169
Preparing functional nachos 170
Preparing object-oriented nachos 171
Classifying Microwave Ovens 171
Why Classify? 172

Chapter 12: Adding Class to C++. **175**

Introducing the Class 175
The Format of a Class 176
Accessing the Members of a Class 177
Activating Our Objects 177
Simulating real-world objects..178
Why bother with member functions?.......................................178

Adding a Member Function 179
Calling a Member Function 180
   Accessing other members from a member function 182
Scope Resolution (And I Don't Mean How Well
   Your Telescope Works) 183
Defining a Member Function in the Class 185
Keeping a Member Function after Class 187
Overloading Member Functions 188

Chapter 13: Point and Stare at Objects **191**
Declaring Arrays of Objects 191
Declaring Pointers to Objects 192
   Dereferencing an object pointer 193
   Pointing toward arrow pointers 194
Passing Objects to Functions 194
   Calling a function with an object value 195
   Calling a function with an object pointer 196
   Calling a function by using the reference operator 198
Why Bother with Pointers or References? 199
Returning to the Heap 199
   Allocating heaps of objects 200
   When memory is allocated for you 201
Linking Up with Linked Lists 201
   Performing other operations on a linked list 203
   Hooking up with a LinkedListData program 203
Ray of Hope: A List of Containers Linked to the C++ Library 206

Chapter 14: Protecting Members: Do Not Disturb **207**
Protecting Members 207
   Why you need protected members 208
   Discovering how protected members work 208
Making an Argument for Using Protected Members 210
   Protecting the internal state of the class 210
   Using a class with a limited interface 211
Giving Non-member Functions Access to Protected Members 211

Chapter 15: "Why Do You Build Me Up,
Just to Tear Me Down, Baby?" **215**
Creating Objects 215
Using Constructors 216
   Constructing a single object 217
   Constructing multiple objects 218
   Constructing a duplex 219
Dissecting a Destructor 221
   Why you need the destructor 221
   Working with destructors 221

Chapter 16: Making Constructive Arguments 225

Outfitting Constructors with Arguments 225
    Using a constructor 226
Placing Too Many Demands on the Carpenter:
    Overloading the Constructor 228
Defaulting Default Constructors 231
Constructing Class Members 233
    Constructing a complex data member 233
    Constructing a constant data member 239
Reconstructing the Order of Construction 239
    Local objects construct in order 240
    Static objects construct only once 240
    All global objects construct before main() 241
    Global objects construct in no particular order 242
    Members construct in the order in which they are declared 243
    Destructors destruct in the reverse order
        of the constructors 243
Constructing Arrays 244
Constructors as a Form of Conversion 245

Chapter 17: The Copy/Move Constructor 247

Copying an Object 247
    Why you need the copy constructor 248
    Using the copy constructor 248
The Automatic Copy Constructor 250
Creating Shallow Copies versus Deep Copies 252
It's a Long Way to Temporaries 256
    Avoiding temporaries, permanently 257
    The move constructor 258

Chapter 18: Static Members: Can Fabric Softener Help? 261

Defining a Static Member 261
    Why you need static members 261
    Using static members 262
    Referencing static data members 263
    Uses for static data members 264
Declaring Static Member Functions 265
What Is this About Anyway? 268

Part IV: Inheritance *271*

Chapter 19: Inheriting a Class 273

Do I Need My Inheritance? 274
How Does a Class Inherit? 275
    Using a subclass 277
    Constructing a subclass 278

    Destructing a subclass 279
    Inheriting constructors 279
   Having a HAS_A Relationship.. 280

Chapter 20: Examining Virtual Member Functions:
Are They for Real?. **281**
   Why You Need Polymorphism.. 284
   How Polymorphism Works.. 284
   When Is a Virtual Function Not? 286
   Considering Virtual Considerations 287

Chapter 21: Factoring Classes.. . . . . **291**
   Factoring... 291
   Implementing Abstract Classes 295
    Describing the abstract class concept............................ 296
    Making an honest class out of an abstract class 298
    Passing abstract classes 298

Part V: Security. *301*

Chapter 22: A New Assignment Operator,
Should You Decide to Accept It **303**
   Comparing Operators with Functions 303
   Inserting a New Operator 304
   Creating Shallow Copies Is a Deep Problem 305
   Overloading the Assignment Operator................................ 306
   Overloading the Subscript Operator 311
   The Move Constructor and Move Operator............................ 312

Chapter 23: Using Stream I/O **315**
   How Stream I/O Works.. 315
    Default stream objects 316
   Stream Input/Output.. 317
    Open modes.. 319
    Hey, file, what state are you in? 320
    Can you show me an example? 320
   Other Methods of the Stream Classes 323
    Reading and writing streams directly 325
    Controlling format 327
    What's up with endl? 329
    Positioning the pointer within a file 329
   Using the stringstream Subclasses 330
   Manipulating Manipulators 333

Chapter 24: Handling Errors — Exceptions 337

Justifying a New Error Mechanism? 339
Examining the Exception Mechanism 340
What Kinds of Things Can I Throw? 342
Just Passing Through 345

Chapter 25: Inheriting Multiple Inheritance 347

Describing the Multiple Inheritance Mechanism 347
Straightening Out Inheritance Ambiguities 349
Adding Virtual Inheritance 350
Constructing the Objects of Multiple Inheritance 356
Voicing a Contrary Opinion 357

Chapter 26: Tempting C++ Templates 359

Generalizing a Function into a Template 360
Class Templates 362
Tips for Using Templates 365
External Template Instantiations 366
Implementing an Initializer List 366

Chapter 27: Standardizing on the Standard Template Library 369

The string Container 370
Iterating through Lists 375
Making your way through a list 376
Operations on an entire list 378
Can you show me an example? 378

Chapter 28: Writing Hacker-Proof Code 381

Understanding the Hacker's Motives 381
Understanding Code Injection 383
Examining an example SQL injection 383
Avoiding code injection 386
Overflowing Buffers for Fun and Profit 386
Can I see an example? 387
How does a call stack up? 389
Hacking BufferOverflow 393
Avoiding buffer overflow — first attempt 397
Avoiding buffer overflow — second attempt 399
Another argument for the string class 402
Why not always use string functions? 403

Part VI: The Part of Tens 407

Chapter 29: Ten Ways to Avoid Adding Bugs to Your Program 409

Enable All Warnings and Error Messages..................................409
Adopt a Clear and Consistent Coding Style 410
Limit the Visibility 411
Comment Your Code While You Write It..................................412
Single-Step Every Path at Least Once 413
Avoid Overloading Operators...413
Manage the Heap Systematically..413
Use Exceptions to Handle Errors..414
Declare Destructors Virtual 414
Avoid Multiple Inheritance..416

Chapter 30: Ten Ways to Protect Your Programs from Hackers.... 417

Don't Make Assumptions about User Input 417
Handle Failures Gracefully 418
Maintain a Program Log...419
Follow a Good Development Process 421
Implement Good Version Control...421
Authenticate Users Securely..423
Manage Remote Sessions 425
Obfuscate Your Code...426
Sign Your Code With a Digital Certificate..............................429
Use Secure Encryption Wherever Necessary 429

Index 431

Introduction

. . . .

*W*elcome to *C++ For Dummies,* 7th Edition. Think of this book as C++: *Reader's Digest Edition,* bringing you everything you need to know to start programming without all the boring stuff.

About This Book

C++ For Dummies is an introduction to the C++ language. I start from the beginning (where else?) and work my way from early concepts through more sophisticated techniques. I don't assume that you have any prior knowledge (at least, not of programming).

The book is full of examples. Every concept is documented in numerous snippets and several complete programs.

Unlike other C++ programming books, *C++ For Dummies* considers the "why" just as important as the "how." The features of C++ are like pieces of a jigsaw puzzle. Rather than just present the features, I think it's important that you understand how they fit together. You can also use the book as a reference: If you want to understand what's going on with all the template stuff, for example, just flip to Chapter 26. Each chapter contains necessary references to other earlier chapters in case you don't read the chapters in sequence.

C++ For Dummies is not operating system–specific. It is just as useful to Macintosh or Linux programmers as it is to Windows-based developers. The book doesn't cover Windows or .NET programming.

You have to master a powerful programming language, like C++, first even if your plan is to become an accomplished Windows application or .NET programmer. Once you've finished *C++ For Dummies* you will be in position to continue in your area of specialization, whatever it might be.

In this modern era of hackerdom, learning defensive programming is important, even for beginners, so I do cover important concepts to keep your program from being hacked.

What is C++?

C++ is an object-oriented, low-level standard programming language. As a low-level language similar to and compatible with its predecessor C, C++ can generate very efficient, very fast programs. It is often used to write games, graphics software, hardware control software, and other applications where performance really counts.

As an object-oriented language, C++ has the power and extensibility to write large-scale programs. C++ is one of the most popular programming languages for all types of programs. Most of the programs you use on your PC every day are written in C++ (or the subset, which is the C language).

C++ has been certified as a 99.9 percent pure standard, which makes it a portable language. A standard C++ compiler exists for every major operating system. Some versions support extensions to the basic language — in particular, Visual Studio and Visual Studio Express from Microsoft includes a C++ compiler that implements several extensions that allow their programs to interface better with other .NET languages. Nevertheless, any student is better off learning the standard C++ first. Learning the extensions is easy once you've mastered the basics demonstrated here.

When I describe a message that you see onscreen, it appears like this:

```
Hi mom!
```

In addition, code listings appear as follows:

```
// some program
int main()
{
    ...
}
```

If you're entering these programs by hand, you must enter the text exactly as shown with one exception: The amount of *whitespace* (spaces, tabs, and newlines) is not critical. You can't put a space in the middle of a keyword, but you don't have to worry about entering one too many or too few spaces.

Case IS critical however. If it says *int*, it does not mean *Int* or *INT*!

C++ words are usually based on English words with similar meanings. This can make reading a sentence containing both English and C++ difficult without a little assistance. To help out, C++ commands and function names appear in a different font, *like this*. In addition, function names are always followed by open and closed parentheses, such as *myFavoriteFunction()*. The arguments to the function are left off except when there's a specific need to make them easier to read.

Sometimes, I'll tell you to use menu commands, such as File➪Open. This notation means to use the keyboard or mouse to open the File menu and then choose the Open option.

Use of gender is always a tricky subject when writing a how-to book. I don't want to appear to be telling gentlemen how ignorant they are while giving the ladies a pass by using *he* and *him* all the time. In this book, I use the pronouns *she* and *her* when referring to the programmer and *he* and *him* when referring to the user of the program. So, she writes a program that he can use.

Each new feature is introduced by answering the following three questions:

- ✔ *What* is this new feature?
- ✔ *Why* was it introduced into the language?
- ✔ *How* does it work?

Small pieces of code are sprinkled liberally throughout the chapters. Each demonstrates some newly introduced feature or highlights some brilliant point I'm making. These snippets may not be complete and certainly don't do anything meaningful. However, every concept is demonstrated in at least one functional program that you can execute and play with on your own computer.

A real-world program can take up lots of pages. However, seeing such a program is an important didactic tool for any reader. I've included a series of programs along with an explanation of how these programs work.

I use one simple example program that I call BUDGET. The program starts life as a simple, functionally oriented BUDGET1. This program maintains a set of simple checking and savings accounts. The reader is encouraged to review this program at the end of Part II. The subsequent version, BUDGET2, adds the object-oriented concepts presented in Part III. The examples work their way using more and more features of the language, culminating with BUDGET5, which you should review after you master all the chapters in the book. The BUDGET programs are included with the book's source code at www.dummies.com/extras/cplusplus.

Icons Used in This Book

This is technical stuff that you can skip on the first reading.

Tips highlight a point that can save you a lot of time and effort.

Remember this. It's important.

Remember this, too. This one can sneak up on you when you least expect it and generate one of those really hard-to-find bugs.

This icon flags some 2011 additions to the language compared to the predecessor standard (which is known as C++ 2003). If you already have some familiarity with C++ and something seems completely new or if something doesn't work with your existing C++ tools, it may be because it's an '11 addition.

This icon flags proposed additions of the C++ 2014 standard. These features are not implemented in the Code::Blocks/gcc that's available as of this writing but they may be available at www.codeblocks.org by the time you read this.

Beyond the Book

C++ For Dummies includes the following goodies online for easy download:

- ✔ A cheat sheet that provides an overview of C++ grammar in one (fairly) easy to read page is available at www.dummies.com/cheatsheet/cplusplus. Beginners will want to print this out and keep it handy as they work through the later chapters. Like creeping socialism, eventually C++ syntax will become second nature and you won't need the cheat sheet anymore.

- ✔ The source code for all of the examples in the book can be downloaded from www.dummies.com/extras/cplusplus. The programs are organized by chapter number. I have included a project file for Code::Blocks (more about Code::Blocks in the next bullet, and I explain project files in Chapter 1).

✔ This book uses the free, open source Code::Blocks environment and GCC C++ compiler. The version of Code::Blocks used in writing this book (Version13.12) is available for download at www.dummies.com/extras/cplusplus. I have included versions for Windows (2000 and later) and for Macintosh (10.6 and later). Versions for Linux are available online as well. Chapter 1 includes instructions for how to download and install Code::Blocks. You can find newer versions of Code::Blocks and versions for different versions of Linux at www.codeblocks.org/downloads/binaries.

If you do go to www.codeblocks.org, be sure to download a version that includes the gcc compiler.

If you already have a C++ compiler installed on your computer that you would prefer to use, feel free to do so as long as it is compatible with the C++ standard (most are). Not all compilers have implemented the 2011 standard yet so I've flagged the '11 extensions in the book. In addition, if you use a different compiler, your screen may not look exactly like the figures in the book.

I don't recommend using the Visual Studio or Visual Studio Express packages with this book. It has many extensions designed to make it compatible with the .NET Framework. Once you've learned C++ on Code::Blocks, you can learn .NET programming with Visual Studio.

Where to Go from Here

Finding out about a programming language is not a spectator sport. I'll try to make it as painless as possible, but you have to power up the ol' PC and get down to some serious programming. Limber up the fingers, break the spine on the book so that it lies flat next to the keyboard (and so that you can't take it back to the bookstore), and dive in.

If you run into a problem, first check the Frequently Asked Questions (FAQ) at www.stephendavis.com.

Part I
Getting Started with C++ Programming

getting started with

C++
Programming

web extras

Visit www.dummies.com for great Dummies content online.

In this part...

- ✔ Explaining the building blocks
- ✔ Declaring variables
- ✔ Defining mathematical operators
- ✔ Using logical operators
- ✔ Visit www.dummies.com for great Dummies content online.

Chapter 1

Writing Your First C++ Program

· ·

In This Chapter

▶ Finding out about C++

▶ Installing Code::Blocks on Windows, Ubuntu Linux, or Macintosh OS X

▶ Creating your first C++ program

▶ Executing your program

· ·

*O*kay, so here we are: No one here but just you and me. Nothing left to do but get started. Might as well lay out a few fundamental concepts.

A computer is an amazingly fast but incredibly stupid machine. A computer can do anything you tell it (within reason), but it does *exactly* what it's told — nothing more and nothing less.

Perhaps unfortunately for us, computers don't understand any reasonable human language — they don't speak English either. Okay, I know what you're going to say: "I've seen computers that could understand English." What you really saw was a computer executing a *program* that could meaningfully understand English.

Computers understand a language variously known as *computer language* or *machine language*. It's possible but extremely difficult for humans to speak machine language. Therefore, computers and humans have agreed to sort of meet in the middle, using intermediate languages such as C++. Humans can speak C++ (sort of), and C++ can be converted into machine language for the computer to understand.

Grasping C++ Concepts

A C++ program is a text file containing a sequence of C++ commands put together according to the laws of C++ grammar. This text file is known as the *source file* (probably because it's the source of all frustration). A C++ source file normally carries the extension .CPP just as an Adobe Acrobat file ends in .PDF or an MS-DOS (remember that?) batch file ends in .BAT.

The point of programming in C++ is to write a sequence of commands that can be converted into a machine-language program that actually *does* what we want done. This conversion is called *compiling* and is the job of the compiler. The machine code that you wrote must be combined with some setup and teardown instructions and some standard library routines in a process known as *linking.* Together, compiling and linking are known as *building.* The resulting *machine-executable* files carry the extension .EXE in Windows. They don't carry any particular extension in Linux or Macintosh.

That sounds easy enough — so what's the big deal? Keep going.

To write a program, you need two specialized computer programs. One (an editor) is what you use to write your code as you build your .CPP source file. The other (a compiler) converts your source file into a machine-executable file that carries out your real-world commands (open spreadsheet, make rude noises, deflect incoming asteroids, whatever).

Nowadays, tool developers generally combine compiler and editor into a single package — a development *environment.* After you finish entering the commands that make up your program, you need only click a button to build the executable file.

Fortunately, there are public-domain C++ environments. I use one of them in this book — the Code::Blocks environment. This editor will work with a lot of different compilers, but the version of Code::Blocks combined with the GNU gcc compiler used to write this book is available for download for Windows, Macintosh, and various versions of Linux, as described in the installation section of this chapter.

Although Code::Blocks is public domain, you're encouraged to pay some small fee to support its further development. You don't *have* to pay to use Code::Blocks, but you can contribute to the cause if you like. See the Code::Blocks website for details.

I have tested the programs in this book with Code::Blocks 13.12 which comes bundled with gcc version 4.7.1. This version of gcc implements most of the C++ 2011 standard.

You can use different versions of gcc or even different compilers if you prefer, but they may not implement the complete '11 standard. For that reason, 2011 extensions are marked with the '11 icon seen here.

The gcc compiler does not implement any of the extensions added in the C++ 2014 standard as of this writing, but I have included them, where applicable, because some day it will.

Okay, I admit it: This book is somewhat Windows-centric. I have tested all of the programs in the book on Windows 2000/XP/Vista/7/8, Ubuntu Linux, and Macintosh OS X. I flag any differences between operating systems in the text.

In addition, I include installation instructions for each of the above three operating systems in this chapter. Versions of Code::Blocks and gcc are available for other flavors of Linux and other versions of the Macintosh OS. The programs should work with these, as well.

The Code::Blocks/gcc package generates 32-bit programs, but it does not easily support creating "windowed" programs. The programs in this book run from a command line prompt and write out to the command line. As boring as that may sound, I strongly recommend that you work through the examples in this book first to learn C++ *before* you tackle windowed development. C++ and windows programming are two separate things and (for the sake of your sanity) should remain so in your mind.

Follow the steps in the next section to install Code::Blocks and build your first C++ program. This program's task is to convert a temperature value entered by the user from degrees Celsius to degrees Fahrenheit.

Installing Code::Blocks

The www.dummies.com/extra/cplusplus website includes the most recent version of the Code::Blocks environment at the time of this writing for Windows, Ubuntu Linux, and Macintosh OS X 10.6 or later. Follow the installation instructions below that apply to your operating system.

Windows

The Code::Blocks environment comes in an easy-to-install, compressed executable file that is compatible with all versions of Windows after Windows 2000. Here's the rundown on installing the environment:

1. **Download the executable `codeblocks-13.12.mingw-setup.exe` from www.dummies.com/extra/cplusplus.**

   Save the executable to your desktop or some other place that you can easily find it.

   This includes the 4.71 version of the GCC compiler. This is not the newest version of GCC but it's the version recommended by Code::Blocks. If you want the newer but perhaps slightly buggy 4.81 version, you can download and install `codeblocks-13.12.mingw-setup-TDM-GCC-481.exe` instead. I tested the programs in this book with both versions but I used 4.71 during its writing.

2. **Double-click the program once it has completed downloading.**

3. **Depending on what version of Windows you're using, you may get the ubiquitous "An unidentified program wants access to your computer" warning pop-up. If so, click Allow to get the installation ball rolling.**

4. **Click Next after closing all extraneous applications as you are warned in the Welcome dialog box to the Code::Blocks Setup Wizard.**

5. **Read the End User License Agreement (commonly known as the EULA) and then click I Agree if you can live with its provisions.**

   It's not like you have much choice — the package really won't install itself if you don't accept. Assuming you *do* click OK, Code::Blocks opens a dialog box showing the installation options. The default options are fine.

6. **Click the Next button.**

   The installation program allows you to install only some subset of the features. You must select at least the Default Install and the MinGW Compiler Suite. The default is to install everything — that's the best choice.

   If the MinGW Compiler Suite is not an option, then you must have downloaded a version of Code::Blocks that does not include gcc. This version will not work correctly.

7. **Click Install and accept the default Destination Folder.**

   Code::Blocks commences to copying a whole passel of files to your hard drive. Code::Blocks then asks "Do you want to run Code::Blocks now?"

8. **Click Yes to start Code::Blocks.**

   Code::Blocks now asks which compiler you intend to use. The default is GNU GCC Compiler, which is the proper selection.

9. **From within Code::Blocks, choose Settings⇨Compiler.**

10. **Select the Compiler Flags tab.**

11. **Make sure that the following three flags are selected, as shown in Figure 1-1:**

    • Enable All Compiler Warnings

    • Have g++ Follow the Coming C++0x ISO C++ Language Standard

    • Have g++ Follow the C++11 ISO C++ Language Standard

    The C++ 2011 standard was originally supposed to be the C++ 2008 or 2009 standard. Since it wasn't clear, the standard became known as the 0x standard. The standard wasn't completely accepted until 2011. Within gcc, C++0x and C++11 refer to the same standard.

Figure 1-1:
Ensure that
the Enable
All Compiler
Warnings
and the C++
2011 flags
are set.

12. **Select the Toolchain Executables tab. Make sure that it appears like Figure 1-2.**

    The default location for the gcc compiler is the MinGW\bin subdirectory of the Code::Blocks directory.

If the default location is empty, then Code::Blocks does not know where the gcc compiler is, and it will not be able to build your programs. Make sure that you downloaded a version of Code::Blocks that includes gcc and that you included MinGW during the installation. If you are using an existing gcc compiler that you've already installed, then you will need to point Code::Blocks to where it is located on your hard drive.

13. **Close the Settings dialog box.**

14. **Click Next in the Code::Blocks Setup dialog box and then click Finish to complete the setup program.**

    The setup program exits.

Ubuntu Linux

Code::Blocks does not include gcc on Linux, so installation is a two-step process. First you will need to install gcc. Then you can install Code::Blocks.

Figure 1-2:
Ensure
that the
Compiler's
installation
directory is
correct.

Installing gcc

The gcc compiler is readily available for Linux. Follow these steps to install it:

1. **Enter the following commands from a command prompt:**

```
sudo apt-get update
sudo apt-get upgrade
sudo apt-get install g++
```

The standard Ubuntu Linux distribution includes a GNU C compiler, but it does not include the C++ extensions and, in particular, not the C++ 2011 standard extensions. The first two commands update and upgrade the tools you already have. The third command installs C++.

2. **Enter the following command from a command prompt:**

```
gcc --version
```

My Ubuntu 13.04 downloaded GNU C++ version 4.7.3. You'll be fine with version 4.7.1 or later. If you have an earlier version, some of the C++ 2011 features may not work properly, but otherwise, it should be okay.

If you are using Debian Linux, the commands are the same. If you're using Red Hat Linux, replace the command *apt-get* with *yum* so that you end up with

```
sudo yum install g++
```

Installing Code::Blocks

Fortunately for all concerned, an Ubuntu-ready version of Code::Blocks is available in the Ubuntu Software Center. Many other versions of Linux include something similar to the Software Center. Follow these steps to install Code::Blocks:

1. **Click on the Software Center icon on the Ubuntu desktop.**

2. **Select Code::Blocks from the list of available software.**

   This will start the installation process.

   Code::Blocks searches your hard drive for your C++ compiler. It should be able to find it without a problem, but if it doesn't, then execute the following steps.

3. **Start Code::Blocks.**

4. **Select Settings⇨Compiler.**

5. **Select the Compiler Flags tab.**

6. **Make sure that the following three flags are selected, as shown in Figure 1-1:**

   • Enable All Compiler Warnings

   • Have g++ Follow the Coming C++0x ISO C++ Language Standard

   • Have g++ Follow the C++11 ISO C++ Language Standard

7. **Select the Toolchain Executables tab.**

8. **Select the ". . ." button.**

9. **Navigate to */usr*, unless you installed your gcc compiler someplace other than the default location of */user/bin*.**

10. **The "C compiler" should be gcc, the "C++ compiler" should be g++ and the "Linker for dynamic libs" should be g++.**

11. **Select OK to close the dialog box.**

Macintosh

The Macintosh version of Code::Blocks relies on the Xcode distribution from Apple for its compiler. I have divided the installation into three separate parts for this reason.

Installing Xcode

Xcode is a free development package offered by Apple that you will need. Follow these steps to install it first:

1. **Open the Safari browser and go to** `http://developer.apple.com`.

2. **Click on Download Xcode to get the most recent version.**

   This will open the Xcode download dialog box shown in Figure 1-3.

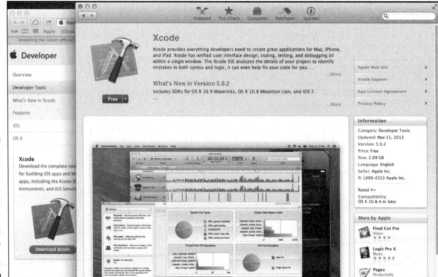

Figure 1-3:
The Xcode download dialog box allows you to install Xcode for free.

3. **Click on the Free icon to change it to Install App. Click on it again.**

4. **Enter your system password (the one you log in with when your Mac boots up).**

   The icon changes to Installing.

   The download and installation takes quite some time, as Xcode is a little over 2GB as of this writing.

Installing the Command Line Tools

As big as Xcode is, you would think that it has everything you need, but you would be wrong. You need one more package from Apple to make your joy complete and to get a working gcc compiler on your Macintosh. Follow these steps to install the Command Line Tools for Xcode:

1. **Open the Safari browser and go to** `http://developer.apple.com/downloads`.

You may be asked to sign up for an Apple Developer ID. Go ahead and do so — it's free.

2. **Search for Command Line Tools for Xcode. Select the application shown in Figure 1-4. Click on the Download icon.**

3. **Double-click on the mpkg package that downloads to install it.**

4. **Accept all of the default values.**

The installation should finish with Installation Was Successful.

Installing Code::Blocks

Now, you can finish your installation by downloading the Code::Blocks editor:

1. **Open the Safari browser and go to www.codeblocks.org/downloads.**

2. **Click on Downloads⇨Binaries.**

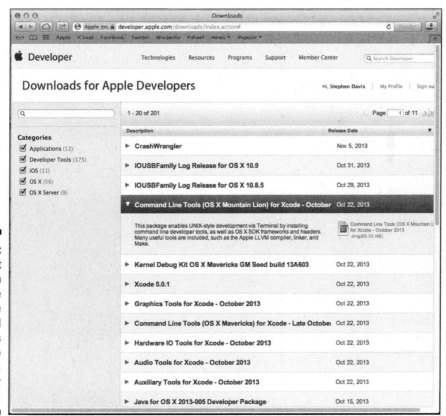

Figure 1-4: You must install both Xcode and the Command Line Tools for Xcode to get the gcc compiler for Macintosh.

3. **Click on Mac OS X.**

4. **Select either the BerliOS or Sourceforge.net mirror for the most recent version.**

   At the time of this writing, *CodeBlocks-13.12 -mac.zip* was the most recent.

5. **Install the downloaded Zip file into the Applications folder.**

   If you have never installed an application from a third-party site, you may need to execute these extra steps before you can do so:

   a. *Click on System Preferences.*

   b. *Click on Security and Privacy.*

   c. *Click the padlock in the lower-left corner of the dialog box to allow changes.*

   d. *Click on Allow Applications Downloaded from: Anywhere, as shown in Figure 1-5.*

   Once you have completed the installation of Code::Blocks, you may choose to return to this dialog box and restore the settings to Mac App Store.

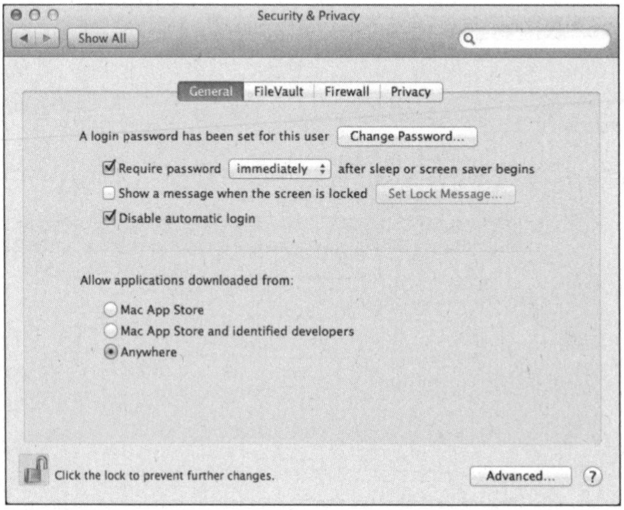

Figure 1-5:
You will
need to
allow
third-party
applica-
tions to be
installed
before you
can install
Code::Blocks
on your
Macintosh.

6. **Double-click on the Code::Blocks icon.**

   The first time you do this, the Mac OS will ask, "Are you sure you want to open it?"

7. **Select Don't Warn Me When Opening Applications on This Disk Image and click Open.**

   Code::Blocks should start and find the gcc compiler installed with the Command Line Tools.

8. **Select the gcc compiler, as shown in Figure 1-6. Click on Set as Default and then click on OK to continue starting Code::Blocks.**

   Code::Blocks will open with a banner page followed by a menu across the top of the dialog box.

9. **Select Settings⇨Compiler, then click the Have g++ Follow the Coming C++0x ISO C++ Language Standard. Click on OK to close the dialog box.**

   You are now ready to build your first C++ program.

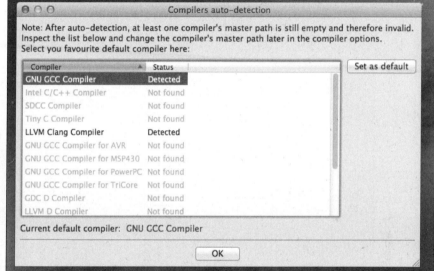

Figure 1-6:
Code::Blocks automatically finds the gcc compiler the first time you execute it.

Creating Your First C++ Program

In this section, you create your first C++ program. You enter the C++ code into a file called *CONVERT.CPP* and then convert the C++ code into an executable program.

Creating a project

The first step to creating a C++ program is to create what is known as a *project*. A *project* tells Code::Blocks the names of the *.CPP* source files to include and what type of program to create. Most of the programs in the book will consist of a single source file and will be command-line style:

1. **Start up the Code::Blocks tool.**

2. **From within Code::Blocks, choose File⇨New⇨Project.**

3. **Select the Console Application icon and then click Go.**

4. **Select C++ as the language you want to use from the next dialog box. Click Next.**

   Code::Blocks and gcc also support plain ol' C programs.

5. **In the Folder to Build Project In field, select the "..." icon.**

6. **Click on Computer and then the C: drive on Windows.**

   On Linux and Macintosh, you can select the Desktop.

7. **Select the Make New Folder button at the lower left of the screen.**

8. **Name the new folder** CPP_Programs_from_Book.

   The result should look like Figure 1-7.

Figure 1-7:
Put your
project in
the C:\CPP_
Programs_
from_Book
folder on
Windows.

9. **In the Project Title field, type the name of the project, in this case** *Conversion.*

   The resulting screen is shown in Figure 1-8 on Windows. The Linux and Macintosh version look the same except for the path.

Figure 1-8: I created the project Conversion for the first program.

10. **Click Next.**

    The next dialog box gives you the option of creating an application for testing or the final version. The default is fine.

11. **Click Finish to create the Conversion project.**

Entering the C++ code

The Conversion project that Code::Blocks creates consists of a single, default `main.cpp` file that displays the message "Hello, world". The next step is to enter our program:

1. **In the Management dialog box on the left, double-click** *main.cpp,* **which is under Sources, which is under Conversion.**

   Code::Blocks opens the empty *main.cpp* program that it created in the code editor, as shown in Figure 1-9.

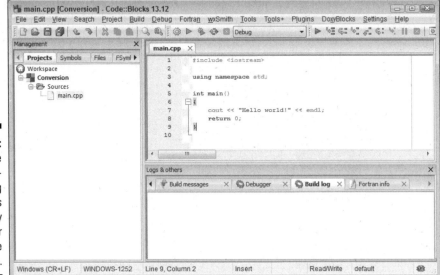

Figure 1-9:
The
Manage-
ment dialog
box displays
a directory
structure for
all available
programs.

2. **Edit *main.cpp* with the following program exactly as written.**

   Don't worry too much about indentation or spacing — it isn't critical whether a given line is indented two or three spaces, or whether there are one or two spaces between two words. C++ is case sensitive, however, so you need to make sure everything is lowercase.

   You can cheat by using the files at www.dummies.com/extra/cplusplus, as described in the next section.

```
//
//  Conversion - Program to convert temperature from
//          Celsius degrees into Fahrenheit:
//          Fahrenheit = Celsius  * (212 - 32)/100 + 32
//
#include <cstdio>
#include <cstdlib>
#include <iostream>
using namespace std;

int main(int nNumberofArgs, char* pszArgs[])
{
    // enter the temperature in Celsius
    int celsius;
    cout << "Enter the temperature in Celsius:";
    cin >> celsius;

    // calculate conversion factor for Celsius
    // to Fahrenheit
    int factor;
    factor = 212 - 32;
```

```
    // use conversion factor to convert Celsius
    // into Fahrenheit values
    int fahrenheit;
    fahrenheit = factor * celsius/100 + 32;

    // output the results (followed by a NewLine)
    cout << "Fahrenheit value is:";
    cout << fahrenheit << endl;

    // wait until user is ready before terminating program
    // to allow the user to see the program results
    cout << "Press Enter to continue..." << endl;
    cin.ignore(10, '\n');
    cin.get();
    return 0;
}
```

3. **Choose File⇨Save to save the source file.**

   I know that it may not seem all that exciting, but you've just created
   your first C++ program!

Cheating

All the programs in the book are included online, along with the project files
to build them. You will need to download them and install them onto your
hard drive before you can use them by following this procedure:

The following instructions are for Windows. The steps to follow for Linux or
Macintosh are very similar.

1. **Open your Internet browser.**

2. **Migrate to** www.dummies.com/extras/cplusplus.

3. **Click on the CPP_programs link.**

   A dialog box appears asking you where you want to download the specified file.

4. **Click on Save File.**

   Windows will copy the *CPP_programs.zip* file to the default download
   location. This may be either your Downloads folder or the Desktop.

5. **Right-click on the CPP_programs.zip file and select Open.**

   A dialog box opens containing the single directory
   CPP_Programs_from_Book.

6. **Copy this folder to the C: drive.**

   This will copy all of the sources used in the book to the directory
   C:\CPP_Programs_from_Book.

You can put the *CPP_Programs_from_Book* folder at some other location, but don't put your source files in a directory that includes a space. On Windows, that means don't put any of your Code::Blocks folders in My Documents or on the Desktop, as they both include a space in their paths.

You can use these files in two ways: One way is to go through all the steps I describe in the book to create the program by hand first, but copy and paste from the provided files into your program if you get into trouble (or your fingers start cramping). This is the preferred technique.

A second approach is that you can use the sources and project file provided as-is:

1. **Double-click *AllPrograms.workspace* in *C:\CPP_Programs_from_Book*.**

   A *workspace* is a single file that references one or more projects. The `AllPrograms.workspace` file contains references to all the projects defined in the book.

2. **Right-click the Conversion project in the Management dialog box on the left. Choose Activate Project from the context-sensitive menu that appears.**

   Code::Blocks turns the Conversion label bold to verify that this is the program you are working on right now. When you subsequently select Build, Code::Blocks, it always builds the active project.

3. **Double-click the `main.cpp` file to open the file in the editor.**

The problem with this approach is that you tend to learn very little about C++ if you don't enter the code yourself.

Building your program

After you've saved your C++ source file to your hard drive, it's time to generate the executable machine instructions.

To build your *Conversion* program, you choose Build➪Build from the menu or press Ctrl-F9. Almost immediately, Code::Blocks takes off, compiling your program with gusto. If all goes well, the happy result of *0 Errors, 0 Warnings* appears in the lower-right dialog box, as shown in Figure 1-10.

Code::Blocks generates a message if it finds any type of error in your C++ program — and coding errors are about as common as ice cubes in Alaska. You'll undoubtedly encounter numerous warnings and error messages, probably even when entering the simple *Conversion.cpp*. To demonstrate the error-reporting process, change Line 16 from *cin >> celsius;* to *cin >>> celsius;*.

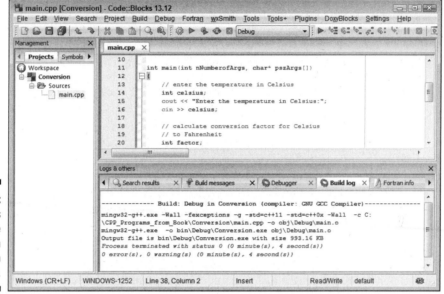

Figure 1-10:
Code::Blocks builds the Conversion program quickly.

This seems an innocent enough offense — forgivable to you and me perhaps, but not to C++. Choose Build⇨Build to start the compile and build process. Code::Blocks almost immediately places a red square next to the erroneous line. The message in the Build Message tab is a rather cryptic *error: expected primary-expression before '>' token*. To get rid of the message, remove the extra > and recompile.

You probably consider the error message generated by the example a little mysterious, but give it time — you've been programming for only about 30 minutes now. Over time, you'll come to understand the error messages generated by Code::Blocks and gcc much better.

Code::Blocks was able to point directly at the error this time, but it isn't always that good. Sometimes it doesn't notice the error until the next line or the one after that, so if the line flagged with the error looks okay, start looking at its predecessor to see if the error is there.

Executing Your Program

It's now time to execute your new creation . . . that is, to run your program. You will run the *Conversion* program file and give it input to see how well it works.

To execute the Conversion program on Windows Code::Blocks, choose Build⇨Build and Run, or press F9. This rebuilds the program if anything has changed and executes the program if the build is successful.

A dialog box opens immediately, requesting a temperature in Celsius. Enter a known temperature, such as 100 degrees. After you press Enter, the program returns with the equivalent temperature of 212 degrees Fahrenheit as follows:

```
Enter the temperature in Celsius:100
Fahrenheit value is:212
Press Enter to continue . . .
```

The message *Press Enter to continue* . . . gives you the opportunity to read what you've entered before it goes away. Press Enter, and the dialog box (along with its contents) disappears. Congratulations! You just entered, built, and executed your first C++ program.

Notice that Code::Blocks is not truly intended for developing windowed programs like those used in Windows. In theory, you can write a Windows application by using Code::Blocks, but it isn't easy. (Building windowed applications is *so* much easier in Visual Studio.)

Windows programs show the user a visually oriented output, all nicely arranged in onscreen windows. *Conversion.exe* is a 32-bit program that executes *under* Windows, but it's not a Windows program in the visual sense.

If you don't know what *32-bit program* means, don't worry about it. As I said, this book isn't about writing Windows programs. The C++ programs you write in this book have a *command line interface* executing within an MS-DOS box.

Budding Windows programmers shouldn't despair — you didn't waste your money. Learning C++ is a prerequisite to writing Windows programs. I think that they should be mastered separately: C++ first, Windows second.

Reviewing the Annotated Program

Entering data in someone else's program is about as exciting as watching someone else drive a car. You really need to get behind the wheel yourself. Programs are a bit like cars, as well. All cars are basically the same with small differences and additions — okay, French cars are a lot different than other cars, but the point is still valid. Cars follow the same basic pattern — steering wheel in front of you, seat below you, roof above you, and stuff like that.

Similarly, all C++ programs follow a common pattern. This pattern is already present in this very first program. We can review the Conversion program by looking for the elements that are common to all programs.

Examining the framework for all C++ programs

Every C++ program you write for this book uses the same basic framework, which looks a lot like this:

```
//
//  Template - provides a template to be used as the
//             starting point
//
// the following include files define the majority of
// functions that any given program will need
#include <cstdio>
#include <cstdlib>
#include <iostream>
using namespace std;

int main(int nNumberofArgs, char* pszArgs[])
{
    // your C++ code starts here

    // wait until user is ready before terminating program
    // to allow the user to see the program results
    cout<< "Press Enter to continue..." <<endl;
    cin.ignore(10, '\n');
    cin.get();
    return 0;
}
```

Without going into all the boring details, execution begins with the code contained in the open and closed braces immediately following the line beginning *main()*.

I've copied this code into a file called *Template.cpp* located in the main *CPP_Programs_from_Book* folder.

Clarifying source code with comments

The first few lines in the Conversion program appear to be freeform text. Either this code was meant for human eyes or C++ is a lot smarter than I give it credit for. These first six lines are known as comments. *Comments* are the programmer's explanation of what she is doing or thinking when writing a particular code segment. The compiler ignores comments. Programmers (*good* programmers, anyway) don't.

A C++ comment begins with a double slash (//) and ends with a newline. You can put any character you want in a comment. A comment may be as long as you want, but it's customary to keep comment lines to no more than 80 characters across. Back in the old days — "old" is relative here — screens were limited to 80 characters in width. Some printers still default to 80 characters across when printing text. These days, keeping a single line to fewer than 80 characters is just a good practical idea (easier to read; less likely to cause eyestrain; the usual).

A newline was known as a *carriage return* back in the days of typewriters — when the act of entering characters into a machine was called *typing* and not *keyboarding*. A *newline* is the character that terminates a command line.

C++ allows a second form of comment in which everything appearing after a /* and before a */ is ignored; however, this form of comment isn't normally used in C++ anymore.

It may seem odd to have a command in C++ (or any other programming language) that's specifically ignored by the computer. However, all computer languages have some version of the comment. It's critical that the programmer explain what was going through her mind when she wrote the code. A programmer's thoughts may not be obvious to the next colleague who tries to use or modify her program. In fact, the programmer herself may forget what her program meant if she looks at it months after writing the original code and has left no clue.

Basing programs on C++ statements

All C++ programs are based on what are known as C++ statements. This section reviews the statements that make up the program framework used by the *Conversion* program.

A statement is a single set of commands. Almost all C++ statements other than comments end in a semicolon. (You see one other exception in Chapter 10.) Program execution begins with the first C++ statement after the open brace and continues through the listing, one statement at a time.

As you look through the program, you can see that spaces, tabs, and newlines appear throughout the program. In fact, I place a newline after every statement in this program. These characters are collectively known as *whitespace* because you can't see them on the monitor.

You may add whitespace anywhere you like in your program to enhance readability — except in the middle of a word:

```
See wha

t I mean?
```

Although C++ may ignore whitespace, it doesn't ignore case. In fact, C++ is case sensitive to the point of obsession. The variable *fullspeed* and the variable *FullSpeed* have nothing to do with each other. The command *int* is completely understandable, but C++ has no idea what *INT* means. See what I mean about fast but stupid compilers?

Writing declarations

The line *int celsius;* is a declaration statement. A *declaration* is a statement that defines a variable. A *variable* is a "holding tank" for a value of some type. A variable contains a *value,* such as a number or a character.

The term *variable* stems from algebra formulas of the following type:

```
x = 10
y = 3 * x
```

In the second expression, *y* is set equal to 3 times *x,* but what is *x?* The variable *x* acts as a holding tank for a value. In this case, the value of *x* is 10, but we could have just as well set the value of *x* to 20 or 30 or –1. The second formula makes sense no matter what the value of *x* is.

In algebra, you're allowed but not required to begin with a statement such as *x = 10.* In C++, the programmer must define the variable *x* before she can use it.

In C++, a variable has a type and a name. The variable defined on line 11 is called *celsius* and declared to hold an integer. (Why they couldn't have just said *integer* instead of *int*, I'll never know. It's just one of those things you learn to live with.)

The name of a variable has no particular significance to C++. A variable must begin with the letters *A* through *Z*, the letters *a* through *z*, or an underscore (_). All subsequent characters must be a letter, a digit 0 through 9, or an underscore. Variable names can be as long as you want to make them.

It's convention that variable names begin with a lowercase letter. Each new word *within* a variable begins with a capital letter, as in *myVariable.*

Try to make variable names short but descriptive. Avoid names such as *x* because *x* has no particular meaning. A variable name such as *lengthOfLine Segment* is much more descriptive.

Generating output

The lines beginning with *cout* and *cin* are known as input/output statements, often contracted to I/O statements. (Like all engineers, programmers love contractions and acronyms.)

The first I/O statement says "Output the phrase *Enter the temperature in Celsius* to *cout*" (pronounced "see-out"). *cout* is the name of the standard C++ output device. In this case, the standard C++ output device is your monitor.

The next line is exactly the opposite. It says, in effect, "Extract a value from the C++ input device and store it in the integer variable *celsius*." The C++ input device is normally the keyboard. What we have here is the C++ analog to the algebra formula *x = 10* just mentioned. For the remainder of the program, the value of *celsius* is whatever the user enters there.

Calculating Expressions

All but the most basic programs perform calculations of one type or another. In C++, an *expression* is a statement that performs a calculation. Said another way, an expression is a statement that has a value. An *operator* is a command that generates a value.

For example, in the Conversion example program — specifically, in the two lines marked as a *calculation expression* — the program declares a variable *factor* and then assigns it the value resulting from a calculation. This particular command calculates the difference of 212 and 32; the operator is the minus sign (–), and the expression is *212–32*.

Storing the results of an expression

The spoken language can be very ambiguous. The term *equals* is one of those ambiguities. The word *equals* can mean that two things have the same value as in "a dollar equals one hundred cents." Equals can also imply assignment, as in math when you say that "*y* equals 3 times *x*."

To avoid ambiguity, C++ programmers call = the *assignment operator,* which says (in effect), "Store the results of the expression to the right of the assignment sign in the variable to the left." Programmers say that "*factor* is assigned the value 212 minus 32." For short, you can say "*factor* gets 212 minus 32."

Never say "*factor* is *equal to* 212 minus 32." You'll hear this from some lazy types, but you and I know better.

Examining the remainder of Conversion

The second expression in the Conversion program presents a slightly more complicated expression than the first. This expression uses the same mathematical symbols: * for multiplication, / for division, and + for addition. In this case, however, the calculation is performed on variables and not simply on constants.

The value contained in the variable called *factor* (which was calculated as the results of 212 – 32, by the way) is multiplied by the value contained in *celsius* (which was input from the keyboard). The result is divided by 100 and summed with 32. The result of the total expression is assigned to the integer variable *fahrenheit*.

The next two commands output the string *Fahrenheit value is:* to the display, followed by the value of *fahrenheit* — and all so fast that the user scarcely knows it's going on.

The final three statements prompt the user to press Enter and then waits for him to do so. This is because on some systems the program can display the results and then close the console dialog box so rapidly you don't even see that anything's happened.

On many systems, you can skip these three lines — Code::Blocks will keep the dialog box open until you press Enter anyway — but these lines never hurt.

The final *return 0* returns control to the operating system.

Chapter 2

Declaring Variables Constantly

In This Chapter

▶ Declaring variables

▶ Declaring different types of variables

▶ Using floating-point variables

▶ Declaring and using other variable types

*T*he most fundamental of all concepts in C++ is the *variable* — a variable is like a small box. You can store things in the box for later use, particularly numbers. The concept of a variable is borrowed from mathematics. A statement such as

```
x = 1
```

stores the value 1 in the variable *x*. From that point forward, the mathematician can use the variable *x* in place of the constant 1 — until he changes the value of *x* to something else.

Variables work the same way in C++. You can make the assignment

```
x = 1;
```

From that point forward in the execution of the program, the value of *x* is 1 until the program changes the value to something else. References to *x* are replaced by the value 1. In this chapter, you will find out how to declare and initialize variables in C++ programs. You will also see the different types of variables that C++ defines and when to use each.

Declaring Variables

A mathematician might write something like the following:

```
(x + 2) = y / 2
x + 4 = y
solve for x and y
```

Any reader who's had algebra realizes right off that the mathematician has introduced the variables *x* and *y*. But C++ isn't that smart. (Computers may be fast, but they're stupid.)

You have to announce each variable to C++ before you can use it. You have to say something soothing like this:

```
int x;
x = 10;

int y;
y = 5;
```

These lines of code *declare* that a variable *x* exists, is of type *int,* and has the value 10; and that a variable *y* of type *int* also exists with the value 5. (The next section discusses variable types.) You can declare variables (almost) anywhere you want in your program — as long as you *declare the variable before you use it.*

Declaring Different Types of Variables

If you're on friendly terms with math (and who isn't?), you probably think of a variable in mathematics as an amorphous box capable of holding whatever you might choose to store in it. You might easily write something like the following:

```
x = 1
x = 2.3
x = "this is a sentence"
```

Alas, C++ is not that flexible. (On the other hand, C++ can do things that people can't do, such as add a billion numbers or so in a second, so let's not get too uppity.) To C++, there are different types of variables just as there are different types of storage bins. Some storage bins are so small that they can handle only a single number. It takes a larger bin to handle a sentence.

Some computer languages try harder to accommodate the programmer by allowing her to place different types of data in the same variable. These languages are called *weakly typed* languages. C++ is a *strongly typed* language — it requires the programmer to specifically declare each variable along with its exact type.

The variable type *int* is the C++ equivalent of an *integer* — a number that has no fractional part. (Integers are also known as *counting numbers* or *whole numbers.*)

Integers are great for most calculations. I made it through most of elementary school with integers. It isn't until I turned 11 or so that my teachers started mucking up the waters with fractions. The same is true in C++: More than 90 percent of all variables in C++ are declared to be of type *int*.

Unfortunately, *int* variables aren't adapted to every problem. For example, if you worked through the temperature-conversion program in Chapter 1, you might have noticed that the program has a potential problem — it can calculate temperatures to the nearest degree. No fractions of a degree are allowed. This integer limitation wouldn't affect daily use because it isn't likely that someone (other than a meteorologist) would get all excited about being off a fraction of a degree. There are plenty of cases, however, where this isn't the case — for example, you wouldn't want to come up a half mile short of the runway on your next airplane trip due to a navigational round-off.

Reviewing the limitations of integers in C++

The *int* variable type is the C++ version of an integer. *int* variables suffer the same limitations as their counting-number integer equivalents in math do.

Integer round-off

Lopping off the fractional part of a number is called *truncation*. Consider the problem of calculating the average of three numbers. Given three *int* variables — *nValue1, nValue2,* and *nValue3* — an equation for calculating the average is

```
int nAverage; int nValue1; int nValue2; int nValue3;
nAverage = (nValue1 + nValue2 + nValue3) / 3;
```

Because all three values are integers, the sum is assumed to be an integer. Given the values 1, 2, and 2, the sum is 5. Divide that by 3, and you get 1⅔, or 1.666. C++ uses slightly different rules: Given that all three variables *nValue1, nValue2,* and *nValue3* are integers, the sum is also assumed to be an integer. The result of the division of one integer by another integer is also an integer. Thus, the resulting value of *nAverage* is the unreasonable but logical value of 1.

The problem is much worse in the following mathematically equivalent formulation:

```
int nAverage; int nValue1; int nValue2; int nValue3;
nAverage = nValue1/3 + nValue2/3 + nValue3/3;
```

Plugging in the same 1, 2, and 2 values, the resulting value of *nAverage* is 0 (talk about unreasonable). To see how this can occur, consider that ⅓ truncates to 0, ⅔ truncates to 0, and ⅔ truncates to 0. The sum of 0, 0, and 0 is 0. You can see that integer truncation can be completely unacceptable.

Limited range

A second problem with the *int* variable type is its limited range. A normal *int* variable can store a maximum value of 2,147,483,647 and a minimum value of –2,147,483,648 — roughly from positive 2 billion to negative 2 billion, for a total range of about 4 billion.

Two billion is a very large number: plenty big enough for most uses. But it's not large enough for some applications, including computer technology. In fact, your computer probably executes faster than 2 gigahertz, depending on how old your computer is. (*Giga* is the prefix meaning billion.) A single strand of communications fiber — the kind that's been strung back and forth from one end of the country to the other — can handle way more than 2 billion bits per second.

Solving the truncation problem

The limitations of *int* variables can be unacceptable in some applications. Fortunately, C++ understands decimal numbers that have a fractional part. (Mathematicians also call those *real numbers*.) Decimal numbers avoid many of the limitations of *int* type integers. To C++ all decimal numbers have a fractional part even if that fractional part is 0. In C++, the number 1.0 is just as much a decimal number as 1.5. The equivalent integer is written simply as 1. Decimal numbers can also be negative, such as –2.3.

When you declare variables in C++ that are decimal numbers, you identify them as floating-point or simply *float* variables. The term *floating-point* means the decimal point is allowed to float back and forth, identifying as many decimal places as necessary to express the value. Floating-point variables are declared in the same way as *int* variables:

```
float fValue1;
```

Once declared, you cannot change the type of a variable. *fValue1* is now a *float* and will be a *float* for the remainder of the program. To see how floating-point numbers fix the truncation problem inherent with integers, convert all the *int* variables to *float*. Here's what you get:

```
float fValue;
fValue = 1.0/3.0 + 2.0/3.0 + 2.0/3.0;
```

is equivalent to

```
fValue = 0.333... + 0.666... + 0.666...;
```

which results in the value

```
fValue = 1.666...;
```

I have written the value *1.6666* . . . as if the number of trailing 6s goes on for-ever. This is not necessarily the case. A *float* variable has a limit to the number of digits of accuracy that we'll discuss in the next section.

A constant that has a decimal point is assumed to be a floating-point value. However, the default type for a floating-point constant is something known as a double precision, which in C++ is called simply *double*, as we'll see in the next section.

The programs *IntAverage* and *FloatAverage* are available from www.dummies. com/extras/cplusplus in the *CPP_Programs_from_Book\Chap02* directory to demonstrate the round-off error inherent in integer variables.

Looking at the limits of floating point numbers

Although floating-point variables can solve many calculation problems, such as truncation, they have some limitations themselves — the reverse of those associated with integer variables. Floating-point variables can't be used to count things, are more difficult for the computer to handle, and also suffer from round-off error (though not nearly to the same degree as *int* variables).

Counting

You cannot use floating-point variables in applications where counting is important. This includes C++ constructs that count. C++ can't verify which whole number value is meant by a given floating-point number.

For example, it's clear to you and me that 1.0 is 1 but not so clear to C++. What about 0.9 or 1.1? Should these also be considered as 1? C++ simply avoids the problem by insisting on using *int* values when counting is involved.

Calculation speed

Historically, a computer processor can process integer arithmetic quicker than it can floating-point arithmetic. Thus, while a processor can add 1 million integer numbers in a given amount of time, the same processor may be able to perform only 200,000 floating-point calculations during the same period.

Calculation speed is becoming less of a problem as microprocessors get faster. In addition, today's general-purpose microprocessors include special floating-point circuitry on board to increase the performance of these opera-tions. However, arithmetic on integer values is just a heck of a lot easier and faster than performing the same operation on floating-point values.

Loss of accuracy

Floating-point *float* variables have a precision of about 6 digits, and an extra-economy size, double-strength version of *float* known as a *double* can handle about 13 significant digits. This can cause round-off problems as well.

Consider that ⅓ is expressed as 0.333 . . . in a continuing sequence. The concept of an infinite series makes sense in math but not to a computer because it has a finite accuracy. The *FloatAverage* program outputs 1.66667 as the average 1, 2, and 2 — that's a lot better than the 0 output by the *IntAverage* version but not even close to an infinite sequence. C++ can correct for round-off error in a lot of cases. For example, on output, C++ can sometimes determine that the user really meant 1 instead of 0.999999. In other cases, even C++ cannot correct for round-off error.

Not-so-limited range

Although the *double* data type has a range much larger than that of an integer, it's still limited. The maximum value for an *int* is a skosh more than 2 billion. The maximum value of a *double* variable is roughly 10 to the 38th power. That's 1 followed by 38 zeroes; it eats 2 billion for breakfast. (It's even more than the national debt, at least at the time of this writing.)

Only the first 13 digits or so of a *double* have any meaning; the remaining 25 digits are noise having succumbed to floating-point round-off error.

Declaring Variable Types

So far in this chapter, I have been trumpeting that variables must be declared and that they must be assigned a type. Fortunately (ta-dah!), C++ provides a number of variable types. See Table 2-1 for a list of variables, their advantages, and limitations.

Table 2-1		Common C++ Variable Types
Variable	*Defining a Constant*	*What It Is*
int	1	A simple counting number, either positive or negative.
short int	---	A potentially smaller version of *int.* It uses less memory but has a smaller range.
long int	10L	A potentially larger version of *int.* There is no difference between *long* and *int* with gcc.

Variable	Defining a Constant	What It Is
long long int	*10LL*	A potentially even larger version of *int*.
float	*1.0F*	A single precision real number. This smaller version takes less memory than a *double* but has less accuracy and a smaller range.
double	*1.0*	A standard floating-point variable.
long double	---	A potentially larger floating-point number. On the PC, *long double* is used for the native size of the 80x86 floating-point processor, which is 80 bits.
char	*'c'*	A single *char* variable stores a single alphabetic or digital character. Not suitable for arithmetic.
wchar_t	*L'c'*	A larger character capable or storing symbols with larger character sets like Chinese.
char string	*"this is a string"*	A string of characters forms a sentence or phrase.
bool	*true*	The only other value is *false*. No, I mean, it's *really* false. Logically *false*. Not *false* as in fake or ersatz or . . . never mind.

The *long long int* and *long double* were officially introduced with C++ '11.

The integer types come in both signed and unsigned versions. Signed is always the default (for everything except *char* and *wchar_t*). The unsigned version is created by adding the keyword *unsigned* in front of the type in the declaration. The unsigned constants include a *U* or *u* in their type designation. Thus, the following declares an *unsigned int* variable and assigns it the value 10:

```
unsigned int uVariable;
uVariable = 10U;
```

The following statement declares the two variables *lVariable1* and *lVariable2* as type *long int* and sets them equal to the value 1, while *dVariable* is a double set to the value 1.0. Notice in the declaration of *lVariable2* that the *int* is assumed and can be left off:

```
// declare two long int variables and set them to 1
long int lVariable1
long lVariable2;      // int is assumed
lVariable1 = lVariable2 = 1;
// declare a variable of type double and set it to 1.0
double dVariable; dVariable = 1.0;
```

You can declare a variable and initialize it in the same statement:

```
int nVariable = 1;   // declare a variable and
                     // initialize it to 1
```

A *char* variable can hold a single character; a character string (which isn't really a variable type but works like one for most purposes) holds a string of characters. Thus, 'C' is a *char* that contains the character C, whereas "C" is a string with one character in it. A rough analogy is that a 'C' corresponds to a nail in your hand, whereas "C" corresponds to a nail gun with one nail left in the magazine. (Chapter 9 describes strings in detail.)

If an application requires a string, you've gotta provide one, even if the string contains only a single character. Providing nothing but the character just won't do the job.

Types of constants

A *constant value* is an explicit number or character (such as 1, 0.5, or 'c') that doesn't change. As with variables, every constant has a type. In an expression such as *n = 1;* the constant value 1 is an *int*. To make 1 a *long* integer, write the statement as *n = 1L;*. The analogy is as follows: 1 represents a pickup truck with one ball in it, whereas *1L* is a dump truck also with one ball. The number of balls is the same in both cases, but the capacity of one of the containers is much larger.

Following the *int* to *long* comparison, 1.0 represents the value 1 but in a floating-point container. Notice, however, that the default for floating-point constants is *double*. Thus, 1.0 is a *double* number and not a *float*.

You can use either uppercase or lowercase letters for your special constants. Thus, 10UL and 10ul are both unsigned long integers.

The constant values *true* and *false* are of type *bool*. In keeping with C++'s attention to case, *true* is a constant but *TRUE* has no meaning.

A variable can be declared constant when it is created via the keyword *const:*

```
const double PI = 3.14159; // declare a constant variable
```

A *const* variable must be initialized with a value when it is declared, and its value cannot be changed by any future statement.

Variables declared *const* don't have to be named with all capitals, but by convention they often are. This is just a hint to the reader that this so-called variable is, in fact, not.

I admit that it may seem odd to declare a variable and then say that it can't change. Why bother? Largely because carefully named *const* variables can make a program a lot easier to understand. Consider the following two equivalent expressions:

```
double dC = 6.28318 * dR;   // what does this mean?
double dCircumference = TWO_PI * dRadius; // this is a
                          // lot easier to understand
```

It should be a lot clearer to the reader of this code that the second expression is multiplying the radius of something by 2π to calculate the circumference.

Range of Numeric Types

It may seem odd, but the C++ standard doesn't say exactly how big a number each of the data types can accommodate. The standard speaks only to the relative size of each data type. For example, it says that the maximum *long int* is at least as large as the maximum *int*.

The authors of C++ weren't trying to be mysterious. They merely wanted to allow the compiler to implement the absolute fastest code possible for the base machine. The standard was designed to work for all different types of processors running different operating systems.

However, it is useful to know the limits for your particular implementation. Table 2-2 shows the size of each number type on a Windows PC using the Code::Blocks/gcc compiler.

Table 2-2		Range of Numeric Types in Code::Block/gcc	
Variable	*Size (bytes)*	*Accuracy*	*Range*
short	2	exact	−32768 to 32767
int	4	exact	−2,147,483,648 to 2,147,483,647
long	4	exact	−2,147,483,648 to 2,147,483,647
long long int	8	exact	−9,223,372,036,854,775,808 to 9,223,372,036,854,775,807
float	4	7 digits	$\pm3.4028 \times 10^{\pm38}$
double	8	16 digits	$\pm1.7977 \times 10^{\pm308}$
long double	12	19 digits	$\pm1.1897 \times 10^{\pm4932}$

Attempting to calculate a number that's beyond the range of its type is known as an *overflow*. The C++ standard generally leaves the results of an overflow as undefined. That's another way that the definers of C++ remained flexible.

TIP

On the PC, a floating-point overflow results in an exception, which if not handled will cause your program to crash. (I don't discuss exceptions until Chapter 24.) As bad as that sounds, an integer overflow is worse — C++ silently generates an incorrect value without complaint.

Special characters

You can store any printable character you want in a *char* or *string* variable. You can also store a set of non-printable characters that are used as character constants. See Table 2-3 for a description of these important non-printable characters.

Table 2-3	Special Characters
Character Constant	*What It Is*
'\n'	newline
'\t'	tab
'\040'	The character whose value is 40 in octal (see Chapter 4 for a discussion of number systems)
'\x20'	The character whose value is 20 in hexadecimal (this is the same as '\040')
'\0'	null (i.e., the character whose value is 0)
'\\'	backslash

You have already seen the newline character at the end of strings. This character breaks a string and puts the parts on separate lines. A newline character may appear anywhere within a string. For example:

```
"This is line 1\nThis is line 2"
```

appears on the output as

```
This is line 1
This is line 2
```

C++ collision with filenames

Windows uses the backslash character to separate folder names in the path to a file. (This is a remnant of MS-DOS that Windows has not been able to shake.) Thus, *Root\FolderA\File* represents *File* within *FolderA,* which is a sub-directory of *Root.*

Unfortunately, MS-DOS's use of the backslash conflicts with the use of the backslash to indicate an escape character in C++. The character \\ is a backslash in C++. The MS-DOS path *Root\ FolderA\File* is represented in C++ as the string *"Root\\FolderA\\File"*.

Similarly, the \t tab character moves output to the next tab position. (This position can vary, depending on the type of computer you're using to run the program.)

The numerical forms allow you to specify any non-printing character that you like, but results may vary. The character represented by *0xFB,* for example, depends on the font and the character set (and may not be a legal character at all).

Because the backslash character is used to signify special characters, a character pair for the backslash itself is required. The character pair \\ represents the backslash.

Wide Loads on Char Highway

The standard *char* variable is a scant 1 byte wide and can handle only 255 different characters. This is plenty enough for European languages but not big enough to handle symbol-based languages such as kanji.

Several standards have arisen to extend the character set to handle the demands of these languages. UTF-8 uses a mixture of 8-, 16-, and 32-bit characters to implement almost every kanji or hieroglyph you can think of but still remain compatible with simple 8-bit ASCII. UTF-16 uses a mixture of 16- and 32-bit characters to achieve an expanded character set, and UTF-32 uses 32 bits for all characters.

UTF stands for Unicode Transformation Format, from which it gets the common nickname Unicode.

Table 2-4 describes the different character types supported by C++. At first, C++ tried to get by with a vaguely defined wide character type, *wchar_t.* This type was intended to be the wide character type native to the application program's environment. C++ '11 introduced specific types for UTF-16 and UTF-32.

Table 2-4		The C++ Character Types
Variable	**Example**	**What It Is**
char	'c'	ASCII or UTF-8 characters
wchar_t	L'c'	Character in wide format
char_16t	u'c'	UTF-16 character
char_32t	U'c'	UTF-32 character

UTF-16 is the standard encoding for Windows applications. The *wchar_t* type refers to UTF-16 in the Code::Blocks/gcc compiler.

Any of the character types in Table 2-4 can be combined into strings as well:

```
wchar_t* wideString = L"this is a wide string";
```

(Ignore the asterisk for now. I have a lot to say about its meaning in Chapter 8.)

Are These Calculations Really Logical?

C++ provides a logical variable called *bool.* The type *bool* comes from *Boole,* the last name of the inventor of the logical calculus. A Boolean variable has two values: *true* and *false.*

There are actually calculations that result in the value *bool.* For example, *"x is equal to y"* is either *true* or *false.*

Mixed Mode Expressions

C++ allows you to mix variable types in a single expression. That is, you are allowed to add an integer with a *double* precision floating-point value. In the following expression, for example, *nValue1* is allowed to be an *int:*

```
// in the following expression the value of nValue1
// is converted into a double before performing the
// assignment
int nValue1 = 1;
nValue1 + 1.0;
```

An expression in which the two operands are not the same type is called a *mixed mode expression.* Mixed mode expressions generate a value whose type is equal to the more capable of the two operands. In this case, *nValue1* is converted to a *double* before the calculation proceeds. Similarly, an expression of one type may be assigned to a variable of a different type, as in the following statement:

```
// in the following assignment, the whole
// number part of fVariable is stored into nVariable
double dVariable = 1.0;
int nVariable;
nVariable = dVariable;
```

You can lose precision or range if the variable on the left side of the assignment is smaller. In the preceding example, C++ truncates the value of *dVariable* before storing it in *nVariable*.

Converting a larger value type into a smaller value type is called *demotion*, whereas converting values in the opposite direction is known as *promotion*. Programmers say that the value of *int* variable *nVariable1* is promoted to a *double* in expressions such as the following:

```
int nVariable1 = 1;
double dVariable = nVariable1;
```

Mixed mode expressions are not a good idea. Avoid forcing C++ to do your conversions for you.

Naming conventions

You may have noticed that the name of each of the variables that I create begins with a special character that seems to have nothing to do with the name. These special characters are not special to C++ at all; they are merely meant to jog the reader's memory and indicate the type of the variable. A partial list of these special characters follows. Using this convention, I can immediately recognize *dVariable* as a variable of type *double*, for example.

Religious wars worse than the True Value of BitCoin have broken out over whether or not this naming convention clarifies C++ code. It helps me, so I stick with it. Try it for awhile. If after a few months, you don't think it helps, feel free to change your naming convention.

Character	Type
n	*int*
l	*long*
f	*float*
d	*double*
c	*character*
sz	*string*

Automatic Declarations

If you are really lazy, you can let C++ determine the types of your variables for you. Consider the following declaration:

```
int nVar = 1;
```

You might ask, "Why can't C++ figure out the type of *nVar?*" The answer is, it will if you ask nicely, as follows:

```
auto var1 = 1;
auto var2 = 2.0;
```

This says, "declare *var1* to be a variable of the same type as the constant value 1 (which happens to be an *int*) and declare *var2* to be the same type as 2.0 (which is a *double*)."

I consider the term *auto* to be a particularly unfortunate choice for this purpose because prior to C++ '11, the keyword *auto* had a completely different meaning. However, *auto* had fallen out of use for at least 20 years, so the standards people figured that it would be safe to usurp the term. Just be aware that if you see the keyword *auto* in some old code, you will need to remove it.

You can also tell C++ that you want a variable to be declared to be of the same type as another variable, whatever that might be, using the keyword *decltype()*.

```
int var1;
decltype(var1) var2; // declare var2 to be of the
                     // same type as var1
```

C++ replaces the *decltype(var1)* with the type of *var1,* again an *int.*

Chapter 3

Performing Mathematical Operations

In This Chapter

▶ Defining mathematical operators in C++

▶ Using the C++ mathematical operators

▶ Identifying expressions

▶ Increasing clarity with special mathematical operators

C++ offers all the common arithmetic operations: C++ programs can multiply, add, divide, and so forth. Programs have to be able to perform these operations to get anything done. What good is a health insurance program if it can't calculate how much you're supposed to (over) pay?

C++ operations look like the arithmetic operations you would perform on a piece of paper, except you have to declare any variables before you can use them (as detailed in Chapter 2):

```
int var1;
int var2 = 1;
var1 = 2 * var2;
```

This code snippet declares two variables, *var1* and *var2*. It initializes *var2* to 1 and then stores the results of multiplying 2 times the value of *var2* into *var1*.

This chapter describes the complete set of C++ mathematical operators.

Performing Simple Binary Arithmetic

A *binary operator* is one that has two arguments. If you can say *var1 op var2*, *op* must be a binary operator. The most common binary operators are the simple operations you performed in grade school. The binary operators are flagged in Table 3-1. (This table also includes the unary operators, which I describe a little later in this chapter.)

Table 3-1	Mathematical Operators in Order of Precedence	
Precedence	*Operator*	*What It Is*
1	+ (unary)	Effectively does nothing
1	- (unary)	Returns the negative of its argument
2	++ (unary)	Increment
2	-- (unary)	Decrement
3	* (binary)	Multiplication
3	/ (binary)	Division
3	% (binary)	Modulo
4	+ (binary)	Addition
4	- (binary)	Subtraction
5	=, *=,%=,+=,-= (special)	Assignment types

Multiplication, division, modulus, addition, and subtraction are the operators used to perform arithmetic. In practice, they work just like the familiar arithmetic operations as well. For example, using the binary operator for division with a floating point *double* variable looks like this:

```
double var = 133.0 / 10.0;
```

The expression 133/10 performs integer division, producing the *int* result 13 rather than the floating-point 13.3.

Each of the binary operators has the conventional meaning that you studied in grammar school — with one exception. You may not have encountered modulus in your studies. The *modulus* operator (%) works much like division, except it produces the remainder *after* division instead of the quotient. For example, 4 goes into 14 three times with a remainder of 2. Thus we say 14 modulus 4 is 2:

```
int var = 14 % 4; // var is set to 2
```

Modulus is not defined for floating point variables. (I discuss round-off errors in Chapter 2.)

Decomposing Expressions

The most common type of statement in C++ is the expression. An *expression* is a C++ statement with a value. Every expression also has a type, such as *int, double,* or *char.* A statement involving any mathematical operator is an expression since all these operators return a value. For example, *1 + 2* is an expression whose value is 3 and type is *int.* (Remember that a constant without a decimal point is of type *int.*)

Expressions can be complex or extremely simple. In fact, the statement 1 is an expression because it has a value (1) and a type (*const int*). The following statement has six expressions:

```
z = x * y + w;
```

The expressions are

```
x
y
w
x * y
x * y + w
z = x * y + w
```

Determining the Order of Operations

All operators perform some defined function. In addition, every operator has a *precedence* — a specified order in which the expressions are evaluated. Consider, for example, how precedence affects solving the following problem:

```
int var = 2 * 3 + 1;
```

If the addition is performed before the multiplication, the value of the expression is 2 times 4, or 8. If the multiplication is performed first, the value is 6 plus 1, or 7.

The precedence of the operators determines who goes first. Table 3-1 shows that multiplication has higher precedence than addition, so the result is 7. (The concept of precedence is also present in arithmetic. C++ adheres to the common arithmetic precedence.)

So what happens when two operators of the same precedence appear in the same expression? For example:

```
int var = 8 / 4 / 2;
```

When operators of the same precedence appear in the same expression, they are evaluated from left to right (the same rule applied in arithmetic). Thus, in this code snippet, *var* is equal to 8 divided by 4 (which is 2) divided by 2 (which is 1).

The expression

```
x / 100 + 32
```

divides *x* by 100 before adding 32. But what if the programmer wanted to divide *x* by *100 plus 32?* The programmer can change the precedence by bundling expressions together in parentheses (shades of algebra!), as follows:

```
x /(100 + 32)
```

This expression has the same effect as dividing *x* by 132. The original expression

```
x / 100 + 32
```

is identical to the expression

```
(x / 100) + 32
```

Performing Unary Operations

Arithmetic binary operators — those operators that take two arguments — are familiar to a lot of us from school days. But consider the *unary operators,* which take a single argument (for example, –*a*). Many unary operations are not so well known.

The unary mathematical operators are plus, minus, plus-plus, and minus-minus (respectively, +, –, ++, and – –). The minus operator changes the sign of its argument. Positive numbers become negative and vice versa. The plus operator does not change the sign of its argument. The plus operator is rarely, if ever, used.

```
int var1 = 10;
int var2 = -var1;   // var2 is now -10
```

The latter expression uses the minus unary operator (–) to calculate the value negative 10.

The ++ and the – – operators might be new to you. These operators (respectively) add one to their arguments or subtract one from their arguments, so they're known (also respectively) as the *increment* and *decrement operators.* Because they're dependent upon numbers that can be counted, they're limited to non-floating point variables. For example, the value of *var* after executing the following expression is 11:

```
int var = 10;   // initalize var
var++;          // now increment it
                // value of var is now 11
```

Why define a separate increment operator?

The authors of C++ noted that programmers add 1 more than any other constant. To provide some convenience, a special *add 1* instruction was added to the language. In addition, most present-day computer processors have an increment instruction that is faster than the addition instruction. Back when C++ was created — with microprocessors being what they were — saving a few instructions was a big deal. Today, not so much.

The increment and decrement operators are peculiar in that both come in two flavors: a *prefix* version and a *postfix* version (known as pre-increment and post-increment, respectively). Consider, for example, the increment operator (the decrement works in the same way).

Suppose that the variable *n* has the value 5. Both ++*n* and *n*++ increment *n* to the value 6. The difference between the two is that the value of ++*n* is the value after incrementing (6) while the value of *n*++ is the value before incrementing (5). The following example illustrates this difference:

```
// declare three integer variables
int n1, n2, n3;


n1 = 5;
n2 = ++n1; // the value of both n1 and n2 is now 6


n1 = 5;
n3 = n1++;// the value of n1 is 6 but the value of n3 is 5
```

Thus *n2* is given the value of *n1* after *n1* has been incremented (using the pre-increment operator), whereas *n3* gets the value of *n1* before it is incremented using the post-increment operator.

Using Assignment Operators

An *assignment operator* is a binary operator that changes the value of its left argument. The equal sign (=), a simple assignment operator, is an absolute necessity in any programming language. This operator puts the value of the right-hand argument into the left-hand argument. The other assignment operators are odd enough that they seem to be someone's whim.

So what about the following:

```
int var1;
int var2 = 2;
var1 = var2 = 1;
```

If we used the left to right rule, *var1* ends up with the value 2 but *var2* with the value 1, which is counterintuitive. To avoid this, multiple assignment operators are evaluated from right to left. Thus, the example snippet assigns the value 1 to *var2* and then copies the same value into *var1*.

The creators of C (from which C++ originated) noticed that assignments often follow the form of

```
variable = variable # constant
```

where # is some binary operator. Thus, to increment an integer operator by 2, the programmer might write

```
nVariable = nVariable + 2;
```

This expression says, "Add 2 to the value of *nVariable* and store the results back into *nVariable*." Doing so changes the value of *nVariable* to 2 more than it was.

Because the same variable appears on both sides of the = sign, the same Fathers of the C Revolution decided to create a version of the assignment operator with a binary operator attached. This says, in effect, "Thou shalt perform whatever operation on a variable and store the results right back into the same variable."

Every binary operator has one of these nifty *assignment versions*. Thus, the assignment just given could have been written this way:

```
nVariable = nVariable + 2;
nVariable += 2;
```

Here the first line says (being very explicit now), "Take the value of *nVariable*, add 2, and store the results back into *nVariable*." The next line says (a bit more abruptly), "Add 2 to the value of *nVariable*."

Other than assignment itself, these assignment operators are not used all that often. However, as odd as they might look, sometimes they can actually make the resulting program easier to read

Chapter 4

Performing Logical Operations

· ·

In This Chapter

▶ Using sometimes-illogical logical operators

▶ Defining logical variables

▶ Operating with bitwise logical operators logically, a bit at a time

· ·

*T*he most common statement in C++ is the expression. Most expressions involve the arithmetic operators, such as addition (+), subtraction (–) and multiplication (*), as demonstrated in Chapter 3.

This chapter describes a whole other class of operators known as the *logical operators*. In comparison with the arithmetic operators, most people don't think nearly as much about this type of operation. It isn't that people don't deal with logical operations such as AND and OR — we compute them constantly. I won't eat cereal unless the bowl contains cereal AND the bowl has milk in it AND the cereal is coated with sugar (lots of sugar). I'll have a Scotch IF it's single-malt AND someone else is paying for it. People use such logical operations all the time, but they don't write them down as machine instructions (or think of them in that light).

Logical operators fall into two types. The AND and OR operators are what I will call *simple logical operators*. The second type of logical operator is the *bitwise* operator. People don't use the bitwise operator in their daily business at all; it's unique to the computer world. We'll start with the simple and sneak up on the bitwise in this chapter.

Why Mess with Logical Operations?

C++ programs have to make decisions. A program that can't make decisions is of limited use. The temperature-conversion program laid out in Chapter 1 is about as complex as you can get without *some* type of decision-making. Invariably a computer program gets to the point where it has to figure out situations such as "Do *this* if the *a* variable is less than some value; do that *other* thing if it's not." The ability to make decisions is what makes a computer appear to be intelligent. (By the same token, that same property makes a computer look really stupid when the program makes the wrong decision.) Making decisions, right or wrong, requires the use of logical operators.

Using the Simple Logical Operators

The simple logical operators, shown in Table 4-1, evaluate to *true* or *false*.

Table 4-1	Simple Operators Representing Daily Logic
Operator	*What It Does*
==	Equality; *true* if the left-hand argument has the same value as the right
!=	Inequality; opposite of equality
>, <	Greater than, less than; *true* if the left-hand argument is greater than or less than the right-hand argument
>=, <=	Greater than or equal to, less than or equal to; *true* if either > or == is *true*, or either < or == is *true*
&&	AND; *true* if both the left- and right-hand arguments are *true*
||	OR; *true* if either the left- or right-hand argument is *true*
!	NOT; *true* if its argument is *false;* otherwise, *false*

The first six entries in Table 4-1 are comparison operators. The equality operator is used to compare two numbers. For example, the following is *true* if the value of *n* is 0, and is *false* otherwise:

```
n == 0;
```

Looks can be deceiving. Don't confuse the equality operator (==) with the assignment operator (=). Not only is this a common mistake, but it's a mistake that the C++ compiler generally cannot catch — that makes it more than twice as bad. The following statement does not initialize *n* to 0; it compares the current value of *n* with 0 and then does nothing with the results of that comparison:

```
n == 0;    // programmer meant to say n = 0
```

The greater-than (>) and less-than (<) operators are similarly common in everyday life. The following logical comparison is true:

```
int n1 = 1;
int n2 = 2;
n1 < n2;
```

The greater-than-or-equal-to operator (>=) and the less-than-or-equal-to operator (<=) are similar to the less-than and greater-than operators, with one major exception. They include equality; the other operators don't.

The && (AND) and || (OR) work in combination with the other logic operators to build more complex logical expressions, like this:

```
// the following is true if n2 is greater than n1
// AND n2 is smaller than n3
// (this is the most common way determining that n2 is in
// the range of n1 to n3, exclusive)
(n1 < n2) && (n2 < n3);
```

Storing logical values

The result of a logical operation can be assigned to a variable of type *bool*. The term *bool* refers to Boolean algebra, which is the algebra of logic. This was invented by a British mathematician, George Boole, in the 19th century.

```
int n1 = 1;
int n2 = 2;
bool b;
b = (n1 == n2);
```

This expression highlights the difference between the assignment operator = and the comparison operator ==. The expression says, "Compare the variables *n1* and *n2*. Store the results of this comparison in the variable *b*."

The following *BoolTest* program demonstrates the use of a *bool* variable:

```
// BoolTest - compare variables input from the
//            keyboard and store the results off
//            into a logical variable
#include <cstdio>
#include <cstdlib>
#include <iostream>
using namespace std;
```

```cpp
int main(int nNumberofArgs, char* pszArgs[])
{
    // set output format for bool variables
    // to true and false instead
    // of 1 and 0
    cout.setf(cout.boolalpha);

    // input two values
    int nArg1;
    cout << "Input value 1: ";
    cin >> nArg1;

    int nArg2;
    cout << "Input value 2: ";
    cin >> nArg2;

    // compare the two variables and store the results
    bool b;
    b = nArg1 == nArg2;

    cout << "The statement, " << nArg1
         << " equals "         << nArg2
         << " is "             << b
         << endl;

    // wait until user is ready before terminating program
    // to allow the user to see the program results
    cout << "Press Enter to continue..." << endl;
    cin.ignore(10, '\n');
    cin.get();
    return 0;
}
```

The first line *cout.setf()* makes sure that our *bool* variable *b* is output as *"true"* or *"false"*. The next section explains why this is necessary.

The program inputs two values from the keyboard and displays the result of the equality comparison:

```
Input value 1: 5
Input value 2: 5
The statement, 5 equals 5 is true
Press Enter to continue...
```

The special value *endl* inserts a newline. The difference between the value *endl* and the character *'\n'* as described in Chapter 2 is subtle and explained in Chapter 23.

Using logical int variables

C++ hasn't always had a *bool* type variable. Back in the old days (when cameras still used actual film), C++ used *int* variables to store logical values. A value of 0 was considered *false* and all other values *true*. By the same token, a logical operator generated a 0 for *false* and a 1 for *true*. (Thus, *10 < 5* returned 0 while *10 > 5* returned 1.)

C++ retains a high degree of compatibility between *bool* and *int* to support the older programs. You get completely different output from the *BitTest* program if you remove the line *cout.setf(cout.boolalpha)*:

```
Input value 1: 5
Input value 2: 5
The statement, 5 equals 5 is 1
Press Enter to continue...
```

Variables of type *int* and *bool* can be mixed in expressions as well. For example, C++ allows the following bizarre statement without batting an eyelid:

```
int n;
n = (nArg1 == nArg2) * 5;
```

This sets *n* to 5 if *nArg1* and *nArg2* are equal and 0 otherwise.

Be careful performing logical operations on floating-point variables

Round-off errors in floating-point computation can create havoc with logical operations. Consider the following example:

```
float f1 = 10.0;
float f2 = f1 / 3;
bool b1 = (f1 == (f2 * 3.0));   // are these two equal?
```

Even though it's obvious to us that *f1* is equal to *f2* times 3, the resulting value of *b1* is not *necessarily true*. A floating-point variable cannot hold an unlimited number of significant digits. Thus, *f2* is not equal to the number we'd call "three-and-a-third," but rather to 3.3333 . . ., stopping after some number of decimal places.

A *float* variable supports about 7 digits of accuracy while a *double* supports a skosh over 16 digits. I say "about" and "skosh" because the computer is likely to generate a number like 3.3333347 due to vagaries in floating-point calculations.

Now, in pure math, the number of 3s after the decimal point is infinite, but no computer built can handle an infinite number of digits. So, after multiplying 3.3333 by 3, you get 9.9999 instead of the 10 you'd get if you multiplied "three-and-a-third" — in effect, a *round-off error.* Such small differences may be unnoticeable to a person but not to the computer. Equality means exactly that — *exact* equality.

Modern processors are sophisticated in performing such calculations. The processor may, in fact, accommodate the round-off error, but from inside C++, you can't predict exactly what any given processor will do.

The safer comparison follows:

```
float f1 = 10.0;
float f2 = f1 / 3;
float f3 = f2 * 3.0;
float delta = f1 - f3;
bool bEqual = -0.0001 < delta && delta < 0.0001;
```

This comparison is *true* if *f1* and *f3* are within some small delta from each other, which should still be *true* even if you take some small round-off error into account.

Short circuits and C++

The logical AND && and logical OR || operators perform what is called *short-circuit evaluation.* Consider the following:

```
condition1 && condition2
```

If *condition1* is not *true,* the overall result is not *true,* no matter what the value of *condition2.* (For example, *condition2* could be *true* or *false* without changing the result.) The same situation occurs in the following:

```
condition1 || condition2
```

If *condition1* is *true,* the result is *true,* no matter what the value of *condition2* is.

To save time, C++ doesn't evaluate *condition2* if it doesn't need to. For example, in the expression *condition1 && condition2,* C++ doesn't evaluate *condition2* if *condition1* is *false.* Likewise, in the expression *condition1 || condition2,* C++ doesn't evaluate *condition2* if *condition1* is *true.* This is known as short-circuit evaluation.

Short-circuit evaluation may mean that *condition2* is not evaluated even if that condition has side effects. Consider the following admittedly contrived code snippet:

```
int nArg1 = 1;
int nArg2 = 2;
int nArg3 = 3;

bool b = (nArg1 > nArg2) && (nArg2++ > nArg3);
```

The variable *nArg2* is never incremented because the comparison *nArg2++ > nArg3* is not performed. There's no need because *nArg1 > nArg2* already returned a *false* so the overall expression must be *false*.

Expressing Binary Numbers

C++ variables are stored internally as so-called binary numbers. Binary numbers are stored as a sequence of 1 and 0 values known as *bits*. Most of the time, you don't really need to deal with which particular bits you use to represent numbers. Sometimes, however, it's practical and convenient to tinker with numbers at the bit level — so C++ provides a set of operators for that purpose.

Fortunately, you won't have to deal too often with C++ variables at the bit level, so it's pretty safe to consider the remainder of this chapter a Deep Techie excursion.

The so-called *bitwise* logical operators operate on their arguments at the bit level. To understand how they work, let's first examine how computers store variables.

The decimal number system

The numbers we've been familiar with from the time we could first count on our fingers are known as *decimal numbers* because they're based on the number 10. (If beer by the six-pack had been invented early enough, our number system might well be based on the number 6.) In general, the programmer expresses C++ variables as decimal numbers. Thus you could specify the value of *var* as (say) 123, but consider the implications.

A number such as 123 refers to *1 * 100 + 2 * 10 + 3 * 1*. All of these base numbers — 100, 10, and 1 — are powers of 10.

```
123 = 1 * 100 + 2 * 10 + 3 * 1
```

Expressed in a slightly different (but equivalent) way, 123 looks like this:

```
123 = 1 * 10² + 2 * 10¹ + 3 * 10⁰
```

Remember that *any* number *to the zero power* is 1.

Other number systems

Well, okay, using 10 as the basis (or *base*) of our counting system probably stems from those 10 human fingers, the original counting tools. An alternative base for a counting system could just as easily have been 20 (maybe the inventor of base 10 had shoes on at the time).

If our numbering scheme had been invented by dogs, it might well be based on 8 (one digit of each paw is out of sight on the back part of the leg). Mathematically, such an *octal* system would have worked just as well:

```
123₁₀ = 1 * 8² + 7 * 8¹ + 3 * 8⁰ = 173₈
```

The small *10* and *8* here refer to the numbering system, *10* for decimal (base 10) and *8* for octal (base 8). A counting system may use any positive base.

The binary number system

Computers have essentially two fingers. (Maybe that's why computers are so stupid: without an opposing thumb, they can't grasp anything. And then again, maybe not.) Computers prefer counting using base 2. The number *123₁₀* would be expressed this way:

```
123₁₀ = 0*2⁷ + 1*2⁶ + 1*2⁵ + 1*2⁴ + 1*2³ + 0*2² + 1*2¹ + 1*2⁰
123₁₀ = 0*128 + 1*64 + 1*32 + 1*16 + 1*8 + 0*4 + 1*2 + 1*1
      = 01111011₂
```

Computer convention expresses binary numbers by using 4, 8, 16, 32, or even 64 binary digits, even if the leading digits are 0. This is also because of the way computers are built internally.

Because the term *digit* refers to a multiple of 10, a *binary digit* is called a *bit* (an abbreviation of *binary digit*). A *byte* is made up of 8 bits. (Calling a binary digit a *byte-it* didn't seem like a good idea.) Memory is usually measured in bytes (like rolls are measured in units of baker's dozen).

With such a small base, you have to use a *large* number of bits to express numbers. Human beings don't want the hassle of using an expression such as 01111011_2 to express such a mundane value as 123_{10}. Programmers prefer to express numbers by using an even number of bits. The octal system — which is based on 3 bits — was the default binary system in the early days of C. We see a vestige of this even today — a constant that begins with a 0 is assumed to be octal in C++. Thus, the line:

```
cout << "0173 = " << 0173 << endl;
```

produces the following output:

```
0173 = 123
```

However, octal has been almost completely replaced by the *hexadecimal* system, which is based on 4-bit digits.

Hexadecimal uses the same digits for the numbers 0 through 9. For the digits between 9 and 16, hexadecimal uses the first six letters of the alphabet: A for 10, B for 11, and so on. Thus, 123_{10} becomes $7B_{16}$, like this:

```
123 = 7 * 16¹ + B (i.e. 11) * 16⁰ = 7B₁₆
```

Programmers prefer to express hexadecimal numbers in multiples of 4 hexadecimal digits even when the leading digit in each case is 0.

Finally, who wants to express a hexadecimal number such as $7B_{16}$ by using a subscript? Terminals don't even *support* subscripts. Even on a word processor such as the one I'm using now, it's a drag to change fonts to and from subscript mode just to type two lousy digits. Therefore, programmers (no fools, they) use the convention of beginning a hexadecimal number with a *0x*. (Why? Well, the reason for such a strange convention goes back to the early days of C, in a galaxy far, far, away . . . never mind.) Thus, *7B* becomes *0x7B*. Using this convention, the hexadecimal number *0x7B* is equal to 123 decimal while *0x123* hexadecimal is equal to 291 decimal. The code snippet

```
cout << "0x7B  = " << 0x7B  << endl;
cout << "0x123 = " << 0x123 << endl;
```

produces the following output:

```
0x7B  = 123
0x123 = 291
```

You can use all the mathematical operators on hexadecimal numbers in the same way you'd apply them to decimal numbers. (Well, okay, most of us can't perform a multiplication such as *0xC * 0xE* in our heads, but that has more to do with the multiplication tables we learned in school than it has to do with any limitation in the number system.)

If you really want to, you can write binary numbers in C++ '14 using the prefix '0b'. Thus, 123 becomes 0b01111011.

Performing Bitwise Logical Operations

All C++ numbers can be expressed in binary form. Binary numbers use only the digits 1 and 0 to represent a value. Table 4-2 defines the set of operations that work on numbers *one bit at a time,* hence the term *bitwise* operators.

Table 4-2	Bitwise Operators
Operator	*Function*
~	NOT: toggle each bit from 1 to 0 and from 0 to 1
&	AND each bit of the left-hand argument with that on the right
|	OR each bit of the left-hand argument with that on the right
^	XOR (exclusive OR) each bit of the left-hand argument with that on the right

Bitwise operations can potentially store a lot of information in a small amount of memory. Many traits in the world have only two possibilities — that are either this way or that way. You are either married or you're not. You are either male or female (at least that's what my driver's license says). In C++, you can store each of these traits in a single bit — in this way, you can pack 32 separate binary properties into a single 32-bit *int*.

In addition, bit operations can be extremely fast. No performance penalty is paid for that 32-to-1 savings.

Even though memory is cheap these days, it's not unlimited. Sometimes, when you're storing large amounts of data, this ability to pack a whole lot of properties into a single word is a big advantage.

The single-bit operators

The bitwise operators — AND (&), OR (|) and NOT (~) — perform logic operations on single bits. If you consider 0 to be *false* and 1 to be *true* (it doesn't *have* to be this way, but it's a common convention), you can say things like the following for the NOT operator:

```
~ 1 (true)  is 0 (false)
~ 0 (false) is 1 (true)
```

The AND operator is defined as following:

```
1 (true) & 1 (true)  is 1 (true)
1 (true) & 0 (false) is 0 (false)
```

It's a similar situation for the OR operator:

```
1 (true)  | 0 (false) is 1 (true)
0 (false) | 0 (false) is 0 (false)
```

The definition of the AND operator appears in Table 4-3. Read one argument as the column head and the other argument as the row head — the result is the intersection. Thus, 1 AND 1 is 1. 0 AND 1 is 0.

Table 4-3	Truth Table for the AND Operator	
AND	*1*	*0*
1	1	0
0	0	0

You read Table 4-3 as the column corresponding to the value of one of the arguments while the row corresponds to the other. Thus, 1 & 0 is 0. (Column 1 and row 0.) The only combination that returns anything other than 0 is 1 & 1. (This is known as a *truth table*.)

Similarly, the truth table for the OR operator is shown in Table 4-4.

Table 4-4	Truth Table for the OR Operator	
OR	*1*	*0*
1	1	1
0	1	0

One other logical operation that is not so commonly used in day-to-day living is the OR ELSE operator, commonly contracted to XOR. XOR is *true* if either argument is *true* but not if both are *true*. The truth table for XOR is shown in Table 4-5.

Table 4-5	Truth Table for the XOR Operator	
XOR	**1**	**0**
1	0	1
0	1	0

Armed with these single-bit operators, we can take on the C++ bitwise logical operations.

Using the bitwise operators

The bitwise operators are used much like any other binary arithmetic operator. The NOT operator is the easiest to understand. To NOT a number is to NOT each bit that makes up that number (and to a programmer, that sentence makes perfect sense — honest). Consider this example:

```
~0110₂ (0x6)
 1001₂ (0x9)
```

Thus we say that *~0x6* equals *0x9* (pronounced "NOT 6 equals 9").

The following calculation demonstrates the & operator:

```
    0110₂
&
    0011₂
    0010₂
```

Beginning with the most significant bit, 0 AND 0 is 0. In the next bit, 1 AND 0 is 0. In bit 3, 1 AND 1 is 1. In the least significant bit, 0 AND 1 is 0. Expressed in hexadecimal, the same expression appears as follows:

```
0x6         0110₂
&           &
0x3         0011₂
0x2         0010₂
```

In shorthand, we say that *0x6 & 0x3* equals *0x2* (pronounced "6 AND 3 equals 2").

A simple test

The following program illustrates the bitwise operators in action. The program initializes two variables and outputs the result of ANDing, ORing, and XORing them:

```
// BitTest - initialize two variables and output the
//           results of applying the ~,& , | and ^
//           operations
#include <cstdio>
#include <cstdlib>
#include <iostream>
using namespace std;

int main(int nNumberofArgs, char* pszArgs[])
{
    // set output format to hexadecimal
    cout.unsetf(cout.dec);
    cout.setf(cout.hex);

    // initialize two arguments
    int nArg1 = 0x78ABCDEF;
    int nArg2 = 0x12345678;

    // now perform each operation in turn
    // first the unary NOT operator
    cout << " nArg1 = 0x" << nArg1  << endl;
    cout << "~nArg1 = 0x" << ~nArg1 << "\n" << endl;
    cout << " nArg2 = 0x" << nArg2  << endl;
    cout << "~nArg2 = 0x" << ~nArg2 << "\n" << endl;

    // now the binary operators
    cout << "  0x" << nArg1 << "\n"
         << "& 0x" << nArg2 << "\n"
         << "  ----------" << "\n"
         << "  0x" << (nArg1 & nArg2) << "\n"
         << endl;

    cout << "  0x" << nArg1 << "\n"
         << "| 0x" << nArg2 << "\n"
         << "  ----------" << "\n"
         << "  0x" << (nArg1 | nArg2) << "\n"
         << endl;

    cout << "  0x" << nArg1 << "\n"
         << "^ 0x" << nArg2 << "\n"
```

```
         << " ----------" << "\n"
         << "   0x" << (nArg1 ^ nArg2) << "\n"
         << endl;

    // wait until user is ready before terminating program
    // to allow the user to see the program results
    cout << "Press Enter to continue..." << endl;
    cin.ignore(10, '\n');
    cin.get();
    return 0;
}
```

The first two expressions in our program, *cout.unsetf(ios::dec)* and *cout. setf(ios::hex),* changes the default output format from decimal to hexadecimal. (You'll have to trust me until Chapter 23 that it works.)

The remainder of the program is straightforward. The program assigns *nArg1* the test value *0x78ABCDEF* and *nArg2* the value *0x12345678.* The program then outputs all combinations of bitwise calculations. The extra newlines, such as in the following line, cause a blank line to appear to help group the output to make it easier to read:

```
cout << "~nArg1 = 0x" << ~nArg1 << "\n" << endl;
```

The output appears as follows:

```
 nArg1 = 0x78abcdef
~nArg1 = 0x87543210

 nArg2 = 0x12345678
~nArg2 = 0xedcba987

  0x78abcdef
& 0x12345678
  ----------
  0x10204468

  0x78abcdef
| 0x12345678
  ----------
  0x7abfdfff

  0x78abcdef
^ 0x12345678
  ----------
  0x6a9f9b97

Press Enter to continue...
```

You can convert each of the digits into binary to check the bitwise arithmetic. For example, from the first digit of each of the examples, you can see that *7 & 1* equals *1, 7 | 1* equals *7,* and *7 ^ 1* equals *6.*

Running through simple and bitwise logical calculations in your head at parties is fun (well, okay, for *some* of us), but a program has to make actual, practical *use* of these values to make them worth the trouble. Coming right up: Chapter 5 demonstrates how logical calculations are used to control program flow.

Chapter 5

Controlling Program Flow

. . . .

In This Chapter

▶ Controlling the flow through the program

▶ Executing a group of statements repetitively

▶ Avoiding infinite loops

. . . .

*T*he simple programs that appear in Chapters 1 through 4 process a fixed number of inputs, output the result of that calculation, and quit. However, these programs lack any form of flow control. They cannot make tests of any sort. Computer programs are all about making decisions. If the user presses a key, the computer responds to the command.

For example, if the user presses Ctrl+C, the computer copies the currently selected area to the Clipboard. If the user moves the mouse, the pointer moves on the screen. If the user clicks the right mouse button with the Windows key depressed, the computer crashes. The list goes on and on. Programs that don't make decisions are necessarily pretty boring.

Flow-control commands allow the program to decide what action to take based on the results of the C++ logical operations performed (see Chapter 4). There are basically three types of flow-control statements: the branch, the loop, and the switch.

Controlling Program Flow with the Branch Commands

The simplest form of flow control is the *branch statement*. This instruction allows the program to decide which of two paths to take through C++ instructions, based on the results of a logical expression (see Chapter 4 for a description of logical expressions).

In C++, the branch statement is implemented using the *if* statement:

```
if (m > n)
{
    // Path 1
    // ...instructions to be executed if
    // m is greater than n
}
else
{
    // Path 2
    // ...instructions to be executed if not
}
```

First, the logical expression *m > n* is evaluated. If the result of the expression is *true,* control passes down the path marked *Path 1* in the previous snippet. If the expression is *false,* control passes to *Path 2.* The *else* clause is optional. If it is not present, C++ acts as if it is present but empty.

Actually, the braces are not required if there's only one statement to execute as part of the *if.* Originally, braces were only used if there were two or more statements that you wanted to treat as one. However, people quickly realized that it was cleaner and less error prone if you used braces every time, no matter how many statements there are.

The following program demonstrates the *if* statement (note all the lovely braces):

```
// BranchDemo - input two numbers. Go down one path of the
//              program if the first argument is greater
//              than the first or the other path if not
#include <cstdio>
#include <cstdlib>
#include <iostream>
using namespace std;

int main(int nNumberofArgs, char* pszArgs[])
{
    // input the first argument...
    int nArg1;
    cout << "Enter arg1: ";
    cin  >> nArg1;

    // ...and the second
    int nArg2;
    cout << "Enter arg2: ";
    cin  >> nArg2;

    // now decide what to do:
    if (nArg1 > nArg2)
```

```
    {
        cout<< "Argument 1 is greater than argument 2"
            << endl;
    }
    else
    {
        cout<< "Argument 1 is not greater than argument 2"
            << endl;
    }

    // wait until user is ready before terminating program
    // to allow the user to see the program results
    cout << "Press Enter to continue..." << endl;
    cin.ignore(10, '\n');
    cin.get();
    return 0;
}
```

Here the program reads two integers from the keyboard and compares them. If *nArg1* is greater than *nArg2*, control flows to the output statement *cout << "Argument 1 is greater than argument 2"*. If *nArg1* is not greater than *nArg2*, control flows to the *else* clause where the statement *cout << "Argument 1 is not greater than argument 2\n"* is executed. Here's what that operation looks like:

```
Enter arg1: 5
Enter arg2: 6
Argument 1 is not greater than argument 2
Press Enter to continue...
```

Notice how the instructions within the *if* blocks are indented slightly. This is strictly for human consumption because C++ ignores whitespace (spaces, tabs, and newlines). It may seem trivial, but a clear coding style increases the readability of your C++ program. The Code::Blocks editor can enforce this style or any one of several other coding styles for you. Select Settings➪Editor, then click on the Source Formatter selection from the scrolled list on the left. I use the ANSI bracket style with four spaces per indent.

Executing Loops in a Program

Branch statements allow you to direct the flow of a program's execution down one path or another. This is a big improvement but still not enough to write full-strength programs.

Consider the problem of updating the computer display. The typical PC must update well over a thousand pixels for each row as it paints an image from left to right. It repeats this process for each of the thousand or so rows on the display. It does this by executing the same small number of instructions, millions of times — once for each pixel.

Looping while a condition is true

The simplest form of looping statement is the *while* loop. Here's what the *while* loop looks like:

```
while(condition)
{
    // ...repeatedly executed as long as condition is true
}
```

The *condition* is tested. This condition could be *if var > 10* or *if var1 == var2* or any other expression you might think of as long as it returns a value of *true* or *false*. If the condition is *true,* the statements within the braces are executed. Upon encountering the closed brace, C++ returns control to the beginning, and the process starts over. If the condition is *false,* control passes to the first statement after the closed brace. The effect is that the C++ code within the braces is executed repeatedly as long as the condition is *true.* (Kind of reminds me of how I get to walk around the yard with my dog until she . . . well, until we're done.)

If the condition were *true* the first time, what would make it be *false* in the future? Consider the following example program:

```
// WhileDemo - input a loop count. Loop while
//             outputting astring arg number of times.
#include <cstdio>
#include <cstdlib>
#include <iostream>
using namespace std;

int main(int nNumberofArgs, char* pszArgs[])
{
    // input the loop count
    int nLoopCount;
    cout << "Enter loop count: ";
    cin  >> nLoopCount;

    // now loop that many times
    while (nLoopCount > 0)
    {
        nLoopCount = nLoopCount - 1;
        cout << "Only " << nLoopCount
             << " loops to go" << endl;
    }
```

```
    // wait until user is ready before terminating program
    // to allow the user to see the program results
    cout << "Press Enter to continue..." << endl;
    cin.ignore(10, '\n');
    cin.get();
    return 0;
}
```

WhileDemo begins by retrieving a loop count from the user, which it stores in the variable *nLoopCount*. The program then executes a *while* loop. The *while* first tests *nLoopCount*. If *nLoopCount* is greater than 0, the program enters the body of the loop (the *body* is the code between the braces), where it decrements *nLoopCount* by 1 and outputs the result to the display. The program then returns to the top of the loop to test whether *nLoopCount* is still positive.

When executed, the program *WhileDemo* outputs the results shown in this next snippet. Here I entered a loop count of **5**. The result is that the program loops five times, each time outputting a countdown:

```
Enter loop count: 5
Only 4 loops to go
Only 3 loops to go
Only 2 loops to go
Only 1 loops to go
Only 0 loops to go
Press Enter to continue...
```

If the user enters a negative loop count, the program skips the loop entirely. That's because the specified condition is never *true,* so control never enters the loop. In addition, if the user enters a very large number, the program loops for a long time before completing.

A separate, less frequently used version of the *while* loop known as the *do . . . while* appears identical except the condition isn't tested until the bottom of the loop:

```
do
{
    // ...the inside of the loop
} while (condition);
```

Because the condition isn't tested until the end, the body of the *do . . . while* is always executed at least once.

The condition is checked only at the beginning of the *while* loop or at the end of the *do . . . while* loop. Even if the condition ceases to be *true* at some time during the execution of the loop, control does not exit the loop until the condition is retested.

Using the autoincrement/ autodecrement feature

Programmers very often use the autoincrement ++ or the autodecrement −− operators with loops that count something. Notice from the following snippet extracted from the *WhileDemo* example that the program decrements the loop count by using assignment and subtraction statements, like this:

```
// now loop that many times
while (nLoopCount > 0)
{
    nLoopCount = nLoopCount - 1;
    cout << "Only " << nLoopCount
        << " loops to go" << endl;
}
```

A more compact version uses the *autodecrement* feature, which does what you may well imagine:

```
while (nLoopCount > 0)
{
    nLoopCount--;
    cout << "Only " << nLoopCount
        << " loops to go" << endl;
}
```

The logic in this version is the same as in the original. The only difference is the way that *nLoopCount* is decremented.

Because the autodecrement both decrements its argument *and* returns its value, the decrement operation can be combined with the *while* loop. In particular, the following version is the smallest loop yet:

```
while (nLoopCount-- > 0)
{
    cout << "Only " << nLoopCount
        << " loops to go" << endl;
}
```

Believe it or not, *nLoopcount-- > 0* is the version that most C++ programmers would use. It's not that C++ programmers like being cute (although they do). In fact, the more compact version (which embeds the autoincrement or autodecrement feature in the logical comparison) is easier to read, especially as you gain experience.

Both *nLoopCount--* and *--nLoopCount* expressions decrement *nLoopCount*. The former expression, however, returns the value of *nLoopCount* before being decremented; the latter expression does so after being decremented.

How often should the autodecrement version of *WhileDemo* execute when the user enters a loop count of 1? If you use the pre-decrement version, the value of *--nLoopCount* is 0, and the body of the loop is never entered. With the post-decrement version, the value of *nLoopCount* is 1, and control enters the loop.

Beware thinking that the version of the program with the autodecrement command executes faster than the simple *"- 1"* version (since it contains fewer statements). It probably executes exactly the same. Modern compilers are good at getting the number of machine-language instructions down to a minimum, no matter which of the decrement instructions shown here you actually use.

Using the for loop

The most common form of loop is the *for* loop. The *for* loop is preferred over the more basic *while* loop because it's generally easier to read (there's really no other advantage).

The *for* loop has the following format:

```
for (initialization; conditional; increment)
{
    // ...body of the loop
}
```

The *for* loop is equivalent to the following *while* loop:

```
{
    initialization;
    while(conditional)
    {
        {
            // ...body of the loop
        }
        increment;
    }
}
```

Execution of the *for* loop begins with the *initialization clause,* which got its name because it's normally where counting variables are initialized. The initialization clause is executed only once, when the *for* loop is first encountered.

Execution continues with the *conditional clause.* This clause works just like the *while* loop: As long as the conditional clause is *true,* the *for* loop continues to execute.

After the code in the body of the loop finishes executing, control passes to the increment clause before returning to check the conditional clause — thereby repeating the process. The increment clause normally houses the autoincrement or autodecrement statements used to update the counting variables.

The *for* loop is best understood by example. The following *ForDemo1* program is nothing more than the *WhileDemo* converted to use the *for* loop construct:

```
// ForDemo1 - input a loop count. Loop while
//            outputting astring arg number of times.
#include <cstdio>
#include <cstdlib>
#include <iostream>
using namespace std;

int main(int nNumberofArgs, char* pszArgs[])
{
    // input the loop count
    int nLoopCount;
    cout << "Enter loop count: ";
    cin  >> nLoopCount;

    // count up to the loop count limit
    for (; nLoopCount > 0;)
    {
        nLoopCount = nLoopCount - 1;
        cout << "Only " << nLoopCount
             << " loops to go" << endl;
    }


    // wait until user is ready before terminating program
    // to allow the user to see the program results
    cout << "Press Enter to continue..." << endl;
    cin.ignore(10, '\n');
    cin.get();
    return 0;
}
```

The program reads a value from the keyboard into the variable *nloopCount*. The *for* starts out comparing *nloopCount* to 0. Control passes into the *for* loop if *nloopCount* is greater than 0. Once inside the *for* loop, the program decrements *nloopCount* and displays the result. That done, the program returns to the *for* loop control. Control skips to the next line after the *for* loop as soon as *nloopCount* has been decremented to 0.

All three sections of a *for* loop may be empty. An empty initialization or increment section does nothing. An empty comparison section is treated like a comparison that returns *true*.

This *for* loop has two small problems. First, it's destructive — not in the sense of what my puppy does to a slipper, but in the sense that it changes the value of *nloopCount*, "destroying" the original value. Second, this *for* loop counts backward from large values down to smaller values. These two problems are addressed by adding a dedicated counting variable to the *for* loop. Here's what it looks like:

```
// ForDemo2 - input a loop count. Loop while
//            outputting astring arg number of times.
#include <cstdio>
#include <cstdlib>
#include <iostream>
using namespace std;

int main(int nNumberofArgs, char* pszArgs[])
{
    // input the loop count
    int nLoopCount;
    cout << "Enter loop count: ";
    cin  >> nLoopCount;

    // count up to the loop count limit
    for (int i = 1; i <= nLoopCount; i++)
    {
        cout << "We've finished " << i
             << " loops" << endl;
    }

    // wait until user is ready before terminating program
    // to allow the user to see the program results
    cout << "Press Enter to continue..." << endl;
    cin.ignore(10, '\n');
    cin.get();
    return 0;
}
```

This modified version of *ForDemo* loops the same as it did before. Instead of modifying the value of *nLoopCount*, however, this *ForDemo2* version uses a new counter variable.

This *for* loop declares a counter variable *i* and initializes it to 0. It then compares this counter variable to *nLoopCount*. If *i* is less than *nLoopCount*, control passes to the output statement within the body of the *for* loop. Once the body has completed executing, control passes to the increment clause where *i* is incremented and compared to *nLoopCount* again, and so it goes.

The following shows example output from the program:

```
Enter loop count: 5
We've finished 1 loops
We've finished 2 loops
We've finished 3 loops
We've finished 4 loops
We've finished 5 loops
Press Enter to continue...
```

When declared within the initialization portion of the *for* loop, the index variable is known only within the *for* loop itself. Nerdy C++ programmers say that the scope of the variable is limited to the *for* loop. In the *ForDemo2* example just given, the variable *i* is not accessible from the *return* statement because that statement is not within the loop.

Avoiding the dreaded infinite loop

An *infinite loop* is an execution path that continues forever. An infinite loop occurs any time the condition that would otherwise terminate the loop can't occur — usually the result of a coding error.

Consider the following minor variation of the earlier loop:

```
while (nLoopCount > 0)
{
    cout << "Only " << nLoopCount
         << " loops to go" << endl;
}
```

The programmer forgot to decrement the variable *nLoopCount.* The result is a loop counter that never changes. The test condition is either always *false* or always *true.* The program executes in a never-ending (infinite) loop.

I realize that nothing's infinite. Eventually the power will fail, the computer will break, Microsoft will go bankrupt, and dogs will sleep with cats. . . . Either the loop will stop executing, or you won't care anymore. But an infinite loop will continue to execute until something outside the control of the program makes it stop.

You can create an infinite loop in many more ways than shown here, most of which are a lot more difficult to spot than this was.

For each his own

New for 2011 is a form of the *for* statement commonly known as the "*for* each" or the "range-based *for* loop." In this *for* loop, the counting variable is followed by a list of values, as shown in the following demo program:

The ForEach does not work on the Macintosh version of Code::Blocks as of this writing.

```cpp
// ForEachDemo - C++ includes a form of the "for each"
//                which iterates through each member of
//                a list
#include <cstdio>
#include <cstdlib>
#include <iostream>
using namespace std;

int main(int nNumberofArgs, char* pszArgs[])
{
    cout << "The primes less than 20 are:" << endl;
    for(int n : {1, 2, 3, 5, 7, 11, 13, 17, 19})
    {
        cout << n << ", ";
    }
    cout << endl;

    // wait until user is ready before terminating program
    // to allow the user to see the program results
    cout << "Press Enter to continue..." << endl;
    cin.ignore(10, '\n');
    cin.get();
    return 0;
}
```

The values within the braces are known as a list. The variable *n* is assigned each value in the list: 1 the first time through the loop, then the value 2, then 3, then 5, and so on. The *for* loop terminates when the list is exhausted. The output of this program appears as follows:

```
The primes less than 20 are:
1, 2, 3, 5, 7, 11, 13, 17, 19,
Press Enter to continue...
```

I touch on initializer lists again in Chapter 7 and discuss in detail in Chapter 26.

The range-based loop example shown here does not work on the Macintosh version of Code::Blocks/gcc. The array-based examples in Chapter 7 do work correctly on the Mac, however.

Applying special loop controls

C++ defines two special flow-control commands known as *break* and *continue*. Sometimes the condition for terminating a loop occurs at neither the beginning nor the end of the loop, but in the middle. Consider a program that accumulates numbers of values entered by the user. The loop terminates when the user enters a negative number.

The challenge with this problem is that the program can't exit the loop until the user has entered a value but must exit before the value is added to the sum.

For these cases, C++ defines the *break* command. When encountered, the *break* causes control to exit the current loop immediately. Control passes from the *break* statement to the statement immediately following the closed brace at the end of the loop.

The format of the *break* commands is as follows:

```
while(condition)  // break works equally well in for loop
{
    if (some other condition)
    {
        break;    // exit the loop
    }
}                 // control passes here when the
                  // program encounters the break
```

Armed with this new *break* command, my solution to the accumulator problem appears as the program *BreakDemo:*

```
// BreakDemo - input a series of numbers.
//             Continue to accumulate the sum
//             of these numbers until the user
//             enters a negative number.
#include <cstdio>
#include <cstdlib>
#include <iostream>
using namespace std;

int main(int nNumberofArgs, char* pszArgs[])
{
    // input the loop count
    int accumulator = 0;
    cout << "This program sums values from the user\n"
         << "Terminate by entering a negative number"
         << endl;

    // loop "forever"
    for(;;)
```

```
    {
        // fetch another number
        int nValue = 0;
        cout << "Enter next number: ";
        cin  >> nValue;

        // if it's negative...
        if (nValue < 0)
        {
            // ...then exit
            break;
        }

        // ...otherwise add the number to the accumulator
        accumulator += nValue;
    }

    // now that we've exited the loop
    // output the accumulated result
    cout << "\nThe total is "
         << accumulator
         << endl;

    // wait until user is ready before terminating program
    // to allow the user to see the program results
    cout << "Press Enter to continue..." << endl;
    cin.ignore(10, '\n');
    cin.get();
    return 0;
}
```

After explaining the rules to the user (entering a negative number to terminate and so on), the program enters what looks like an infinite *for* loop. Once
within the loop, *BreakDemo* retrieves a number from the keyboard. Only after
the program has read the number can it test to see whether that number
matches the exit criteria. If the input number is negative, control passes to
the *break,* causing the program to exit the loop. If the input number is **not**
negative, control skips over the *break* command to the expression that sums
the new value into the accumulator. After the program exits the loop, it outputs the accumulated value and then exits.

When performing an operation on a variable repeatedly in a loop, make sure
that the variable is initialized properly before entering the loop. In this case,
the program zeros *accumulator* before entering the loop where *nValue* is added
to it.

The result of an example run appears as follows:

```
This program sums values from the user
Terminate by entering a negative number
Enter next number: 1
Enter next number: 2
Enter next number: 3
Enter next number: -1

The total is 6
Press Enter to continue...
```

The similar *continue* command is used less frequently. When the program encounters the *continue* command, it immediately moves back to the top of the loop. The rest of the statements in the loop are ignored for the current iteration.

The following example snippet ignores negative numbers that the user might input. Only a 0 terminates this version (the complete program appears on the website as *ContinueDemo*):

```
while(true) // this while() has the same effect as for(;;)
{
    // input a value
    cout << "Input a value:";
    cin  >> nValue;

    // if the value is negative...
    if (nValue < 0)
    {
        // ...output an error message...
        cout << "Negative numbers are not allowed\n";

        // ...and go back to the top of the loop
        continue;
    }

    // ...continue to process input like normal
}
```

Nesting Control Commands

Return to our PC-screen-repaint problem. Surely it must need a loop structure of some type to write each pixel from left to right on a single line. (Do Middle Eastern terminals scan from right to left? I have no idea.) What about repeatedly repainting each scan line from top to bottom? (Do PC screens in Australia scan from bottom to top?) For this particular task, you need to include a left-to-right scan loop within the top-to-bottom scan loop.

A loop command within another loop is known as a *nested loop*. As an example, I have modified the *BreakDemo* program to accumulate any number of sequences. In this *NestedDemo* program, the inner loop sums numbers entered from the keyboard until the user enters a negative number. The outer loop continues accumulating sequences until the sum is 0. Here's what it looks like:

```
// NestedDemo - input a series of numbers.
//              Continue to accumulate the sum
//              of these numbers until the user
//              enters a 0. Repeat the process
//              until the sum is 0.
#include <cstdio>
#include <cstdlib>
#include <iostream>
using namespace std;

int main(int nNumberofArgs, char* pszArgs[])
{
    // the outer loop
    cout << "This program sums multiple series\n"
         << "of numbers. Terminate each sequence\n"
         << "by entering a negative number.\n"
         << "Terminate the series by entering two\n"
         << "negative numbers in a row\n";

    // continue to accumulate sequences
    int accumulator;
    for(;;)
    {
        // start entering the next sequence
        // of numbers
        accumulator = 0;
        cout << "Start the next sequence\n";

        // loop forever
        for(;;)
        {
            // fetch another number
            int nValue = 0;
            cout << "Enter next number: ";
            cin  >> nValue;

            // if it's negative...
            if (nValue < 0)
            {
                // ...then exit
                break;
            }
```

```
                    // ...otherwise add the number to the
                    // accumulator
                    accumulator += nValue;
            }

            // exit the loop if the total accumulated is 0
            if (accumulator == 0)
            {
                break;
            }

            // output the accumulated result and start over
            cout << "The total for this sequence is "
                 << accumulator << endl << endl;
        }

        // wait until user is ready before terminating program
        // to allow the user to see the program results
        cout << "Press Enter to continue..." << endl;
        cin.ignore(10, '\n');
        cin.get();
        return 0;
}
```

Notice the inner *for* loop looks like the earlier accumulator example. Immediately after that loop, however, is an added test. If *accumulator* is equal to 0, the program executes a break statement that exits the outer loop. Otherwise, the program outputs the accumulated value and starts over.

Switching to a Different Subject?

One last control statement is useful in a limited number of cases. The *switch* statement resembles a compound *if* statement by including a number of different possibilities rather than a single test:

```
switch(expression)
{
    case c1:
        // go here if the expression == c1
        break;
    case c2:
        // go here if expression == c2
        break;
    default:
        // go here if there is no match
}
```

The value of expression must be an integer (*int*, *long*, or *char*). The case values must be constants.

As of the '14 standard, they can also be a constant expression. I don't describe constant expressions until Chapter 10.

When the *switch* statement is encountered, the expression is evaluated and compared to the various case constants. Control branches to the case that matches. If none of the cases matches, control passes to the *default* clause.

Consider the following example code snippet:

```
int choice;
cout << "Enter a 1, 2 or 3:";
cin  >> choice;

switch(choice)
{
    case 1:
       // do "1" processing
       break;

    case 2:
       // do "2" processing
       break;

    case 3:
       // do "3" processing
       break;

    default:
       cout << "You didn't enter a 1, 2 or 3\n";
}
```

Once again, the *switch* statement has an equivalent; in this case, multiple *if* statements. However, when there are more than two or three cases, the *switch* structure is easier to understand.

The *break* statements are necessary to exit the *switch* command. Without the *break* statements, control falls through from one case to the next. (Look out below!)

Part II

Becoming a Functional C++ Programmer

Visit www.dummies.com/extras/cplusplus for great Dummies content online.

In this part...

- Writing functions
- Using arrays
- Passing pointers
- Defining constants and macros
- Visit `www.dummies.com/extras/cplusplus` for great Dummies content online

Chapter 6

Creating Functions

• •

In This Chapter

▶ Writing functions

▶ Passing data to functions

▶ Naming functions with different arguments

▶ Creating function prototypes

▶ Passing by value versus passing by reference

▶ Providing default values for arguments

• •

*T*he programs developed in prior chapters have been small enough that they can be easily read as a single unit. Larger, real-world programs are often many thousands if not millions of lines long. Developers need to break up these monster programs into smaller chunks that are easier to conceive, describe, develop, and maintain.

C++ allows programmers to divide their code into just such chunks known as functions. A *function* is a small block of code that can be executed as a single entity. This allows the programmer to divide her program into a number of such entities, each that implements some well-defined subset of the overall program. Functions are themselves broken up into smaller, more detailed functions in a pyramid of ever smaller, more detailed solutions that make up the complete program.

This divide-and-conquer approach reduces the complexity of creating a working program of significant size to something achievable by a mere mortal.

Writing and Using a Function

Functions are best understood by example. This section starts with the example program *FunctionDemo*, which simplifies the *NestedDemo* program I discussed in Chapter 5 by defining a function to contain part of the logic. Then this section explains how the function is defined and how it is invoked, using *FunctionDemo* as a pattern for understanding both the problem and the solution.

The *NestedDemo* program in Chapter 5 contains at least three parts that can be easily separated both in your mind and in fact:

- An explanation to the operator as to how data is to be entered
- An inner loop that sums up a single sequence of numbers
- An outer loop that repeatedly invokes the inner loop until the accumulated value is 0

Separating the program along these lines allows the programmer to concentrate on each piece of the program separately. The following *FunctionDemo* program shows how *NestedDemo* can be broken up by creating the functions *displayExplanation()* and *sumSequence():*

```cpp
// FunctionDemo - demonstrate the use of functions
//                by breaking the inner loop of the
//                NestedDemo program off into its own
//                function
#include <cstdio>
#include <cstdlib>
#include <iostream>
using namespace std;

// displayExplanation - prompt the user as to the rules
//                      of the game
void displayExplanation(void)
{
    cout << "This program sums multiple series\n"
         << "of numbers. Terminate each sequence\n"
         << "by entering a negative number.\n"
         << "Terminate the series by entering an\n"
         << "empty sequence.\n"
         << endl;
    return;
}

// sumSequence - add a sequence of numbers entered from
//               the keyboard until the user enters a
//               negative number.
//               return - the summation of numbers entered
int sumSequence(void)
{
    // loop forever
    int accumulator = 0;
    for(;;)
    {
        // fetch another number
        int nValue = 0;
        cout << "Enter next number: ";
        cin  >> nValue;
```

```cpp
            // if it's negative...
            if (nValue < 0)
            {
                // ...then exit from the loop
                break;
            }

            // ...otherwise add the number to the
            // accumulator
            accumulator += nValue;
    }

    // return the accumulated value
    return accumulator;
}

int main(int nNumberofArgs, char* pszArgs[])
{
    // display prompt to the user
    displayExplanation();

    // accumulate sequences of numbers...
    for(;;)
    {
        // sum a sequence of numbers entered from
        // the keyboard
        cout << "Enter next sequence" << endl;
        int accumulatedValue = sumSequence();

        // terminate the loop if sumSequence() returns
        // a zero
        if (accumulatedValue == 0)
        {
            break;
        }

        // now output the accumulated result
        cout << "The total is " << accumulatedValue
             << endl << endl;
    }

    // wait until user is ready before terminating program
    // to allow the user to see the program results
    cout << "Press Enter to continue..." << endl;
    cin.ignore(10, '\n');
    cin.get();
    return 0;
}
```

Defining our first function

The statement *void displayExplanation(void)* is known as a *function declaration* — it introduces the function definition that immediately follows. A function declaration always starts with the name of the function preceded by the type of value the function returns and followed by a pair of open and closed parentheses containing any arguments to the function.

The return type *void* means that *displayExplanation()* does not return a value. The *void* within the argument list means that it doesn't take any arguments either. (We'll get to what that means very soon.) The body of the function is contained in the braces immediately following the function declaration.

Function names are normally written as a multiword description with all the words rammed together. I start function names with lowercase but capitalize all intermediate words. Function names almost always appear followed by an open and close parenthesis pair.

A function doesn't do anything until it is invoked. Our program starts executing with the first line in *main()* just like always. The first non-comment line in *main()* is the call to *displayExplanation()*:

```
displayExplanation();
```

This passes program control to the first line in the *displayExplanation()* function. The computer continues to execute there until it reaches the return statement at the end of *displayExplanation()* or until control reaches the closed brace at the end of the function.

Defining the sumSequence ( ) function

The declaration *int sumSequence(void)* begins the definition of the *sumSequence()* function. This declaration says that the function does not expect any arguments but returns a value of type *int* to the caller. The body of this function contains the same code previously found in the inner loop of the *NestedDemo* example.

The *sumSequence()* function also contains a return statement to exit the program. This return is not optional since it contains the value to be returned, *accumulator.* The type of value returned must match the type of the function in the declaration, in this case *int.*

Calling the function sumSequence ( )

Return back to the *main()* function in *FunctionDemo* again. This section of code looks similar to the outer loop in *NestedDemo.*

The main difference is the expression *accumulatedValue = sumSequence()*; that appears where the inner loop would have been. The *sumSequence()* statement invokes the function of that name. The value of the expression *sumSequence()* is the value returned by the function. This value is stored in the variable *accumulatedValue* and then displayed. The main program continues to loop until *sumSequence()* returns a sum of 0, which indicates that the user has finished calculating sums.

Divide and conquer

The *FunctionDemo* program has split the outer loop in *main()* from the inner loop into a function *sumSequence()* and created a *displayExplanation()* to get things kicked off. This division wasn't arbitrary: Both functions in *FunctionDemo* perform a logically separate operation.

A good function is easy to describe. You shouldn't have to use more than a single sentence, with a minimum of such words as *and, or, unless, until* or *but*. For example, here's a simple, straightforward definition: "The function *sumSequence* accumulates a sequence of integer values entered by the user." This definition is concise and clear. It's a world away from the *NestedDemo* program description: "The program explains to the user how the program works AND then sums a sequence of positive values AND displays the sum AND starts over again UNTIL the user enters a zero-length sum."

The output of a sample run of this program appears identical to that generated by the *NestedDemo* program.

Understanding the Details of Functions

Functions are so fundamental to creating C++ programs that getting a handle on the details of defining, creating, and testing them is critical. Armed with the example *FunctionDemo* program, consider the following definition of function: A *function* is a logically separated block of C++ code.

The function construct has the following form:

```
<return type> name(<arguments to the function>)
{
    // ...
    return <expression>;
}
```

The *arguments* to a function are values that can be passed to the function to be used as input information. The *return* value is a value that the function returns. For example, in the call to the function *square(10)*, the value 10 is an argument to the function *square()*. The returned value is 100 (if it's not, this is one poorly named function).

Both the arguments and the return value are optional. If either is absent, the keyword *void* is used instead. That is, if a function has a *void* argument list, the function does not take any arguments when called (this was the case with the *FunctionDemo* program). If the return type is *void,* the function does not return a value to the caller.

The default argument type to a function is *void,* meaning that it takes no arguments. A function *int fn(void)* may be declared as *int fn().*

Understanding simple functions

The simple function *sumSequence()* returns an integer value that it calculates. Functions may return any of the intrinsic variable types described in Chapter 2. For example, a function might return a *double* or a *char.* If a function returns no value, the return type of the function is labeled *void.*

A function may be labeled by its return type — for example, a function that returns an *int* is often known as an integer function. A function that returns no value is known as a void function.

For example, the following *void* function performs an operation but returns no value:

```
void echoSquare()
{
    int value;
    cout << "Enter a value:";
    cin >> value;
    cout << "\nThe square is:" << (value * value) << "\n";
    return;
}
```

Control begins at the open brace and continues through to the return statement. The return statement in a *void* function is not followed by a value. The return statement in a *void* function is optional. If it isn't present, execution returns to the calling function when control encounters the close brace.

Understanding functions with arguments

Functions without arguments are of limited use because the communication from such functions is one-way — through the return value. Two-way communication is through function arguments.

Functions with arguments

A *function argument* is a variable whose value is passed to the calling function during the call operation. The following *SquareDemo* example program defines and uses a function *square()* that returns the square of a double-precision float passed to it:

```
// SquareDemo - demonstrate the use of a function
//              which processes arguments

#include <cstdio>
#include <cstdlib>
#include <iostream>
using namespace std;

// square - returns the square of its argument
//          doubleVar - the value to be squared
//          returns - square of doubleVar
double square(double doubleVar)
{
    return doubleVar * doubleVar;
}

// displayExplanation - prompt the user as to the rules
//                      of the game
void displayExplanation(void)
{
    cout << "This program sums the square of multiple\n"
         << "series of numbers. Terminate each sequence\n"
         << "by entering a negative number.\n"
         << "Terminate the series by entering an\n"
         << "empty sequence.\n"
         << endl;
    return;
}


// sumSquareSequence - accumulate the square of the number
//                     entered at the keyboard into a sequence
//                     until the user enters a negative number
double sumSquareSequence(void)
{
    // loop forever
    double accumulator = 0.0;
    for(;;)
    {
        // fetch another number
        double dValue = 0;
        cout << "Enter next number: ";
        cin  >> dValue;
```

```cpp
        // if it's negative...

        if (dValue < 0)
        {
            // ...then exit from the loop
            break;
        }

        // ...otherwise calculate the square
        double value = square(dValue);

        // now add the square to the
        // accumulator
        accumulator += value;
    }

    // return the accumulated value
    return accumulator;
}

int main(int nNumberofArgs, char* pszArgs[])
{
    displayExplanation();

    // Continue to accumulate numbers...
    for(;;)
    {
        // sum a sequence of numbers entered from
        // the keyboard
        cout << "Enter next sequence" << endl;
        double accumulatedValue = sumSquareSequence();

        // terminate if the sequence is zero or negative
        if (accumulatedValue <= 0.0)
        {
            break;
        }

        // now output the accumulated result
        cout << "\nThe total of the values squared is "
             << accumulatedValue << endl << endl;
    }

    // wait until user is ready before terminating program
    // to allow the user to see the program results
    cout << "Press Enter to continue..." << endl;
    cin.ignore(10, '\n');
    cin.get();
    return 0;
}
```

This is essentially the same *FunctionDemo* program, except that the *sumSquare Sequence()* function accumulates the square of the values entered and returns them as a *double* rather than an *int.* The function *square()* returns the value of its one argument multiplied by itself. The change to the *sumSequence()* function is simple: Rather than accumulate the value entered, the function now accumulates the result returned from *square()*.

Functions with multiple arguments

Functions may have multiple arguments that are separated by commas. Thus, the following function returns the product of its two arguments:

```
int product(int arg1, int arg2)
{
    return arg1 * arg2;
}
```

main ( ) exposed

The "keyword" *main()* from our standard program template is nothing more than a function — albeit a function with strange arguments but a function nonetheless.

When C++ builds a program from source code, it adds some boilerplate code that executes before your program ever starts. (You can't see this code without digging into the bowels of the C++ library functions.) This code sets up the environment in which your program operates. For example, this boilerplate code opens the default input and output channels *cin* and *cout.*

After the environment has been established, the C++ boilerplate code calls the function *main()*, thereby beginning execution of your code. When your program finishes, it exits from *main()*. This enables the C++ boilerplate to clean up a few things before turning control over to the operating system that kills the program.

The arguments to *main()* are complicated — we'll review those later. The *int* returned from *main()* is a status indicator. The program returns a 0 if the program terminates normally. Any other value can be used to indicate an error — the actual value returned indicates the nature of the error that caused the program to quit.

Overloading Function Names

C++ must have a way of telling functions apart. Thus, two functions cannot share the same name and argument list, known as the *extended name* or the *signature.* The following extended function names are all different and can reside in the same program:

```
void someFunction(void)
{
    // ....perform some function
}
void someFunction(int n)
{
    // ...perform some different function
}
void someFunction(double d)
{
    // ...perform some very different function
}
void someFunction(int n1, int n2)
{
    // ....do something different yet
}
```

C++ knows that the functions *someFunction(void), someFunction(int), someFunction(double),* and *someFunction(int, int)* are not the same.

This multiple use of names is known as function *overloading.*

Programmers often refer to functions by their shorthand name, which is the name of the function without its arguments, such as *someFunction(),* in the same way that I have the shorthand name Stephen (actually, my nickname is Randy, but work with me on this one). But if there's any doubt, I can be differentiated from other Stephens by including my family name. In the same way, overloaded functions can be differentiated by their argument lists.

Here's a typical application that uses overloaded functions with unique extended names:

```
int intVariable1, intVariable2;
double doubleVariable;

// functions are distinguished by the type of
// the argument passed
someFunction();                 // calls someFunction(void)
```

```
someFunction(intVariable1);   // calls someFunction(int)
someFunction(doubleVariable);// calls someFunction(double)
someFunction(intVariable1, intVariable2); // calls
                             // someFunction(int, int)

// this works for constants as well
someFunction(1);              // calls someFunction(int)
someFunction(1.0);            // calls someFunction(double)
someFunction(1, 2);           // calls someFunction(int, int)
```

In each case, the type of the arguments matches the extended names of the three functions.

The return type is not part of the extended name of the function. The following two functions have the same name, so they can't be part of the same program:

```
int someFunction(int n);     // full name of the function
                             // is someFunction(int)
double someFunction(int n);  // same name
long l = someFunction(10);   // call which function?
```

Here C++ does not know whether to convert the value returned from the *double* version of *someFunction()* to a long or promote the value returned from *int* version.

Defining Function Prototypes

A function must be declared before it can be used. That's so C++ can compare the call against the declaration to make sure that any necessary conversions are performed. However, a function does not have to be defined when it is first declared. A function may be defined anywhere in the module. (A *module* is another name for a C++ source file.)

Consider the following code snippet:

```
int main(int nNumberofArgs, char* pszArgs[])
{
    someFunc(1, 2);
}
int someFunc(double dArg1, int nArg2)
{
    // ...do something
}
```

main() doesn't know the proper argument types of the function *someFunc()* at the time of the call. C++ might surmise from the call that the full function definition is *someFunc(int, int)* and that its return type is *void;* however, the definition of the function that appears immediately after *main()* shows that the programmer wants the first argument converted to a floating point and that the function does actually return a value.

I know, I know — C++ could be less lazy and look ahead to determine the extended name of *someFunc()* on its own, but it doesn't. What is needed is some way to inform *main()* of the full name of *someFunc()* before it is used. This is handled by what we call a *function prototype* declaration.

A prototype declaration appears the same as a function with no body. In use, a prototype declaration looks like this:

```
int someFunc(double, int);
int main(int nNumberofArgs, char* pszArgs[])
{
    someFunc(1, 2);
}
int someFunc(double dArg1, int nArg2)
{
    // ...do something
}
```

The prototype declaration tells the world (at least that part of the world after the declaration) that the extended name for *someFunc()* is *someFunction(double, int)*. The call in *main()* now knows to cast the 1 to a *double* before making the call. In addition, *main()* knows that *someFunc()* returns an *int* value to the caller.

It is common practice to include function prototypes for every function in a module either at the beginning of the module or, more often, in a separate file that can be included within other modules at compile-time. That's the function of the *include* statements that appear at the beginning of the Official *C++ For Dummies* program template:

```
#include <cstdio>
#include <cstdlib>
#include <iostream>
```

These three files *cstdio, cstdlib,* and *iostream* include prototype declarations for the common system functions that we've been using, such as *cout <<* *"string"*. The contents of these files are inserted at the point of the #*include* statement by the compiler as part of its normal duties.

Chapter 10 is dedicated to include files and other so-called preprocessor commands.

Defaulting Arguments

You can provide default values for arguments in your function declaration. Consider the following simple example:

```
// isLegal - return true if the age is greater
//           than or equal to the minimum age
//           which defaults to 21
bool isLegal(int age, int minAge = 21)
{
    return age >= minAge;
}
```

This function returns a *true* if the first argument passed, *age*, is greater than the second argument, *minAge*, and the second argument defaults to 21 if you don't say otherwise in the function call. Thus, the following calls are both legal:

```
legal = isLegal(age); // same as isLegal(age, 21)
if (inLouisiana())
{
    legal = isLegal(age, 18);
}
```

The call *isLegal(age)* is completely equivalent to *isLegal(age, 21)*. C++ just provides the default argument for you. The call to *isLegal(age, 18)* ignores the default value.

Normally the defaults are provided in the prototype declarations.

You can default more than one argument, but defaults must be defined from right to left and filled in from left to right:

```
// the following is legal
bool isWorkingAge(int age, int minAge=18, int maxAge=65);

// check if the worker is between 18 and 65
legal = isWorkingAge(age);

// check if worker is between 21 and 65
legal = isWorkingAge(age, 21);

// check if work is between 21 and 60
legal = isWorkingAge(age, 21, 60);

// the following does NOT check if the worker is
// between 18 and 60
legal = isWorkingAge(age, 60);
```

The first call uses the default values for both the minimum and maximum age (18 and 65, respectively). The second call uses the default maximum age of 65 but supplies a different minimum age of 21. The third call provides both an explicit minimum and maximum age.

The last call does not check whether age is between 18 and 60 as you might expect. In this case, the call is made with a minimum age of 60 and a maximum age of 65.

Default arguments can sometimes confuse C++ when combined with function overloading. For example, the following is not legal:

```
bool isLegal(int age);
bool isLegal(int age, int minAge = 21); // not allowed
```

The problem is that if you called *isLegal(10)*, C++ wouldn't know which one of the two functions to call: the first function with just one argument or the second function with the second argument defaulted.

Passing by Value and Passing by Reference

C++ normally passes arguments to functions by value. That is, if I call a function *fn(n)*, it is the value of *n* that gets passed to the function. This allows me to make calls like the following:

```
fn(a + b);    // pass the value of a + b
```

What gets passed in this snippet is the result of the expression *a + b*.

This has a perhaps surprising side effect demonstrated by the following snippet:

```
void multiplyByTwo(int m)
{
    m *= 2;
}

int n = 1;
multiplyByTwo(n);

cout << "n = " << n << endl;
```

You may be surprised to find out that this example prints out *n = 1.*

Let's go through the example one step at a time:

1. The main program declares the variable *n* and initializes it to 1.

2. The program then passes the value of *n (1)* to the function *multiplyByTwo()* and calls it *m.*

3. The function multiplies the value passed it by two and stores the result in the local variable

4. *multiplyByTwo()* discards *m* upon returning.

5. The main program displays the unchanged value of *n (1)*.

This is called *pass by value* — the alternative is called *pass by reference.*

You can tell C++ that you want to pass not the value of a variable but a reference to a variable by adding an ampersand *(&)* to the type, as in the following snippet:

```
void multiplyByTwo(int& m)    // referential argument
{
     m *= 2;
}

int n = 1;
multiplyByTwo(n);

cout << "n = " << n << endl;
```

This example does the following:

1. The main program declares the variable *n* and initializes it to 1.

2. The program then passes a reference to *n* to the function *multiplyByTwo()* which calls that reference *m.*

3. The function multiplies by two the variable referenced by *m* and saves the results back into the variable referenced by *m* (in other words, the variable *n*).

4. The main program displays the changed value of *n (2)*.

Arrays (which I introduce in the next chapter) are always passed by reference for reasons that I will explain in Chapter 8.

I will have a lot more to say about reference arguments in Chapter 8.

Variable Storage Types

Variables are also assigned a storage type depending on where and how they are defined in the function, as shown in the following example:

```
int globalVariable;
void fn()
{
    int localVariable;
    static int staticVariable = 1;
}
```

Variables declared within a function like *localVariable* are said to be local. The variable *localVariable* doesn't exist until execution passes through its declaration within the function *fn()*. *localVariable* ceases to exist when the function returns. Upon return, whatever value that is stored in *localVariable* is lost. In addition, only *fn()* has access to *localVariable* — other functions cannot reach into the function to access it.

By comparison, the variable *globalVariable* is created when the program begins execution and exists as long as the program is running. All functions have access to *globalVariable* all the time.

The keyword *static* can be used to create a sort of mishling — something between a global and local variable. The static variable *staticVariable* is created when execution reaches the declaration the first time that function *fn()* is called, just like a local variable. The static variable is not destroyed when program execution returns from the function, however. Instead, it retains its value from one call to the next. If *fn()* assigns a value to *staticVariable* once, it'll still be there the next time *fn()* is called. The initialization portion of the declaration is ignored every subsequent time execution passes through.

Chapter 7

Storing Sequences in Arrays

- -

In This Chapter

▶ Considering the need for something like an array

▶ Introducing the array data type

▶ Using an array

▶ Using the most common type of array — the character string

- -

*A*n *array* is a sequence of variables that shares the same name and that is referenced using an index. Arrays are useful little critters that allow you to store a large number of values of the same type that are related in some way — for example, the batting averages of all the players on the same team might be a good candidate for storage within an array. Arrays can be multi-dimensional, too, allowing you, for example, to store an array of batting averages within an array of months, which allows you to work with the batting averages of the team as they occur by month.

In this chapter, you find out how to initialize and use arrays for fun and profit. You also find out about an especially useful form of array called a *char string*.

Arraying the Arguments for Arrays

Consider the following problem. You need a program that can read a sequence of numbers from the keyboard and display their sum. You guessed it — the program stops reading in numbers as soon as you enter a negative number. Unlike similar programs in Chapters 5 and 6, however, this program will output all the numbers entered before displaying the average.

You could try to store numbers in a set of independent variables, as in

```
cin >> value1;
if (value1 >= 0)
{
    cin >> value2;
    if (value2 >= 0)
    {
        ...
```

You can see that this approach can't handle sequences involving more than just a few numbers. Besides, it's ugly. What we need is some type of structure that has a name like a variable but that can store more than one value. May I present to you, Ms. A. Ray.

An array solves the problem of sequences nicely. For example, the following snippet declares an array *valueArray* that has storage for up to 128 *int* values. It then populates the array with numbers entered from the keyboard:

```
int nValue;

// declare an array capable of holding up to 128 ints
int nValueArray[128];

// define an index used to access subsequent members of
// of the array; don't exceed the 128 int limit
for (int i = 0; i < 128; i++)
{
    cin >> nValue;

    // exit the loop when the user enters a negative
    // number
    if (nValue < 0)
    {
        break;
    }
    nValueArray[i] = nValue;
}
```

The second line of this snippet declares an array *nValueArray*. Array declarations begin with the type of the array members: in this case, *int*. This is followed by the name of the array. The last elements of an array declaration are open and closed brackets containing the maximum number of elements that the array can hold. In this code snippet, *nValueArray* can store up to 128 integers.

The size of an array must be a constant expression — this means an expression that C++ can calculate when it does the build.

The 2014 standards allows the program to declare the size of an array with any expression as long as its value is known when the declaration is encountered. However, once declared, the size of the array is fixed.

This snippet reads a number from the keyboard and stores it into each subsequent member of the array *nValueArray*. You access an individual element of an array by providing the name of the array followed by brackets containing the index. The first integer in the array is *nValueArray[0]*, the second is *nValueArray[1]*, and so on.

In use, *nValueArray[i]* represents the *i*th element in the array. The index variable *i* must be a counting variable — that is, *i* must be a *char*, an *int*, or a *long*. If *nValueArray* is an array of *int*s, *nValueArray[i]* is an *int*.

Using an array

The following program inputs a sequence of integer values from the keyboard until the user enters a negative number. The program then displays the numbers input and reports their sum.

```
// ArrayDemo - demonstrate the use of arrays
//             by reading a sequence of integers
//             and then displaying them and their sum
#include <cstdio>
#include <cstdlib>
#include <iostream>
using namespace std;

// prototype declarations
int readArray(int integerArray[], int maxNumElements);
int sumArray(int integerArray[], int numElements);
void displayArray(int integerArray[], int numElements);

int main(int nNumberofArgs, char* pszArgs[])
{
    // input the loop count
    cout << "This program sums values entered "
         << "by the user\n";
    cout << "Terminate the loop by entering "
         << "a negative number\n";
    cout << endl;

    // read numbers to be summed from the user into a
    // local array
    int inputValues[128];
    int numberOfValues = readArray(inputValues, 128);

    // now output the values and the sum of the values
    displayArray(inputValues, numberOfValues);
    cout << "The sum is "
         << sumArray(inputValues, numberOfValues)
         << endl;

    // wait until user is ready before terminating program
    // to allow the user to see the program results
    cout << "Press Enter to continue..." << endl;
    cin.ignore(10, '\n');
    cin.get();
    return 0;
}

// readArray - read integers from the operator into
//             'integerArray' until operator enters neg.
//             Return the number of elements stored.
int readArray(int integerArray[], int maxNumElements)
```

```
{
    int numberOfValues;
    for(numberOfValues = 0;
        numberOfValues < maxNumElements;
        numberOfValues++)
    {
        // fetch another number
        int integerValue;
        cout << "Enter next number: ";
        cin  >> integerValue;

        // if it's negative...
        if (integerValue < 0)
        {
            // ...then exit
            break;
        }

        // ... otherwise store the number
        // into the  storage array
        integerArray[numberOfValues] = integerValue;
    }

    // return the number of elements read
    return numberOfValues;
}

// displayArray - display the members of an
//                array of length sizeOfloatArray
void displayArray(int integerArray[], int numElements)
{
    cout << "The value of the array is:" << endl;
    for (int i = 0; i < numElements; i++)
    {
        cout << i << ": " << integerArray[i] << endl;
    }
    cout << endl;
}

// sumArray - return the sum of the members of an
//            integer array
int sumArray(int integerArray[], int numElements)
{
    int accumulator = 0;
    for (int i = 0; i < numElements; i++)
    {
        accumulator += integerArray[i];
    }
    return accumulator;
}
```

The program *ArrayDemo* begins with prototype declarations of the functions *readArray()*, *sumArray()*, and *displayArray()*, which it will need later. The main program starts with a prompt to the user to input data to be summed.

The program then declares an array *inputValues[ ]* to be used to store the values input by the user. The main program passes this array to *readArray()*, along with the length of the array — *readArray()* cannot read more than 128 values even if the user does not enter a negative number since that's all the room allocated in the *inputValues[ ]* array.

The array *inputValues* is declared as 128 integers long. If you're thinking that this must be more than enough, don't count on it. No matter how large you make the array, always put a check to make sure that you do not exceed the limits of the array. Writing more data than an array can hold causes your program to perform erratically and often to crash. This is discussed in detail in Chapter 28.

The main function then calls *displayArray()* to print the contents of the array. Finally, the function calls *sumArray()* to add the elements in the array.

The *readArray()* function takes two arguments: the *integerArray[ ]* into which to store the values it reads and *maxNumElements,* the maximum number of integer values for which there is room at the inn. The function begins with a *for* loop that reads integer values. Every non-negative value that the function reads is saved into *integerArray[ ]*. The first element goes into *integerArray[0],* the second into *integerArray[1],* and so forth.

Once the user enters a negative number, the program breaks out of the loop and returns the total *numberOfValues* input.

The *displayArray()* function also uses a *for* loop to traverse the elements of the array, starting at 0 and continuing to the last element, which is *numElements - 1.* The final function, *sumArray(),* also iterates through the array but sums the elements stored there into *accumulator,* which it then returns to the caller.

Notice, yet again, that the index *i* in the *displayArray()* and *sumArray()* functions is initialized to 0 and not to 1. In addition, notice how the *for* loop terminates as soon as *i* reaches *numElements.* The output from a sample run appears as follows:

```
This program sums values entered by the user
Terminate the loop by entering a negative number

Enter next number: 10
Enter next number: 20
Enter next number: 30
Enter next number: 40
Enter next number: -1
The value of the array is:
0: 10
1: 20
2: 30
3: 40

The sum is 100
Press Enter to continue...
```

Just to keep non-programmers guessing, the term *iterate* means to traverse through a set of objects such as an array. Programmers say that the preceding functions iterate through the array.

Initializing an array

A local variable does not start life with a valid value, not even the value 0. Said another way, a local variable contains garbage until you actually store something in it. Locally declared arrays are the same — each element contains garbage until you actually assign something to it. You should initialize local variables when you declare them. This rule is even truer for arrays. It is far too easy to access uninitialized array elements thinking that they are valid values.

By "local variable", I'm talking about the normal variables declared within a function. C++ purists actually call these *automatic variables* to differentiate them from static variables (discussed in Chapter 18).

Fortunately, a small array may be initialized at the time it is declared with an initializer list. The following code snippet demonstrates how this is done:

```
float floatArray[5] = {0.0, 1.0, 2.0, 3.0, 4.0};
```

This initializes *floatArray[0]* to 0, *floatArray[1]* to 1.0, *floatArray[2]* to 2.0, and so on.

C++ pads the initialization list with 0s if the number of elements in the list is less than the size of the array. In fact, an empty initializer list can be used to initialize an array to 0:

```
int nArray[128] = {}; // initialize array to all 0's
```

The number of initialization constants can determine the size of the array. For example, you could have determined that *floatArray* has five elements just by counting the values within the braces. C++ can count as well (here's at least one thing C++ can do for itself).

```
float floatArray[] = {0.0, 1.0, 2.0, 3.0, 4.0};
```

Accessing too far into an array

Mathematicians start counting arrays with 1. Most program languages start with an offset of 1 as well. C++ arrays begin counting at 0. The first member of a C++ array is *valueArray[0]*. That makes the last element of a 128-integer array *integerArray[127]* and not *integerArray[128]*.

Unfortunately for the programmer, C++ does not check to see whether the index you are using is within the range of the array. C++ is perfectly happy giving you access to *integerArray[200]*. Our *integerArray* yard is only 128 integers long — 200 is 72 integers into someone else's yard. No telling who lives there and what he's storing at that location. Reading from *integerArray[200]* will return some unknown and unpredictable value. Writing to that location generates unpredictable results. It may do nothing — the house may be abandoned and the yard unused. On the other hand, it might overwrite some data, thereby confusing the neighbor and making the program act in a seemingly random fashion. Or it might crash the program.

The most common wrong way to access an array is to read or write location *integerArray[128]*. Although it's only one element beyond the end of the array, reading or writing this location is just as dangerous as using any other incorrect address.

Arraying range-based for loops

You can access the elements of an array using a range-based *for* loop in some cases. The following *for* loop initializes all of the members of *nArray* to 0:

```
int nArray[128];
for(int& n: nArray)
{
    n = 0;
}
```

This *for* loop says assign the variable *n* to be a reference to each element of *nArray* in turn. A 0 is then assigned to each element in *nArray* through the reference *n*.

The following range-based *for* loop has no effect:

```
int nArray[128];
for(int n: nArray)
{
    n = 0;
}
```

Without the ampersand (&), *n* is assigned the value of each element of *nArray* in turn. The variable *n* is then overwritten with a 0, leaving the value of *nArray* unchanged. Compare this to passing arguments to functions by value versus passing by reference, as described in Chapter 6.

Range-based *for* loops can be used only where C++ knows the size of the array at build time. A range-based *for* loop would not work within the *displayArray()* function, for example. This function is built to handle arrays of any size. You get really strange build time error messages when you use range-based *for* loops on arrays where the size is not known. I have more to say about this in Chapter 26.

Defining and using arrays of arrays

Arrays are adept at storing sequences of numbers. Some applications require sequences of sequences. A classic example of this matrix configuration is the spreadsheet. Laid out like a chessboard, each element in the spreadsheet has both an *x* and a *y* offset.

C++ implements the matrix as follows:

```
int intMatrix[10][5];
```

This matrix is 10 elements in one dimension and 5 in another, for a total of 50 elements. In other words, *intMatrix* is a 10-element array, each element of which is a 5-*int* array. As you might expect, one corner of the matrix is in *intMatrix[0][0]*, while the other corner is *intMatrix[9][4]*.

Whether you consider *intMatrix* to be 10 elements long in the *x* dimension or in the *y* dimension is a matter of taste. A matrix can be initialized in the same way that an array is:

```
int intMatrix[2][3] = {{1, 2, 3}, {4, 5, 6}};
```

This line initializes the 3-element array *intMatrix[0]* to 1, 2, and 3; and the 3-element array *intMatrix[1]* to 4, 5, and 6.

Using Arrays of Characters

The elements of an array can be of any type. Arrays of *floats*, *doubles*, and *longs* are all possible; however, arrays of characters have particular significance.

Creating an array of characters

Human words and sentences can be expressed as an array of characters. An array of characters containing my first name would appear as

```
char sMyName[] = {'S', 't', 'e', 'p', 'h', 'e', 'n'};
```

The following small program displays my name:

```
// CharDisplay - output a character array to
//               standard output, the MS-DOS window
#include <cstdio>
#include <cstdlib>
#include <iostream>
using namespace std;

// prototype declarations
void displayCharArray(char charArray[], int sizeOfArray);

int main(int nNumberofArgs, char* pszArgs[])
{
    char charMyName[]={'S', 't', 'e', 'p', 'h', 'e', 'n'};
    displayCharArray(charMyName, 7);
    cout << endl;

    // wait until user is ready before terminating program
    // to allow the user to see the program results
    cout << "Press Enter to continue..." << endl;
    cin.ignore(10, '\n');
    cin.get();
    return 0;
}

// displayCharArray - display an array of characters
//                    by outputing one character at
//                    a time
void displayCharArray(char charArray[], int sizeOfArray)
{
    for(int i = 0; i< sizeOfArray; i++)
    {
        cout << charArray[i];
    }
}
```

The program declares a fixed array of characters *charMyName* containing —
you guessed it — my name (what better name?). This array is passed to the
function *displayCharArray()* along with its length. The *displayCharArray()*
function is identical to the *displayArray()* function in the earlier example
program except that this version displays *char*s rather than *int*s.

This program works fine; however, it is inconvenient to pass the length of the
array with the array itself. If we could come up with a rule for determining
the end of the string of characters, we wouldn't need to pass its length — you
would know that the string was complete when you encountered the special
rule that told you so.

Creating a string of characters

In many cases, all values for each element are possible. However, C++ reserves the special "character" 0 as the non-character. You can use '\0' to mark the end of a character array. (The numeric value of '\0' is 0, but the type of '\0' is *char*.)

The character '\y' is the character whose octal value is y. The character '\0' is the character with a value of 0, otherwise known as the null character. Using that rule, the previous small program becomes

```cpp
// DisplayString - output a character array to
//                 standard output, the MS-DOS window
#include <cstdio>
#include <cstdlib>
#include <iostream>
using namespace std;

// prototype declarations
void displayString(char stringArray[]);

int main(int nNumberofArgs, char* pszArgs[])
{
    char charMyName[] =
            {'S', 't', 'e', 'p', 'h', 'e', 'n', '\0'};
    displayString(charMyName);
    cout << endl;

    // wait until user is ready before terminating program
    // to allow the user to see the program results
    cout << "Press Enter to continue..." << endl;
    cin.ignore(10, '\n');
    cin.get();
    return 0;
}

// displayString - display a character string
//                 one character at a time
void displayString(char stringArray[])
{
    for(int i = 0; stringArray[i] != '\0'; i++)
    {
        cout << stringArray[i];
    }
}
```

The declaration of *charMyName* declares the character array with the extra null character '\0' on the end. The *displayString* program iterates through the character array until a null character is encountered.

The function *displayString()* is simpler to use than its *displayCharArray()* predecessor because it is no longer necessary to pass along the length of the character array. This secret handshake of terminating a character array with a null is so convenient that it is used throughout the C++ language. C++ even gives such an array a special name.

A *string of characters* is a null-terminated character array. It is officially known as a *null-terminated byte string,* or *NTBS.* The simpler term *C-string* is also used to differentiate from the C++ type *string.*

The choice of '\0' as the terminating character was not random. Remember that 0 is the only numeric value that converts to *false;* all other values translate to *true.* This means that the *for* loop could be (and usually is) written as

```
for(int i = 0; stringArray[i]; i++)
```

This whole business of null-terminated character strings is so ingrained in the C++ language psyche that C++ uses a string of characters surrounded by double quotes to be an array of characters automatically terminated with a '\0' character. The following are identical declarations:

```
char szMyName[] = "Stephen";
char szAlsoMyName[] =
            {'S', 't', 'e', 'p', 'h', 'e', 'n', '\0'};
```

The naming convention used here is exactly that, a convention. C++ does not care. The prefix *sz* stands for *zero-terminated string.*

The string *Stephen* is eight characters long and not seven — the null character after the *n* is assumed. The string "" is one character long, consisting of just the null character.

Manipulating Strings with Character

The following *Concatenate* program inputs two strings from the keyboard and concatenates them into a single string:

```
// Concatenate - concatenate two strings
//                with a " - " in the middle
#include <cstdio>
#include <cstdlib>
#include <iostream>
using namespace std;

// prototype declarations
void concatString(char szTarget[], const char szSource[]);
```

```cpp
int main(int nNumberofArgs, char* pszArgs[])
{
    // read first string...
    char szString1[256];
    cout << "Enter string #1:";
    cin.getline(szString1, 128);

    // ...now the second string...
    char szString2[128];
    cout << "Enter string #2:";
    cin.getline(szString2, 128);

    // ...concatenate a " - " onto the first...
    concatString(szString1, " - ");

    // ...now add the second string...
    concatString(szString1, szString2);

    // ...and display the result
    cout << "\n" << szString1 << endl;

    // wait until user is ready before terminating program
    // to allow the user to see the program results
    cout << "Press Enter to continue..." << endl;
    cin.ignore(10, '\n');
    cin.get();
    return 0;
}

// concatString - concatenate the szSource string
//                onto the end of the szTarget string
void concatString(char szTarget[], const char szSource[])
{
    // find the end of the first string
    int targetIndex = 0;
    while(szTarget[targetIndex])
    {
        targetIndex++;
    }

    // tack the second onto the end of the first
    int sourceIndex = 0;
    while(szSource[sourceIndex])
    {
        szTarget[targetIndex] =
            szSource[sourceIndex];
        targetIndex++;
        sourceIndex++;
    }

    // tack on the terminating null
    szTarget[targetIndex] = '\0';
}
```

The *Concatenate* program reads two character strings and appends them together with a *" - "* in the middle.

The program begins by reading a string from the keyboard. The program does not use the normal *cin >> szString1* for two reasons. First, the *cin >>* operation stops reading when any type of whitespace is encountered. Characters up to the first whitespace are read, the whitespace character is tossed, and the remaining characters are left in the input hopper for the next *cin >>* statement. Thus, if I were to enter "the Dog", *szString2* would be filled with "the" and the word "Dog" would be left in the input buffer.

The second reason is that the *getline()* allows the programmer to specify the size of the buffer. The call to *getline(szString2, 128)* will not read more than 128 bytes no matter how many are input.

Instead, the call to *getline()* inputs an entire line up to but not including the newline at the end. We'll review this function with other file I/O functions in detail in Chapter 23.

After reading the first string into *szString1[]*, the program appends *" - "* onto the end by calling *concatString()*. It concatenates the second string by calling *concatString()* with *szString2[]*.

The *concatString()* function accepts a target string, *szTarget,* and a source string, *szSource.* The function begins by scanning *szTarget* for the terminating null character, which it stores in *targetIndex.* The function then enters a second loop in which it copies characters from the *szSource* into *szTarget* starting at the terminating null. The final statement in *concatString()* slaps a terminating null on the completed string.

An example output from the program appears as follows:

```
Enter string #1:this is a string
Enter string #2:THIS IS A STRING

this is a string - THIS IS A STRING
Press Enter to continue...
```

Adding Some Library Functions

The C++ programmer is often required to manipulate zero-terminated strings. C++ provides a number of standard string-manipulation functions to make the job easier. A few of these functions are listed in Table 7-1.

Table 7-1	String-Handling Functions
Name	*Operation*
int strlen(string)	Returns the number of characters in a string (not including the terminating null).
char* strcpy(target, source)	Copies the source string into a target array.
char* strcat(target, source)	Concatenates the source string onto the end of the target string.
char* strncpy(target, source, n)	Copies a string up to *n* characters from the source string into a target array.
char* strncat(target, source, n)	Concatenates the source string onto the end of the target string or *n* characters, whichever comes first.
char* strstr(string, pattern)	Returns the address of the first occurrence of pattern in string. Returns a null if pattern is not found.
int strcmp(source1, source2)	Compares two strings. Returns –1 if *source1* occurs before *source2* in the dictionary and 1 if later. Returns 0 if the two strings match exactly.
int strncmp(source1, source2, n)	Compares the first *n* characters in two strings.

You need to add the statement *#include <cstring>* to the beginning of any program that uses a *str...* function because this include file contains the prototype declarations that C++ requires to check up on your work.

The arguments to the *str...()* functions appear backward to any reasonable individual (you might consider this an acid test for "reasonable"). For example, the function *strcat(target, source)* tacks the second string *source* onto the end of the first argument *target.*

The *strncpy()* and *strncat()* functions are similar to their *strcpy()* and *strcat()* counterparts except that they accept the length of the target buffer as one of their arguments. The call *strncpy(szTarget, szSource, 128)* says "copy the characters in *szSource* into *szTarget* until you copy a null character or until you've copied 128 characters, whichever comes first." This avoids inadvertently writing beyond the end of the source string array.

Making Room for Wide Strings

The standard C++ library includes similar functions to handle wide character strings. A few of these functions are listed in Table 7-2.

Table 7-2	Wide String-Handling Functions
Name	*Operation*
int wcslen(string)	Returns the number of wide characters in a string, not including the terminating null.
wchar_t* wcscpy(target, source)	Copies the source wide string into a target array.
wchar_t* wcscat(target, source)	Concatenates the source wide string onto the end of the target wide string.
wchar_t* wcsncpy(target, source, n)	Copies a wide string up to *n* characters from the source string into a target array.
wchar_t* wcsncat(target, source, n)	Concatenates the source string onto the end of the target string or *n* characters, whichever comes first.
wchar_t* wcsstr(string, pattern)	Finds the address of the first occurrence of pattern in string. Returns a null if pattern is not found.
int wcscmp(source1, source2)	Compares two wide strings. Returns –1 if *source1* occurs before *source2* in the dictionary and 1 if later. Returns 0 if the two strings match exactly.
int wcsncmp(source1, source2, n)	Compares the first *n* wide characters in two wide strings.

Remember from Chapter 2 that wide characters are used for applications that must support foreign languages, where a measly 255 different characters may not be enough.

The following shows a wide character version of the *Concatenate* program:

```
// ConcatenateWide - concatenate two wide strings
//      with a " - " in the middle using library routines
#include <cstdio>
#include <cstdlib>
#include <iostream>
using namespace std;

int main(int nNumberofArgs, char* pszArgs[])
{
    // read first string...
    wchar_t wszString1[260];
    cout << "Enter string #1:";
    wcin.getline(wszString1, 128);

    // ...now the second string...
    wchar_t wszString2[128];
```

```
cout << "Enter string #2:";
wcin.getline(wszString2, 128);

// now tack the second onto the end of the first
// with a dash in between
wcsncat(wszString1, L" - ", 260);
wcsncat(wszString1, wszString2, 260);

wcout << L"\n" << wszString1 << endl;

// wait until user is ready before terminating program
// to allow the user to see the program results
cout << "Press Enter to continue..." << endl;
cin.ignore(10, '\n');
cin.get();
return 0;
}
```

The wide character string program looks similar to its single-byte character string cousin except for the following differences:

✔ Variables are declared *wchar_t* rather than *char*.

✔ Constant characters and constant strings appear preceded by an *L*, as in *L"This is a wide string"*.

✔ The objects *wcin* and *wcout* are used in place of *cin* and *cout* for input and output.

✔ The *wcs* . . . functions appear in place of the narrow *str* . . . functions.

The output from *ConcatenateWide* appears identical to that of the *char*-based *Concatenate* program to those of us who do most of their input/output in European languages. The topic of writing programs capable of handling multiple languages with different alphabets and rules of grammar is known as *localization* and beyond the scope of a beginning book.

ANSI C++ includes a type *string* designed to make it easier to manipulate strings of text. However, this type makes use of features of the language that you haven't seen yet. I return to the *string* type in Chapter 13.

Chapter 8

Taking a First Look at C++ Pointers

. . . .

In This Chapter

▶ Addressing variables in memory

▶ Declaring and using pointer variables

▶ Recognizing the inherent dangers of pointers

▶ Passing pointers to functions

▶ Allocating objects off the heap (whatever that is)

. . . .

So far, the C++ language has been fairly conventional compared with other programming languages. Sure, some computer languages lack (il-)logical operators like those in Chapter 4, and C++ has its own unique symbols for things, but there's been nothing new in the way of concepts. C++ really separates itself from the crowd in its use of pointer variables. A *pointer* is a variable that "points at" other variables. I realize that's a circular argument, but suspend your disbelief at least until you can get into the chapter.

This chapter introduces the pointer variable type. It begins with some concept definitions, flows through pointer syntax, and then introduces some of the reasons for the pointer mania that grips the C++ programming world.

Variable Size

My weight goes up and down all the time, but here I'm really referring to the size of a variable, not my own variable size. Memory is measured in bytes or bits. The keyword *sizeof* returns the size of its argument in bytes. The following program uses this to determine the size of the different variable types:

```
// VariableSize - output the size of each type of variable
#include <cstdio>
#include <cstdlib>
#include <iostream>
using namespace std;
```

```
int main(int nNumberofArgs, char* pszArgs[])
{
    bool        b; char  c; int    n; long           l;
    long long  ll; float f; double d; long double ld;

    cout << "sizeof a bool        = " << sizeof b << endl;
    cout << "sizeof a char        = " << sizeof c << endl;
    cout << "sizeof an int        = " << sizeof n << endl;
    cout << "sizeof a long        = " << sizeof l << endl;
    cout << "sizeof a long long   = " << sizeof ll<< endl;
    cout << "sizeof a float       = " << sizeof f << endl;
    cout << "sizeof a double      = " << sizeof d << endl;
    cout << "sizeof a long double = " << sizeof ld<< endl;

    // wait until user is ready before terminating program
    // to allow the user to see the program results
    cout << "Press Enter to continue..." << endl;
    cin.ignore(10, '\n');
    cin.get();
    return 0;
}
```

The *VariableSize* program generates the following output:

```
sizeof a bool        = 1
sizeof a char        = 1
sizeof an int        = 4
sizeof a long        = 4
sizeof a long long   = 8
sizeof a float       = 4
sizeof a double      = 8
sizeof a long double = 12
Press Enter to continue...
```

As they say, "Your results may vary." You may get different results if using a compiler other than gcc for Windows. For example, you may find that an *int* is smaller than a *long*. C++ doesn't say exactly how big a variable type must be; it just says that a *long* is the same size as or larger than an *int* and that a *double* is the same size as or larger than a *float*. The sizes shown here are typical for a 32-bit 80-x-86 processor.

What's in an Address?

Like the saying goes, "Everyone has to be somewhere." Every C++ variable is stored somewhere in the computer's memory. Memory is broken into individual bytes, with each byte carrying its own address numbered 0, 1, 2, and so on.

A variable *intReader* might be at address 0x100, whereas *floatReader* might be over at location 0x180. (By convention, memory addresses are expressed in hexadecimal.) Of course, *intReader* and *floatReader* might be somewhere else in memory entirely — only the computer knows for sure and only at the time that the program is executed.

This is somewhat analogous to a hotel. When you make your reservation, you may be assigned room 0x100. (I know that suite numbers are normally *not* expressed in hexadecimal, but bear with me.) Your buddy may be assigned 80 doors down in room 0x180. Each variable is assigned an address when it is created (more on that in this chapter when we talk about scope).

Address Operators

The two pointer-related operators are shown in Table 8-1. The & operator says "tell me your address," and * says "the value at the following address."

Table 8-1	Pointer Operators
Operator	*Meaning*
& (unary)	(In an expression) the address of
& (unary)	(In a declaration) reference to
* (unary)	(In an expression) the thing pointed at by
* (unary)	(In a declaration) pointer to

These are not to be confused with the binary & and * operators discussed in Chapters 3 and 4.

The following *Layout* program demonstrates how the & operator can be used to display the layout of variables in memory:

```
// Layout - this program tries to give the
//          reader an idea of the layout of
//          local memory in her compiler
#include <cstdio>
#include <cstdlib>
#include <iostream>
using namespace std;
```

```
int main(int nNumberofArgs, char* pszArgs[])
{
    int   start;
    int     n; long     l; long long   ll;
    float  f; double   d; long double ld;
    int   end;

    // set output to hex mode
    cout.setf(ios::hex);
    cout.unsetf(ios::dec);

    // output the address of each variable
    // in order to get an idea of how variables are
    // laid out in memory
    cout << "--- = " << &start << endl;
    cout << "&n  = " << &n       << endl;
    cout << "&l  = " << &l       << endl;
    cout << "&ll = " << &ll      << endl;
    cout << "&f  = " << &f       << endl;
    cout << "&d  = " << &d       << endl;
    cout << "&ld = " << &ld      << endl;
    cout << "--- = " << &end     << endl;

    // wait until user is ready before terminating program
    // to allow the user to see the program results
    cout << "Press Enter to continue..." << endl;
    cin.ignore(10, '\n');
    cin.get();
    return 0;
}
```

The program declares a set of variables of different types. It then applies the & operator to each one to find out its address. The results of one execution of this program with Code::Blocks appear as follows:

```
--- = 0x28fefc
&n  = 0x28fef8
&l  = 0x28fef4
&ll = 0x28fee8
&f  = 0x28fee4
&d  = 0x28fed8
&ld = 0x28fec0
--- = 0x28febc
Press Enter to continue...
```

Your results may vary. The absolute address of program variables depends on a lot of factors. The C++ standard certainly doesn't specify how variables are to be laid out in memory.

Notice how the variable *n* is exactly 4 bytes from the first variable declared *(start),* which corresponds to the size of an *int* (4 bytes). Similarly, the variable *l* appears 4 bytes down from that, which is also the size of a *long.* However, the *float* variable *f* is a full 12 bytes from its neighboring variable *d* (0x28fee4 – 0x28fed8 = 0x000c). That's way more than the 4 bytes required for a *float.*

There is no requirement that the C++ compiler pack variables in memory with no spaces between them. In fact, you often see these gaps in memory when mixing variables of different size.

The Code::Blocks/gcc compiler could be storing variables for its own use in between our variables. Or, more likely, a peculiarity in the way the variables are being laid out in memory is causing the compiler to waste a small amount of space.

Using Pointer Variables

A *pointer variable* is a variable that contains an address, usually the address of another variable. Returning to the analogy of hotel room numbers, I might tell my son that I will be in room 0x100 on my trip. My son can act as a pointer variable of sorts. Anyone can ask him at any time, "Where's your father staying?" Include $5 with that question, and he'll spill his guts without hesitation.

By the way, notice something about pointer variables: No matter where my son is, and no matter how many other people he tells of my whereabouts, I'm still in room 0x100.

The following pseudo-C++ demonstrates how the two address operators shown in Table 8-1 are used:

```
mySon = &DadsRoom; // tell mySon the address of Dad's Room
room = *mySon;      // "Dad's room number is"
```

The following C++ code snippet shows these operators used correctly:

```
void fn()
{
   int  nVar;
   int* pnVar;

   pnVar  = &nVar; // pnVar now points to nVar
   *pnVar = 10;    // stores 10 into the int location
}                  // pointed at by pnVar
```

The function *fn()* begins with the declaration of *nVar*. The next statement declares the variable *pnVar* to be a variable of type pointer to an *int*.

Pointer variables are declared like normal variables except for the addition of the unary * character. This * character can appear anywhere between the base type name — the following two declarations are equivalent:

```
int* pnVar1;
int *pnVar2;
```

Which you use is a matter of personal preference.

The * character is called the *asterisk character* (that's logical enough), but because *asterisk* is hard to say, many programmers have come to call it the star or, less commonly, the *splat* character. Thus, they would say "star pnVar" or "splat pnVar."

In an expression, the unary operator & means "the address of." Thus, we would read the assignment *pnVar = &nVar;* as "pnVar gets the address of nVar."

Using different types of pointers

Every expression has a type as well as a value. The type of the expression *nVar* is *int;* the type of *&nVar* is "pointer to an integer," written *int*.* Comparing this with the declaration of *pVar,* you see that the types match exactly:

```
int* pnVar = &nVar; // both sides of the assignment
                    // are of type int*
```

Similarly, because *pnVar* is of type *int*,* the type of **pnVar* is *int:*

```
*pnVar = 10;        // both sides of the assignment are
                    // of type int
```

The type of the thing pointed to by *pnVar* is *int.* This is equivalent to saying that if *houseAddress* is the address of a house, the thing pointed at by *houseAddress* must be a house. Amazing, but true.

Pointers to other types of variables are expressed the same way:

```
double doubleVar;
double* pdoubleVar = &doubleVar;
*pdoubleVar = 10.0;
```

A pointer on a Pentium class machine takes 4 bytes no matter what it points to. That is, an address on a Pentium is 4 bytes long, period.

Passing Pointers to Functions

One of the uses of pointer variables is in passing arguments to functions. To understand why this is important, you need to understand how arguments are passed to a function. (I touched on this in Chapter 6, but you're now in a much better place to understand this armed with your new understanding of pointers.)

Passing by value

By default, arguments are passed to functions by value. This has the some-what surprising result that changing the value of a variable in a function does not normally change its value in the calling function. Consider the following example code segment:

```
void fn(int nArg)
{
    nArg = 10;
    // value of nArg at this point is 10
}

void parent(void)
{
    int n1 = 0;
    fn(n1);
    // value of n1 at this point is still 0
}
```

Here the *parent()* function initializes the integer variable *n1* to 0. The value of *n1* is then passed to *fn()*. Upon entering the function, *nArg* is equal to 0, the value passed. *fn()* changes the value of *nArg* to 10 before returning to *parent()*. Upon returning to *parent()*, the value of *n1* is still 0.

The reason for this behavior is that C++ doesn't pass a variable to a function. (I'm not even sure what that would mean.) Instead, C++ passes the value contained in the variable at the time of the call. That is, the expression is evaluated, even if it is just a variable name, and the result is passed.

In the example, the value of *n1,* which is 0, was passed to *fn()*. What the function does with that value has no effect on *n1*.

Passing pointer values

Like any other intrinsic type, a pointer may be passed as an argument to a function:

```
void fn(int* pnArg)
{
  *pnArg = 10;
}

void parent(void)
{
    int n = 0;

    fn(&n);        // this passes the address of i
                   // now the value of n is 10
}
```

In this case, the address of *n* is passed to the function *fn()* rather than the value of *n*. The significance of this difference is apparent when you consider the assignment within *fn()*.

Suppose *n* is located at address 0x100. Rather than the value 10, the call *fn(&n)* passes the value 0x100. Within *fn()*, the assignment **pnArg = 10* stores the value 10 in the *int* variable located at location 0x100, thereby overwriting the value 0. Upon returning to *parent()*, the value of *n* is 10 because *n* is just another name for 0x100.

Passing by reference

C++ provides a shorthand for passing arguments by address — a shorthand that enables you to avoid having to hassle with pointers. The following declaration creates a variable *n1* and a second reference to the same *n1* but with a new name, *nRef:*

```
int n1;             // declare an int variable
int& nRef = n1;     // declare a second reference to n1

nRef = 1;           // now accessing the reference
                    // has the same effect as accessing n1;
                    // n1 is now equal to 1
```

A reference variable like *nRef* must be initialized when it is declared because every subsequent time that its name is used, C++ will assume that you mean the variable that *nRef* refers to.

Reference variables find their primary application in function calls:

```
void fn(int& rnArg)// declare reference argument
{
    rnArg = 10;     // change the value of the variable...
}                   //...that rnArg refers to

void parent(void)
{
    int n1 = 0;
    fn(n1);         // pass a reference to n1
                    // here the value of n1 is 10
}
```

This is called *passing by reference*. The declaration *int& rnArg* declares *rnArg* to be a reference to an integer argument. The *fn()* function stores the value 10 into the *int* location referenced by *rnArg*.

Passing by reference is the same as passing the address of a variable. The reference syntax puts the onus on C++ to apply the "address of" operator to the reference rather than requiring the programmer to do so.

You cannot overload a pass by value function with its pass by reference equivalent. Thus, you could not define the two functions *fn(int)* and *fn(int&)* in the same program. C++ would not know which one to call.

Constant const Irritation

The keyword *const* means that a variable cannot be changed once it has been declared and initialized.

```
const double PI = 3.1415926535;
```

Arguments to functions can also be declared *const,* meaning that the argument cannot be changed within the function. However, this introduces an interesting dichotomy in the case of pointer variables. Consider the following declaration:

```
const int* pInt;
```

Exactly what is the constant here? What can we not change? Is it the variable *pInt* or the integer pointed at by *pInt?* It turns out that both are possible, but this declaration declares a variable pointer to a constant memory location. Thus the following:

```
const int* pInt;    // declare a pointer to a const int
int nVar;
pInt = &nVar;       // this is allowed
*pInt = 10;         // but this is not
```

We can change the value of *pInt,* for example, assigning it the address of *nVar.* But the final assignment in the example snippet generates a compiler error since we cannot change the *const int* pointed at by *pInt.*

What if I had intended to create a pointer variable with a constant value? The following snippet shows this in action:

```
int nVar;
int * const cpInt = &nVar; // declare a constant pointer
                           // to a variable integer
*cpInt = 10;               // now this is legal...
cpInt++;                   // ...but this is not
```

The variable *cpInt* is a constant pointer to a variable *int.* The programmer cannot change the value of the pointer, but she can change the value of the integer pointed at.

The *const*-ness can be added via an assignment or initialization but cannot be (readily) cast away. Thus, the following:

```
int nVar = 10;
int pVar = &nVar;
const int* pcVar = pVar;    // this is legal
int* pVar2 = pcVar;         // this is not
```

The assignment *pcVar = pVar;* is okay — this is adding the *const* restriction. The final assignment in the snippet is not allowed since it attempts to remove the *const*-ness restriction of *pcVar.*

A variable can be implicitly recast as part of a function call, as in the following example:

```
void fn(const int& nVar);

void mainFn()
{
    int n;

    fn(10);   // calls fn(const int&)
    fn(n);    // calls the same function by treating n
              // as if it were const
}
```

The declaration *fn(const int&)* says that the function *fn()* does not modify the value of its argument. That's important when passing a reference to the constant 10. It isn't important when passing a reference to the variable *n,* but it doesn't hurt anything either.

Finally, *const* can be used as a discriminator between functions of the same name:

```
void fn(const int& nVar);
void fn(int& nVar);

void mainFn()
{
    int n;

    fn(10);   // calls the first function
    fn(n);    // calls the second function
}
```

Making Use of a Block of Memory Called the Heap

The *heap* is an amorphous block of memory that your program can access as necessary. This section describes why it exists and how to use it.

Just as it is possible to pass a pointer to a function, it is possible for a function to return a pointer. A function that returns the address of a *double* is declared as follows:

```
double* fn(void);
```

However, you must be very careful when returning a pointer. To understand the dangers, you must know something about variable scope. (No, I don't mean a variable zoom rifle scope.)

Limited scope

Besides being a mouthwash, *scope* is the range over which a variable is defined. Consider the following code snippet:

```
// the following variable is accessible to
// all functions and defined as long as the
// program is running(global scope)
int intGlobal;

// the following variable intChild is accessible
// only to the function and is defined only
// as long as C++ is executing child() or a
// function which child() calls (function scope)
void child(void)
{
    int intChild;
}

// the following variable intParent has function
// scope
void parent(void)
{
    int intParent = 0;
    child();

    int intLater = 0;
    intParent = intLater;
}

int main(int nArgs, char* pArgs[])
{
    parent();
}
```

This program fragment starts with the declaration of a variable *intGlobal*. This variable exists from the time the program begins executing until it terminates. We say that *intGlobal* "has program scope." We also say that the variable "goes into scope" even before the function *main()* is called.

The function *main()* immediately invokes *parent()*. The first thing that the processor sees in *parent()* is the declaration of *intParent*. At that point, *intParent* goes into scope — that is, *intParent* is defined and available for the remainder of the function *parent()*.

The second statement in *parent()* is the call to *child()*. Once again, the function *child()* declares a local variable, this time *intChild*. The scope of the variable *intChild* is limited to the function *child()*. Technically, *intParent* is not defined within the scope of *child()* because *child()* doesn't have access to *intParent;* however, the variable *intParent* continues to exist while *child()* is executing.

When *child()* exits, the variable *intChild* goes out of scope. Not only is *intChild* no longer accessible, it no longer exists. (The memory occupied by *intChild* is returned to the general pool to be used for other things.)

As *parent()* continues executing, the variable *intLater* goes into scope at the declaration. At the point that *parent()* returns to *main()*, both *intParent* and *intLater* go out of scope.

Because *intGlobal* is declared globally in this example, it is available to all three functions and remains available for the life of the program.

Examining the scope problem

The following code segment compiles without error but doesn't work (don't you just hate that?):

```
double* child(void)
{
    double dLocalVariable;
    return &dLocalVariable;
}

void parent(void)
{
    double* pdLocal;
    pdLocal   = child();
    *pdLocal = 1.0;
}
```

The problem with this function is that *dLocalVariable* is defined only within the scope of the function *child()*. Thus, by the time the memory address of *dLocalVariable* is returned from *child()*, it refers to a variable that no longer exists. The memory that *dLocalVariable* formerly occupied is probably being used for something else.

This error is very common because it can creep up in a number of ways. Unfortunately, this error does not cause the program to instantly stop. In fact, the program may work fine most of the time — that is, the program continues to work as long as the memory formerly occupied by *dLocalVariable* is not reused immediately. Such intermittent problems are the most difficult ones to solve.

Providing a solution using the heap

The scope problem originated because C++ took back the locally defined memory before the programmer was ready. What is needed is a block of memory controlled by the programmer. She can allocate the memory and put it back when she wants to — not because C++ thinks it's a good idea. Such a block of memory is called the *heap*.

Heap memory is allocated using the *new* keyword followed by the type of object to allocate. The *new* command breaks a chunk of memory off the heap big enough to hold the specified type of object and returns its address. For example, the following allocates a *double* variable off the heap:

```
double* child(void)
{
    double* pdLocalVariable = new double;
    return pdLocalVariable;
}
```

This function now works properly. Although the variable *pdLocalVariable* goes out of scope when the function *child()* returns, the memory to which *pdLocalVariable* refers does not. A memory location returned by *new* does not go out of scope until it is explicitly returned to the heap using the keyword *delete,* which is specifically designed for that purpose:

```
void parent(void)
{
    // child() returns the address of a block
    // of heap memory
    double* pdMyDouble = child();

    // store a value there
    *pdMyDouble = 1.1;

    // ...

    // now return the memory to the heap
    delete pdMyDouble;
    pdMyDouble = 0;

    // ...
}
```

Here the pointer returned by *child()* is used to store a double value. After the function is finished with the memory location, it is returned to the heap. The function *parent()* sets the pointer to 0 after the heap memory has been returned — this is not a requirement, but it is a very good idea. If the programmer mistakenly attempts to store something in ** pdMyDouble* after the *delete,* the program will crash immediately with (I hope) a meaningful error message.

You can use *new* to allocate arrays from the heap as well, but you must return an array using the *delete[ ]* keyword:

```
int* nArray = new int[10];

nArray[0] = 0;

delete[] nArray;
```

Technically *new int[10]* invokes the *new[ ]* operator but it works the same as *new.*

I have more to say about the relationship between pointers and arrays in Chapter 9.

Chapter 9

Taking a Second Look at C++ Pointers

....

In This Chapter

▶ Performing arithmetic operations on character pointers

▶ Examining the relationship between pointers and arrays

▶ Increasing program performance

▶ Extending pointer operations to different pointer types

▶ Explaining the arguments to *main()* in our C++ program template

....

C++ allows the programmer to operate on pointer variables much as she would on simple types of variables. (The concept of pointer variables is introduced in Chapter 8.) How and why this is done, along with its implications, are the subjects of this chapter.

Defining Operations on Pointer Variables

Some of the same arithmetic operators I cover in Chapter 3 can be applied to pointer types. This section examines the implications of applying these operators both to pointers and to the array types (I discuss arrays in Chapter 7). Table 9-1 lists the three fundamental operations that are defined on pointers. In Table 9-1, *pointer, pointer1,* and *pointer2* are all of some pointer type, say *char**;, and *offset* is an integer, for example, *long*. C++ also supports the other operators related to addition and subtraction, such as ++ and +=., although they are not listed in Table 9-1.

Table 9-1	The Three Basic Operations Defined on Pointer Types	
Operation	*Result*	*Meaning*
pointer + offset	pointer	Calculate the address of the object *offset* entries from *pointer*.
pointer – offset	pointer	The opposite of addition.
pointer2 – pointer1	offset	Calculate the number of entries between *pointer2* and *pointer1*.

The neighborhood memory model is useful to explain how pointer arithmetic works. Consider a city block in which all houses are numbered sequentially. The house at 123 Main Street has 122 Main Street on one side and 124 Main Street on the other.

Now it's pretty clear that the house four houses down from 123 Main Street must be 127 Main Street; thus, you can say *123 Main + 4 = 127 Main*. Similarly, if I were to ask how many houses there are from 123 Main to 127 Main, the answer would be four — *127 Main – 123 Main = 4*. (Just as an aside, a house is zero houses from itself: *123 Main – 123 Main = 0*.)

But it makes no sense to ask how far away from 123 Main Street is 4 or what the sum of 123 Main and 127 Main is. In similar fashion, you can't add two addresses. Nor can you multiply an address, divide an address, square an address, or take the square root — you get the idea. You can perform any operation that can be converted to addition or subtraction. For example, if you increment a pointer to 123 Main Street, it now points to the house next door (at 124 Main, of course!).

Reexamining arrays in light of pointer variables

Now return to the wonderful array for just a moment. Consider the case of an array of 32 1-byte characters called *charArray*. If the first byte of this array is stored at address 0x100, the array will extend over the range 0x100 through 0x11f. *charArray[0]* is located at address 0x100, *charArray[1]* is at 0x101, *charArray[2]* at 0x102, and so on.

After executing the expression

```
char* ptr = &charArray[0];
```

the pointer *ptr* contains the address 0x100. The addition of an integer offset to a pointer is defined such that the relationships shown in Table 9-2 are true. Table 9-2 also demonstrates why adding an offset *n* to *ptr* calculates the address of the *n*th element in *charArray*.

Table 9-2	Adding Offsets	
Offset	*Result*	*Is the Address Of*
+ 0	0x100	*charArray[0]*
+ 1	0x101	*charArray[1]*
+ 2	0x102	*charArray[2]*
. . .	. . .	. . .
+ n	0x100 + n	*charArray[n]*

The addition of an offset to a pointer is identical to applying an index to an array.

Thus, if

```
char* ptr = &charArray[0];
```

then

```
*(ptr + n)  ←  corresponds with  →  charArray[n]
```

Because * has higher precedence than addition, * *ptr* + *n* adds *n* to the character that *ptr* points to. The parentheses are needed to force the addition to occur before the indirection. The expression **(ptr + n)* retrieves the character pointed at by the pointer *ptr* plus the offset *n*.

In fact, the correspondence between the two forms of expression is so strong that C++ considers *array[n]* nothing more than a simplified version of **(ptr + n)*, where *ptr* points to the first element in *array*.

```
array[n]  --  C++ interprets as  →  *(&array[0] + n)
```

To complete the association, C++ takes a second shortcut. If given

```
char charArray[20];
```

charArray is defined as *&charArray[0];*. That is, the name of an array without a subscript present is the address of the array itself. Thus, you can further simplify the association to

```
array[n] -- C++ interprets as → *(array + n)
```

The type of *charArray* is actually *char const**; that is, "constant pointer to a character" since its address cannot be changed.

Applying operators to the address of an array

The correspondence between indexing an array and pointer arithmetic is useful. For example, a *displayArray()* function used to display the contents of an array of integers can be written as follows:

```cpp
// displayArray - display the members of an
//                array of length nSize
void displayArray(int intArray[], int nSize)
{
    cout << "The value of the array is:\n";

    for(int n = 0; n < nSize; n++)
    {
        cout << n << ": " << intArray[n] << "\n";
    }
    cout << endl;
}
```

This version uses the array operations with which you are familiar. A pointer version of the same appears as follows:

```cpp
// displayArray - display the members of an
//                array of length nSize
void displayArray(int intArray[], int nSize)
{
    cout << "The value of the array is:\n";

    // initialize the pointer pArray with the
    // the address of the array intArray
    int* pArray = intArray;
    for(int n = 0; n < nSize; n++, pArray++)
    {
        cout << n << ": " << *pArray << "\n";
    }
    cout << endl;
}
```

The new *displayArray()* begins by creating a pointer to an integer *pArray* that points at the first element of *intArray*.

The name *intArray* by itself is of type *int** and refers to the address of the array.

The function then loops through each element of the array. On each loop, *displayArray()* outputs the current integer (that is, the integer pointed at by *pArray*) before incrementing the pointer to the next entry in *intArray*. *displayArray()* can be tested using the following version of *main()*:

```cpp
int main(int nNumberofArgs, char* pszArgs[])
{
    int array[] = {4, 3, 2, 1};
    displayArray(array, 4);

    // wait until user is ready before terminating program
    // to allow the user to see the program results
    cout << "Press Enter to continue..." << endl;
    cin.ignore(10, '\n');
    cin.get();
    return 0;
}
```

The output from this program is

```
The value of the array is:
0: 4
1: 3
2: 2
3: 1

Press Enter to continue...
```

You may think this pointer conversion is silly; however, the pointer version of *displayArray()* is actually more common than the array version among C++ programmers in the know. For some reason, C++ programmers don't seem to like arrays, but they love pointer manipulation.

The use of pointers to access arrays is nowhere more common than in the accessing of character arrays.

Expanding pointer operations to a string

A null-terminated string is simply a constant character array whose last character is a null. C++ uses the null character at the end to serve as a terminator. This null-terminated array serves as a quasi-variable type of its own. (See Chapter 7 for an explanation of null-terminated string arrays.) Often C++ programmers use character pointers to manipulate such strings. The following code examples compare this technique to the earlier technique of indexing in the array.

Character pointers enjoy the same relationship with a character array that any other pointer and array share. However, the fact that strings end in a terminating null makes them especially amenable to pointer-based manipulation, as shown in the following *DisplayString* program:

```cpp
// DisplayString - display an array of characters both
//                 using a pointer and an array index
#include <cstdio>
#include <cstdlib>
#include <iostream>
using namespace std;

int main(int nNumberofArgs, char* pszArgs[])
{
    // declare a string
    const char* szString = "Randy";
    cout << "The array is '" << szString << "'" << endl;

    // display szString as an array
    cout << "Display the string as an array: ";
    for(int i = 0; i < 5; i++)
    {
      cout << szString[i];
    }
    cout << endl;

    // now using typical pointer arithmetic
    cout << "Display string using a pointer: ";
    const char* pszString = szString;
    while(*pszString)
    {
      cout << *pszString;
      pszString++;
    }
    cout << endl;

    // wait until user is ready before terminating program
    // to allow the user to see the program results
    cout << "Press Enter to continue..." << endl;
    cin.ignore(10, '\n');
    cin.get();
    return 0;
}
```

The program first makes its way through the array *szString* by indexing into the array of characters. The *for* loop chosen stops when the index reaches 5, the length of the string.

The second loop displays the same string using a pointer. The program sets the variable *pszString* equal to the address of the first character in the array. It then enters a loop that will continue until the *char* pointed at by *pszString* is equal to *false* — in other words, until the character is a *null*.

The integer value 0 is interpreted as *false* — all other values are *true*.

The program outputs the character pointed at by *pszString* and then increments the pointer so that it points to the next character in the string before being returned to the top of the loop.

The dereference and increment can be (and usually are) combined into a single expression as follows:

```
cout << *pszString++;
```

The output of the program appears as follows:

```
The array is 'Randy'
Display the string as an array: Randy
Display string using a pointer: Randy
Press Enter to continue...
```

Justifying pointer-based string manipulation

The sometimes-cryptic nature of pointer-based manipulation of character strings might lead the reader to wonder, "Why?" That is, what advantage does the *char** pointer version have over the easier-to-read index version?

The answer is partially (pre-)historic and partially human nature. When C, the progenitor to C++, was invented, compilers were pretty simplistic. These compilers could not perform the complicated optimizations that modern compilers can. As complicated as it might appear to the human reader, a statement such as **pszString++* could be converted into an amazingly small number of machine-level instructions even by a stupid compiler.

Older computer processors were not very fast by today's standards. In the early days of C, saving a few computer instructions was a big deal. This gave C a big advantage over other languages of the day, notably Fortran, which did not offer pointer arithmetic.

In addition to the efficiency factor, programmers like to generate clever program statements. After C++ programmers learn how to write compact and cryptic but efficient statements, there is no getting them back to accessing arrays with indices.

Do not generate complex C++ expressions to create a more efficient program. There is no obvious relationship between the number of C++ statements and the number of machine instructions generated.

Applying operators to pointer types other than char

It is not too hard to convince yourself that *szTarget + n* points to *szTarget [n]* when *szTarget* is an array of *char*s. After all, a *char* occupies a single byte. If *szTarget* is stored at 0x100, *szTarget[5]* is located at 0x105.

It is not so obvious that pointer addition works in exactly the same way for an *int* array because an *int* takes 4 bytes for each *char*'s 1 byte (at least it does on a 32-bit Intel processor). If the first element in *intArray* were located at 0x100, then *intArray[5]* would be located at 0x114 *(0x100 + (5 * 4) = 0x114)* and not 0x104.

Fortunately for us, *array + n* points at *array[n]* no matter how large a single element of *array* might be. C++ takes care of the element size for us — it's clever that way.

Once again, the dusty old house analogy works here as well. (I mean dusty analogy, not dusty house.) The third house down from 123 Main is 126 Main, no matter how large the buildings might be, whether they're bungalows or mansions.

Contrasting a pointer with an array

There are some differences between an array and a pointer. For one, the array allocates space for the data, whereas the pointer does not, as shown here:

```
void arrayVsPointer()
{
    // allocate storage for 128 characters
    char charArray[128];

    // allocate space for a pointer but not for
    // the thing pointed at
    char* pArray;
}
```

Here *charArray* allocates room for 128 characters. *pArray* allocates only 4 bytes — the amount of storage required by a pointer.

Consider the following example:

```
char charArray[128];
charArray[10] = '0'; // this works fine

char* pArray;
pArray[10] = '0';    // this writes into random location
```

Strings have me constantly confused

You may have noticed that I slipped a *const* declaration into the earlier *DisplayString* example program. This was necessary to account for differences between an array and a pointer. A string such as "this is a string" is considered a constant address of a string of constant characters. In other words, neither the address of the string nor the characters themselves can be changed. Why is that?

One problem is that you don't know where C++ stores its local strings nor do you know how many times it reuses the same string. Often C++ stores constant strings in the same memory locations as source code, and it very often reuses the same string in several places in the program. For this reason, C++ often marks constant strings as unwritable.

The initialization of a pointer variable is similar to initializing any other simple variable:

```
int i = 1;
const char* pString = "this is a string";
```

Both declarations initialize the variable on the left with the constant value on the right. However, since *pString* points directly at the immutable string "this is a string" it's important that *pString* be declared *const char**, that is, a pointer to constant characters.

The equivalent array is more complicated than it first appears:

```
char sChars[] = "this is a string"; // declare and init array
```

This declares and allocates memory for an array *sChars[]* and then copies the initialization string into it. Thus, the letter *t* that is the first character in *sChars* is not the same letter *t* that makes up the immutable initialization string.

In fact, the preceding is shorthand for the more long-winded but descriptive

```
char sChars[17];                    // declare the array and...
strcpy(sChars, "this is a string"); // ...then initialize it
```

Remember that *strcpy()* copies the string of characters represented by the second argument into the array pointed at by the first argument. And also remember to allocate space for the terminating null.

The expression *pArray[10]* is syntactically equivalent to *charArray[10]*, but *pArray* has not been initialized so *pArray[10]* references some random (garbage) location in memory.

The mistake of referencing memory with an uninitialized pointer variable is generally caught by the CPU when the program executes, resulting in the dreaded *segment violation* error that from time to time issues from your favorite applications under your favorite, or not-so-favorite, operating system. This problem is not generally the fault of the processor or the operating system, but of the application.

Another implication of this difference is that you can use a range-based *for* loop on an array where the size of the array is known but not on a pointer where the number of elements is not known:

```
char charArray[128];
for(char& c : charArray) { c = '\0';} // initialize array

char* pArray = charArray;
for(char& c : pArray) {c = '\0';} //not legal
```

The first range-based *for* loop can be used to initialize the *charArray* to null characters. The second *for* loop does not compile, however. Even though *pArray* is assigned the address of the character array with its 128 characters, C++ doesn't keep that size information with the pointer, so it doesn't know how far to iterate in the range-based *for* loop. (See Chapter 5 for a description of the range-based *for* loop.)

A second difference between a pointer and the address of an array is that *charArray* is a constant, whereas *pArray* is not. Thus, the following *for* loop used to initialize the array *charArray* does not work:

```
char charArray[10];
for (int i = 0; i < 10; i++)
{
    *charArray = '\0';     // this makes sense...
    charArray++;           // ...this does not
}
```

The expression *charArray*++ makes no more sense than *10*++. The following version is correct:

```
char charArray[10];
char* pArray = charArray;
for (int i = 0; i < 10; i++)
{
    *pArray = '\0'; // this works great
    pArray++;       // this is ok - not a const pointer
}
```

When Is a Pointer Not?

C++ is completely quiet about what is and isn't a legal address, with one exception. C++ predefines the constant *nullptr* with the following properties:

✔ It is a constant value.

✔ It can be assigned to any pointer type.

✔ It evaluates to *false*.

✔ It is never a legal address.

The constant *nullptr* is used to indicate when a pointer has not been initialized. It is also often used to indicate the last element in an array of pointers in much the same way that a null character is used to terminate a character string.

Actually the keyword *nullptr* was introduced in the 2011 standard. Before that, the constant 0 was used to indicate a null pointer.

It is a safe practice to initialize pointers to the *nullptr* (or 0 if your compiler doesn't support *nullptr* yet). You should also clear out the contents of a pointer to heap memory after you invoke *delete* to avoid deleting the same memory block twice:

```
delete pHeap;      // return memory to the heap
pHeap = nullptr;   // now clear out the pointer
```

Passing the same address to delete twice will always cause your program to crash. Passing a *nullptr* (or 0) to *delete* has no effect.

Declaring and Using Arrays of Pointers

If pointers can point to arrays, it seems only fitting that the reverse should be *true*. Arrays of pointers are a type of array of particular interest.

Just as arrays may contain other data types, an array may contain pointers. The following declares an array of pointers to *int*s:

```
int* pInts[10];
```

Given the preceding declaration, *pInts[0]* is a pointer to an *int* value. Thus, the following is true:

```
void fn()
{
    int n1;
    int* pInts[3];
    pInts[0] = &n1;
    *pInts[0] = 1;
}
```

or

```
void fn()
{
    int n1, n2, n3;
    int* pInts[3] = {&n1, &n2, &n3};
    for (int i = 0; i < 3; i++)
    {
        *pInts[i] = 0;
    }
}
```

or even

```
void fn()
{
    int* pInts[3] = { (new int),
                      (new int),
                      (new int) };
    for (int i = 0; i < 3; i++)
    {
        *pInts[i] = 0;
    }
}
```

The latter declares three *int* objects off the heap. This type of declaration isn't used very often except in the case of an array of pointers to character strings. The following two examples show why arrays of character strings are useful.

Utilizing arrays of character strings

Suppose I need a function that returns the name of the month corresponding to an integer argument passed to it. For example, if the program is passed a 1, it returns a pointer to the string *"January"*; if 2, it reports *"February"*, and so on. The month 0 and any numbers greater than 12 are assumed to be invalid. I could write the function as follows:

```
// int2month() - return the name of the month
const char* int2month(int nMonth)
{
    const char* pszReturnValue;

    switch(nMonth)
    {
        case 1: pszReturnValue = "January";
                break;
        case 2: pszReturnValue = "February";
                break;
        case 3: pszReturnValue = "March";
                break;
        // ...and so forth...
        default: pszReturnValue = "invalid";
    }
    return pszReturnValue;
}
```

The *switch()* control command is like a sequence of *if* statements.

A more elegant solution uses the integer value for the month as an index into an array of pointers to the names of the months. In use, this appears as follows:

```
// define an array containing the names of the months
const char *const pszMonths[] = {"invalid",
                                  "January",
                                  "February",
                                  "March",
                                  "April",
                                  "May",
                                  "June",
                                  "July",
                                  "August",
                                  "September",
                                  "October",
                                  "November",
                                  "December"};

// int2month() - return the name of the month
const char* int2month(int nMonth)
{
    // first check for a value out of range
    if (nMonth < 1 || nMonth > 12)
    {
        return "invalid";
    }

    // nMonth is valid - return the name of the month
    return pszMonths[nMonth];
}
```

Here *int2month()* first checks to make sure that *nMonth* is a number between 1 and 12, inclusive (the *default* clause of the *switch* statement handled that in the previous example). If *nMonth* is valid, the function uses it as an offset into an array containing the names of the months.

This technique of referring to character strings by index is especially useful when writing your program to work in different languages. For example, a program may declare a *ptrMonths* of pointers to Julian months in different languages. The program would initialize *ptrMonth* to the proper names, be they in English, French, or German (for example), at execution time. In that way, *ptrMonth[1]* points to the correct name of the first Julian month, irrespective of the language.

A program that demonstrates *int2Month()* is included in the extras at www. dummies.com/extras/cplusplus as *DisplayMonths*.

Accessing the arguments to main ( )

Now the truth can be told — what are all those funny argument declarations to *main()* in our program template? The second argument to *main()* is an array of pointers to null-terminated character strings. These strings contain the arguments to the program. The arguments to a program are the strings that appear with the program name when you launch it. These arguments are also known as *parameters*. The first argument to *main()* is the number of parameters passed to the program. For example, suppose that I entered the following command at the command prompt:

```
MyProgram file.txt /w
```

The operating system executes the program contained in the file *MyProgram* (or *MyProgram.exe* on a Windows machine), passing it the arguments *file.txt* and */w*.

Consider the following simple program:

```cpp
// PrintArgs - write the arguments to the program
//             to the standard output
#include <cstdio>
#include <cstdlib>
#include <iostream>
using namespace std;

int main(int nNumberofArgs, char* pszArgs[])
{
    // print a warning banner
    cout << "The arguments to "
         << pszArgs[0] << " are:\n";

    // now write out the remaining arguments
    for (int i = 1; i < nNumberofArgs; i++)
    {
        cout << i << ":" << pszArgs[i] << "\n";
    }

    // that's it
    cout << "That's it" << endl;

    // wait until user is ready before terminating program
    // to allow the user to see the program results
    cout << "Press Enter to continue..." << endl;
    cin.ignore(10, '\n');
    cin.get();
    return 0;
}
```

As always, the function *main()* accepts two arguments. The first argument is an *int* that I have been calling (quite descriptively, as it turns out) *nNumberofArgs*. This variable is the number of arguments passed to the program. The second argument is an array of pointers of type *char** that I have been calling *pszArgs*.

Accessing program arguments DOS-style

If I were to execute the *PrintArgs* program from the command prompt window as

```
PrintArgs arg1 arg2 arg3 /w
```

nArgs would be 5 (one for each argument). The first argument is the name of the program itself. This could be anywhere from the simple "PrintArgs" to the slightly more complicated "PrintArgs.exe" to the full path — the C++ standard doesn't specify. The environment can even supply a null string " " if it doesn't have access to the name of the program.

The remaining elements in *pszArgs* point to the program arguments. For example, the element *pszArgs[1]* points to "arg1" and *pszArgs[2]* to "arg2". Because Windows does not place any significance on "/w", this string is also passed as an argument to be processed by the program.

Actually, C++ includes one final value. The last value in the array, the one after the pointer to the last argument of the program, contains *nullptr*.

To demonstrate how argument passing works, you need to build the program from within Code::Blocks and then execute the program directly from a command prompt. First ensure that Code::Blocks has built an executable by opening the PrintArgs projects and choosing Build⇨Rebuild.

Next, open a command prompt window. If you are running Unix or Linux, you're already there. If you are running Windows, choose Programs⇨ Accessories⇨Command Prompt to open an 80-character-wide window with a command prompt.

Now you need to use the *CD* command to navigate to the directory where Code::Blocks placed the PrintArgs program. If you used the default settings when installing Code::Blocks, that directory will be *C:\CPP_Programs_from_ Book\Chap09\PrintArgs\bin\Debug*.

You can now execute the program by typing its name followed by your arguments. The following shows what happened when I did it in Windows 7:

```
C:\Users\Randy>cd \cpp_programs_from_book\chap09\printargs\bin\debug

C:\CPP_Programs_from_book\Chap09\PrintArgs\bin\Debug>PrintArgs arg1 arg2 arg3 /n
The arguments to PrintArgs are:
1:arg1
2:arg2
3:arg3
4:/n
That's it
Press Enter to continue...
```

Wild cards such as *.* may or may not be expanded before being passed to the program — the standard is silent on this point. The Code::Blocks/gcc compiler does perform such expansion on Windows, as the following example shows:

```
C:\CPP_Programs_from_book\Chap09\PrintArgs>bin\debug\PrintArgs *.*
The arguments to bin\debug\PrintArgs are:
1:bin
2:main.cpp
3:obj
4:PrintArgs.cbp
That's it
Press Enter to continue...
```

Here you see the names of the files in the current directory in place of the *.* that I entered.

Wild-card expansion is performed under all forms of Linux, as well as on the Macintosh.

Accessing program arguments Code::Blocks–style

You can add arguments to your program when you execute it from Code::Blocks as well. Choose *Project⇨Set programs' arguments* from within Code::Blocks. Enter the command line you would like in the *Program arguments* window.

Accessing program arguments Windows-style

Windows passes arguments as a means of communicating with your program as well. Try the following experiment: Build your program as you would normally. Find the executable file using Windows Explorer. (As noted earlier, the default location for the *PrintArgs* program is *C:\CPP_Programs_from_book\Chap09\PrintArgs\bin\Debug.*) Now grab a file and drop it onto the filename.

(It doesn't matter what file you choose because the program won't hurt it anyway.) Bam! The *PrintArgs* program starts right up, and the name of the file that you dropped on the program appears.

Now try again, but drop several files at once. Select multiple filenames while pressing the Ctrl key or by using the Shift key to select a group. Now drag the lot of them onto *PrintArgs.exe* and let go. The name of each file appears as output.

I dropped a few of the files that appear in my *\Program Files\WinZip* folder onto PrintArgs as an example:

```
The arguments to
              C:\CPP_Programs_from_book\Chap09\PrintArgs\bin\Debug\PrintArgs.
          exe are:
1:C:\Program Files\WinZip\VENDOR.TXT
2:C:\Program Files\WinZip\WHATSNEW.TXT
3:C:\Program Files\WinZip\WINZIP.CHM
4:C:\Program Files\WinZip\WINZIP.TXT
5:C:\Program Files\WinZip\WINZIP32.EXE
6:C:\Program Files\WinZip\WZ.COM
That's it
Press Enter to continue...
```

Notice that the name of each file appears as a single argument, even though the filename may include spaces. Also note that Windows passes the full pathname of the file.

Chapter 10

The C++ Preprocessor

In This Chapter

▶ Including source files

▶ Defining constants and macros

▶ Enumerating alternatives to constants

▶ Inserting compile-time checks

▶ Simplifying declarations via *typedef*

*Y*ou only thought that all you had to learn was C++. It turns out that C++ includes a preprocessor that works on your source files before the "real C++ compiler" ever gets to see it. Unfortunately, the syntax of the preprocessor is completely different than that of C++ itself.

Before you despair, however, let me hasten to add that the preprocessor is very basic and the C++ '11 standard has added a number of features that make the preprocessor almost unnecessary. Nevertheless, if the conversation turns to C++ at your next Coffee Club meeting, you'll be expected to understand the preprocessor.

What Is a Preprocessor?

Up until now, you may have thought of the C++ compiler as munching on your source code and spitting out an executable program in one step, but that isn't quite true.

First, the preprocessor makes a pass through your program looking for preprocessor instructions. The output of this preprocessor step is an intermediate file that has all the preprocessor commands expanded. This intermediate file gets passed to the C++ compiler for processing. The output from the C++ compiler is an object file that contains the machine instruction equivalent to your C++ source code. During the final step, a separate program known as the linker combines a set of standard libraries with your object file (or files, as we'll see in Chapter 21) to create an executable program. (More on the standard library in the next section of this chapter.)

Object files normally carry the extension *.o*. Executable programs always carry the extension *.exe* in Windows and have no extension under Linux or Mac OS X. Code::Blocks stores the object and executable files in their own folders. For example, if you've already built the *IntAverage* program from Chapter 2, you will have on your hard disk a folder *C:\CPP_Programs_from_book\IntAverage\obj\Debug* containing *main.o* and a folder *C:\CPP_Programs_from_book\IntAverage\bin\Debug* that contains the executable program.

All preprocessor commands start with a # symbol in column 1 and end with the newline.

Like almost all rules in C++, this rule has an exception. You can spread a preprocessor command across multiple lines by ending the line with a back-slash character: \. We won't have any preprocessor commands that are that complicated, however.

In this book, we'll be working with three preprocessor commands:

- ✔ *#include* includes the contents of the specified file in place of the #include statement.
- ✔ *#define* defines a constant or macro.
- ✔ *#if* includes a section of code in the intermediary file if the following condition is true.

Each of these preprocessor commands is covered in the following sections.

Including Files

The C++ standard library consists of functions that are basic enough that almost everyone needs them. It would be silly to force every programmer to have to write them for herself. For example, the I/O functions, which we have been using to read input from the keyboard and write out to the console, are contained in the standard library.

However, C++ requires a prototype declaration for any function you call, whether it's in a library or not (see Chapter 6 if that doesn't make sense to you). Rather than force the programmer to type all these declarations by hand, the library authors created include files that contain little more than prototype declarations. All you have to do is *#include* the source file that contains the prototypes for the library routines you intend to use.

Take the following simple example. Suppose I had created a library that contains the trigonometric functions *sin(), cosin(), tan(),* and a whole lot more. I would likely create an include file *mytrig* with the following contents to go along with my standard library:

```
// include prototype declarations for my library
double sin(double x);
double cosin(double x);
double tan(double x);
// ...more prototype declarations...
```

Any program that wanted to make use of one of these math functions would *#include* that file, enclosing the name of the include file either in brackets or quotes as in

```
#include <mytrig>
```

or

```
#include "mytrig"
```

The difference between the two forms of *#include* is a matter of where the preprocessor goes to look for the *mytrig* file. When the file is enclosed in quotes, the preprocessor assumes that the include file is locally grown, so it starts looking for the file in the same directory in which it found the source file. If it doesn't find the file there, it starts looking in its own include file directories. The preprocessor assumes that include files in angle brackets are from the C++ library, so it skips looking in the source file directory and goes straight to the standard include file folders. Use quotes for any include file that you create and angle brackets for C++ library include files.

Thus, you might write a source file like the following:

```
// MyProgram - is very intelligent
#include "mytrig"

int main(int nArgc, char* pArguments[])
{
    cout << "The sin of .5 is " << sin(0.5) << endl;
    return 0;
}
```

Playing in your own name sandbox

(This is truly technical, so feel free to skip this sidebar and come back to it later.) The authors of the C++ standard worry a lot about name collisions. For example, besides my mathematical function *log(x)* that returns the logarithm of *x*, suppose in another context I had written a function *log(x)* that writes status information to a system log. Clearly, two different functions with the same arguments can't coexist in one program. This is known as a *name collision*.

To avoid this, C++ allows the programmer to bundle declarations into a namespace using the key-word of the same name:

```
namespace Mathematics
{
    double log(double x)
    {
        // ...the definition of the function...
    }
}
namespace SystemLog
{
    int log(double x)
    {
        // ...log the value to file...
    }
}
```

The namespace becomes part of the extended name of the function. Thus, the following code snip-pet actually logs the logarithm of a value:

```
void myFunc(double x)
{
    // invoke the logarithm function...
    double dl = Mathematics::log(x);

    // ...now log it to disk
    SystemLog::log(dl);
}
```

Fortunately, you don't have to specify the namespace every single time. The keyword *using* allows the programmer to specify a default namespace for a given function:

```
using double Mathematics::log(double);
void myFunc(double x)
{
    // the default is the mathematics version...
    double dl = log(x);

    // ...however, the other version is still accessible by
    // explicitly specifying the namespace
    SystemLog::log(dl);
}
```

You can automatically default every declaration within a namespace:

```
using namespace Mathematics;
void myFunc(double x)
{
    // look in the Mathematics namespace first...
    double dl = log(x);

    // ...however, the other version is still accessible by
    // explicitly specifying the namespace
    SystemLog::log(dl);
}
```

See the program *NamespaceExample* in the extras at www.dummies.com/extras/ cplusplus for an example of the use of namespaces.

The standard library functions reside in the *std* namespace; the statement *using namespace std;* included at the beginning of each of the programs in this book gives the programs access to the standard library functions without the need to specify the namespace explicitly.

The C++ compiler sees the following intermediary file after the preprocessor gets finished expanding the *#include*:

```
// MyProgram - is very intelligent
// include prototype declarations for my library
double sin(double x);
double cosin(double x);
double tan(double x);
// ...more prototype declarations...

int main(int nArgc, char* pArguments[])
{
    cout << "The sin of .5 is " << sin(0.5) << endl;
    return 0;
}
```

Historically, the convention was to end include files with *.h.* C still uses that standard. However, C++ dropped the extension when it revamped the include file structure. Now, C++ standard include files have no extension.

#Defining Things

The preprocessor also allows the programmer to *#define* expressions that get expanded during the preprocessor step. For example, you can *#define* a constant to be used throughout the program.

In usage, you pronounce the # sign as "pound," so you say "pound-define a constant" to distinguish from defining a constant in some other way.

```
#define TWO_PI 6.2831852
```

This makes the following statement much easier to understand:

```
double diameter = TWO_PI * radius;
```

than the equivalent expression, which is actually what the C++ compiler sees after the preprocessor has replaced *TWO_PI* with its definition:

```
double diameter = 6.2831852 * radius;
```

Another advantage is the ability to *#define* a constant in one place and use it everywhere. For example, I might include the following *#define* in an include file:

```
#define MAX_NAME_LENGTH 512
```

Throughout the program, I can truncate the names that I read from the keyboard to a common and consistent *MAX_NAME_LENGTH.* Not only is this easier to read, but it also provides a single place in the program to change should I want to increase or decrease the maximum name length that I choose to process.

The preprocessor also allows the program to *#define* function-like macros with arguments that are expanded when the definition is used:

```
#define SQUARE(X) X * X
```

In use, such macro definitions look a lot like functions:

```
// calculate the area of a circle
double dArea = HALF_PI * SQUARE(dRadius);
```

Remember that the C++ compiler actually sees the file generated from the expansion of all macros. This can lead to some unexpected results. Consider the following code snippets (these are all taken from the program *MacroConfusion,* which is included among the extra programs at www.dummies.com/extras/cplusplus):

```
int nSQ = SQUARE(2);
cout << "SQUARE(2) = " << nSQ << endl;
```

Reassuringly, this generates the expected output:

```
SQUARE(2) = 4
```

However, the following lines

```
int nSQ = SQUARE(1 + 2);
cout << "SQUARE(1 + 2) = " << nSQ << endl;
```

generate the surprising result

```
SQUARE(1 + 2) = 5
```

The preprocessor simply replaced X in the macro definition with $1 + 2$. What the C++ compiler actually sees is

```
int nSQ = 1 + 2 * 1 + 2;
```

Since multiplication has higher precedence than addition, this is turned into $1 + 2 + 2$ which, of course, is 5. This confusion could be solved by liberal use of parentheses in the macro definition:

```
#define SQUARE(X) ((X) * (X))
```

This version generates the expected

```
SQUARE(1 + 2) → ((1 + 2) * (1 + 2)) → 9
```

However, some unexpected results cannot be fixed no matter how hard you try. Consider the following snippet:

```
int i = 2;
cout << "i = " << i << endl;
int nSQ = SQUARE(i++);
cout << "SQUARE(i++) = " << nSQ << endl;
cout << "now i = " << i << endl;
```

This generates the following:

```
i = 3;
SQUARE(i++) = 9
now i = 5
```

The value generated by *SQUARE* is correct, but the variable *i* has been incremented twice. The reason is obvious when you consider the expanded macro:

```
int i = 3;
nSQ = i++ * i++;
```

Since autoincrement has precedence, the two *i*++ operations are performed first. Both return the current value of *i,* which is 3. These two values are then multiplied together to return the expected value of 9. However, *i* is then incremented twice to generate a resulting value of 5.

Okay, how about not #defining things?

The sometimes unexpected results from the preprocessor have created heartburn for the fathers (and mothers) of C++ almost from the beginning. C++ has included features over the years to make most uses of *#define* unnecessary.

For example, C++ defines the inline function to replace the macro. This looks just like any other function declaration with the addition of the keyword *inline* tacked to the front:

```
inline int SQUARE(int x) { return x * x; }
```

This inline function definition looks very much like the previous macro definition for *SQUARE()* (I have written this definition on one line to highlight the similarities). However, an inline function is processed by the C++ compiler rather than by the preprocessor. This definition of *SQUARE()* does not suffer from any of the strange effects noted previously.

The *inline* keyword is supposed to suggest to the compiler that it "expand the function inline" rather than generate a call to some code somewhere to perform the operation. This was to satisfy the speed freaks, who wanted to avoid the overhead of performing a function call compared to a macro definition that generates no such call. The best that can be said is that inline functions may be expanded in place, but then again, they may not. There's no way to be sure without performing detailed timing analysis or examining the machine code output by the compiler.

C++ allows programmers to use a variable declared *const* to take the place of a *#define* constant so long as the value of the constant is spelled out at compile time:

```
const int MAX_NAME_LENGTH = 512;
int szName[MAX_NAME_LENGTH];
```

The '11 standard goes so far as to allow you to declare a function to be a *constexpr:*

```
constexpr int square(int n1, int n2)
    {return n1 * n1 + n2 * n2;}
```

This makes a declaration like the following legal:

```
int matrix[square(5)];
```

However, '11 puts a lot of significant restrictions on what can go into a *const* expression. For example, such a function is pretty much limited to a single line.

The '14 standard loosens the rules concerning *const* expressions quite a bit. In general, a function can be declared a *constexpr* if all of the sub-expressions can be calculated at compile time.

Enumerating other options

C++ provides a mechanism for defining constants of a separate, user-defined type. Suppose, for example, that I were writing a program that manipulated States of the Union. I could refer to the states by their name, such as "Texas" or "North Dakota." In practice, this is not convenient since repetitive string comparisons are computationally intensive and subject to error.

I could define a unique value for each state as follows:

```
#define DC_OR_TERRITORY 0
#define ALABAMA   1
#define ALASKA    2
#define ARKANSAS 3
// ...and so on...
```

Not only does this avoid the clumsiness of comparing strings; it allows me to use the name of the state as an index into an array of properties such as population:

```
// increment the population of ALASKA (they need it)
population[ALASKA]++;
```

A statement such as this is much easier to understand than the semantically identical *population[2]*++. This is such a common thing to do that C++ allows the programmer to define what's known as an enumeration:

```
enum STATE {DC_OR_TERRITORY,   // gets 0
            ALABAMA,           // gets 1
            ALASKA,            // gets 2
            ARKANSAS,
            // ...and so on...
```

Each element of this enumeration is assigned a value starting at 0, so *DC_OR_TERRITORY* is defined as 0, *ALABAMA* is defined as 1, and so on. You can override this incremental sequencing by using as assign statement as follows:

```
enum STATE {DC,
            TERRITORIES = 0,
            ALABAMA,
            ALASKA,
            // ...and so on...
```

This version of *STATE* defines an element *DC*, which is given the value 0. It then defines a new element *TERRITORIES*, which is also assigned the value 0. *ALABAMA* picks up with 1 just as before.

The '11 standard extends enumerations by allowing the programmer to create a user-defined enumerated type as follows (note the addition of the keyword *class* in the snippet):

```
enum class STATE {DC,
                  TERRITORIES = 0,
                  ALABAMA,
                  ALASKA,
                  // ...and so on...
```

This declaration creates a new type *STATE* and assigns it 52 members (*ALABAMA* through *WYOMING* plus *DC* and *TERRITORIES*). The programmer can now use *STATE* as she would any other variable type. A variable can be declared to be of type *STATE*:

```
STATE s = STATE::ALASKA;
```

Function calls can be differentiated by this new type:

```
int getPop(STATE s);          // return population
int setPop(STATE s, int pop); // set the population
```

The type *STATE* is not just another word for *int*: Arithmetic is not defined for members of type *STATE*. The following attempt to use *STATE* as an index into an array is not legal:

```
int getPop(STATE s)
{
    return population[s];  // not legal
}
```

However, the members of *STATE* can be converted to their integer equivalent (0 for *DC* and *TERRITORIES*, 1 for *ALABAMA*, 2 for *ALASKA*, and so on) through the application of a cast:

```
int getPop(STATE s)
{
    return population[(int)s];  // is legal
}
```

Including Things #if I Say So

The third major class of preprocessor statement is the #*if*, which is a preprocessor version of the C++ *if* statement:

```
#if constexpression
// included if constexpression evaluates to other than 0
#else
// included if constexpression evaluates to 0
#endif
```

This is known as *conditional compilation* because the set of statements between the *#if* and the *#else* or *#endif* are included in the compilation only if a condition is true. The *constexpression* phrase is limited to simple arithmetic and comparison operators. That's okay because anything more than an equality comparison and the occasional addition is rare.

For example, the following is a common use for *#if*. I can include the following definition within an include file with a name such as *LogMessage:*

```
#if DEBUG == 1
inline void logMessage(const char *pMessage)
        { cout << pMessage << endl; }
#else
#define logMessage(X) (0)
#endif
```

I can now sprinkle error messages throughout my program wherever I need them:

```
#define DEBUG 1
#include "LogMessage"
void testFunction(char *pArg)
{
    logMessage(pArg);
    // ...function continues...
```

With *DEBUG* set to 1, the *logMessage()* is converted into a call to an inline function that outputs the argument to the display. Once the program is working properly, I can remove the definition of *DEBUG*. Now the references to *logMessage()* invoke a macro that does nothing.

A second version of the conditional compilation is the *#ifdef* (which is pronounced "if def"):

```
#ifdef DEBUG
// included if DEBUG has been #defined
#else
// included if DEBUG has not been #defined
#endif
```

There is also an *#ifndef* (pronounced "if not def"), which is the logical reverse of *#ifdef.*

Intrinsically Defined Objects

C++ defines a set of intrinsic constants, which are shown in Table 10-1. These are constants that C++ thinks are just too cool to be without — and that you would have trouble defining for yourself anyway.

Table 10-1		Predefined Preprocessor Constants
Constant	*Type*	*Meaning*
__FILE__	const char const *	The name of the source file.
__LINE__	const int	The current line number.
__func__	const char const *	The name of the current function (C++ '11 only).
__DATE__	const char const *	The current date.
__TIME__	const char const *	The current time.
__TIMESTAMP__	const char const *	The current date and time.
__STDC__	int	Set to 1 if the C++ compiler is compliant with the standard.
__cplusplus	int	Set to 1 if the compiler is a C++ compiler (as opposed to a C compiler). This allows include files to be shared across environments.

These internal macros are particularly useful when generating error messages. You would think that C++ generates plenty of error messages on its own and doesn't need any more help, but sometimes you want to create your own compiler errors. For you, C++ offers not one, not two, but three options: *#error, assert(),* and *static_assert().* Each of these three mechanisms works slightly differently.

The *#error* command is a preprocessor directive (as you can tell by the fact that it starts with the # sign). It causes the preprocessor to stop and output a message. Suppose that your program just won't work with anything but standard C++. You could add the following to the beginning of your program:

```
#if !__cplusplus || !__STDC__
#error This is a standard C++ program.
#endif
```

Now if someone tries to compile your program with anything other than a C++ compiler that strictly adheres to the standards, she will get a single neat error message rather than a raft of potentially meaningless error messages from a confused non-standard compiler.

Unlike *#error*, *assert()* performs its test when the resulting program is executed. For example, suppose that I had written a factorial program that calculates *N * (N - 1) * (N - 2)* and so on down to 1 for whatever *N* I pass it. Factorial is only defined for positive integers; passing a negative number to a factorial is always a mistake. To be careful, I should add a test for a non-positive value at the beginning of the function:

```
int factorial(int N)
{
    assert(N > 0);
    // ...program continues...
```

The program now checks the argument to *factorial()* each time it is called. At the first sign of negativity, *assert()* halts the program with a message to the operator that the assertion failed, along with the file and line number.

Liberal use of *assert()* throughout your program is a good way to detect problems early during development, but constantly testing for errors that have already been found and removed during testing slows the program needlessly. To avoid this, C++ allows the programmer to "remove" the tests when creating the version of the program to be shipped to users: *#define* the constant *NDEBUG* (for "not debug mode"). This causes the preprocessor to convert all the calls to *assert()* in your module to "do nothings" (universally known as NO-OPs).

The preprocessor cannot perform certain compile-time tests. For example, suppose that your program works properly only if the default integer size is 32 bits. The preprocessor is of no help since it knows nothing about integers or floating points. To address this situation, C++ introduced the keyword *static_assert()*, which is interpreted by the compiler (rather than the preprocessor). It accepts two arguments: a *const* expression and a string, as in the following example:

```
static_assert(sizeof(int) == 4, "int is not 32-bits.");
```

If the *const* expression evaluates to 0 or *false* during compilation, the compiler outputs the string and stops. The *static_assert()* does not generate any run-time code. Remember, however, that the expression is evaluated at compile time, so it cannot contain function calls or references to things that are known only when the program executes.

Typedef

The *typedef* keyword allows the programmer to create a shorthand name for a declaration. The careful application of *typedef* can make the resulting program easier to read. (Note that *typedef* is not actually a preprocessor command, but it's largely associated with include files and the preprocessor.)

```
typedef int* IntPtr;
typedef const IntPtr IntConstPtr;

int i;
int *const ptr1 = &i;
IntConstPtr ptr2= ptr1; // ptr1 and ptr2 are the same type
```

The first two declarations in this snippet give a new name to existing types. Thus, the second declaration declares *IntConstPtr* to be another name for *int const**. When this new type is used in the declaration of *ptr2*, it has the same effect as the more complicated declaration of *ptr1*.

Although *typedef* does not introduce any new capability, it can make some complicated declarations a lot easier to read.

Part III
Introduction to Classes

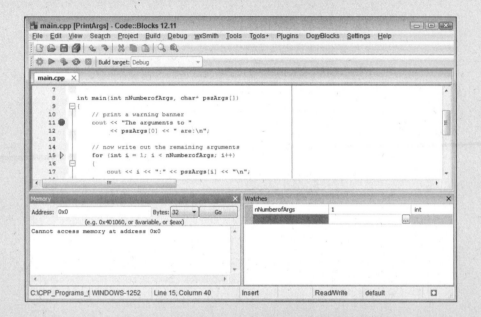

In this part...

✔ Reviewing object-oriented programming

✔ Declaring and defining class members

✔ Declaring constructors and destructors

✔ Defining static member functions

✔ Visit www.dummies.com/extras/cplusplus for great Dummies content online

Chapter 11

Examining Object-Oriented Programming

In This Chapter

▶ Making nachos

▶ Reviewing object-oriented programming

▶ Introducing abstraction and classification

▶ Discovering why object-oriented programming is important

*W*hat, exactly, is object-oriented programming? Object-oriented programming, or OOP as those in the know prefer to call it, relies on two principles you learned before you ever got out of Pampers: abstraction and classification. To explain, let me tell you a little story.

Abstracting Microwave Ovens

Sometimes when my son and I are watching football (which only happens when my wife can't find the switcher), I whip up a terribly unhealthy batch of nachos. I dump some chips on a plate, throw on some beans, cheese, and lots of jalapeños, and nuke the whole mess in the microwave oven for five minutes. To use my microwave, I open the door, throw the stuff in, and punch a few buttons. After a few minutes, the nachos are done.

Now think for a minute about all the things I don't do to use my microwave:

✔ I don't rewire or change anything inside the microwave to get it to work. The microwave has an interface — the front panel with all the buttons and the little time display — that lets me do everything I need to do.

✔ I don't have to reprogram the software used to drive the little processor inside my microwave, even if I cooked a different dish the last time I used the microwave.

✔ I don't look inside my microwave's case.

✔ Even if I were a microwave designer and knew all about the inner workings of a microwave, including its software, I would still use it the same way to heat my nachos without thinking about all that stuff inside.

These are not profound observations. You can deal with only so much stress in your life. To reduce the number of things that you deal with, you work at a certain level of detail.

In object-oriented (OO) computerese, the level of detail at which you are working is called the *level of abstraction*. To introduce another OO term while I have the chance, I *abstract away* the details of the microwave's innards.

When I'm working on nachos, I view my microwave oven as a box. (I can't worry about the innards of the microwave oven and still follow the Cowboys on the tube.) As long as I operate the microwave only through its interface (the keypad), there should be nothing I can do to

✔ Cause the microwave to enter an inconsistent state and crash.

✔ Turn my nachos into a blackened, flaming mass.

✔ Make the microwave (along with the surrounding house) burst into flames!

Preparing functional nachos

Suppose that I were to ask my son to write an algorithm for how Dad makes nachos. After he understood what I wanted, he would probably write "open a can of beans, grate some cheese, cut the jalapeños," and so on. When it came to the part about microwaving the concoction, he would write something like "cook in the microwave for five minutes."

That description is straightforward and complete. But it's not the way a functional programmer would code a program to make nachos. Functional programmers live in a world devoid of objects such as microwave ovens and other appliances. They tend to worry about flow charts with their myriad functional paths. In a functional solution to the nachos problem, the flow of control would pass through my finger to the front panel and then to the internals of the microwave. Pretty soon, flow would be wiggling around through complex logic paths about how long to turn on the microwave tube and whether to sound the "come and get it" tone.

In a world like this, it's difficult to think in terms of levels of abstraction. There are no objects, no abstractions behind which to hide inherent complexity.

Preparing object-oriented nachos

In an object-oriented approach to making nachos, I would first identify the types of objects in the problem: chips, beans, cheese, and an oven. Then I would begin the task of modeling these objects in software, without regard to the details of how they will be used in the final program.

While I am doing this, I'm said to be working (and thinking) at the level of the basic objects. I need to think about making a useful oven, but I don't have to think about the logical process of making nachos yet. After all, the microwave designers didn't think about the specific problem of my making a snack. Rather, they set about the problem of designing and building a useful microwave.

After the objects I need have been successfully coded and tested, I can ratchet up to the next level of abstraction. I can start thinking at the nacho-making level, rather than the microwave-making level. At this point, I can pretty much translate my son's instructions directly into C++ code.

Classifying Microwave Ovens

Critical to the concept of abstraction is that of classification. If I were to ask my son, "What's a microwave?" he would probably say, "It's an oven that . . ." If I then asked, "What's an oven?" he might reply, "It's a kitchen appliance that . . ." (If I then asked, "What's a kitchen appliance?" he would probably say, "Why are you asking so many stupid questions?")

The answers my son gave to my questions stem from his understanding of our particular microwave as an example of the type of things called microwave ovens. In addition, my son sees microwave ovens as just a special type of oven, which itself is just a special type of kitchen appliance.

In object-oriented computerese, the microwave in my kitchen is an *instance* of the *class* microwave. The class microwave is a *subclass* of the class oven, and the class oven is a subclass of the class kitchen appliances. We say that microwaves *inherit* their cooking properties from oven.

Humans classify. Everything about our world is ordered into taxonomies. We do this to reduce the number of things we have to remember. Take, for example, the first time you saw a hybrid car. The advertisement probably called the hybrid "unique, the likes of which have never been seen." But you and I know that that just isn't so. I like hybrids and I will grant you that they have a lot of differences under the hood, but hey, a hybrid is still a car. As such, it shares all of (or at least most of) the properties of other cars. It has a steering wheel, seats, a motor, brakes, and so on. I bet I could even drive one without first reading the owner's manual.

I don't have to clutter my limited storage with all the things that a hybrid has in common with other cars. All I have to remember is "a hybrid is a car that . . ." and tack on those few things that are unique to a hybrid (like the price tag). I can go further. Cars are a subclass of wheeled vehicles along with other members, such as trucks and pickups. Maybe wheeled vehicles are a subclass of vehicles, which includes boats and planes. And on and on and on.

Why Classify?

Why do we classify? It sounds like a lot of trouble. Besides, people have been using the functional approach for so long, why change now?

It may seem easier to design and build a microwave oven specifically for this one problem, rather than build a separate, more generic oven object. Suppose, for example, that I want to build a microwave to cook nachos and nachos only. I wouldn't need to put a front panel on it, other than a Start button. I always cook nachos the same amount of time, so I could dispense with all that Defrost and Temp Cook nonsense. My nachos-only microwave needs to hold only one flat little plate. Three cubic feet of space would be wasted on nachos.

For that matter, I can dispense with the concept of "microwave oven" altogether. All I really need is the guts of the oven. Then, in the recipe, I put the instructions to make it work: "Put nachos in the box. Connect the red wire to the black wire. Bring the radar tube up to about 3,000 volts. Notice a slight hum. Try not to stand too close if you intend to have children." Stuff like that.

But the functional approach has some problems:

- **Too complex:** I don't want the details of oven building mixed into the details of nacho building. If I can't define the objects and pull them out of the morass of details to deal with separately, I must deal with all the complexities of the problem at the same time.

- **Not flexible:** Someday I may need to replace the microwave oven with some other type of oven. I should be able to do so as long as its interface is the same. Without being clearly delineated and developed separately, it becomes impossible to cleanly remove an object type and replace it with another.

- **Not reusable:** Ovens are used to make lots of different dishes. I don't want to create a new oven every time I encounter a new recipe. Having solved a problem once, it would be nice to be able to reuse the solution in future programs.

The remaining chapters in this part demonstrate how the object-oriented language features of C++ address these problems.

In real life, it isn't quite as pure as I make it sound here. I can't spend the time to build the software equivalent of a generic microwave oven. After all, teams of engineers spends thousands of developer hours designing microwave ovens (and still the front panel comes out incomprehensible!). When I build my classes, I generally only build in the capabilities that I will need for the particular problem at hand, but still the principle is the same. When I am building the microwave oven, I need only think about the oven. When I am making nachos, I only have to think about using the oven. It's simpler that way.

Chapter 12

Adding Class to C++

In This Chapter

▶ Grouping data into classes

▶ Declaring and defining class members

▶ Adding active properties to the class

▶ Accessing class member functions

▶ Overloading member functions

*P*rograms often deal with groups of data: a person's name, rank, and serial number, stuff like that. Any one of these values is not sufficient to describe a person — only in the aggregate do the values make any sense. A simple structure such as an array is great for holding standalone values, but it doesn't work well for data groups. This makes good ol' arrays inadequate for storing complex data (such as personal credit records that the Web companies maintain so they can lose them to hackers).

For reasons that will become clear shortly, I'll call such a grouping of data an *object*. A microwave oven is an object (see Chapter 11 if that doesn't make sense). You are an object (no offense). Your savings account information in a database is an object.

Introducing the Class

How nice it would be if we could create objects in C++ that have the relevant properties of the real-world objects we're trying to model. What we need is a structure that can hold all the different types of data necessary to describe a single object. C++ calls the structure that combines multiple pieces of data into a single object a *class*.

The Format of a Class

A class consists of the keyword *class* followed by a name and an open and closed brace. A class used to describe a savings account including account number and balance might appear as follows:

```
class SavingsAccount
{
  public:
    unsigned accountNumber;
    double balance;
};
```

The statement after the open brace is the keyword *public.* (Hold off asking about the meaning of the *public* keyword. I'll make its meaning public a little later.)

The alternative keyword *struct* can be used in place of *class.* The two keywords are identical except that the *public* declaration is assumed in the *struct* and can be omitted. You should stick with *class* for most programs for reasons that will become clear later in this chapter.

Following the *public* keyword are the entries it takes to describe the object. The *SavingsAccount* class contains two elements: an unsigned integer *accountNumber* and the account *balance.* We can also say that *accountNumber* and *balance* are members or properties of the class *SavingsAccount.*

To create an actual savings account object, I type something like the following:

```
SavingsAccount mySavingsAccount;
```

We say that *mySavingsAccount* is an *instance* of the class *SavingsAccount.*

The naming convention used here is common: Class names are normally capitalized. In a class name with multiple words such as *SavingsAccount,* each word is capitalized, and the words are jammed together without an underscore. Object names follow the same rule of jamming multiple words together, but they normally start with a small letter, as in *mySavingsAccount.* As always, these norms (I hesitate to say rules) are to help out the human reader — C++ doesn't care one way or the other.

Accessing the Members of a Class

The following syntax is used to access the property of a particular object:

```
// Create a savings account object
SavingsAccount mySave;
mySave.accountNumber = 1234;
mySave.balance = 0.0;

// Input a second savings account from the keyboard
cout << "Input your account number and balance" << endl;
SavingsAccount urSave;
cin >> urSave.accountNumber;
cin >> urSave.balance;
```

This code snippet declares two objects of class *SavingsAccount, mySave* and *urSave.* The snippet initializes *mySave* by assigning a value to the account number and a 0 to the balance (as per usual for my savings account). It then creates a second object of the same class, *urSave.* The snippet reads the account number and balance from the keyboard.

An important point to note in this snippet is that *mySave* and *urSave* are separate, independent objects. Manipulating the members of one has no effect on the members of the other (lucky for *urSave*).

In addition, the name of the member without an associated object makes no sense. I cannot say either of the following:

```
balance = 0.0;                    // illegal; no object
SavingsAccount.balance = 0.0;// class but still no object
```

Every savings account has its own unique account number and maintains a separate balance. (There may be properties that are shared by all savings accounts — we'll get to those in Chapter 18 — but account and balance don't happen to be among them.)

Activating Our Objects

You use classes to simulate real-world objects. The *Savings* class tries to represent a savings account. This allows you to think in terms of objects rather than simply lines of code. The closer C++ objects are to modeling the real world, the easier it is to deal with them in programs. This sounds simple enough. However, the *Savings* class doesn't do a very good job of simulating a savings account.

Simulating real-world objects

Real-world accounts have data-type properties such as account numbers and balances, the same as the *Savings* class. This makes *Savings* a good starting point for describing a real account. But real-world accounts do things. Savings accounts accumulate interest; CDs charge a substantial penalty for early withdrawal — stuff like that.

Functional programs "do things" through functions. A C++ program might call *strcmp()* to compare two character strings or *max()* to return the maximum of two values. In fact, Chapter 23 explains that even stream I/O (*cin* >> and *cout* <<) is a special form of function *call*.

The *Savings* class needs active properties of its own if it's to do a good job of representing a real concept:

```
class Savings
{
  public:
    double deposit(double amount)
    {
        balance += amount;
        return balance;
    }

    unsigned accountNumber;
    double balance;
};
```

In addition to the account number and balance, this version of *Savings* includes the function *deposit()*. This gives *Savings* the ability to control its own future. The class *Savings* needs a function *accumulateInterest()*, and the class *CD* a function to *penalizeForEarlyWithdrawal()*.

Functions defined in a class are called *member functions*.

Why bother with member functions?

Why should you bother with member functions? What's wrong with the good ol' days of functional programming?

I'm using the term "functional programming" synonymously with "procedural programming", the way programming was done before object-oriented programming came along.

```
class Savings
{
  public:
    unsigned accountNumber;
    double balance;
};
double deposit(Savings& s, double amount)
{
    s.balance += amount;
    return s.balance;
}
```

Here, *deposit()* implements the "deposit into savings account" function. This functional solution relies on an outside function, *deposit()*, to implement an activity that savings accounts perform but that *Savings* lacks. This gets the job done, but it does so by breaking the object-oriented (OO) rules.

The microwave oven has internal components that it "knows" how to use to cook, defrost, and burn to a crisp. Class data members are similar to the parts of a microwave — the member functions of a class perform cook-like functions.

When I make nachos, I don't have to start hooking up the internal components of the oven in a certain way to make it work. Nor do I rely on some external device to reach into a mess of wiring for me. I want my classes to work the same way my microwave does (and, no, I don't mean "not very well"). I want my classes to know how to manipulate their internals without outside intervention.

Adding a Member Function

To demonstrate member functions, start by defining a class *Student*. One possible representation of such a class follows (taken from the program *CallMemberFunction*):

```
class Student
{
  public:
    // add a completed course to the record
    double addCourse(int hours, double grade)
    {
        // calculate the sum of all courses times
        // the average grade
        double weightedGPA;
        weightedGPA = semesterHours * gpa;

        // now add in the new course
        semesterHours += hours;
        weightedGPA += grade * hours;
```

```
        gpa = weightedGPA / semesterHours;

        // return the new gpa
        return gpa;
    }

    int  semesterHours;
    double gpa;
};
```

The function *addCourse(int, double)* is called a member function of the class *Student*. In principle, it's a property of the class like the data members *semesterHours* and *gpa*.

Sometimes functions that are not members of a class are class "plain ol' functions," but I'll refer to them simply as *nonmembers*.

The member functions do not have to precede the data members as in this example. The members of a class can be listed in any order — I just prefer to put the functions first.

For historical reasons, member functions are also called *methods*. This term originated in one of the original object-oriented languages. The name made sense there, but it makes no sense in C++. Nevertheless, the term has gained popularity in OO circles because it's easier to say than "member function." (The fact that it sounds more impressive probably doesn't hurt, either.) So, if your friends start spouting off at a dinner party about "methods of the class," just replace *methods* with *member functions* and reparse anything they say.

Calling a Member Function

The following *CallMemberFunction* program shows how to invoke the member function *addCourse()*:

```
//  CallMemberFunction - define and invoke a function
//                 that's a member of the class Student
//
#include <cstdio>
#include <cstdlib>
#include <iostream>
using namespace std;

class Student
{
  public:
    // add a completed course to the record
    double addCourse(int hours, double grade)
    {
        // calculate the sum of all courses times
```

```
            // the average grade
            double weightedGPA;
            weightedGPA = semesterHours * gpa;

            // now add in the new course
            semesterHours += hours;
            weightedGPA += grade * hours;
            gpa = weightedGPA / semesterHours;

            // return the new gpa
            return gpa;
        }

        int   semesterHours;
        double gpa;
};

int main(int nNumberofArgs, char* pszArgs[])
{
    // create a Student object and initialize it
    Student s;
    s.semesterHours = 3;
    s.gpa = 3.0;

    // the values before the call
    cout << "Before: s = (" << s.semesterHours
         << ", " << s. gpa   << ")" << endl;

    // the following subjects the data members of the s
    // object to the member function addCourse()
    cout << "Adding 3 hours with a grade of 4.0" << endl;
    s.addCourse(3, 4.0); // call the member function

    // the values are now changed
    cout << "After: s = (" << s.semesterHours
         << ", " << s. gpa   << ")" << endl;

    // wait until user is ready before terminating program
    // to allow the user to see the program results
    cout << "Press Enter to continue..." << endl;
    cin.ignore(10, '\n');
    cin.get();
    return 0;
}
```

The syntax for calling a member function looks like a cross between the syntax for accessing a data member and that used for calling a function. The right side of the dot looks like a conventional function call, but an object is on the left of the dot.

In the call *s.addCourse()*, we say that "*addCourse()* operates on the object *s*" or, said another way, "*s* is the student to which the course is to be added." You can't fetch the number of semester hours without knowing from which student to fetch those hours — you can't add a student to a course without knowing which student to add. Calling a member function without an object makes no more sense than referencing a data member without an object.

Accessing other members from a member function

I can see it clearly: You repeat to yourself, "Accessing a member without an object makes no sense. Accessing a member without an object makes no sense. Accessing . . ." Just about the time you've accepted this, you look at the member function *Student::addCourse()* and *Wham!* It hits you: *addCourse()* accesses other class members without reference to an object. So how do they do that?

Okay, which is it, can you or can't you? Believe me, you can't. When you reference a member of *Student* from *addCourse()*, that reference is against the *Student* object with which the call to *addCourse()* was made. Huh? Go back to the *CallMemberFunction* example. A stripped-down version appears here:

```
int main(int nNumberofArgs, char* pszArgs[])
{
    Student s;
    s.semesterHours = 10;
    s.gpa       = 3.0;
    s.addCourse(3, 4.0); // call the member function

    Student t;
    t.semesterHours = 6;
    t.gpa       = 1.0;    // not doing so good
    t.addCourse(3, 1.5); // things aren't getting
                         // much better

    return 0;
}
```

When *addCourse()* is invoked with the object *s*, all of the otherwise unqualified member references in *addCourse()* refer to *s* as well. Thus, the reference to *semesterHours* in *addCourse()* refers to *s.semesterHours,* and *gpa* refers to *s.gpa*. But when *addCourse()* is invoked with the *Student t* object, these same references are to *t.semesterHours* and *t.gpa* instead.

The object with which the member function was invoked is the "current" object, and all unqualified references to class members refer to this object. Put another way, unqualified references to class members made from a member function are always against the current object.

Naming the current object

How does the member function know what the current object is? It's not magic — the address of the object is passed to the member function as an implicit and hidden first argument. In other words, the following conversion is taking place:

```
s.addCourse(3, 2.5)
```

is like

```
Student::addCourse(&s, 3, 2.5)
```

(Note that you can't actually use the explicit syntax; this is just the way C++ sees it.)

Inside the function, this implicit pointer to the current object has a name, in case you need to refer to it. It is called *this,* as in "Which object? *This* object." Get it? The type of *this* is always a pointer to an object of the appropriate class.

Anytime a member function refers to another member of the same class without providing an object explicitly, C++ assumes that the programmer meant *this*. You also can refer to *this* explicitly, if you like. I could have written *Student::addCourse()* as follows:

```
double Student::addCourse(int hours, double grade)
{
    double weightedGPA;
    weightedGPA = this->semesterHours * this->gpa;

    // now add in the new course
    this->semesterHours += hours;
    weightedGPA += hours * grade;
    this->gpa = weightedGPA / this->semesterHours;
    return this->gpa;
}
```

The effect is the same whether you explicitly include *this,* as in the preceding example, or leave it implicit, as you did before.

Scope Resolution (And I Don't Mean How Well Your Telescope Works)

The *::* between a member and its class name is called the *scope resolution operator* because it indicates the class to which a member belongs. The class name before the colons is like the family last name, while the function name after the colons is like the first name — the order is similar to a Chinese name, family name first.

You use the *::* operator to describe a non-member function by using a null class name. The non-member function *addCourse,* for example, can be referred to as *::addCourse(int, double),* if you prefer. This is like a function without a home.

Normally the *::* operator is optional, but there are a few occasions when this is not so, as illustrated here:

```
// addCourse - combine the hours and grade into
//             a weighted grade
double addCourse(int hours, double grade)
{
    return hours * grade;
}

class Student
{
  public:
    // add a completed course to the record
    double addCourse(int hours, double grade)
    {
        // call some external function to calculate the
        // weighted grade
        double weightedGPA=::addCourse(semesterHours,gpa);

        // now add in the new course
        semesterHours += hours;

        // use the same function to calculate the weighted
        // grade of this new course
        weightedGPA += ::addCourse(hours, grade);
        gpa = weightedGPA / semesterHours;

        // return the new gpa
        return gpa;
    }

    int   semesterHours;
    double gpa;
};
```

Here, I want the member function *Student::addCourse()* to call the non-member function *::addCourse()*. Without the *::* operator, however, a call to *addCourse()* from *Student* refers to *Student::addCourse()*. This would result in the function calling itself.

Defining a Member Function in the Class

A member function can be defined either in the class or separately. When defined in the class definition, the function looks like the following, which is contained in the include file *Savings.h:*

```cpp
// Savings - define a class that includes the ability
//           to make a deposit
class Savings
{
  public:
    // define a member function deposit()
    double deposit(double amount)
    {
        balance += amount;
        return balance;
    }

    unsigned int accountNumber;
    double  balance;
};
```

Using an include like this is pretty slick. Now a program can include the class definition (along with the definition for the member function), as follows in the venerable SavingsClass_inline program:

```cpp
//
//   SavingsClassInline - invoke a member function that's
//                        both declared and defined within
//                        the class Student
//
#include <cstdio>
#include <cstdlib>
#include <iostream>

using namespace std;
#include "Savings.h"

int main(int nNumberofArgs, char* pszArgs[])
{
    Savings s;
    s.accountNumber = 123456;
    s.balance = 0.0;

    // now add something to the account
    cout << "Depositing 10 to account "
         << s.accountNumber << endl;
    s.deposit(10);
    cout << "Balance is " << s.balance << endl;
```

```
      // wait until user is ready before terminating program
      // to allow the user to see the program results
      cout << "Press Enter to continue..." << endl;
      cin.ignore(10, '\n');
      cin.get();
      return 0;
}
```

This is cool because everyone other than the programmer of the *Savings* class can concentrate on the act of performing a deposit rather than the details of banking. These details are neatly tucked away in their own include files.

The *#include* directive inserts the contents of the file during the compilation process. The C++ compiler actually "sees" your source file with the contents of the *Savings.h* file included. See Chapter 10 for details on include files.

Inlining member functions

Member functions defined in the class default to inline (unless they have been specifically outlined by a compiler switch or for any number of very technical reasons). Mostly, this is because a member function defined in the class is usually very small, and small functions are prime candidates for inlining.

Remember that an inline function is expanded where it is invoked. (See Chapter 10 for a comparison of inline functions and macros.) An inline function executes faster because the processor doesn't have to jump over to where the function is defined — inline functions usually take up more memory because they are copied into every call instead of being defined just once.

There is another good but more technical reason to inline member functions defined within a class. Remember that C++ structures are normally defined in include files, which are then included in the .CPP source files that need them. Such include files should not contain data or functions because these files are compiled multiple times. Including an inline function is okay, however, because it (like a macro) expands in place in the source file. The same applies to C++ classes. By defaulting member functions defined in classes inline, you avoid the preceding problem.

Keeping a Member Function after Class

For larger functions, putting the code directly in the class definition can lead to some large, unwieldy class definitions. To prevent this, C++ lets you define member functions outside the class.

A function that is defined outside the class is said to be an *outline function*. This term is meant to be the opposite of an inline function that has been defined within the class. Your basic functions such as those we have defined since Chapter 5 are also outline functions.

When written outside the class declaration, the *Savings.h* file declares the *deposit()* function without defining it as follows:

```
// Savings - define a class that includes the ability
//           to make a deposit
class Savings
{
  public:
    // declare but don't define member function
    double deposit(double amount);
    unsigned int accountNumber;
    double  balance;
};
```

The definition of the *deposit()* function must be included in one of the source files that make up the program. For simplicity, I defined it within `main.cpp`.

You would not normally combine the member function definition with the rest of your program. It is more convenient to collect the outlined member function definitions into a source file with an appropriate name (such as `Savings.cpp`). This source file is combined with other source files as part of building the executable program. I describe this in Chapter 21.

```
//   SavingsClassOutline - invoke a member function that's
//                         declared within a class but
//                         defined in a separate file
//
#include <cstdio>
#include <cstdlib>
#include <iostream>

using namespace std;
#include "Savings.h"

// define the member function Savings::deposit()
// (normally this is contained in a separate file that is
// then combined with a different file that is combined)
double Savings::deposit(double amount)
```

```
{
    balance += amount;
    return balance;
}

// the main program
int main(int nNumberofArgs, char* pszArgs[])
{
    Savings s;
    s.accountNumber = 123456;
    s.balance = 0.0;

    // now add something to the account
    cout << "Depositing 10 to account "
         << s.accountNumber << endl;
    s.deposit(10);
    cout << "Balance is " << s.balance << endl;

    // wait until user is ready before terminating program
    // to allow the user to see the program results
    cout << "Press Enter to continue..." << endl;
    cin.ignore(10, '\n');
    cin.get();
    return 0;
}
```

This class definition contains nothing more than a prototype declaration for the function *deposit()*. The function definition appears separately. The member function prototype declaration in the structure is analogous to any other prototype declaration and, like all prototype declarations, is required.

Notice how the function nickname *deposit()* was good enough when the function was defined within the class. When defined outside the class, however, the function requires its extended name, *Savings::deposit()*.

Overloading Member Functions

Member functions can be overloaded in the same way that conventional functions are overloaded. (See Chapter 6 if you don't remember what that means.) Remember, however, that the class name is part of the extended name. Thus, the following functions are all legal:

```
class Student
{
  public:
    // grade -- return the current grade point average
    double grade();
```

```
        // grade -- set the grade and return previous value
        double grade(double newGPA);
        // ...data members and other stuff...
};
class Slope
{
  public:
    // grade -- return the percentage grade of the slope
    double grade();
    // ...stuff goes here too...
};

// grade - return the letter equivalent of a number grade
char grade(double value);

int main(int argcs, char* pArgs[])
{
    Student s;
    s.grade(3.5);            // Student::grade(double)
    double v = s.grade();  // Student::grade()

    char c = grade(v);     // ::grade(double)

    Slope o;
    double m = o.grade(); // Slope::grade()
    return 0;
}
```

Each call made from *main()* is noted in the comments with the extended name of the function called.

When calling overloaded functions, not only the arguments of the function but also the type of the object (if any) with which the function is invoked are used to resolve the call. (The term *resolve* is object-oriented talk for "decide at compile time which overloaded function to call." A mere mortal might say "differentiate.")

Chapter 13

Point and Stare at Objects

In This Chapter

▶ Examining the object of arrays of objects

▶ Getting a few pointers on object pointers

▶ Strong typing — getting picky about our pointers

▶ Navigating through lists of objects

C++ programmers are forever generating arrays of things — arrays of *ints*, arrays of *doubles* — so why not arrays of students? Students stand in line all the time — a lot more than they care to. The concept of *Student* objects all lined up quietly awaiting their names to jump up to perform some mundane task is just too attractive to pass up.

Declaring Arrays of Objects

Arrays of objects work the same way arrays of simple variables work. (Chapter 7 goes into the care and feeding of arrays of simple — intrinsic — variables, and Chapters 8 and 9 describe simple pointers in detail.) Take, for example, the following snippet from the ArrayOfStudents program:

```
// ArrayOfStudents - define an array of student objects
//                   and access an element in it. This
//                   program doesn't do anything
#include <cstdio>
#include <cstdlib>
#include <iostream>
using namespace std;

class Student
{
  public:
    int   semesterHours;
    double gpa;
    double addCourse(int hours, double grade){return 0.0;}
};
```

```
void someFn()
{
    // declare an array of 10 students
    Student s[10];

    // assign the 5th student a gpa of 4.0 (lucky guy)
    s[4].gpa = 4.0;
    s[4].semesterHours = 32;

    // add another course to the 5th student;
    // this time he failed - serves him right
    s[4].addCourse(3, 0.0);
}
```

Here *s* is an array of *Student* objects. *s[4]* refers to the fifth *Student* object in the array. By extension, *s[4].gpa* refers to the GPA of the fifth student. Further, *s[4].addCourse()* adds a course to the fifth *Student* object.

Declaring Pointers to Objects

Pointers to objects work like pointers to simple types, as you can see in the example program ObjPtr:

```
// ObjPtr - define and use a pointer to a Student object
#include <cstdio>
#include <cstdlib>
#include <iostream>
using namespace std;

class Student
{
  public:
    int    semesterHours;
    double gpa;
    double addCourse(int hours, double grade);
};

int main(int argc, char* pArgs[])
{
    // create a Student object
    Student s;
    s.gpa = 3.0;

    // now create a pointer pS to a Student object
    Student* pS;

    // make pS point to our Student object
    pS = &s;
```

```
        // now output the gpa of the object, once thru
        // the variable name and a second time thru pS
        cout << "s.gpa   = " << s.gpa   << "\n"
             << "pS->gpa = " << pS->gpa << endl;

        // wait until user is ready before terminating program
        // to allow the user to see the program results
        cout << "Press Enter to continue..." << endl;
        cin.ignore(10, '\n');
        cin.get();
        return 0;
}
```

The program declares a variable *s* of type *Student*. It then goes on to declare
a pointer variable *pS* of type "pointer to a *Student* object," also written as
Student*. The program initializes the value of one of the data members in *s*.
It then proceeds to assign the address of *s* to the variable *pS*. Finally, it refers
to the same *Student* object, first using the object's name, *s,* and then using the
pointer to the object, *pS*. I explain the strange notation *pS->gpa;* in the next
section of this chapter.

Dereferencing an object pointer

By analogy of pointers to simple variables, you might think that the following
refers to the GPA of student *s:*

```
int main(int argc, char* pArgs[])
{
    Student s;
    Student* pS = &s; // create a pointer to s

    // access the gpa member of the obj pointed at by pS
    // (this doesn't work)
    *pS.gpa = 3.5;

    return 0;
}
```

As the comments indicate, this doesn't work. The problem is that the dot
operator *(.)* is evaluated before the pointer *(*)*. Thus, **ps.gpa* is interpreted as
if written **(ps.gpa)*. Parentheses are necessary to force the pointer operator to
be evaluated before the dot:

```
int main(int argc, char* pArgs[])
{
    Student s;
    Student* pS = &s; // create a pointer to s
```

```
    // access the gpa member of the obj pointed at by pS
    // (this works as expected)
    (*pS).gpa = 3.5;

    return 0;
}
```

The **pS* evaluates to the pointer's *Student* object pointed at by *pS*. The *.gpa* refers to the *gpa* member of that object.

Pointing toward arrow pointers

Using the asterisk operator together with parentheses works just fine for dereferencing pointers to objects; however, even the most hardened techies would admit that this mixing of asterisks and parentheses is a bit tortured.

C++ offers a more convenient operator for accessing members of an object to avoid clumsy object pointer expressions. The -> operator is defined as follows:

```
ps->gpa is equivalent to (*pS).gpa
```

This leads to the following:

```
int main(int argc, char* pArgs[])
{
    Student s;
    Student* pS = &s; // create a pointer to s

    // access the gpa member of the obj pointed at by pS
    pS->gpa = 3.5;

    return 0;
}
```

The arrow operator is used almost exclusively because it is easier to read; however, the two forms are completely equivalent.

Passing Objects to Functions

Passing pointers to functions is just one of the many ways to entertain yourself with pointer variables.

Calling a function with an object value

As you know, C++ passes arguments to functions by reference when the argument type is flagged with the & property (see Chapter 8). However, by default, C++ passes arguments to functions by value. (You can check Chapter 6 on this one, if you insist.)

Complex, user-defined class objects are passed the same as simple *int* values, as shown in the following PassObjVal program:

```
// PassObjVal - attempts to change the value of an object
//              in a function fail when the object is
//              passed by value
#include <cstdio>
#include <cstdlib>
#include <iostream>
using namespace std;

class Student
{
  public:
    int    semesterHours;
    double gpa;
};

void someFn(Student copyS)
{
    copyS.semesterHours = 10;
    copyS.gpa           = 3.0;
    cout << "The value of copyS.gpa = "<<copyS.gpa<< endl;
}

int main(int argc, char* pArgs[])
{
    Student s;
    s.gpa = 0.0;

    // display the value of s.gpa before calling someFn()
    cout << "The value of s.gpa = " << s.gpa << endl;

    // pass the address of the existing object
    cout << "Calling someFn(Student)" << endl;
    someFn(s);
    cout << "Returned from someFn(Student)" << endl;

    // the value of s.gpa remains 0
    cout << "The value of s.gpa = " << s.gpa << endl;
```

```
      // wait until user is ready before terminating program
      // to allow the user to see the program results
      cout << "Press Enter to continue..." << endl;
      cin.ignore(10, '\n');
      cin.get();
      return 0;
}
```

The function *main()* creates an object *s* and then passes *s* to the function *someFn()*.

It is not the object *s* itself that is passed, but a copy of *s*.

The object *copyS* in *someFn()* begins life as an exact copy of the variable *s* in *main()*. Since it is a copy, any change to *copyS* made within *someFn()* has no effect on *s* back in *main()*. Executing this program generates the following understandable but disappointing response:

```
The value of s.gpa = 0
Calling someFn(Student)
The value of copyS.gpa = 3
Returned from someFn(Student)
The value of s.gpa = 0
Press Enter to continue...
```

Calling a function with an object pointer

Most of the time, the programmer wants any changes made in the function to be reflected in the calling function as well. For this, the C++ programmer must pass either the address of an object or a reference to the object. The following PassObjPtr program uses the address approach:

```
// PassObjPtr - change the contents of an object in
//              a function by passing a pointer
#include <cstdio>
#include <cstdlib>
#include <iostream>
using namespace std;

class Student
{
  public:
    int    semesterHours;
    double gpa;
};
```

```
void someFn(Student* pS)
{
    pS->semesterHours = 10;
    pS->gpa           = 3.0;
    cout << "The value of pS->gpa = " << pS->gpa << endl;
}

int main(int nNumberofArgs, char* pszArgs[])
{
    Student s;
    s.gpa = 0.0;

    // display the value of s.gpa before calling someFn()
    cout << "The value of s.gpa = " << s.gpa << endl;

    // pass the address of the existing object
    cout << "Calling someFn(Student*)" << endl;
    someFn(&s);
    cout << "Returned from someFn(Student*)" << endl;

    // the value of s.gpa is now 3.0
    cout << "The value of s.gpa = " << s.gpa << endl;

    // wait until user is ready before terminating program
    // to allow the user to see the program results
    cout << "Press Enter to continue..." << endl;
    cin.ignore(10, '\n');
    cin.get();
    return 0;
}
```

The type of the argument to *someFn()* is a pointer to a *Student* object (otherwise known as *Student**). This is reflected in the way that the program calls *someFn()*, passing the address of *s* rather than the value of *s*. Giving *someFn()* the address of *s* allows him to modify whatever value that is stored there. Conceptually, this is akin to writing down the address of the house *s* on the piece of paper *pS* and then passing that paper to *someFn()*. The function *someFn()* uses the arrow syntax for dereferencing the *pS* pointer.

The output from PassObjPtr is much more satisfying (to me, anyway):

```
The value of s.gpa = 0
Calling someFn(Student*)
The value of pS->gpa = 3
Returned from someFn(Student*)
The value of s.gpa = 3
Press Enter to continue...
```

Calling a function by using the reference operator

Chapter 6 introduces the concept of passing simple argument types to functions by reference using the "&" operator. The following PassObjRef demonstrates the same for user-defined objects:

```cpp
// PassObjRef - change the contents of an object in
//              a function by using a reference
#include <cstdio>
#include <cstdlib>
#include <iostream>
using namespace std;

class Student
{
  public:
    int    semesterHours;
    double gpa;
};

// same as before, but this time using references
void someFn(Student& refS)
{
    refS.semesterHours = 10;
    refS.gpa          = 3.0;
    cout << "The value of copyS.gpa = " <<refS.gpa<< endl;
}

int main(int nNumberofArgs, char* pszArgs[])
{
    Student s;
    s.gpa = 0.0;

    // display the value of s.gpa before calling someFn()
    cout << "The value of s.gpa = " << s.gpa   << endl;

    // pass the address of the existing object
    cout << "Calling someFn(Student*)" << endl;
    someFn(s);
    cout << "Returned from someFn(Student&)" << endl;

    // the value of s.gpa is now 3.0
    cout << "The value of s.gpa = " << s.gpa << endl;

    // wait until user is ready before terminating program
    // to allow the user to see the program results
    cout << "Press Enter to continue..." << endl;
    cin.ignore(10, '\n');
    cin.get();
    return 0;
}
```

In this example, C++ passes a reference to *s* rather than a copy. The output from this version is identical to the PassObjPtr program — changes made in *someFn()* are retained in *main()*.

Why Bother with Pointers or References?

Okay, so both pointers and references provide relative advantages, but why bother with either one? Why not just always pass the object? I mentioned one obvious answer earlier in this chapter: You can't modify the object from a function that gets nothing but a copy of the structure object.

Here's a second reason: Some objects are large — I mean *really* large. An object representing a screen image can be many megabytes in length. Passing such an object by value means copying the entire thing into the function's memory.

The object will need to be copied again should that function call another, and so on. After a while, you can end up with dozens of copies of this object. That consumes memory, and copying all the objects can make execution of your program slower than booting up Windows.

The problem of copying objects gets worse. You see in Chapter 17 that making a copy of an object can be even more painful than simply copying some memory around.

Passing a pointer (or a reference) is very fast. A pointer is 4 bytes, no matter how big the object being pointed at is.

Returning to the Heap

The problems that exist for simple types of pointers plague class object pointers as well. In particular, you must make sure that the pointer you're using actually points to a valid object. For example, don't return a reference to an object defined local to the function:

```
MyClass* myFunc()
{
    // the following does not work
    MyClass  mc;
    MyClass* pMC = &mc;
    return pMC;
}
```

Upon return from *myFunc()*, the *mc* object goes out of scope. The pointer returned by *myFunc()* is not valid in the calling function.

The problem of returning memory that's about to go out of scope is discussed in Chapter 9.

Allocating the object off the heap solves the problem:

```
MyClass* myFunc()
{
    MyClass* pMC = new MyClass;
    return pMC;
}
```

Here the memory allocated off the heap is not returned when the variable *pMC* goes out of scope.

Programmers allocate memory from the heap if they don't want the memory to be lost when any particular variable goes out of scope. The programmer is responsible for both allocating and returning heap memory.

Allocating heaps of objects

It is also possible to allocate an array of objects off the heap using the following syntax:

```
class MyClass
{
  public:
    int nValue;
};
void fn()
{
    MyClass* pMC = new MyClass[5]

    // reference individual members like any array
    for (int i = 0; i < 5; i++)
    {
        pMC[i].nValue = i;
    }

    // uses a different delete keyword to return memory
    // to the heap
    delete[] pMC;
};
```

Notice that once allocated, *pMC* can be used like any other array, with *pMC[i]* referring to the *i*th object of type *MyClass*. Notice also that you use the slightly different keyword *delete[]* to return arrays of class objects to the heap.

When memory is allocated for you

Many classes (particularly the containers described in Chapter 27) manage heap memory for you. For example, the *string* class maintains a character string in memory that it allocates off of the heap. The authors of these classes are careful to return heap memory in all the right places so that it's safe to write a function like the following:

```
string myFunc()
{
    string localString;
    localString << cin;
    return localString;
}
```

The object *localString* allocates heap memory when it is created but carefully returns said memory when it goes out of scope at the end of the function. (You will see in Chapters 16 and 17 how this magic is performed.)

Linking Up with Linked Lists

The second most common structure after the array is called a *list*. Lists come in different sizes and types; however, the most common one is the *linked list*. In the linked list, each object points to the next member in a sort of chain that extends through memory. The program can simply point the last element in the list to an object to add it to the list. This means that the user doesn't have to declare the size of the linked list at the beginning of the program — you can add and remove objects from the list by merely unlinking them. In addition, you can sort the members of a linked list — without actually moving data objects around — by changing the links.

The cost of such flexibility is speed of access. You can't just reach in and grab the tenth element, for example, like you would in the case of an array. Instead, you have to start at the beginning of the list and link ten times from one object to the next.

A linked list has one other feature besides its run-time expandability (that's good) and its difficulty in accessing an object at random (that's bad): A linked list makes significant use of pointers. This makes linked lists a great tool for giving you experience in manipulating pointer variables (that's very good).

The C++ standard library offers a number of different types of lists. You can see them in action in Chapter 27; however, it's always good to implement your first linked list yourself to get practice in manipulating pointers.

Not every class can be used to create a linked list. You declare a linkable class as follows:

```
class LinkableClass
{
    public:
        LinkableClass* pNext;

        // other members of the class
};
```

The key to a linkable class is the *pNext* pointer. At first blush, this seems odd indeed — a class contains a pointer to itself? Actually, *pNext* is not a pointer to itself but to another, different object of the same type.

A linked list is similar to a chain of school children crossing the street. The *pNext* pointer corresponds to a child's arm reaching out and grabbing the child next to him.

Somewhere outside the linked list is a pointer to the first element of the list, the *head pointer*. The head pointer is simply a pointer of type *LinkableClass*:*, sort of like the teacher holding onto the first kid in the chain.

Always initialize any pointer to *nullptr,* the pointer that doesn't point to anything, the non-pointer.

```
LinkableClass* pHead = nullptr;
```

For C++ compilers prior to the '11 standard that don't implement *nullptr,* use a hardcoded 0 or an equivalent #*define* instead:#define NULLPTR 0.

LinkableClass* pHead = NULLPTR;

To see how linked lists work in practice, consider the following function, which adds the argument passed it to the beginning of a list:

```
void addHead(LinkableClass* pLC)
{
    pLC->pNext = pHead;
    pHead = pLC;
}
```

Here, the *pNext* pointer of the object is set to point to the first member of the list. This is akin to grabbing the hand of the first kid in the chain. For one instruction, both you and the teacher have hold of this first kid in the list. The second line points the head pointer to the object, sort of like having the teacher let go of the kid you're holding onto and grabbing you. That makes you the first kid in the chain.

Performing other operations on a linked list

Adding an object to the head of a list is the simplest operation on a linked list. Moving through the elements in a list gives you a better idea about how a linked list works:

```
// navigate through a linked list
LinkableClass* pL = pHead;
while(pL)
{
    // perform some operation here

    // get the next entry
    pL = pL->pNext;
}
```

The program initializes the *pL* pointer to the first object of a list of *LinkableClass* objects through the pointer *pHead*. (Grab the first kid's hand.) The program then enters the *while* loop. If the *pL* pointer is non-null, it points to some *LinkableClass* object. Control enters the loop, where the program can then perform whatever operations it wants on the object pointed at by *pL*.

The assignment *pL = pL->pNext* "moves" the *pL* pointer over to the next kid in the list of objects. The program checks to see if *pL* is null, meaning that we've exhausted the list . . . I mean run out of kids, not exhausted all the kids in the list.

Hooking up with a LinkedListData program

The LinkedListData program shown here implements a linked list of objects containing a person's name. The program could easily contain whatever other data you might like, such as Social Security number, grade point average, height, weight, and bank account balance. I've limited the information to just a name to keep the program as simple as possible.

```
// LinkedListData - store data in a linked list of objects
#include <cstdio>
#include <cstdlib>
#include <iostream>

using namespace std;

// NameDataSet - stores a person's name (these objects
//               could easily store any other information
//               desired).
```

```cpp
class NameDataSet
{
  public:
    string sName;

    // the link to the next entry in the list
    NameDataSet* pNext;
};

// the pointer to the first entry in the list
NameDataSet* pHead = nullptr;

// add - add a new member to the linked list
void add(NameDataSet* pNDS)
{
    // point the current entry to the beginning of list
    pNDS->pNext = pHead;

    // point the head pointer to the current entry
    pHead = pNDS;
}

// getData - read a name and social security
//           number; return null if no more to read
NameDataSet* getData()
{
    // read the first name
    string name;
    cout << "Enter name:";
    cin  >> name;

    // if the name entered is 'exit'...
    if (name == "exit")
    {
        // ...return a null to terminate input
        return nullptr;
    }

    // get a new entry and fill in values
    NameDataSet* pNDS = new NameDataSet;
    pNDS->sName = name;
    pNDS->pNext = nullptr; // zero link

    // return the address of the object created
    return pNDS;
}

int main(int nNumberofArgs, char* pszArgs[])
{
    cout << "Read names of students\n"
         << "Enter 'exit' for first name to exit"
         << endl;
```

```
// create (another) NameDataSet object
NameDataSet* pNDS;
while (pNDS = getData())
{
    // add it to the list of NameDataSet objects
    add(pNDS);
}

// to display the objects, iterate through the
// list (stop when the next address is NULL)
cout << "\nEntries:" << endl;
for(NameDataSet *pIter = pHead;
                    pIter; pIter = pIter->pNext)
{
    // display name of current entry
    cout << pIter->sName << endl;
}

// wait until user is ready before terminating program
// to allow the user to see the program results
cout << "Press Enter to continue..." << endl;
cin.ignore(10, '\n');
cin.get();
return 0;
}
```

Although somewhat lengthy, the LinkedListData program is simple if you take it in parts. The *NameDataSet* structure has room for a person's name and a link to the next *NameDataSet* object in a linked list. I mentioned earlier that this class would have other members in a real-world application.

I have used the class *string* to contain the person's name. Although I don't describe all the methods of the *string* class until Chapter 27, it is much easier to use than zero-terminated character strings. You will see the *string* class used in preference to character strings in most applications these days. The *string* class has become about as close to an intrinsic type in the C++ language as possible.

The *main()* function starts looping, calling *getData()* on each iteration to fetch another *NameDataSet* entry from the user. The program exits the loop if *getData()* returns a null, the "nonaddress," for an address.

The *getData()* function prompts the user for a name and reads in whatever the user enters. If the string entered is equal to *exit,* the function returns a null to the caller, thereby exiting the *while* loop. If the string entered is not *exit,* the program creates a new *NameDataSet* object, populates the name, and zeroes out the *pNext* pointer.

Never leave link pointers uninitialized. Use the old programmer's wives' tale: "When in doubt, zero it out." (I mean "Old tale," not "Tale of an old wife.")

Finally, *getData()* returns the object's address to *main().*

main() adds each object returned from *getData()* to the beginning of the linked list pointed at by the global variable *pHead*. Control exits the initial *while* loop when *getData()* returns a null. *main()* then enters a second section that iterates through the completed list, displaying each object.

This time I used a *for* loop that is functionally equivalent to the earlier *while* loop. The *for* loop initializes the iteration pointer *pIter* to point to the first element in the list through the assignment *pIter = pHead*. It next checks to see if *pIter* is null, which will be the case when the list is exhausted. It then enters the loop. On each round trip through the *for* loop, the third clause moves *pIter* from one object to the next with the assignment *pIter = pIter->pNext* before repeating the test and the body of the loop. This pattern is commonly followed for all list types.

The output of a sample run of the program appears as follows:

```
Read names of students
Enter 'exit' for first name to exit
Enter name:Randy
Enter name:Loli
Enter name:Bodi
Enter name:exit

Entries:
Bodi
Loli
Randy
Press Enter to continue...
```

The program outputs the names in the opposite order in which they were entered. This is because each new object is added to the beginning of the list. Alternatively, the program could have added each object to the end of the list — doing so just takes a little more code. I included just such a version in the programs on the web site. Called LinkedListForward, it links newly added objects to the end of the list so that the list comes out in the same order it was entered. The only difference is in the *add()* function. See if you can create this forward version before you peek at my solution.

Ray of Hope: A List of Containers Linked to the C++ Library

I believe everyone should walk before they run, should figure out how to perform arithmetic in their heads before using a calculator, and should write a linked list program before using a list class written by someone else. That being said, in Chapter 27, I describe the list class provided by the C++ environment.

Chapter 14

Protecting Members:
Do Not Disturb

. . . .

In This Chapter

▶ Declaring members protected

▶ Accessing protected members from within the class

▶ Accessing protected members from outside the class

. . . .

Chapter 12 introduces the concept of the class. That chapter describes the *public* keyword as though it were part of the class declaration — just something you do. In this chapter, you find out about an alternative to *public*.

Protecting Members

The members of a class can be marked protected, which makes them inaccessible outside the class. The alternative is to make the members public. Public members are accessible to all.

Please understand the term *inaccessible* in a weak sense. Any programmer can go into the source code, remove the *protected* keyword, and do whatever she wants. Further, any hacker worth his salt can code into a protected section of code. The *protected* keyword is designed to protect a programmer from herself by preventing inadvertent access.

Why you need protected members

To understand the role of protected, think about the goals of object-oriented programming:

- ✓ **To protect the internals of the class from outside functions.** Suppose, for example, that you have a plan to build a software microwave (or whatever), provide it with a simple interface to the outside world, and then put a box around it to keep others from messing with the insides. The protected keyword is that box.

- ✓ **To make the class responsible for maintaining its internal state.** It's not fair to ask the class to be responsible if others can reach in and manipulate its internals (any more than it's fair to ask a microwave designer to be responsible for the consequences of my mucking with a microwave's internal wiring).

- ✓ **To limit the interface of the class to the outside world.** It's easier to figure out and use a class that has a limited interface (the public members). Protected members are hidden from the user and need not be learned. The interface becomes the class; this is called *abstraction* (see Chapter 11 for more on abstraction).

- ✓ **To reduce the level of interconnection between the class and other code.** By limiting interconnection, you can more easily replace one class with another or use the class in other programs.

Now, I know what you non-object oriented types out there are saying: "You don't need some fancy feature to do all that. Just make a rule that says certain members are publicly accessible and others are not."

Although that is true in theory, it doesn't work. People start out with all kinds of good intentions, but as long as the language doesn't at least discourage direct access of protected members, these good intentions get crushed under the pressure to get the product out the door.

Discovering how protected members work

By default, the members of a class are protected, which means they are not accessible by nonmembers of the class. Adding the keyword *public* to a class makes subsequent members public, which means that they are accessible by nonmember functions. Adding the keyword *protected* makes subsequent members of the class protected. You can switch between *public* and *protected* as often as you like.

Suppose you have a class named *Student*. In this example, the following capabilities are all that a fully functional, upstanding *Student* needs (notice the absence of *spendMoney()* and *drinkBeer()* — this is a highly stylized student):

> *addCourse(inthours, double grade)* — adds a course
>
> *grade()* — returns the current grade point average
>
> *hours()* — returns the number of hours earned toward graduation

The remaining members of *Student* can be declared protected to keep other functions' prying expressions out of *Student*'s business.

```
class Student
{
  public:
    // grade - return the current grade point average
    double grade() { return gpa;}

    // hours - return the number of semester hours
    int hours() {      return semesterHours; }
    // addCourse - add a course to the student's record
    double addCourse(int hours, double grade);

    // the following members are off-limits to others
  protected:
    int  semesterHours; // hours earned toward graduation
    double gpa;          // grade point average
};
```

Now the members *semester hours* and *gpa* are accessible only to other members of *Student*. Thus, the following doesn't work:

```
Student s;
int main(int argcs, char* pArgs[])
{
  // raise my grade (don't make it too high; otherwise, no
  // one would believe it)
  s.gpa = 3.5;             // <- generates compiler error
  double gpa = s.grade();// <- this public function reads
                           // a copy of the value, but you
  return 0;                // can't change it from here
}
```

The application's attempt to change the value of *gpa* is flagged with a compiler error.

A class member can also be protected by declaring it *private*. In this book, I use the *protected* keyword exclusively. The difference between private and protected has to do with inheritance, which is presented in Chapter 19.

Making an Argument for Using Protected Members

Now that you know a little more about how to use protected members in an actual class, I can replay the arguments for using protected members.

Protecting the internal state of the class

Making the *gpa* member protected precludes the application from setting the grade point average to some arbitrary value. The application can add courses, but it can't change the grade point average directly.

If the application has a legitimate need to set the grade point average directly, the class can provide a member function for that purpose, as follows:

```
class Student
{
  public:
    // same as before
    double grade() { return gpa; }
    // here we allow the grade to be changed
    double grade(double newGPA)
    {
        double oldGPA = gpa;
        // only if the new value is valid
        if (newGPA > 0 && newGPA <= 4.0)
        {
            gpa = newGPA;
        }
        return oldGPA;
    }
    // ...other stuff is the same including the data
    //        members:
  protected:
    int  semesterHours; // hours earned toward graduation
    double gpa;
};
```

The addition of the member function *grade(double)* allows the application to set the *gpa*. Notice, however, that the class still hasn't given up control completely. The application can't set *gpa* to any old value; only a *gpa* in the legal range of values (from 0 through 4.0) is accepted.

Thus, the *Student* class has provided access to an internal data member without abdicating its responsibility to make sure that the internal state of the class is valid.

Using a class with a limited interface

A class provides a limited interface. To use a class, you need to know only its public members as well as what they do and their arguments. This can drastically reduce the number of things you need to master and remember to use the class.

As conditions change or as bugs are found, you want to be able to change the internal workings of a class. Changes to those details are less likely to require changes in the external application code if you can hide the internal workings of the class.

A second, perhaps more important, reason lies in the limited ability of humans (I can't speak for dogs and cats) to keep a large number of things in their minds at any given instant. Using a strictly defined class interface allows the programmer to forget the details that go on behind it. Likewise, a programmer building the class need not concentrate to quite the same degree on exactly how each of the functions is being used.

Giving Non-member Functions Access to Protected Members

Occasionally, you want a non-member function to have access to the protected members of a class. You do so by declaring the function to be a friend of the class by using the keyword *friend*.

The *friend* declaration appears in the class that contains the protected member. The *friend* declaration is like a prototype declaration in that it includes the extended name and the return type. In the following example, the function *initialize()* can now access anything it wants in *Student*:

```
class Student
{
    friend void initialize(Student*);
  public:
    // same public members as before...
  protected:
    int   semesterHours; // hours earned toward graduation
    double gpa;
};
// the following function is a friend of Student
// so it can access the protected members
void initialize(Student *pS)
{
    pS->gpa = 0;         // this is now legal...
    pS->semesterHours = 0;  // ...when it wasn't before
}
```

A single function can be declared a friend of two classes at the same time. Although this can be convenient, it tends to bind the two classes together. This binding of classes is normally considered bad because it makes one class dependent on the other. If the two classes naturally belong together, however, it's not all bad, as shown here:

```
class Student;    // forward declaration
class Teacher
{
    friend void registration(Teacher& t, Student& s);
  public:
    void assignGrades();
  protected:
    int    noStudents;
    Student *pList[100];
};
class Student
{
    friend void registration(Teacher& t, Student& s);
  public:
    // same public members as before...
  protected:
    Teacher *pT;
    int    semesterHours; // hours earned toward graduation
    double gpa;
};

void registration(Teacher& t, Student& s)
{
    // initialize the Student object
    s.semesterHours = 0;
    s.gpa = 0;

    // if there's room...
    if (t.noStudents < 100)
    {
        // ...add it onto the end of the list
        t.pList[t.noStudents] = &s;
        t.noStudents++;
    }
}
```

In this example, the *registration()* function can reach into both the *Student* and *Teacher* classes to tie them together at registration time, without being a member function of either one.

The first line in the example declares the class *Student,* but none of its members. This is called a *forward declaration* and just defines the name of the class so that other classes, such as *Teacher,* can define a pointer to it. Forward declarations are necessary when two classes refer to each other.

A member function of one class may be declared a friend of another class, as shown here:

```
class Teacher
{
    // ...other members as well...
  public:
    void assignGrades();
};
class Student
{
    friend void Teacher::assignGrades();
  public:
    // same public members as before...
  protected:
    int  semesterHours; // hours earned toward graduation
    double gpa;
};
void Teacher::assignGrades()
{
    // can access protected members of Teacher from here
}
```

Unlike in the non-member example, the member function *assignGrades()* must be declared before the class *Student* can declare it to be a friend.

An entire class can be named a friend of another. This has the effect of making every member function of the class a friend:

```
class Student;    // forward declaration
class Teacher
{
  protected:
    int   noStudents;
    Student *pList[100];
  public:
    void assignGrades();
};
class Student
{
    friend class Teacher; // make entire class a friend
  public:
    // same public members as before...
  protected:
    int  semesterHours; // hours earned toward graduation
    double gpa;
};
```

Now, any member function of *Teacher* has access to the protected members of *Student*. Declaring one class a friend of the other inseparably binds the two classes together.

Chapter 15

"Why Do You Build Me Up, Just to Tear Me Down, Baby?"

In This Chapter

▶ Creating and destroying objects

▶ Declaring constructors and destructors

▶ Invoking constructors and destructors

*O*bjects in programs are built and scrapped just like objects in the real world. If the class is to be responsible for its well-being, it must have some control over this process. As luck would have it (I suppose some planning was involved as well), C++ provides just the right mechanism. But first, a discussion of what it means to create an object.

Creating Objects

Some people get a little sloppy in using the terms *class* and *object*. What's the difference? What's the relationship?

I can create a class *Dog* that describes the relevant properties of man's best friend. At my house, we have two dogs. Thus, my single class *Dog* has two instances, *Jack* and *Scruffy*. (Well, I *think* there are two instances — I haven't seen Scruffy in a few days.)

A class describes a type of thing. An object is one of those things. An object is an instance of a class. There is only one class *Dog*, no matter how many dogs I have.

Objects are created and destroyed, but classes simply exist. My pets come and go, but the class *Dog* (evolution aside) is perpetual.

Different types of objects are created at different times. *Global objects* are created when the program first begins execution. *Local objects* are created when the program encounters their declaration.

A global object is one that is declared outside a function. A local object is one that is declared within a function and is, therefore, local to the function. In the following example, the variable *me* is global, and the variable *notMe* is local to the function *pickOne()*:

```
int me = 0;
void pickOne()
{
    int notMe;
        }
```

According to the rules, global objects are initialized to all zeros when the program starts executing. Objects declared local to a function have no particular initial value. Having all data members have a random state may not be a valid condition for all classes.

C++ allows the class to define a special member function that is invoked automatically when an object of that class is created. This member function, called the *constructor,* initializes the object to a valid initial state. In addition, the class can define a destructor to handle the destruction of the object. These two functions are the topics of this chapter.

Using Constructors

The constructor is a member function that is called automatically when an object is created. Its primary job is to initialize the object to a legal initial value for the class. (It's the job of the remaining member functions to ensure that the state of the object stays legal.)

The constructor carries the same name as the class to differentiate it from the other members of the class. The designers of C++ could have made up a different rule, such as: "The constructor must be called *init()*." It wouldn't have made any difference, as long as the compiler can recognize the constructor. In addition, the constructor has no return type, not even *void,* because it is called only automatically — if the constructor did return something, there would be no place to put it. A constructor cannot be invoked manually.

Constructing a single object

With a constructor, the class *Student* appears as follows:

```
//   Constructor - example that invokes a constructor
//
#include <cstdio>
#include <cstdlib>
#include <iostream>
using namespace std;

class Student
{
  public:
    Student()
    {
        cout << "constructing student" << endl;
        semesterHours = 0;
        gpa = 0.0;
    }
    // ...other public members...
  protected:
    int   semesterHours;
    double gpa;
};

int main(int nNumberofArgs, char* pszArgs[])
{
    cout << "Creating a new Student object" << endl;
    Student s;

    cout << "Creating a new object off the heap" << endl;
    Student* pS = new Student;

    // wait until user is ready before terminating program
    // to allow the user to see the program results
    cout << "Press Enter to continue..." << endl;
    cin.ignore(10, '\n');
    cin.get();
    return 0;
}
```

At the point of the declaration of *s*, the compiler inserts a call to the constructor *Student::Student()*. Allocating a new *Student* object from the heap has the same effect, as demonstrated by the output from the program:

```
Creating a new Student object
constructing student
Creating a new object off the heap
constructing student
Press Enter to continue...
```

This simple constructor was written as an inline member function. Constructors can be written also as outline functions, as shown here:

```
class Student
{
  public:
    Student();
    // ...other public members...
  protected:
    int   semesterHours;
    double gpa;
};
Student::Student()
{
    cout << "constructing student" << endl;
    semesterHours = 0;
    gpa = 0.0;
}
```

Constructing multiple objects

Each element of an array must be constructed on its own. For example, the following ConstructArray program creates five *Student* objects by declaring a single five-element array:

```
//  ConstructArray - example that invokes a constructor
//                   on an array of objects
//
#include <cstdio>
#include <cstdlib>
#include <iostream>
using namespace std;

class Student
{
  public:
    Student()
    {
        cout << "constructing student" << endl;
    }
};

int main(int nNumberofArgs, char* pszArgs[])
{
    cout << "Creating an array of 5 Student objects"
         << endl;
    Student s[5];
```

```
        // wait until user is ready before terminating program
        // to allow the user to see the program results
        cout << "Press Enter to continue..." << endl;
        cin.ignore(10, '\n');
        cin.get();
        return 0;
}
```

Executing the program generates the following output:

```
Creating an array of 5 Student objects
constructing student
constructing student
constructing student
constructing student
constructing student
Press Enter to continue...
```

Constructing a duplex

If a class contains a data member that is an object of another class, the constructor for that class is called automatically as well. Consider the following ConstructMembers example program. I added output statements so that you can see the order in which the objects are invoked.

```
//   ConstructMembers - the member objects of a class
//                      are each constructed before the
//                      container class constructor gets
//                      a shot at it
//
#include <cstdio>
#include <cstdlib>
#include <iostream>
using namespace std;

class Course
{
  public:
    Course(){ cout << "constructing course" << endl;}
};

class Student
{
  public:
    Student()
    {
        cout << "constructing student" << endl;
        semesterHours = 0;
        gpa = 0.0;
    }
```

```
     protected:
       int   semesterHours;
       double gpa;
   };
   class Teacher
   {
     public:
       Teacher(){cout << "constructing teacher" << endl;}
     protected:
       Course c;
   };
   class TutorPair
   {
     public:
       TutorPair()
       {
           cout << "constructing tutorpair" << endl;
           noMeetings = 0;
       }
     protected:
       Student student;
       Teacher teacher;
       int   noMeetings;
   };

   int main(int nNumberofArgs, char* pszArgs[])
   {
       cout << "Creating TutorPair object" << endl;
       TutorPair tp;

       // wait until user is ready before terminating program
       // to allow the user to see the program results
       cout << "Press Enter to continue..." << endl;
       cin.ignore(10, '\n');
       cin.get();
       return 0;
   }
```

Executing this program generates the following output:

```
Creating TutorPair object
constructing student
constructing course
constructing teacher
constructing tutorpair
Press Enter to continue...
```

Creating the object *tp* in *main* automatically invokes the constructor for *TutorPair*. Before control passes into the body of the *TutorPair* constructor, however, the constructors for the two-member objects, *student* and *teacher*, are invoked.

The constructor for *Student* is called first because it is declared first. Then the constructor for *Teacher* is called.

The member *Teacher.c* of class *Course* is constructed as part of building the *Teacher* object. The *Course* constructor gets a shot first. Each object within a class must construct itself before the class constructor can be invoked. Otherwise, the main constructor would not know the state of its data members.

After all member data objects have been constructed, control returns to the open brace, and the constructor for *TutorPair* is allowed to construct the remainder of the object.

Dissecting a Destructor

Just as objects are created, so are they destroyed (ashes to ashes, dust to dust). If a class can have a constructor to set things up, it should also have a special member function to take the object apart. This member is called the *destructor*.

Why you need the destructor

A class may allocate resources in the constructor; these resources need to be deallocated before the object ceases to exist. For example, if the constructor opens a file, the file needs to be closed before leaving that class or the program. Or, if the constructor allocates memory from the heap, this memory must be freed before the object goes away. The destructor allows the class to do these cleanup tasks automatically without relying on the application to call the proper member functions.

Working with destructors

The destructor member has the same name as the class but with a tilde (~) added at the front. (C++ is being cute again — the tilde is the symbol for the logical NOT operator. Get it? A destructor is a "not constructor." Très clever.) Like a constructor, the destructor has no return type. For example, the class *Student* with a destructor added appears as follows:

```
class Student
{
  public:
    Student()
    {
        semesterHours = 0;
        gpa = 0.0;
    }
```

```
    ~Student()
    {
        // ...whatever assets are returned here...
    }
protected:
    int   semesterHours;
    double gpa;
};
```

The destructor is invoked automatically when an object is destroyed, or in C++ parlance, when an object is *destructed*. That sounds sort of circular ("the destructor is invoked when an object is destructed"), so I've avoided the term until now. For non-heap memory, you can also say, "when the object goes out of scope." A local object goes out of scope when the function returns. A global or static object goes out of scope when the program terminates.

But what about heap memory? An object that has been allocated off the heap is destructed when it's returned to the heap using the *delete* command. This is demonstrated in the following DestructMembers program:

```
//   DestructMembers - this program both constructs and
//                     destructs a set of data members
//
#include <cstdio>
#include <cstdlib>
#include <iostream>
using namespace std;

class Course
{
  public:
    Course()  { cout << "constructing course" << endl; }
    ~Course() { cout << "destructing course" << endl;  }
};

class Student
{
  public:
    Student() { cout << "constructing student" << endl;}
    ~Student() { cout << "destructing student" << endl; }
};
class Teacher
{
  public:
    Teacher()
    {
        cout << "constructing teacher" << endl;
        pC = new Course;
    }
```

```
        ~Teacher()
        {
            cout << "destructing teacher" << endl;
            delete pC;
        }
    protected:
        Course* pC;
};
class TutorPair
{
    public:
        TutorPair(){cout << "constructing tutorpair" << endl;}
        ~TutorPair(){cout << "destructing tutorpair" << endl; }
    protected:
        Student student;
        Teacher teacher;
};

TutorPair* fn()
{
    cout << "Creating TutorPair object in function fn()"
         << endl;
    TutorPair tp;

    cout << "Allocating TutorPair off the heap" << endl;
    TutorPair*  pTP = new TutorPair;

    cout << "Returning from fn()" << endl;
    return pTP;
}


int main(int nNumberofArgs, char* pszArgs[])
{
    // call function fn() and then return the
    // TutorPair object returned to the heap
    TutorPair* pTPReturned = fn();
    cout << "Return heap object to the heap" << endl;
    delete pTPReturned;

    // wait until user is ready before terminating program
    // to allow the user to see the program results
    cout << "Press Enter to continue..." << endl;
    cin.ignore(10, '\n');
    cin.get();
    return 0;
}
```

The function *main()* invokes a function *fn()* that defines the object *tp* — this is to allow you to watch the variable go out of scope when control exits the function. *fn()* also allocates heap memory that it returns to *main()* where the memory is returned to the heap.

If you execute this program, it generates the following output:

```
Creating TutorPair object in function fn()
constructing student
constructing teacher
constructing course
constructing tutorpair
Allocating TutorPair off the heap
constructing student
constructing teacher
constructing course
constructing tutorpair
Returning from fn()
destructing tutorpair
destructing teacher
destructing course
destructing student
Return heap object to the heap
destructing tutorpair
destructing teacher
destructing course
destructing student
Press Enter to continue...
```

Each constructor is called in turn as the *TutorPair* object is built up, starting from the smallest data member and working up to the *TutorPair::TutorPair()* constructor function.

Two *TutorPair* objects are created. The first, *tp*, is defined locally to the function *fn()*; the second, *pTP*, is allocated off the heap. *tp* goes out of scope and is destructed when control passes out of the function. The heap memory whose address is returned from *fn()* is not destructed until *main()* deletes it.

When an object is destructed, the sequence of destructors is invoked in the reverse order in which the constructors were called.

C++ provides a separate keyword for deleting arrays, *delete[]*:

```
Student* pS = new Student[5];   // construct 5 Students

// ...later in the program...
delete[] pS;                    // delete heap memory and invoke
                                // destructor on each object
```

Only the *delete[]* keyword knows to invoke the destructor for each object allocated.

Chapter 16

Making Constructive Arguments

In This Chapter

▶ Making argumentative constructors

▶ Overloading the constructor

▶ Creating objects by using constructors

▶ Invoking member constructors

▶ Constructing the order of construction and destruction

A class represents a type of object in the real world. For example, in earlier chapters, I use the class *Student* to represent the properties of a student. Just like students, classes are autonomous. Unlike a student, a class is responsible for its own care and feeding — a class must keep itself in a valid state at all times.

The default constructor presented in Chapter 15 isn't always enough. For example, a default constructor can initialize the student ID to 0 so that it doesn't contain a random value; however, a *Student* ID of 0 is probably not valid.

C++ programmers require a constructor that accepts some type of argument to initialize an object to other than its default value. This chapter examines constructors with arguments.

Outfitting Constructors with Arguments

C++ enables programmers to define a constructor with arguments, as shown here:

```
class Student
{
  public:
    Student(const char *pName);

    // ...class continues...
};
```

Using a constructor

Conceptually, the idea of adding an argument is simple. A constructor is a member function, and member functions can have arguments. Therefore, constructors can have arguments.

Remember, though, that you don't call the constructor like a normal function. Therefore, the only time to pass arguments to the constructor is when the object is created. For example, the following program creates an object *s* of the class *Student* by calling the *Student(const char*)* constructor. The object *s* is destructed when the function *main()* returns.

```cpp
//  ConstructorWArg - a class may pass along arguments
//                    to the members' constructors
//
#include <cstdio>
#include <cstdlib>
#include <iostream>
using namespace std;

class Student
{
  public:
    Student(const char* pName)
    {
        cout << "constructing Student " << pName << endl;
        name = pName;
        semesterHours = 0;
        gpa = 0.0;
    }

  // ...other public members...
  protected:
    string  name;
    int     semesterHours;
    double  gpa;
};

int main(int argcs, char* pArgs[])
{
    // create a student locally and one off of the heap
    Student s1("Jack");
    Student* pS2 = new Student("Scruffy");

    // be sure to delete the heap student
    delete pS2;

    // wait until user is ready before terminating program
    // to allow the user to see the program results
```

```
cout << "Press Enter to continue..." << endl;
cin.ignore(10, '\n');
cin.get();
return 0;
}
```

The *Student* constructor here looks like the constructors shown in Chapter 15 except for the addition of the *const char** argument *pName*. The constructor initializes the data members to their empty start-up values, except for the data member *name*, which gets its initial value from *pName* because a *Student* object without a name is not a valid student.

The object *s1* is created in *main()*. The argument to be passed to the constructor appears in the declaration of *s1*, right next to the name of the object. Thus, the student *s1* is given the name *Jack* in this declaration.

A second student is allocated off the heap on the very next line. The arguments to the constructor in this case appear next to the name of the class.

The third executable line in the program returns the newly allocated object to the heap before exiting the program. This may not be necessary; for example, Windows or Unix will close any files you may have open and return all heap memory when a program terminates even if you forget to do so yourself. However, it's good practice to delete your heap memory when you're finished.

The *const* in the constructor declaration *Student::Student(const char*)* is necessary to allow statements such as the following:

```
Student s1("Jack");
```

The type of "Jack" is *const char**. I could not pass a pointer to a constant character string to a constructor declared *Student(char*)*. A function, including a constructor, declared this way might attempt to modify the character string, which would not be good. You cannot strip away the *const* part of a declaration.

You can add *const*-ness, however, as in the following:

```
void fn(char* pName)
{
    // the following is allowed even though constructor
    // declared Student(const char*)
    Student s(pName);
    // ...do whatever...
}
```

The function *fn()* passes a *char** string to a constructor that promises to treat the string as if it were a constant. No harm there!

Placing Too Many Demands on the Carpenter: Overloading the Constructor

I can draw one more parallel between constructors and other more normal member functions in this chapter: Constructors can be overloaded.

Overloading a function means to define two functions with the same short name but with different types of arguments. See Chapter 6 for the latest news on function overloading.

C++ chooses the proper constructor based on the arguments in the declaration of the object. For example, the class *Student* can have all three constructors shown in the following snippet at the same time:

```
//  OverloadConstructor - provide the class multiple
//                        ways to create objects by
//                        overloading the constructor
//
#include <cstdio>
#include <cstdlib>
#include <iostream>
#include <string.h>

using namespace std;
class Student
{
  public:
    Student()
    {
        cout << "constructing student No Name" << endl;
        name = "No Name";
        semesterHours = 0;
        gpa = 0.0;
    }
    Student(const char *pName)
    {
        cout << "constructing student " << pName << endl;
        name = pName;
        semesterHours = 0;
        gpa = 0;
    }
    Student(const char *pName, int xfrHours, float xfrGPA)
    {
        cout << "constructing student " << pName << endl;
        name = pName;
        semesterHours = xfrHours;
        gpa = xfrGPA;
    }
```

```
   protected:
      string  name;
      int     semesterHours;
      float   gpa;
};

int main(int argcs, char* pArgs[])
{
    // the following invokes three different constructors
    Student noName;
    Student freshman("Marian Haste");
    Student xferStudent("Pikup Andropov", 80, 2.5);

    // wait until user is ready before terminating program
    // to allow the user to see the program results
    cout << "Press Enter to continue..." << endl;
    cin.ignore(10, '\n');
    cin.get();
    return 0;
}
```

Because the object *noName* appears with no arguments, it's constructed using the constructor *Student::Student()*. This constructor is called the default constructor. The *freshman* is constructed using the constructor that has only a *const char** argument, and the *xferStudent* uses the constructor with three arguments.

Notice the similarity in all three constructors. The number of semester hours and the GPA default to 0 if only the name is provided. Otherwise, there is no difference between the two constructors. You wouldn't need both constructors if you could just specify a default value for the two arguments.

C++ enables you to specify a default value for a function argument in the declaration to be used in the event that the argument is not present. By adding defaults to the last constructor, all three constructors can be combined into one. For example, the following class combines all three constructors into a single, clever constructor:

```
//  ConstructorWDefaults - multiple constructors can often
//                         be combined with the definition
//                         of default arguments
//
#include <cstdio>
#include <cstdlib>
#include <iostream>
using namespace std;
```

```
class Student
{
  public:
    Student(const char *pName   = "No Name",
            int xfrHours = 0,
            double xfrGPA = 0.0)
    {
        cout << "constructing student " << pName << endl;
        name = pName;
        semesterHours = xfrHours;
        gpa = xfrGPA;
    }

  protected:
    string  name;
    int     semesterHours;
    double  gpa;
};
// ...the rest is the same...
```

Now all three objects are constructed using the same constructor; defaults are provided for non-existent arguments in *noName* and *freshman*.

A slightly more flexible alternative added in the 2011 standard is to invoke one constructor from another as shown in *ConstructorsCallingEachOther*. This is known as *delegating constructors:*

```
// ConstructorsCallingEachOther - new for 2011,
//         one constructor can invoke another constructor
//         in the same class
//
#include <cstdio>
#include <cstdlib>
#include <iostream>
using namespace std;

class Student
{
  public:
    Student(const char *pName,
            int xfrHours,
            double xfrGPA)
    {
        cout << "constructing student " << pName << endl;
        name = pName;
        semesterHours = xfrHours;
        gpa = xfrGPA;
    }
```

```
     Student() : Student("No Name", 0, 0.0) {}
     Student(const char *pName): Student(pName, 0, 0.0){}

  protected:
     string    name;
     int       semesterHours;
     double    gpa;
};
// ...the rest is the same as before...
```

Here the declaration *Student noName* invokes the no argument constructor which turns around and calls the generic constructor, providing default arguments. The *Student freshman* declaration invokes the *Student(const char*)* constructor.

This is more flexible because you can default arguments other than the last one. In addition, you have more control over how arguments are defaulted. For example, it makes no sense to construct a student with semester hours but no GPA. This version would not allow such an object to be constructed since no *Student(const char*, int)* is provided.

The somewhat bizarre syntax will seem a lot more reasonable by the time you reach the end of this chapter.

Defaulting Default Constructors

As far as C++ is concerned, every class must have a constructor; otherwise, you can't create objects of that class. If you don't provide a constructor for your class, C++ should probably just generate an error, but it doesn't. To provide compatibility with existing C code, which knows nothing about constructors, C++ automatically provides a default constructor (sort of a default default constructor).

If you define a constructor for your class, C++ doesn't provide the automatic default constructor on its own. By creating a constructor, the author is in effect telling C++ that the default constructor is not good enough.

The following code snippets help demonstrate this point. This is legal:

```
class Student
{

    string    name;
};

int main(int argcs, char* pArgs[])
```

```
    {
        Student noName;
        return 0;
    }
```

The automatically provided default constructor invokes the default *string* constructor to create an empty *name* object. The following code snippet does not compile properly:

```
class Student
{
  public:
    Student(const char *pName) {name = pName;}

    string name;
};

int main(int argcs, char* pArgs[])
{
    Student noName;      // doesn't compile
    return 0;
}
```

The seemingly innocuous addition of the *Student(const char*)* constructor precludes C++ from automatically providing a *Student()* constructor with which to build object *noName*.

The C++ '11 standard allows you to "get the default constructor back" via the new keyword *default*, as follows:

```
class Student
{
  public:
    Student(const char *pName) { name = pName; }
    Student() = default;

    string name;
};

int main(int argcs, char* pArgs[])
{
    Student noName;
    return 0;
}
```

The *default* keyword says, in effect, "I know that I defined a constructor but I still want my automatic default constructor back."

The '11 standard also allows a default method such as the default constructor to be explicitly removed using the new keyword *delete:*

```
class Student
{
  public:
    Student() = delete; // remove the default constructor

    string name;
};
```

Constructing Class Members

In the previous examples, all data members are of simple types, such as *int* and *double*. With simple types, it's sufficient to assign a value to the variable within the constructor. Problems arise when initializing certain types of data members, however.

Constructing a complex data member

Members of a class have the same problems as any other variable. It makes no sense for a *Student* object to have some default ID of 0. This is true even if the object is a member of a class. Consider the following example that creates a new class, *StudentId*, to manage the student identification numbers instead of relying on a plain ol' integer variable:

```
//
//  ConstructingMembers - a class may pass along arguments
//                        to the members' constructors
//
#include <cstdio>
#include <cstdlib>
#include <iostream>
using namespace std;

int nextStudentId = 1000; // first legal Student ID
class StudentId
{
  public:
    // default constructor assigns id's sequentially
    StudentId()
    {
        value = nextStudentId++;
        cout << "Take next student id " << value << endl;
    }
```

```
      // int constructor allows user to assign id
      StudentId(int id)
      {
          value = id;
          cout << "Assign student id " << value << endl;
      }
   protected:
      int value;
};

class Student
{
   public:
      Student(const char* pName)
      {
          cout << "constructing Student " << pName << endl;
          name = pName;
          semesterHours = 0;
          gpa = 0.0;
      }

   // ...other public members...
   protected:
      string    name;
      int       semesterHours;
      double    gpa;
      StudentId id;
};

int main(int argcs, char* pArgs[])
{
    // create a couple of students
    Student s1("Jack");
    Student s2("Scruffy");

    // wait until user is ready before terminating program
    // to allow the user to see the program results
    cout << "Press Enter to continue..." << endl;
    cin.ignore(10, '\n');
    cin.get();
    return 0;
}
```

A student ID is assigned to each student as the *Student* object is constructed. In this example, the default constructor for *StudentId* assigns IDs sequentially using the global variable *nextStudentId* to keep track.

The *Student* class invokes the default constructor for the two students *s1* and *s2*. The output from the program shows that this is working properly:

```
Take next student id 1000
constructing Student Jack
Take next student id 1001
constructing Student Scruffy
Press Enter to continue...
```

Notice that the message from the *StudentId* constructor appears before the output from the *Student* constructor. This implies that the constructor *StudentId* was invoked even before the *Student* constructor got underway.

If the programmer does not provide a constructor, the default constructor provided by C++ automatically invokes the default constructors for data members. The same is true come harvesting time. The destructor for the class automatically invokes the destructor for data members that have destructors. The C++–provided destructor does the same.

Okay, this is all great for the default constructor. But what if you want to invoke a constructor other than the default? Where do you put the object? The *StudentId* class provides a second constructor that allows the student ID to be assigned to any arbitrary value. The question is, how do you invoke it?

Let me first show you what doesn't work. Consider the following program segment (only the relevant parts are included here — the entire program, ConstructSeparateID, is with the material that accompanies this book at www.dummies.com/extras/cplusplus):

```cpp
class Student
{
  public:
    Student(const char *pName, int ssId)
    {
        cout << "constructing student " << pName << endl;
        name = pName;
        // don't try this at home kids. It doesn't work
        StudentId id(ssId);     // construct a student id
    }
  protected:
    string    name;
    StudentId id;
};

int main(int argcs, char* pArgs[])
{
    Student s("Jack", 1234);
    cout << "This message from main" << endl;

    // wait until user is ready before terminating program
    // to allow the user to see the program results
    cout << "Press Enter to continue..." << endl;
    cin.ignore(10, '\n');
    cin.get();
}
```

Within the constructor for *Student, the* programmer (that's me) has (cleverly) attempted to construct a *StudentId* object named *id.* (I also added a destructor to *StudentId* that does nothing but output the ID of the object being destroyed.)

If you look at the output from this program, you can see the problem:

```
take next student id 1000
constructing student Jack
assign student id 1234
destructing 1234
This message from main
Press Enter to continue...
```

We seem to be constructing two *StudentId* objects: The first one is created with the default constructor as before. After control enters the constructor for *Student,* a second *StudentId* is created with the assigned value of 1234. Mysteriously, this 1234 object is then destroyed as soon as the program exits the *Student* constructor.

The explanation for this rather bizarre behavior is clear. The data member *id* already exists by the time the body of the constructor is entered. Instead of constructing the existing data member *id,* the declaration provided in the constructor creates a local object of the same name. This local object is destructed upon returning from the constructor.

Somehow, we need a different mechanism to indicate "construct the existing member; don't create a new one." This mechanism needs to appear after the function argument list but before the open brace. C++ provides a construct for this, as shown in the following subset taken from the *ConstructDataMembers* program (the only change between this program and its predecessor is to the *Student* class constructor — the entire program is with the accompanying material at www.dummies.com/extras/cplusplus):

```
class Student
{
  public:
    Student(const char *pName, int ssId)
      : name(pName), id(ssId)
    {
        cout << "constructing student " << pName << endl;
    }
  protected:
    string name;
    StudentId id;
};
```

Notice in particular the first line of the constructor. Here's something you haven't seen before. The *:* means that what follows are calls to the constructors of data members of the current class. To the C++ compiler, this line reads "Construct the members *name* and *id* using the arguments *pName* and *ssId*, respectively, of the *Student* constructor. Whatever data members are not called out in this fashion are constructed using their default constructor."

The *string* type is actually a conventional class defined in an include file which is included by *iostream*. Programs prior to this example have been using the default *string* constructor to create an empty *name* and then copying the student's name into the object within the body of the constructor. It is more efficient to assign the *string* object a value when it's created, if possible.

This new program generates the expected result:

```
assign student id 1234
constructing student Jack
This message from main
Press Enter to continue...
```

Now you can see where the syntax for invoking one constructor from another came from!

Combining this with member initialization

So what happens when a constructor competes with a C++ '11-style member initializer? Consider the following contrived example:

```cpp
//   ConstructMembersWithInitializers - this program
//            demonstrates what happens when a data member
//            with an initializer is constructed
//
#include <cstdio>
#include <cstdlib>
#include <iostream>
using namespace std;

class StudentId
{
  public:
    StudentId(int id) : value(id)
    {
        cout << "id = " << value << endl;
    }

  protected:
    int value;
};
```

```
int nextStudentId = 1000;
class Student
{
  public:
    Student(const char *pName, int ssId)
      : name(pName), id(ssId)
    {
        cout << "constructing student " << pName << endl;
    }
    Student(const char *pName): name(pName)
    {
        cout << "constructing student " << pName << endl;
    }
  protected:
    string name;
    StudentId id = nextStudentId++;
};

int main(int argcs, char* pArgs[])
{
    Student s1("Jack", 1234);
    Student s2("Scruffy");

    // wait until user is ready before terminating program
    // to allow the user to see the program results
    cout << "Press Enter to continue..." << endl;
    cin.ignore(10, '\n');
    cin.get();
    return 0;
}
```

Here I have provided the *StudentID* class with a single constructor. It is now up to the *Student* class to decide which *id* to use. The output from this program is enlightening:

```
id = 1234
constructing student Jack
id = 1000
constructing student Scruffy
Press Enter to continue...
```

In the first case, the student Jack is created using the student ID 1234 provided in the constructor. The student Scruffy accepts the default student ID, the next value starting with 1000. But this is curious — if the member initializer had been invoked when Jack was constructed, then Scruffy should have been assigned the ID 1001.

The moral to this story is that the member initializer (that's the *StudentId id = nextStudentId++*) is ignored if the member is constructed in the class constructor.

Constructing a constant data member

Argument construction solves a similar problem with *const* data members as shown in the following example:

```
class Mammal
{
  public:
    Mammal(int nof) : numberOfFeet(nof) {}
  protected:
    const int numberOfFeet;
};
```

Ostensibly, a given *Mammal* has a fixed number of feet (barring amputation). The number of feet can, and should, be declared *const*. This constructor definition assigns a value to the variable *numberOfFeet* when the object is created. The *numberOfFeet* cannot be modified once it's been declared and initialized.

Reconstructing the Order of Construction

When there are multiple objects, all with constructors, programmers usually don't care about the order in which things are built. If one or more of the constructors has side effects, however, the order can make a difference.

The rules for the order of construction are as follows:

- ✔ Local and static objects are constructed in the order in which their declarations are invoked.
- ✔ Static objects are constructed only once.
- ✔ All global objects are constructed before *main()*.
- ✔ Global objects are constructed in no particular order.
- ✔ Members are constructed in the order in which they are declared in the class within a given access type (that is, all the public members are declared in order declared and all the protected members in the order that they're declared)
- ✔ Objects are destructed in the opposite order in which they were constructed.

A *static variable* is a variable that is local to a function but retains its value from one function invocation to the next. A *global variable* is a variable declared outside a function.

Now we'll consider each of the preceding rules in turn.

Local objects construct in order

Local objects are constructed in the order in which the program encounters their declaration. Normally, this is the same as the order in which the objects appear in the function, unless the function jumps around particular declarations. (By the way, jumping around declarations is a bad thing. It confuses the reader and the compiler.)

Static objects construct only once

Static objects are similar to local variables, except that they are constructed only once. C++ waits until the first time control passes through the static's declaration before constructing the object. Consider the following trivial *ConstructStatic* program:

```cpp
//  ConstructStatic - demonstrate that statics are only
//                    constructed once
//
#include <cstdio>
#include <cstdlib>
#include <iostream>
using namespace std;

class DoNothing
{
  public:
    DoNothing(int initial) : nValue(initial)
    {
        cout << "DoNothing constructed with a value of "
             << initial << endl;
    }
    ~DoNothing()
    {
        cout << "DoNothing object destructed" << endl;
    }
    int nValue;
};
void fn(int i)
{
```

```
        cout << "Function fn passed a value of " << i << endl;
        static DoNothing dn(i);
}

int main(int argcs, char* pArgs[])
{
    fn(10);
    fn(20);
    cout << "Press Enter to continue..." << endl;
    cin.ignore(10, '\n');
    cin.get();
    return 0;
}
```

Executing this program generates the following results:

```
Function fn passed a value of 10
DoNothing constructed with a value of 10
Function fn passed a value of 20
Press Enter to continue...
DoNothing object destructed
```

Notice that the message from the function *fn()* appears twice, but the message from the constructor for *DoNothing* appears only the first time *fn()* is called. This indicates that the object is constructed the first time that *fn()* is called but not thereafter. Also notice that the destructor is not invoked until the program returns from *main()* as part of the program shutdown process.

All global objects construct before main ()

All global variables go into scope as soon as the program starts. Thus, all global objects are constructed before control is passed to *main()*.

Initializing global variables can cause real debugging headaches. Some debuggers try to execute up to *main()* as soon as the program is loaded and before they hand over control to the user. This can be a problem because the constructor code for all global objects has already been executed by the time you can wrest control of your program. If one of these constructors has a fatal bug, you never even get a chance to find the problem. In this case, the program appears to die before it even starts!

The best way I've found to detect this type of problem is to set a breakpoint in every constructor that you even remotely suspect as well as the first statement in *main()*. You will hit a breakpoint for each global object declared as soon as you start the program. Press Continue after each breakpoint until the program crashes — now you know that you pressed Continue once too often.

Restart the program and repeat the process, but stop on the constructor that caused the program to crash. You can now single-step through the constructor until you find the problem. If you make it all the way to the breakpoint in *main()*, the program did not crash while constructing global objects.

Global objects construct in no particular order

Figuring out the order of construction of local objects is easy. An order is implied by the flow of control. With globals, no such flow is available to give order. All globals go into scope simultaneously — remember? Okay, you argue, why can't the compiler just start at the top of the file and work its way down the list of global objects?

That would work fine for a single file (and I presume that's what most compilers do). Most programs in the real world consist of several files that are compiled separately and then linked. Because the compiler has no control over the order in which these files are linked, it cannot affect the order in which global objects are constructed from file to file.

Most of the time, the order of global construction is pretty ho-hum stuff. Once in a while, though, global variables generate bugs that are extremely difficult to track down. (It happens just often enough to make it worth mentioning in a book.)

Consider the following example:

```
class Student
{
  public:
    Student (int id) : studentId(id) {}
    const int studentId;
};
class Tutor
{
  public:
    Tutor(Student& s) : tutoredId(s.studentId) {}
    int tutoredId;
};

// set up a student
Student randy(1234);

// assign that student a tutor
Tutor    janet(randy);
```

Here the constructor for *Student* assigns a student ID. The constructor for *Tutor* records the ID of the student to help. The program declares a student *randy* and then assigns that student a tutor *janet.*

The problem is that the program makes the implicit assumption that *randy* is constructed before *janet.* Suppose it were the other way around. Then *janet* would be constructed with a block of memory that had not yet been turned into a *Student* object and, therefore, had garbage for a student ID.

The preceding example is not too difficult to figure out and more than a little contrived. Nevertheless, problems deriving from global objects being constructed in no particular order can appear in subtle ways. To avoid this problem, don't allow the constructor for one global object to refer to the contents of another global object.

Members construct in the order in which they are declared

Members of a class are constructed according to the order in which they're declared within the class. This isn't quite as obvious as it may sound. Consider the following example:

```
class Student
{
  public:
    Student (int id, int age) : nAge(age), nId(id){}
    const int    nId;
    const int    nAge;
         double dAverage = 0.0;
};
```

In this example, *nId* is constructed before *nAge,* even though *nId* appears second in the constructor's initialization list because it appears before *nAge* in the class definition. The data member *dAverage* is constructed last for the same reason. The only time you might detect a difference in the construction order is when both data members are an instance of a class that has a constructor that has some mutual side effect.

Destructors destruct in the reverse order of the constructors

Finally, no matter in what order the constructors kick off, you can be assured that the destructors are invoked in the reverse order. (It's nice to know that at least one rule in C++ has no ifs, ands, or buts.)

Constructing Arrays

When you declare an array, each element of the array must be constructed. For example, the following declaration calls the default *Student* constructor five times, once for each member of the array:

```
Student s[5];
```

The 2011 standard allows you to invoke a constructor other than the default constructor using an initializer list, as shown in this truncated example program (the full program is available in the online material at www.dummies.com/extras/cplusplus):

```
//
//  ConstructArray - construct an array of objects
//

// ...same Student class with overloaded constructors...

int main(int argcs, char* pArgs[])
{
    // the following invokes three different constructors
    Student s[]{"Marian Haste", "Pikup Andropov"};
    Student t[]{{"Jack", 0, 0.0}, {"Scruffy", 12, 2.5}};

    // wait until user is ready before terminating program
    // to allow the user to see the program results
    cout << "Press Enter to continue..." << endl;
    cin.ignore(10, '\n');
    cin.get();
    return 0;
}
```

The array *s* is created with two members by calling the *Student(const char*)* constructor twice. The array *t* is constructed with the *Student(const char*, int, double)* constructor. The output of this program appears as follows:

```
constructing freshman Marian Haste
constructing freshman Pikup Andropov
constructing transfer Jack
constructing transfer Scruffy
Press Enter to continue...
```

A string of objects contained within braces is known as an initializer list.

Constructors as a Form of Conversion

C++ views constructors with a single argument as a way of converting from one type to another. Consider a user-defined type *Complex* designed to represent complex numbers. Without getting too technical (for me, not for you), there is a natural conversion between real numbers and complex numbers just like the conversion from integers to real numbers, as in the following example:

```
double d = 1;    // this is legal
Complex c = d;   // this should be allowed as well
```

In fact, C++ looks for ways to try to make sense out of statements like this. If the class *Complex* has a constructor that takes as its argument a *double*, C++ will use that constructor as a form of conversion, as if the preceding statement had been written as follows:

```
double d = 1;
Complex c(d);
```

Some constructor-introduced conversions do not make sense. For example, you may not want C++ to convert an integer into a *Student* object just because a *Student(int)* constructor exists. Unexpected conversions can lead to strange run-time errors when C++ tries to make sense out of simple coding mistakes.

The programmer can use the keyword *explicit* to avoid creating unexpected and unintended conversion paths. A constructor marked *explicit* cannot be used as an implicit conversion path:

```
class Student
{
  public:
    // the following "No Name" constructor cannot be used
    // as an implicit conversion path from int to Student
    explicit Student(int nStudentID);
};

Student s = 1;          // generates compiler error
Student t(123456);      // this is still allowed
```

The declaration of *s* does not implicitly invoke the *Student(int)* constructor since it is flagged as "explicitly invokable only." The explicit invoking of the constructor to create the object *t* is still okay.

A complete *TypeConversion* program to demonstrate this principle is included with the online material at www.dummies.com/extras/cplusplus.

Chapter 17

The Copy/Move Constructor

● ●

In This Chapter

▶ Introducing the copy/move constructor

▶ Making copies

▶ Having copies made for you automatically

▶ Creating shallow copies versus deep copies

▶ Avoiding all those copies with a move constructor

● ●

*T*he constructor is a special function that C++ invokes automatically when an object is created to allow the object to initialize itself. Chapter 15 introduces the concept of the constructor, whereas Chapter 16 describes other types of constructors. This chapter examines two particular variations of the constructor known as the *copy* and *move constructors.*

Copying an Object

A copy constructor is the constructor that C++ uses to make copies of objects. It carries the name *X::X(const X&),* where *X* is the name of the class. That is, it's the constructor of class *X,* which takes as its argument a reference to an object of class *X.* Now, I know that this sounds really useless, but just give me a chance to explain why C++ needs such beasties.

The move constructor is unique to C++ 2011. Most of this chapter concerns the copy constructor. I present the details of the move constructor towards the end of this chapter.

Why you need the copy constructor

Think for a moment about what happens when you call a function like the following:

```
void fn(Student fs)
{
    // ...same scenario; different argument...
}
int main(int argcs, char* pArgs[])
{
    Student ms;
    fn(ms);
    return 0;
}
```

In the call to *fn()*, C++ passes a copy of the object *ms* and not the object itself.

Now consider what it means to create a copy of an object. First, it takes a constructor to create an object, even a copy of an existing object. C++ could create a default copy constructor that copies the existing object into the new object one byte at a time. That's what older languages such as C do. But what if the class doesn't want a simple copy of the object? What if something else is required? (Ignore the "why?" for a little while.) The class needs to be able to specify exactly how the copy should be created.

Thus, C++ uses a copy constructor in the preceding example to create a copy of the object *ms* on the stack during the call of function *fn()*. This particular copy constructor would be *Student::Student(Student&)* — say that three times quickly.

Using the copy constructor

The best way to understand how the copy constructor works is to see one in action. Consider the following CopyConstructor program:

```
// CopyConstructor - demonstrate a copy constructor
//
#include <cstdio>
#include <cstdlib>
#include <iostream>
using namespace std;

class Student
{
```

```cpp
public:
    // conventional constructor
    Student(const char *pName = "no name", int ssId = 0)
      : name(pName), id(ssId)
    { cout << "Constructed " << name << endl; }

    // copy constructor
    Student(const Student& s)
      : name("Copy of " + s.name), id(s.id)
    { cout << "Constructed " << name << endl; }

    ~Student() { cout << "Destructing " << name << endl; }

  protected:
    string name;
    int  id;
};

// fn - receives its argument by value
void fn(Student copy)
{
    cout << "In function fn()" << endl;
}

int main(int nNumberofArgs, char* pszArgs[])
{
    Student scruffy("Scruffy", 1234);
    cout << "Calling fn()" << endl;
    fn(scruffy);
    cout << "Back in main()" << endl;

    // wait until user is ready before terminating program
    // to allow the user to see the program results
    cout << "Press Enter to continue..." << endl;
    cin.ignore(10, '\n');
    cin.get();
    return 0;
}
```

The output from executing this program appears as follows:

```
Constructed Scruffy
Calling fn()
Constructed Copy of Scruffy
In function fn()
Destructing Copy of Scruffy
Back in main()
Press Enter to continue...
```

The normal *Student* constructor generates the first message from the declaration on the first line of *main()* about creating *scruffy. main()* then outputs the *Calling . . .* message before calling *fn()*. As part of the function call process, C++ invokes the copy constructor to make a copy of *scruffy* to pass to *fn()*. The copy constructor prepends the string "Copy of" to the student's name before displaying it on the console. The function *fn()* outputs the *In function . . . message*. The copied *Student* object *copy* is destructed at the return from *fn()*. (You can tell it's the copy because of the "Copy of" prepended to the front.) The original object, *scruffy,* is destructed at the end of *main()*.

The Automatic Copy Constructor

Like the default constructor, the copy constructor is important; important enough that C++ thinks no class should be without one. If you don't provide your own copy constructor, C++ generates one for you. (This differs from the default constructor that C++ provides unless your class has constructors defined for it.)

The copy constructor provided by C++ performs a member-by-member copy of each data member. You can see this in the following DefaultCopyConstructor program. (I left out the definition of the *Student* class to save space — it's identical to that shown in the CopyConstructor program. The entire DefaultCopyConstructor program is available online at www.dummies.com/extras/cplusplus.)

```
class Tutor
{
  public:
    Tutor(Student& s)
       : student(s), id(0)
    { cout << "Constructing Tutor object" << endl; }
  protected:
    Student student;
    int id;
};

void fn(Tutor tutor)
{
    cout << "In function fn()" << endl;
}

int main(int argcs, char* pArgs[])
{
    Student scruffy("Scruffy");
    Tutor tutor(scruffy);
```

```
        cout << "Calling fn()" << endl;
        fn(tutor);
        cout << "Back in main()" << endl;

        // wait until user is ready before terminating program
        // to allow the user to see the program results
        cout << "Press Enter to continue..." << endl;
        cin.ignore(10, '\n');
        cin.get();
        return 0;
}
```

Executing this program generates the following output:

```
Constructed Scruffy
Constructed Copy of Scruffy
Constructing Tutor object
Calling fn()
Constructed Copy of Copy of Scruffy
In function fn()
Destructing Copy of Copy of Scruffy
Back in main()
Press Enter to continue...

Destructing Copy of Scruffy
Destructing Scruffy
```

Constructing the *scruffy* object generates the first output message from the "plain Jane" constructor. The constructor for the *tutor* object invokes the *Student* copy constructor to generate its own *Student* data member and then outputs its own message. This accounts for the next two lines of output.

The program then passes a copy of the *Tutor* object to the function *fn()*. Because the *Tutor* class does not define a copy constructor, the program invokes the default copy constructor to make a copy to pass to *fn()*.

The default *Tutor* copy constructor invokes the copy constructor for each data member. The copy constructor for *int* does nothing more than copy the value. You've already seen how the *Student* copy constructor works. This is what generates the *Constructed Copy of Copy of Scruffy* message. The destructor for the copy is invoked as part of the return from function *fn()*. The final destructors are invoked when the program returns from *main()*.

Creating Shallow Copies versus Deep Copies

Performing a member-by-member copy seems the obvious thing to do in a copy constructor. Other than adding the capability to tack on silly things such as *Copy of* to the front of students' names, when would you ever want to do anything but a member-by-member copy?

Consider what happens if the constructor allocates an asset, such as memory off the heap. If the copy constructor simply makes a copy of that asset without allocating its own asset, you end up with a troublesome situation: two objects thinking they have exclusive access to the same asset. This becomes nastier when the destructor is invoked for both objects and they both try to put the same asset back. To make this more concrete, consider the following example class:

```cpp
//   ShallowCopy - performing a byte-by-byte (shallow) copy
//                 is not correct when the class holds assets
//
#include <cstdio>
#include <cstdlib>
#include <iostream>
using namespace std;

class Person
{
  public:
    Person(const char *pN)
    {
        cout << "Constructing " << pN << endl;
        pName = new string(pN);
    }
    ~Person()
    {
        cout << "Destructing " << pName
             << " (" << *pName << ")" << endl;
        *pName = "already destructed memory";
        // delete pName;
    }
  protected:
    string *pName;
};

void fn()
{
    // create a new object
    Person p1("This_is_a_very_long_name");
```

```
        // copy the contents of p1 into p2
        Person p2(p1);
}

int main(int argcs, char* pArgs[])
{
    cout << "Calling fn()" << endl;
    fn();
    cout << "Back in main()" << endl;

    // wait until user is ready before terminating program
    // to allow the user to see the program results
    cout << "Press Enter to continue..." << endl;
    cin.ignore(10, '\n');
    cin.get();
    return 0;
}
```

This program generates the following output:

```
Calling fn()
Constructing This_is_a_very_long_name
Destructing 0x3f2bb8 (This_is_a_very_long_name)
Destructing 0x3f2bb8 (already destructed memory)
Back in main()
Press Enter to continue...
```

The constructor for *Person* allocates memory off the heap to store the person's name. The destructor would normally return this memory to the heap using the *delete* keyword; however, in this case, I've replaced the call to *delete* with a statement that replaces the name with a message. The main program calls the function *fn()*, which creates one person, *p1*, and then makes a copy of that person, *p2*. Both objects are destructed automatically when the program returns from the function.

Only one constructor output message appears when this program is executed. That's not too surprising because the C++–provided copy constructor used to build *p2* performs no output. The *Person* destructor is invoked twice, however, as both *p1* and *p2* go out of scope. The first destructor outputs the expected *This_is_a_very_long_name*. The second destructor indicates that the memory has already been deleted. Notice also that the address of the memory block is the same for both objects (*0x3F2BB8*).

If the program really were to delete the name, the program would become unstable after the second delete and might not even complete properly without crashing.

The problem is shown graphically in Figure 17-1. The object *p1* is copied into the new object *p2,* but the assets are not. Thus, *p1* and *p2* end up pointing to the same assets (in this case, heap memory). This is known as a shallow copy because it just "skims the surface," copying the members themselves.

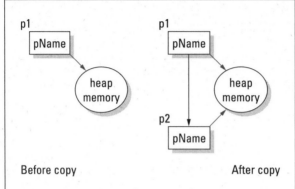

Figure 17-1:
Shallow
copy of p1
to p2.

The solution to this problem is demonstrated visually in Figure 17-2. This figure represents a copy constructor that allocates its own assets to the new object.

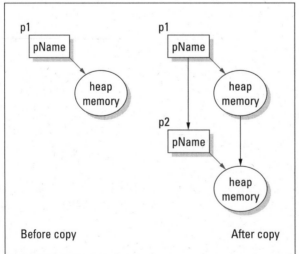

Figure 17-2:
Deep copy
of p1 to p2.

The following shows an appropriate copy constructor for class *Person,* the type you've seen up until now. (This class is embodied in the program DeepCopy, which is on this book's online material at www.dummies.com/extras/cplusplus.)

```
class Person
{
  public:
    Person(const char *pN)
    {
        cout << "Constructing " << pN << endl;
        pName = new string(pN);
    }
    Person(Person& person)
    {
        cout << "Copying " << *(person.pName) << endl;
        pName = new string(*person.pName);
    }
    ~Person()
    {
        cout << "Destructing " << pName
             << " (" << *pName << ")" << endl;
        *pName = "already destructed memory";
        // delete pName;
    }
  protected:
    string *pName;
}
```

Here you see that the copy constructor allocates its own memory block for the name and then copies the contents of the source object name into this new name block. This is a situation similar to that shown in Figure 17-2. *Deep copy* is so named because it reaches down and copies all the assets. (Okay, the analogy is pretty strained, but that's what they call it.)

The output from this program is as follows:

```
Calling fn()
Constructing This_is_a_very_long_name
Copying This_is_a_very_long_name
Destructing 0x9f2be0 (This_is_a_very_long_name)
Destructing 0x9f2ba0 (This_is_a_very_long_name)
Back in main()
Press Enter to continue...
```

The destructor for *Person* now indicates that the string pointers in *p1* and *p2* don't point to the same block of memory: the addresses of the two objects are different, and the name in the version owned by the copy has not been overwritten indicating that it's been deleted.

The real *~Person* destructor should *delete pName*.

It's a Long Way to Temporaries

Passing arguments by value to functions is the most obvious but not the only example of the use of the copy constructor. C++ creates a copy of an object under other conditions as well.

Consider a function that returns an object by value. In this case, C++ must create a copy using the copy constructor. This situation is demonstrated in the following code snippet:

```
Student fn();            // returns object by value
int main(int argcs, char* pArgs[])
{
    Student s;
    s = fn();            // call to fn() creates temporary

    // how long does the temporary returned by fn() last?
    return 0;
}
```

The function *fn()* returns an object by value. Eventually, the returned object is copied to *s*, but where does it reside until then?

C++ creates a temporary object into which it stuffs the returned object. "Okay," you say. "C++ creates the temporary, but how does it know when to destruct it?" Good question. In this example, it doesn't make much difference because you'll be through with the temporary when the copy constructor copies it into *s*. But what if *s* is defined as a reference? It makes a big difference how long temporaries live because *refS* exists for the entire function:

```
int main(int argcs, char* pArgs[])
{
    Student& refS = fn();
    // ...now what?...
    return 0;
}
```

Temporaries created by the compiler are valid throughout the extended expression in which they were created and no further.

In the following function, I mark the point at which the temporary is no longer valid:

```
Student fn1();
int fn2(Student&);
int main(int argcs, char* pArgs[])
{
```

```
    int x;
    // create a Student object by calling fn1().
    // Pass that object to the function fn2().
    // fn2() returns an integer that is used in some
    // silly calculation.
    // All this time the temporary returned from fn1()
    // remains valid.
    x = 3 * fn2(fn1()) + 10;

    // the temporary returned from fn1() is now no longer
          valid
    // ...other stuff...
    return 0;
}
```

This makes the reference example invalid because the object may go away before *refS* does, leaving *refS* referring to a non-object.

Avoiding temporaries, permanently

It may have occurred to you that all this copying of objects hither and yon can be a bit time-consuming. What if you don't want to make copies of everything? The most straightforward solution is to pass objects to functions and return objects from functions by reference. Doing so avoids the majority of temporaries.

But what if you're still not convinced that C++ isn't out there craftily constructing temporaries that you know nothing about? Or what if your class allocates unique assets that you don't want copied? What do you do then?

You can add an output statement to your copy constructor. The presence of this message when you execute the program warns you that a copy has just been made.

A more clever approach is to declare the copy constructor protected, as follows:

```
class Student
{
  protected:
    Student(Student&s){}

  public:
    // ...everything else normal...
};
```

The C++ '11 standard also allows the programmer to delete the copy constructor:

```
class Student
{
    Student(Student&s) = delete;

    // ...everything else normal...
};
```

Either declaring the copy constructor protected or deleting it entirely precludes any external functions, including C++, from constructing a copy of your *Student* objects. If no one can invoke the copy constructor, no copies are being generated. Voilà.

The move constructor

Under certain conditions, C++ can create a copy of an object that is used only for the duration of a single statement. Such objects, known as temporaries, are destructed as soon as the expression is completed. It doesn't make sense to make copies of temporary objects that are about to be destructed anyway.

C++ '11 allows the programmer to create a constructor known as a move constructor that simply moves assets from the source to the destination rather than making unnecessary copies. Move constructors have the format *X::X(X&&)*. This is a new use of *"&&"*.

Consider the following highly contrived example.

C++ '11 includes several return optimizations to avoid the creation of unnecessary copies of objects which this example has to defeat to demonstrate the move constructor. You'll see much less contrived examples in the discussion of overloading operators in Chapter 22.

```
//
//  MoveCopy  - demonstrate the principle of moving a
//              temporary rather than creating a copy
//
#include <cstdio>
#include <cstdlib>
#include <iostream>
using namespace std;

class Person
{
  public:
```

```
    Person(const char *pN)
    {
        pName = new string(pN);
        cout << "Constructing " << *pName << endl;
    }
    Person(Person& p)
    {
        cout << "Copying " << *p.pName << endl;
        pName = new string("Copy of ");
        *pName += *p.pName;
    }
    Person(Person&& p)
    {
        cout << "Moving " << *p.pName << endl;
        pName = p.pName;
        p.pName = nullptr;
    }
    ~Person()
    {
        if (pName)
        {
            cout << "Destructing " << *pName << endl;
            delete pName;
        }
        else
        {
            cout << "Destructing null object" << endl;
        }
    }
protected:
    string* pName;
};

Person fn2(Person p)
{
    cout << "Entering fn2" << endl;
    return p;
}

Person fn1(char* pName)
{
    cout << "Entering fn1_ << endl;
    return fn2(*new Person(pName));
}

int main(int argcs, char* pArgs[])
{
    Person s(fn1("Scruffy"));

    // wait until user is ready before terminating program
    // to allow the user to see the program results
```

```
        cout << "Press Enter to continue..." << endl;
        cin.ignore(10, '\n');
        cin.get();
        return 0;
}
```

Notice how the move constructor assigns the *pName* pointer from the source object *p* and then zeroes out that pointer so that the destructor does not return the memory when the temporary is destructed. This is much more efficient than allocating yet another string object off of the heap and copying the contents of *p.pName* to this new string.

The output from this program appears as follows:

```
Entering fn1
Constructing Scruffy
Copying Scruffy
Entering fn2
Moving Copy of Scruffy
Destructing null object
Press Enter to continue...

Destructing Copy of Scruffy
```

In this case, *fn1()* creates a *Person* object. It then copies this object in the call to *fn2()* using the copy constructor. The function *fn2()* does nothing more than return a copy of this object to *fn1();* however, this copy is just a temporary object that *fn1()* returns to *main()*. Rather than use the copy constructor to create a "Copy of copy of Scruffy," C++ '11 invokes the move constructor to take the contents of the temporary object. When this temporary is subsequently destructed, it is a "null object" because its *pName* has been taken away and reassigned.

You don't have to create a move constructor. The program would have worked just fine, albeit a hair slower, with just the copy constructor. Move constructors should be considered an advanced topic. You will see examples that are less contrived in Chapter 22.

Chapter 18

Static Members: Can Fabric Softener Help?

. . . .

In This Chapter

▶ Declaring static member data

▶ Defining and using static member functions

▶ Understanding why my static member function can't call my other member functions

. . . .

*B*y default, data members are allocated on a per-object basis. For example, each person has his or her own name. You can also declare a member to be shared by all objects of a class by declaring that member static. The term *static* applies to both data members and member functions, although the meaning is slightly different. This chapter describes both types, beginning with static data members.

Defining a Static Member

The programmer can make a data member common to all objects of the class by adding the keyword *static* to the declaration. Such members are called *static data members*. (I would be a little upset if they were called something else.)

Why you need static members

Most properties are properties of the object. Using the well-worn (one might say, threadbare) student example, properties such as name, ID number, and courses are specific to the individual student. However, all students share some properties — for example, the number of students currently enrolled, the highest grade of all students, or a pointer to the first student in a linked list.

It's easy enough to store this type of information in a common, ordinary, garden-variety global variable. For example, you could use a lowly *int* variable to keep track of the number of *Student* objects. The problem with this solution, however, is that global variables are outside the class. It's like putting the voltage regulator for my microwave outside the enclosure. Sure, I could do it, and it would probably work — the only problem is that I wouldn't be too happy if my dog got into the wires and I had to peel him off the ceiling (the dog wouldn't be thrilled about it, either).

If a class is going to be held responsible for its own state, objects such as global variables must be brought inside the class, just as the voltage regulator must be inside the microwave lid, away from prying paws. This is the idea behind static members.

You may hear static members referred to as *class members;* this is because all objects in the class share them. By comparison, normal members are referred to as *instance members,* or *object members,* because each object receives its own copy of these members.

Using static members

A static data member is one that has been declared with the *static* storage class, as shown here:

```
class Student
{
  public:
    Student(char *pName = "no name") : name(pName)
    {
        noOfStudents++;
    }
    ~Student(){ noOfStudents--; }

    static int noOfStudents;
    string name;
};

Student s1;
Student s2;
```

The data member *noOfStudents* is part of the class *Student* but is not part of either *s1* or *s2*. That is, for every object of class *Student,* there is a separate *name,* but there is only one *noOfStudents,* which all *Students* must share.

"Well then," you ask, "if the space for *noOfStudents* is not allocated in any of the objects of class *Student,* where is it allocated?" The answer is, "It isn't." You have to specifically allocate space for it, as follows:

```
int Student::noOfStudents = 0;
```

This somewhat peculiar-looking syntax allocates space for the static data member and initializes it to 0. (You don't have to initialize a static member when you declare it; C++ will invoke the default constructor if you don't.) Static data members must be global — a static variable cannot be local to a function.

The name of the class is required for any member when it appears outside its class boundaries.

This business of allocating space manually is somewhat confusing until you consider that class definitions are designed to go into files that are included by multiple source code modules. C++ has to know in which of those .cpp source files to allocate space for the static variable. This is not a problem with non-static variables because space is allocated in every object created.

Referencing static data members

The access rules for static members are the same as the access rules for normal members. From within the class, static members are referenced like any other class member. Public static members can be referenced from outside the class, whereas well-protected static members can't. Both types of reference are shown in the following code snippet using the declaration of *Student* from the previous section:

```
void fn(Student& s1, Student& s2)
{
    // reference public static
    cout << "No of students "
         << s1.noOfStudents // reference from outside
         << endl;           // of the class
}
```

In *fn()*, *noOfStudents* is referenced using the object *s1*. But *s1* and *s2* share the same member *noOfStudents*. How did I know to choose *s1?* Why didn't I use *s2* instead? It doesn't make any difference. You can reference a static member using any object of that class.

In fact, you don't need an object at all. You can use the class name directly instead, if you prefer, as in the following:

```
// ...class defined the same as before...
void fn(Student& s1, Student& s2)
{
   // the following produce identical results
   cout << "Number of students "
        << Student::noOfStudents
        << endl;
}
```

If you do use an object name when accessing a static member, C++ uses only the declared class of the object.

This is a minor technicality, but in the interest of full disclosure: The object used to reference a static member is not evaluated even if it's an expression. For example, consider the following case:

```
class Student
{
   public:
     static int noOfStudents;
     Student& nextStudent();
     // ...other stuff the same...
};

void fn(Student& s)
{
     cout << s.nextStudent().noOfStudents << "\n"
}
```

The member function *nextStudent()* is not actually called. All C++ needs to access *noOfStudents* is the return type, and it can get that without bothering to evaluate the expression. This is true even if *nextStudent()* should do other things, such as wash windows or shine your shoes. None of those things will be done. Although the example is obscure, it does happen. That's what you get for trying to cram too much stuff into one expression.

Uses for static data members

Static data members have umpteen uses, but let me touch on a few here. First, you can use static members to keep count of the number of objects floating about. In the *Student* class, for example, the count is initialized to 0, the constructor increments it, and the destructor decrements it. At any given instant, the static member contains the count of the number of existing

Student objects. Remember, however, that this count reflects the number of *Student* objects (including any temporaries) and not necessarily the number of students.

A closely related use for a static member is as a flag to indicate whether a particular action has occurred. For example, a class *Radio* may need to initialize hardware before sending the first *tune* command but not before subsequent *tunes*. A flag indicating that this is the first *tune* is just the ticket. This includes flagging when an error has occurred.

Another common use is to provide space for the pointer to the first member of a list — the so-called head pointer (see Chapter 13 if this doesn't sound familiar). Static members can allocate bits of common data that all objects in all functions share (overuse of this common memory is a really bad idea because doing so makes tracking errors difficult).

Declaring Static Member Functions

Member functions can be declared static as well. Static member functions are useful when you want to associate an action to a class, but you don't need to associate that action with a particular object. For example, the member function *Duck::fly()* is associated with a particular *duck,* whereas the rather more drastic member function *Duck::goExtinct()* is not.

Like static data members, static member functions are associated with a class and not with a particular object of that class. This means that, like a reference to a static data member, a reference to a static member function does not require an object. If an object is present, only its type is used.

Thus, both calls to the static member function *number()* in the following example are legal. This brings us to our first static program — I mean our first program using static members — CallStaticMember:

```
// CallStaticMember - demonstrate two ways to call a
//                    static member function
//
#include <cstdio>
#include <cstdlib>
#include <iostream>
using namespace std;

class Student
{
  public:
    Student(const char* pN = "no name") : sName(pN)
```

```
      {
          noOfStudents++;
      }
      ~Student() { noOfStudents--; }
      const string& name() { return sName; }
      static int number() { return noOfStudents; }

    protected:
      string sName;
      static int noOfStudents;
};
int Student::noOfStudents = 0;

int main(int argcs, char* pArgs[])
{
    // create two students and ask the class "how many?"
    Student s1("Chester");
    Student* pS2 = new Student("Scooter");

    cout << "Created " << s1.name()
         << " and " << pS2->name() << endl;
    cout << "Number of students is "
         << s1.number() << endl;

    // now get rid of a student and ask again
    cout << "Deleting " << pS2->name() << endl;
    delete pS2;
    cout << "Number of students is "
         << Student::number() << endl;

    // wait until user is ready before terminating program
    // to allow the user to see the program results
    cout << "Press Enter to continue..." << endl;
    cin.ignore(10, '\n');
    cin.get();
    return 0;
}
```

This program creates two *Student* objects, one locally and one off the heap. It then displays their names and the count of the number of students. Next the program deletes one of the students and asks the class how many students are out there. The output from the program appears as follows:

```
Created Chester and Scooter
Number of students is 2
Deleting Scooter
Number of students is 1
Press any key to continue...
```

This class keeps its data members protected and provides access functions that allow outside (non-*Student*) code to read but not modify them.

Declaring the return type of *name()* method to be *string&* rather than simply *string* causes the function to return a reference to the object's existing name rather than create a temporary string object. (See Chapter 17 for a brilliant treatise on constructing and avoiding temporaries.) Adding the *const* to the declaration keeps the caller from modifying the class's name member.

Notice how the static member function *number()* can access the static data member *noOfStudents*. In fact, that's the only member of the class that it can access — a static member function is not associated with any object. Were I to declare *name()* to be static, I could refer to *Student::name()*, which would immediately beg the question, "Which name?"

The following snippet is only one case that I'm aware of where a static method can refer directly to a non-static member:

```
class Student
{
  public:
    static int elementsInName()
    {
        int sizeOfArray = sizeof(name);
        return sizeOfArray/sizeof(char);
    }

  protected:
    char name[MAX_NAME_SIZE];
};
```

Here the static method *elementsInName()* refers to *name* without referencing any object. This was not legal prior to the 2011 standard. It's allowed now because the *sizeof* name is the same for all objects. Thus, it doesn't matter which object you refer to.

You may wonder why I divided *sizeof(name)* by *sizeof(char)*. The *sizeof(name)* returns the number of bytes in the array name. But what we want is the number of elements in *name,* so we have to divide by the size of each element in name. But isn't *sizeof(char)* equal to 1? Well, maybe, but maybe not. Dividing the sizeof the array by the sizeof a single element always works for all array types.

What Is this About Anyway?

How does a non-static object method know what object it's referring to? In other words, when I ask the *Student* object for its name, how does *name()* know which *sName* to return?

The address of the current object is passed as an implied first argument to every non-static method. When it is necessary to refer to this object, C++ gives it the name *this*. *this* is a keyword in every object method meaning "the current object." This is illustrated in the following code snippet:

```
class SC
{
  public:
    void dyn(int a); // like SC::dyn(SC *this, int a)
    static void stat(int a); // like SC::stat(int a)
};

void fn(SC& s)
{
    s.dyn(10);  // -converts to-> SC::dyn(&s, 10);
    s.stat(10); // -converts to-> SC::stat(10);
}
```

That is, the function *dyn()* is interpreted almost as though it were declared *void SC::dyn(SC *this, int a)*. The call to *dyn()* is converted by the compiler as shown, with the address of *s* passed as the first argument. (You can't actually write the call this way, but this is what the compiler is doing.)

References to other non-static members within *SC::dyn()* automatically use the *this* argument as the pointer to the current object. When *SC::stat()* was called, no object address was passed. Thus, it has no *this* pointer to use when referencing non-static functions, which is why I say that a static member function is not associated with any current object.

You can see *this* used explicitly in an object-oriented version of the linked list program from Chapter 13; called LinkedLIstData. The entire program is available with the online material at www.dummies.com/extras/cplusplus; the *NameDataSet* class appears here:

```
// NameDataSet - stores a person's name (these objects
//               could easily store any other information
//               desired).
class NameDataSet
{
  public:
    NameDataSet(string& refName)
      : sName(refName), pNext(nullptr) {}
```

```
    // add self to beginning of list
    void add()
    {
        this->pNext = pHead;
        pHead = this;
    }

    // access methods
    static NameDataSet* first() { return pHead; }
           NameDataSet* next()  { return pNext; }
         const string& name()   { return sName; }
  protected:
    string sName;

    // the link to the first and next member of list
    static NameDataSet* pHead;
    NameDataSet* pNext;
};

// allocate space for the head pointer
NameDataSet* NameDataSet::pHead = nullptr;
```

Here you can see that the *pHead* pointer to the beginning of the list has been
converted into a static data member because it applies to the entire class.
In addition, *pNext* has been made a data member and access methods have
been provided to give other programs access to the now protected members
of the class.

The *add()* method adds the current object to the list by first setting its *pNext*
pointer to the beginning of the list. The next statement causes the head
pointer to point to the current object via the assignment *pHead = this.*

Part IV
Inheritance

Visit www.dummies.com/extras/cplusplus for great Dummies content online.

In this part...

- ✔ Inheriting a base class
- ✔ Exploring relationships
- ✔ Factoring common properties
- ✔ Declaring abstract classes
- ✔ Visit www.dummies.com/extras/cplusplus for great Dummies content online

Chapter 19

Inheriting a Class

. . . .

In This Chapter

▶ Defining inheritance

▶ Inheriting a base class

▶ Constructing the base class

▶ Exploring meaningful relationships: The IS_A versus the HAS_A relationship

. . . .

*T*his chapter discusses *inheritance,* the ability of one class to inherit capabilities or properties from another class.

Inheritance is a common concept. I am a human (except when I first wake up in the morning). I inherit certain properties from the class *Human,* such as my ability to converse (more or less) intelligently and my dependence on air, water, and carbohydrate-based nourishment (a little too dependent on the latter, I'm afraid). These properties are not unique to humans. The class *Human* inherits the dependencies on air, water, and nourishment from the class *Mammal,* which inherited it from the class *Animal.*

The capability of passing down properties is a powerful one. It enables you to describe things in an economical way. For example, if my son asks, "What's a duck?" I can say, "It's a bird that goes quack." Despite what you may think, that answer conveys a considerable amount of information. He knows what a bird is, and now he knows all those same things about a duck plus the duck's additional property of "quackness." (Refer to Chapter 11 for a further discussion of this and other profound observations.)

Object-oriented (OO) languages express this inheritance relationship by allowing one class to inherit from another. OO languages can generate a model that's closer to the real world (remember that real-world stuff!) than the model generated by languages that don't support inheritance.

C++ allows one class to inherit another class as follows:

```
class Student
{
};

class GraduateStudent : public Student
{
};
```

Here, a *GraduateStudent* inherits all the members of *Student*. Thus, a *Graduate Student* IS_A *Student*. (The capitalization of IS_A stresses the importance of this relationship.) Of course, *GraduateStudent* may also contain other members that are unique to a *GraduateStudent*.

Do I Need My Inheritance?

Inheritance was introduced into C++ for several reasons. Of course, the major reason is the capability of expressing the inheritance relationship. (I'll return to that in a moment.) A minor reason is to reduce the amount of typing. Suppose that you have a class *Student,* and you're asked to add a new class called *GraduateStudent.* Inheritance can drastically reduce the number of things you have to put in the class. All you really need in the class *GraduateStudent* are things that describe the differences between students and graduate students.

Another minor side effect has to do with software modification. Suppose you inherit from some existing class. Later, you find that the base class doesn't do exactly what the subclass needs. Or perhaps the class has a bug. Modifying the base class might break other code that uses that base class. Creating and using a new subclass that overloads the incorrect feature with a corrected version solves your problem without causing someone else further problems.

This IS_A-mazing

To make sense of our surroundings, humans build extensive taxonomies. Fido is a special case of dog, which is a special case of canine, which is a special case of mammal, and so it goes. This shapes our understanding of the world.

To use another example, a student is a (special type of) person. Having said this, I already know a lot of things about students (American students, anyway). I know they have social security numbers, they watch too much TV, and they daydream about the opposite sex (the male ones, anyway). I know all these things because these are properties of all people.

In C++, we say that the class *Student* inherits from the class *Person*. Also, we say that *Person* is a *base class* of *Student,* and *Student* is a *subclass* of *Person*. One final phrase and then I'll stop: *Student* extends the class *Person*.

Finally, we say that a *Student* IS_A *Person* (using all caps is a common way of expressing this unique relationship — I didn't make it up). C++ shares this terminology with other object-oriented languages.

Notice that although *Student* IS_A *Person,* the reverse is not true. A *Person* IS not a *Student.* (A statement like this always refers to the general case. It could be that a particular *Person* is, in fact, a *Student.*) A lot of people who are members of class *Person* are not members of

class *Student.* In addition, class *Student* has properties it does not share with class *Person.* For example, *Student* has a grade point average, but *Person* does not.

The inheritance property is transitive. For example, if I define a new class *GraduateStudent* as a subclass of *Student, GraduateStudent* must also be *Person.* It has to be that way: If a *GraduateStudent* IS_A *Student* and a *Student* IS_A *Person,* a *GraduateStudent* IS_A *Person.*

How Does a Class Inherit?

Here's the *GraduateStudent* example filled out into a program InheritanceExample:

```
//   InheritanceExample - demonstrate an inheritance
//               relationship in which the subclass
//               constructor passes argument information
//               to the constructor in the base class
//
#include <cstdio>
#include <cstdlib>
#include <iostream>
using namespace std;
class Advisor {}; // define an empty class

class Student
{
  public:
    Student(const char *pName = "no name")
       : name(pName), average(0.0), semesterHours(0)
    {
        cout << "Constructing student " << name << endl;
    }

    void addCourse(int hours, float grade)
    {
        cout << "Adding grade to " << name << endl;
        average = semesterHours * average + grade;
        semesterHours += hours;
        average = average / semesterHours;
    }

    int hours() { return semesterHours;}
    float gpa() { return average;}
```

```
   protected:
      string name;
      double average;
      int     semesterHours;
};

class GraduateStudent : public Student
{
  public:
    GraduateStudent(const char *pName, Advisor adv,
                    double qG = 0.0)
         : Student(pName), advisor(adv), qualifierGrade(qG)
    {
        cout << "Constructing graduate student "
             << pName << endl;
    }

    double qualifier() { return qualifierGrade; }

  protected:
    Advisor advisor;
    double qualifierGrade;
};

int main(int nNumberofArgs, char* pszArgs[])
{
    // create a dummy advisor to give to GraduateStudent
    Advisor adv;

    // create two Student types
    Student llu("Cy N Sense");
    GraduateStudent gs("Matt Madox", adv, 1.5);

    // now add a grade to their grade point average
    llu.addCourse(3, 2.5);
    gs.addCourse(3, 3.0);

    // display the graduate student's qualifier grade
    cout << "Matt's qualifier grade = "
         << gs.qualifier() << endl;

    // wait until user is ready before terminating program
    // to allow the user to see the program results
    cout << "Press Enter to continue..." << endl;
    cin.ignore(10, '\n');
    cin.get();
    return 0;
}
```

This program demonstrates the creation and use of two objects, one of class *Student* and a second of *GraduateStudent.* The output of this program is as follows:

```
Constructing student Cy N Sense
Constructing student Matt Madox
Constructing graduate student Matt Madox
Adding grade to Cy N Sense
Adding grade to Matt Madox
Matt's qualifier grade = 1.5
Press Enter to continue...
```

Using a subclass

The class *Student* has been defined in the conventional fashion. The class *GraduateStudent* is a bit different, however. The colon followed by the phrase *public Student* at the beginning of the class definition declares *GraduateStudent* to be a subclass of *Student.*

The appearance of the keyword *public* implies that there is probably protected inheritance as well. All right, it's true, but *protected* inheritance is rarely used and beyond the scope of this book.

Programmers love inventing new terms or giving new meaning to existing terms. Heck, programmers even invent new terms and then give them a second meaning. Here is a set of equivalent expressions that describes the same relationship:

- *GraduateStudent* is a subclass of *Student.*
- *Student* is the base class or is the parent class of *GraduateStudent.*
- *GraduateStudent* inherits or is derived from *Student.*
- *GraduateStudent* extends *Student.*

As a subclass of *Student, GraduateStudent* inherits all its members. For example, a *GraduateStudent* has a *name* even though that member is declared up in the base class. However, a subclass can add its own members, for example *qualifierGrade.* After all, *gs* quite literally IS_A *Student* plus a little bit more.

The *main()* function declares two objects, *llu* of type *Student* and *gs* of type *GraduateStudent.* It then proceeds to access the *addCourse()* member function for both types of students. *main()* then accesses the *qualifier()* function that is only a member of the subclass.

Constructing a subclass

Even though a subclass has access to the protected members of the base class and could initialize them, each subclass is responsible for initializing itself.

Before control passes beyond the open brace of the constructor for *Graduate Student,* control passes to the proper constructor of *Student.* If *Student* were based on another class, such as *Person,* the constructor for that class would be invoked before the *Student* constructor got control. Like a skyscraper, the object is constructed starting at the "base"-ment class and working its way up the class structure one story at a time.

Just as with member objects, you often need to be able to pass arguments to the base class constructor. The example program declares the subclass constructor as follows:

```
GraduateStudent(const char *pName, Advisor adv,
                double qG = 0.0)
    : Student(pName), advisor(adv), qualifierGrade(qG)
{
    // whatever else the constructor does
}
```

Here the constructor for *GraduateStudent* invokes the *Student* constructor, passing it the argument *pName.* C++ then initializes the members *advisor* and *qualifierGrade* before executing the statements within the constructor's open and close braces.

The default constructor for the base class is executed if the subclass makes no explicit reference to a different constructor. Thus, in the following code snippet, the *Pig* base class is constructed before any members of *LittlePig,* even though *LittlePig* makes no explicit reference to that constructor:

```
class House {};
class Pig
{
  public:
    Pig() : pHouse(nullptr) {}
  protected:
    House* pHouse;
};
class LittlePig : public Pig
{
  public:
    LittlePig(double volStraw, int numSticks,
              int numBricks)
      : straw(volStraw), sticks(numSticks),
        bricks(numBricks) { }
```

```
protected:
   double straw;
   int sticks;
   int bricks;
};
```

Similarly, the copy constructor for a base class is invoked automatically.

Destructing a subclass

Following the rule that destructors are invoked in the reverse order of the constructors, the destructor for *GraduateStudent* is given control first. After it's given its last full measure of devotion, control passes to the destructor for *Advisor* and then to the destructor for *Student*. If *Student* were based on a class *Person,* the destructor for *Person* would get control after *Student.*

This is logical. The blob of memory is first converted to a *Student* object. Only then is it the job of the *GraduateStudent* constructor to transform this simple *Student* into a *GraduateStudent*. The destructor simply reverses the process.

Inheriting constructors

As of the 2011 standard, subclass can inherit the constructor of its base class as well, as shown in the following snippet:

```
class Student
{
  public:
    Student(string name);
};
class GraduateStudent : public Student
{
  public:
    using Student::Student; // inherit base constructors
};
```

This creates a *GraduateStudent(string)* constructor exactly as if the following had been entered:

```
class GraduateStudent : public Student
{
  public:
    GraduateStudent(string name) : Student(name) {}
};
```

The advantage of inheriting the constructors of the base class is that the subclass inherits all of the base class constructors. This is useful when building a subclass that extends an important base class in some trivial way.

Having a HAS_A Relationship

Notice that the class *GraduateStudent* includes the members of class *Student* and *Advisor*, but in a different way. By defining a data member of class *Advisor*, you know that a *Student* has all the data members of an *Advisor* within it. However, you can't say that a *GraduateStudent* is an *Advisor* — instead you say that a *GraduateStudent* HAS_A *Advisor*. What's the difference between this and inheritance?

Use a car as an example. You could logically define a car as being a subclass of vehicle, so it inherits the properties of other vehicles. At the same time, a car has a motor. If you buy a car, you can logically assume that you are buying a motor as well. (Unless you go to the used-car lot where I got my last junk heap.)

If friends ask you to show up at a rally on Saturday with your vehicle of choice and you go in your car, they can't complain (even if someone else shows up on a bicycle) because a car IS_A vehicle. But, if you appear on foot carrying a motor, your friends will have reason to laugh at you because a motor is not a vehicle. A motor is missing certain critical properties that all vehicles share — such as a place to ride.

From a programming standpoint, the HAS_A relationship is just as straight-forward. Consider the following:

```
class Vehicle {};
class Motor {};
class Car : public Vehicle
{
  public:
    Motor motor;
};

void VehicleFn(Vehicle& v);
void MotorFn(Motor& m);

int main(int nNumberofArgs, char* pszArgs[])
{
    Car car;
    VehicleFn(car);     // this is allowed
    MotorFn(car);       // this is not allowed
    MotorFn(car.motor);// this is allowed
    return 0;
}
```

The call *VehicleFn(c)* is allowed because *car* IS_A *vehicle*. The call *MotorFn(car)* is not because *car* is not a *Motor*, even though it contains a *Motor*. If the intention were to pass the *Motor* portion of *c* to the function, this must be expressed explicitly, as in the call *MotorFn(car.motor)*.

Chapter 20

Examining Virtual Member Functions: Are They for Real?

● ●

In This Chapter

▶ Discovering how polymorphism (a.k.a. late binding) works

▶ Finding out how safe polymorphic nachos are

▶ Overriding member functions in a subclass

▶ Checking out special considerations with polymorphism

● ●

*T*he number and type of a function's arguments are included in its full, or *extended,* name. This enables you to give two functions the same name as long as the extended name is different:

```
void someFn(int);
void someFn(char*);
void someFn(char*, double);
```

In all three cases, the short name for these functions is *someFn()* (hey! this is some fun). The extended names for all three differ: *someFn(int)* versus *someFn(char*),* and so on. C++ is left to figure out which function is meant by the arguments during the call.

Member functions can be overloaded. The number of arguments, the type of arguments, and the class name are all part of the extended name.

Inheritance introduces a whole new wrinkle, however. What if a function in a base class has the same name as a function in the subclass? Consider, for example, the following simple code snippet:

```
class Student
{
  public:
    double calcTuition();
};
```

```
class GraduateStudent : public Student
{
  public:
    double calcTuition();
};

int main(int argcs, char* pArgs[])
{
    Student s;
    GraduateStudent gs;
    s.calcTuition(); //calls Student::calcTuition()
    gs.calcTuition();//calls GraduateStudent::calcTuition()
    return 0;
}
```

As with any overloading situation, when the programmer refers to *calcTuition()*, C++ has to decide which *calcTuition()* is intended. Obviously, if the two functions differed in the type of arguments, there's no problem. Even if the arguments were the same, the class name should be sufficient to resolve the call, and this example is no different. The call *s.calcTuition()* refers to *Student::calcTuition()* because *s* is declared locally as a *Student*, whereas *gs.calcTuition()* refers to *GraduateStudent::calcTuition()*.

But what if the exact class of the object can't be determined at compile-time? To demonstrate how this can occur, change the preceding program in a seemingly trivial way:

```
// OverloadOverride - demonstrate when a function is
//      overloaded at compile time vs. overriden at runtime
//
#include <cstdio>
#include <cstdlib>
#include <iostream>
using namespace std;

class Student
{
  public:
    // uncomment one or the other of the next
    // two lines; one binds calcTuition() early and
    // the other late
//          void calcTuition()
    virtual void calcTuition()
    {
        cout << "We're in Student::calcTuition" << endl;
    }
};
```

```
class GraduateStudent : public Student
{
  public:
    void calcTuition()
    {
      cout<<"We're in GraduateStudent::calcTuition"<<endl;
    }
};

void fn(Student& x)
{
    x.calcTuition(); // which calcTuition()?
}

int main(int nNumberofArgs, char* pszArgs[])
{
    // pass a base class object to function
    // (to match the declaration)
    Student s;
    fn(s);

    // pass a specialization of the base class instead
    GraduateStudent gs;
    fn(gs);

    // wait until user is ready before terminating program
    // to allow the user to see the program results
    cout << "Press Enter to continue..." << endl;
    cin.ignore(10, '\n');
    cin.get();
    return 0;
}
```

Instead of calling *calcTuition()* directly, the call is now made through an intermediate function, *fn()*. Depending on how *fn()* is called, *x* can be a *Student* or a *GraduateStudent*. A *GraduateStudent* IS_A *Student*.

Refer to Chapter 19 if you don't remember why a *GraduateStudent* IS_A *Student*.

The argument *x* passed to *fn()* is declared to be a reference to *Student*.

Passing an object by reference can be a lot more efficient than passing it by value. See Chapter 17 for a treatise on making copies of objects.

You might want *x.calcTuition()* to call *Student::calcTuition()* when *x* is a *Student* but to call *GraduateStudent::calcTuition()* when *x* is a *GraduateStudent*. It would be really cool if C++ were that smart.

The type that you've been accustomed to until now is called the *static*, or *compile-time*, type. The compile-time type of *x* is *Student* in both cases because that's what the declaration in *fn()* says. The other kind is the *dynamic*, or *run-time*, type. In the case of the example function *fn()*, the run-time type of *x* is *Student* when *fn()* is called with *s* and *GraduateStudent* when *fn()* is called with *gs*. Aren't we having fun?

The capability of deciding at runtime which of several overloaded member functions to call based on the run-time type is called *polymorphism*, or *late binding*. Deciding which overloaded function to call at compile-time is called *early binding* because that sounds like the opposite of late binding.

Overloading a base class function polymorphically is called *overriding the base class function*. This new name is used to differentiate this more complicated case from the normal overload case.

Why You Need Polymorphism

Polymorphism is key to the power of object-oriented programming. It's so important that languages that don't support polymorphism can't advertise themselves as OO languages. (I think it's a government regulation — you can't label a language OO if it doesn't support polymorphism unless you add a disclaimer from the Surgeon General, or something like that.)

Without polymorphism, inheritance has little meaning. Remember how I made nachos in the oven? In this sense, I was acting as the late binder. The recipe read: Heat the nachos in the oven. It didn't read: If the type of oven is microwave, do this; if the type of oven is conventional, do that; if the type of oven is convection, do this other thing. The recipe (the code) relied on me (the late binder) to decide what the action (member function) heat means when applied to the oven (the particular instance of class *Oven*) or any of its variations (subclasses), such as a microwave oven (*Microwave*). This is the way people think, and designing a language along the lines of the way people think allows the programming model to more accurately describe the world in which people live.

How Polymorphism Works

Any given language can support either early or late binding based upon the whims of its developers. Older languages like C tend to support early binding alone. Recent languages like Java and C# support only late binding. As a fence straddler, C++ supports both early and late binding.

You may be surprised that the default for C++ is early binding. The output of the *OverloadOverride* program the way it appears is as follows:

```
We're in Student::calcTuition
We're in Student::calcTuition
Press Enter to continue...
```

The reason is simple, if a little dated. First, C++ has to act as much like C as possible by default to retain upward compatibility with its predecessor. Second, polymorphism adds a small amount of overhead to every function call both in terms of data storage and code needed to perform the call. The founders of C++ were concerned that any additional overhead would be used as a reason not to adopt C++ as the system's language of choice, so they made the more efficient early binding the default.

To make a member function polymorphic, the programmer must flag the function with the C++ keyword *virtual,* as shown in the following modification to the declaration in the *OverloadOveride* program:

```
class Student
{
  public:
    virtual void calcTuition()
    {
        cout << "We're in Student::calcTuition" << endl;
    }
};
```

The keyword *virtual* that tells C++ that *calcTuition()* is a polymorphic member function. That is to say, declaring *calcTuition()* virtual means that calls to it will be bound late if there is any doubt as to the run-time type of the object with which *calcTuition()* is called.

Executing the *OverloadOveride* program with *calcTuition()* declared virtual generates the following output:

```
We're in Student::calcTuition
We're in GraduateStudent::calcTuition
Press Enter to continue...
```

If you're comfortable with the debugger that comes with your C++ environment, you really should single-step through this example. It's so cool to see the program single-step into *Student::calcTuition()* the first time that *fn()* is called but into *GraduateStudent::calcTuition()* on the second call. I don't think that you can truly appreciate polymorphism until you've tried it.

You need to declare the function virtual only in the base class. The "virtual-ness" is carried down to the subclass automatically. In this book, however, I follow the coding standard of declaring the function virtual everywhere (virtually).

When Is a Virtual Function Not?

Just because you think that a particular function call is bound late doesn't mean that it is. If not declared with the same arguments in the subclasses, the member functions are not overridden polymorphically, whether or not they are declared virtual.

One exception to the identical declaration rule is that if the member function in the base class returns a pointer or reference to a base class object, an overridden member function in a subclass may return a pointer or reference to an object of the subclass. In other words, the function *makeACopy()* is polymorphic, even though the return type of the two functions differ:

```
class Base
{
  public:
    // return a copy of the current object
    Base* makeACopy();
};

class SubClass : public Base
{
  public:
    // return a copy of the current object
    SubClass* makeACopy();
};

void fn(Base& bc)
{
    Base* pCopy = bc.makeACopy();

    // proceed on...
}
```

In practice, this is quite natural. A *makeACopy()* function should return an object of type *SubClass,* even though it might override *BaseClass::makeACopy().*

This business of silently deciding when a function is overridden and when not is a source of error in C++; so much so that the 2011 standard introduced the descriptor *override* that the programmer can use to indicate her intent to override a base class function. C++ generates a compiler error if a function is declared override but does not, in fact, override a base class function for some reason (such as a mismatched argument) as in the following example:

```
class Student
{
  public:
    virtual void addCourseGrade(double grade);
};
class GradStudent : public Student
{
  public:
    virtual void addCourseGrade(float grade) override;
};
```

This snippet generates a compile-time error because the method *GradStudent:: addCourseGrade(float)* was declared *override* but it does not, in fact, override the base class function *Student::addCourseGrade(double)* because the argument types don't match.

The programmer can also declare a function as not overrideable using the *final* keyword, even if that function itself overrides some earlier base class function, as demonstrated in the following additional *PostDoc* class:

```
class GradStudent : public Student
{
  public:
    virtual void addCourseGrade(double grade) final;
};
class PostDoc : public GradStudent
{
  public:
    virtual void addCourseGrade(double grade);
};
```

Since *Student::addCourseGrade()* is marked *final*, the declaration of *PostDoc:: addCourseGrade()* generates an error because it attempts to override the *Student* method.

In addition, an entire class can be declared *final:*

```
class GradStudent final: public Student
```

This affects more than just the virtual methods of the class. A *final* class cannot be inherited from at all.

Considering Virtual Considerations

You need to keep in mind a few things when using virtual functions. First, static member functions cannot be declared virtual. Because static member functions are not called with an object, there is no runtime object upon which to base a binding decision.

Second, specifying the class name in the call forces a call to bind early, whether or not the function is virtual. For example, the following call is to *Base::fn()* because that's what the programmer indicated, even if *fn()* is declared virtual:

```
void test(Base& b)
{
    b.Base::fn();      // this call is not bound late
}
```

Finally, constructors cannot be virtual because there is no (completed) object to use to determine the type. At the time the constructor is called, the memory that the object occupies is just an amorphous mass. It's only after the constructor has finished that the object is a member of the class in good standing.

By comparison, the destructor should almost always be declared virtual. If not, you run the risk of improperly destructing the object, as in the following circumstance:

```
class Base
{
  public:
    ~Base();
};

class SubClass : public Base
{
  public:
    ~SubClass();
};

void finishWithObject(Base* pHeapObject)
{
    // ...work with object...
    // now return it to the heap
    delete pHeapObject; // this calls ~Base() no matter
}                       // the runtime type of
                        // pHeapObject
```

If the pointer passed to *finishWithObject()* really points to a *SubClass,* the *SubClass* destructor is not invoked properly — because the destructor has not been declared virtual, it's always bound early. Declaring the destructor virtual solves the problem.

So when would you not want to declare the destructor virtual? There's only one case. Virtual functions introduce a "little" overhead. Let me be more specific: When the programmer defines the first virtual function in a class,

C++ adds an additional, hidden pointer — not one pointer per virtual function, just one pointer if the class has any virtual functions. A class that has no virtual functions (and does not inherit any virtual functions from base classes) does not have this pointer.

Now, one pointer doesn't sound like much, and it isn't unless the following two conditions are true:

✔ The class doesn't have many data members (so that one pointer represents a lot compared to what's there already).

✔ You intend to create a lot of objects of this class (otherwise, the overhead doesn't make any difference).

If these two conditions are met and your class doesn't already have virtual member functions, you may not want to declare the destructor virtual.

Except for this one case, always declare destructors to be virtual, even if a class is not subclassed (yet) — you never know when someone will come along and use your class as the base class for her own. If you don't declare the destructor virtual, then declare the class final (if your compiler supports this feature) and document it!

Chapter 21

Factoring Classes

● ●

In This Chapter

▶ Factoring common properties into a base class

▶ Using abstract classes to hold factored information

▶ Declaring abstract classes

▶ Inheriting from an abstract class

▶ Dividing a program into multiple modules using a project file

● ●

*T*he concept of inheritance allows one class to inherit the properties of a base class. Inheritance has a number of purposes, including paying for my son's college. The main benefit of inheritance is the ability to point out the relationship between classes. This is the so-called IS_A relationship — a *MicrowaveOven IS_A Oven* and stuff like that.

Factoring is great stuff if you make the correct correlations. For example, the microwave versus conventional oven relationship seems natural. Claim that microwave is a special kind of toaster, and you're headed for trouble. True, they both make things hot, they both use electricity, and they're both found in the kitchen, but the similarity ends there — a microwave can't make toast and a toaster can't make nachos.

Identifying the classes inherent in a problem and drawing the correct relationships among these classes is a process known as *factoring*. (The word is related to the arithmetic that you were forced to do in grade school: factoring out the least common denominators, for example, 12 is equal to 2 times 2 times 3.)

Factoring

This section describes how you can use inheritance to simplify your programs using a bank account example. Suppose that you were asked to write a simple bank program that implemented the concept of a savings account and a checking account.

I can talk until I'm blue in the face about these classes; however, object-oriented programmers have come up with a concise way to describe the salient points of a class in a drawing. The *Checking* and *Savings* classes are shown in Figure 21-1. (This is only one of several ways to graphically express the same thing.)

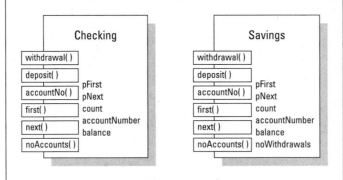

Figure 21-1:
Independent
classes
Checking
and
Savings.

To read this figure and the other figures, remember the following:

- ✔ The big box is the class, with the class name at the top.

- ✔ The names in boxes are member functions.

- ✔ The names not in boxes are data members.

- ✔ The names that extend partway out of the boxes are publicly accessible members; that is, these members can be accessed by functions that are not part of the class or any of its descendents. Those members that are completely within the box are not accessible from outside the class.

- ✔ A thick arrow (see Figure 21-2) represents the IS_A relationship.

- ✔ A thin arrow represents the HAS_A relationship.

A *Car* IS_A *Vehicle,* but a *Car* HAS_A *Motor.*

You can see in Figure 21-1 that the *Checking* and *Savings* classes have a lot in common. For example, both classes have a *withdrawal()* and *deposit()* member function. Because the two classes aren't identical, however, they must remain as separate classes. (In a real-life bank application, the two classes would be a good deal more different than in this example.) Still, there should be a way to avoid this repetition.

You could have one of these classes inherit from the other. *Savings* has more members than *Checking,* so you could let *Savings* inherit from *Checking.* This arrangement is shown in Figure 21-2. The *Savings* class inherits all the members. The class is completed with the addition of the data member *noWithdrawals* and by overriding the function *withdrawal()*. You have to override *withdrawal()* because the rules for withdrawing money from a savings account are different from those for withdrawing money from a checking account.

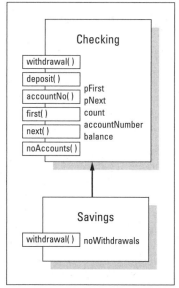

Figure 21-2:
Savings implemented as a subclass of *Checking.*

Although letting *Savings* inherit from *Checking* is laborsaving, it's not completely satisfying. The main problem is that, like the weight listed on my driver's license, it misrepresents the truth. This inheritance relationship implies that a savings account is a special type of checking account, which it is not.

"So what?" you say. "Inheriting works, and it saves effort." True, but my reservations are more than stylistic trivialities — my reservations are at some of the best restaurants in town (at least that's what all the truckers say). Such misrepresentations are confusing to the programmer, both today's and tomorrow's. Someday, a programmer unfamiliar with our programming tricks will have to read and understand what our code does. Misleading representations are difficult to reconcile and understand.

In addition, such misrepresentations can lead to problems down the road. Suppose, for example, that the bank changes its policies with respect to checking accounts. Say it decides to charge a service fee on checking accounts only if the minimum balance dips below a given value during the month.

A change like this can be easily handled with minimal changes to the class *Checking.* You'll have to add a new data member to the class *Checking* to keep track of the minimum balance during the month. Let's go out on a limb and call it *minimumBalance.*

But now you have a problem. Because *Savings* inherits from *Checking, Savings* gets this new data member as well. It has no use for this member because the minimum balance does not affect savings accounts, so it just sits there. Remember that every checking account object has this extra *minimumBalance* member. One extra data member may not be a big deal, but it adds further confusion.

Changes like this accumulate. Today it's an extra data member — tomorrow it's a changed member function. Eventually, the savings account class is carrying a lot of extra baggage that is applicable only to checking accounts.

Now the bank comes back and decides to change some savings account policy. This requires you to modify some function in *Checking*. Changes like this in the base class automatically propagate down to the subclass unless the function is already overridden in the subclass *Savings*. For example, suppose that the bank decides to give away toasters for every deposit into the checking account. (Hey — it could happen!) Without the bank (or its programmers) knowing it, deposits to checking accounts would automatically result in toaster donations. Unless you're very careful, changes to *Checking* may unexpectedly appear in *Savings*.

How can you avoid these problems? Claiming that *Checking* is a special case of *Savings* changes but doesn't solve our problem. What you need is a third class (call it *Account,* just for grins) that embodies the things that are common between *Checking* and *Savings,* as shown in Figure 21-3.

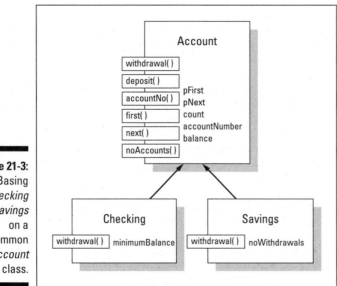

Figure 21-3:
Basing
Checking
and *Savings*
on a
common
Account
class.

How does building a new account solve the problems? First, creating a new *Account* class is a more accurate description of the real world (whatever that is). In our concept of things (or at least in mine), there really is something known as an account. Savings accounts and checking accounts are special cases of this more fundamental concept.

In addition, the class *Savings* is insulated from changes to the class *Checking* (and vice versa). If the bank institutes a fundamental change to all accounts, you can modify *Account,* and all subclasses will automatically inherit the change. But if the bank changes its policy only for checking accounts, you can modify just the *Checking* account class without affecting *Savings*.

This process of culling common properties from similar classes is the essence of class factoring.

Factoring is legitimate only if the inheritance relationship corresponds to reality. Factoring together a class *Mouse* and *Joystick* because they're both hardware pointing devices is legitimate. Factoring together a class *Mouse* and *Display* because they both make low-level operating system calls is not.

Implementing Abstract Classes

As intellectually satisfying as factoring is, it introduces a problem of its own. Return one more time to the bank account classes, specifically the common base class *Account*. Think for a minute about how you might go about defining the different member functions defined in *Account*.

Most *Account* member functions are no problem because both account types implement them in the same way. Implementing those common functions with *Account::withdrawal()* is different, however. The rules for withdrawing from a savings account are different than those for withdrawing from a checking account. You'll have to implement *Savings::withdrawal()* differently than you do *Checking::withdrawal()*. But how are you supposed to implement *Account::withdrawal()?*

Let's ask the bank manager for help. I imagine the conversation going something like the following:

"What are the rules for making a withdrawal from an account?" you ask.

"What type of account? Savings or checking?" comes the reply.

"From an account," you say. "Just an account."

Blank look. (One might say a "blank bank look" . . . then again, maybe not.)

The problem is that the question doesn't make sense. There's no such thing as "just an account." All accounts (in this example) are either checking accounts or savings accounts. The concept of an account is an abstract one that factors out properties common to the two concrete classes. It is incomplete because it lacks the critical property *withdrawal()*. (After you get further into the details, you may find other properties that a simple account lacks.)

An *abstract class* is one that exists only in subclasses. A *concrete class* is a class that is not abstract.

Describing the abstract class concept

An abstract class is a class with one or more pure virtual functions. Oh, great! That helps a lot.

Okay, a *pure virtual* function is a virtual member function that is marked as having no implementation. Most likely it has no implementation because no implementation is possible with the information provided in the class, including any base classes. A conventional, run-of-the-mill non-pure virtual function is known as a *concrete function* (note that a concrete function may be virtual — unfortunately, C++ uses this term to mean polymorphic. See Chapter 20).

The syntax for declaring a function pure virtual is demonstrated in the following class *Account:*

```
// Account - this class is an abstract class
class Account
{
  public:
    Account(unsigned accNo, double initialBalance = 0.0);

    // access functions
    unsigned int accountNo( );
    double acntBalance( );
    static int noAccounts( );

    // transaction functions
    void deposit(double amount);

    // the following is a pure virtual function
    virtual void withdrawal(double amount) = 0;
```

```
protected:
    // keep accounts in a linked list so there's no limit
    // to the number of accounts
    static int  count;        // number of accounts
    unsigned    accountNumber;
    double      balance;
};
```

The *= 0* after the declaration of *withdrawal()* indicates that the programmer does not intend to define this function. The declaration is a placeholder for the subclasses. The subclasses of *Account* are expected to override this function with a concrete function. The programmer must provide an implementation for each member function not declared pure virtual.

I think this notation is silly, and I don't like it any more than you do. But it's here to stay, so you just have to learn to live with it. There is a reason, if not exactly a justification, for this notation. Every virtual function must have an entry in a special table. This entry contains the address of the function. Presumably, at least at one time, the entry for a pure virtual function was 0. In any case, it's the syntax we're stuck with now.

An abstract class cannot be instanced with an object; that is, you can't make an object out of an abstract class. For example, the following declaration is not legal:

```
void fn( )
{
    // declare an account with 100 dollars
    Account acnt(1234, 100.00);// this is not legal
    acnt.withdrawal(50);        // what would you expect
}                               // this call to do?
```

If the declaration were allowed, the resulting object would be incomplete, lacking in some capability. For example, what should the preceding call do? Remember, there is no *Account::withdrawal()*.

Abstract classes serve as base classes for other classes. An *Account* contains all the properties associated with a generic bank account. You can create other types of bank accounts by inheriting from *Account*.

The technical term is to *instantiate*. We say that the *Account* class cannot be instantiated with an object or a given object instantiates the *Savings* class.

Making an honest class out of an abstract class

The subclass of an abstract class remains abstract until all pure virtual functions have been overridden. The class *Savings* is not abstract because it overrides the pure virtual function *withdrawal()* with a perfectly good definition. The class *Savings* knows how to perform *withdrawal()* when called on to do so. So does the class *Checking*, even if the answer is different. Neither class is virtual because the function *withdrawal()* overrides the pure virtual function in the base class.

Passing abstract classes

Because you can't instantiate an abstract class, it may sound odd that it's possible to declare a pointer or a reference to an abstract class. With polymorphism, however, this isn't as crazy as it sounds. Consider the following code snippet:

```
void fn(Account *pAccount);   // this is legal
void otherFn( )
{
    Savings s; Checking c;

    // this is legitimate because Savings IS_A Account
    fn(&s);
    // same here
    fn(&c);
}
```

Here, *pAccount* is declared as a pointer to an *Account*. However, it's understood that when the function is called, it will be passed the address of some non-abstract subclass object such as *Savings* or *Checking*.

All objects received by *fn()* will be of either class *Savings* or class *Checking* (or some future equally non-abstract subclass of *Account*). The function is assured that you will never pass an actual object of class *Account* because you could never create one to pass in the first place.

The online material at www.dummies.com/extras/cplusplus includes a set of programs *Budget1* through *Budget5*. Each program solves essentially the same problem. Each program allows the user to create and collect the balance of a series of checking and savings accounts. However, each program in the sequence is a bit more object-oriented than its predecessors. *Budget1* is a completely functional implementation with no concept of classes. *Budget2* implements separate *Savings* and *Checking* classes. The *Budget3* program factors the similarities in these two classes into a common, abstract *Account* class using the techniques presented in this chapter. *Budget4* and *Budget5* go on to use features presented in the following chapters.

Part V
Security

Visit www.dummies.com/extras/cplusplus for great Dummies content online.

In this part...

- ✔ Introducing the assignment operator
- ✔ Performing input/output
- ✔ Handling program errors
- ✔ Introducing multiple inheritance
- ✔ Applying templates
- ✔ Evading hackers
- ✔ Visit `www.dummies.com/extras/cplusplus` for great Dummies content online

Chapter 22

A New Assignment Operator, Should You Decide to Accept It

In This Chapter

▶ Introducing the assignment operator

▶ Knowing why and when the assignment operator is necessary

▶ Understanding similarities between the assignment operator and the copy constructor

▶ Comparing copy semantics with move semantics

*T*he *intrinsic* data types are built into the language, such as *int, float,* and *double* and the various pointer types. Chapters 3 and 4 describe the operators that C++ defines for the intrinsic data types. C++ enables the programmer to define the operators for classes that the programmer has created in addition to these intrinsic operators. This is called *operator overloading*.

Normally, operator overloading is optional and not attempted by beginning C++ programmers. A lot of experienced C++ programmers (including me) don't think operator overloading is such a great idea either. However, you will have to learn how to overload one operator: the assignment operator.

Comparing Operators with Functions

An operator is nothing more than a built-in function with a peculiar syntax. The following addition operation

```
a + b
```

could be understood as though it were written

```
operator+(a, b)
```

In fact, C++ gives each operator a function-style name. The functional name of an operator is the operator symbol preceded by the keyword *operator* and followed by the appropriate argument types. For example, the + operator that adds an *int* to an *int* generating an *int* is called *int operator+(int, int)*.

Any existing operator can be defined for a user-defined class. Thus, I could create a *Complex operator*(const Complex&, const Complex&)* that would allow me to multiply two objects of type *Complex*. The new operator may have the same semantics as the operator it overloads, but it doesn't have to. The following rules apply when overloading operators:

✔ The programmer cannot overload the . (dot), :: (colon), . *, *->, *sizeof* and *?:* (ternary) operators.

✔ The programmer cannot invent a new operator. For example, you cannot invent the operation *x $ y.*

✔ The syntax of an operator cannot be changed. Thus, you cannot define an operation *%i* because *%* is already defined as a binary operator.

✔ The operator precedence cannot change. A program cannot force *operator+* to be evaluated before *operator**.

✔ The operators cannot be redefined when applied to intrinsic types — you can't change the meaning of 1 + 2. Existing operators can be overloaded only for newly defined types.

Overloading operators is one of those things that seems like a much better idea than it really is. In my experience, operator overloading introduces more problems than it solves, with three notable exceptions that are the subject of this chapter.

Inserting a New Operator

The insertion and extraction operators << and >> are nothing more than the left and right shift operators overloaded for a set of input/output classes. These definitions are found in the include file *iostream* (which is why every program includes that file). Thus, *cout << "some string"* becomes *operator<<(cout, "some string")*. Our old friends *cout* and *cin* are predefined objects that are tied to the console and keyboard, respectively. I discuss this in detail in Chapter 23.

Creating Shallow Copies
Is a Deep Problem

No matter what anyone may think of operator overloading, you'll need to overload the assignment operator for many classes that you generate. C++ provides a default definition for *operator=()* for all classes. This default definition performs a member-by-member copy. This works great for an intrinsic type like an *int* where the only "member" is the integer itself.

```
int i;
i = 10;    // "member by member" copy
```

This same default definition is applied to user-defined classes. In the following example, each member of *source* is copied over the corresponding member in *destination:*

```
void fn()
{
    MyStruct source, destination;
    destination = source;
}
```

The default assignment operator works for most classes; however, it is not correct for classes that allocate resources, such as heap memory. The programmer must overload *operator=()* to handle the transfer of resources.

The assignment operator is much like the copy constructor (see Chapter 17). In use, the two look almost identical:

```
void fn(MyClass& mc)
{
    MyClass newMC(mc);      //of course, this uses the
                            //copy constructor
    MyClass newerMC = mc;   //less obvious, this also invokes
                            //the copy constructor
    MyClass newestMC;       //this creates a default object
    newestMC = mc;          //and then overwrites it with
                            //the argument passed
}
```

The creation of *newMC* follows the standard pattern of creating a new object as a mirror image of the original using the copy constructor *MyClass(const MyClass&)*. Not so obvious is that *newerMC* is also created using the copy constructor. *MyClass a = b* is just another way of writing *MyClass a(b)* — in particular, this declaration does *not* involve the assignment operator despite its appearance. However, *newestMC* is created using the default constructor and then overwritten with *mc* using the assignment operator.

TIP

The rule is this: The copy constructor is used when a new object is being created. The assignment operator is used if the left-hand object already exists.

Like the copy constructor, an assignment operator should be provided whenever a shallow copy is not appropriate. (Chapter 17 discusses shallow versus deep copy constructors.) A simple rule is to provide an assignment operator for classes that have a user-defined copy constructor.

Notice that the default copy constructor does work for classes that contain members that themselves have copy constructors, like in the following example:

```
class Student
{
  public:
    int nStudentID;
    string sName;
};
```

The C++ library class *string* does allocate memory off the heap, so the authors of that class include a copy constructor and an assignment operator that (one hopes) perform all the operations necessary to create a successful copy of a *string*. The default copy constructor for *Student* invokes the *string* copy constructor to copy *sName* from one student to the next. Similarly, the default assignment operator for *Student* does the same.

Overloading the Assignment Operator

The *DemoAssignmentOperator* program demonstrates how to provide an assignment operator. The program also includes a copy constructor to provide a comparison:

```
//DemoAssignmentOperator - demonstrate the assignment
//                          operator on a user defined class
#include <cstdio>
#include <cstdlib>
#include <iostream>
using namespace std;

// DArray - a dynamically sized array class used to
//          demonstrate the assignment and copy constructor
//          operators
class DArray
{
```

```cpp
public:
  DArray(int nLengthOfArray = 0)
    : nLength(nLengthOfArray), pArray(nullptr)
  {
      cout << "Creating DArray of length = "
           << nLength << endl;
      if (nLength > 0)
      {
          pArray = new int[nLength];
      }
  }
  DArray(DArray& da)
  {
      cout << "Copying DArray of length = "
           << da.nLength << endl;
      copyDArray(da);
  }
  ~DArray()
  {
      deleteDArray();
  }

  //assignment operator
  DArray& operator=(const DArray& s)
  {
      cout << "Assigning source of length = "
           << s.nLength
           << " to target of length = "
           << this->nLength << endl;

      //delete existing stuff...
      deleteDArray();
      //...before replacing with new stuff
      copyDArray(s);
      //return reference to existing object
      return *this;
  }

  int& operator[](int index)
  {
      return pArray[index];
  }

  int size() { return nLength; }

  void display(ostream& out)
  {
      if (nLength > 0)
      {
          out << pArray[0];
          for(int i = 1; i < nLength; i++)
```

```cpp
            {
                out << ", " << pArray[i];
            }
        }
    }

  protected:
    void copyDArray(const DArray& da);
    void deleteDArray();

    int nLength;
    int* pArray;
};

//copyDArray() - create a copy of a dynamic array of ints
void DArray::copyDArray(const DArray& source)
{
    nLength = source.nLength;
    pArray = nullptr;
    if (nLength > 0)
    {
        pArray = new int[nLength];
        for(int i = 0; i < nLength; i++)
        {
            pArray[i] = source.pArray[i];
        }
    }
}

//deleteDArray() - return heap memory
void DArray::deleteDArray()
{
    nLength = 0;
    delete pArray;
    pArray = nullptr;
}

int main(int nNumberofArgs, char* pszArgs[])
{
    // a dynamic array and assign it values
    DArray da1(5);
    for (int i = 0; i < da1.size(); i++)
    {
        // uses user defined index operator to access
        // members of the array
        da1[i] = i;
    }
    cout << "da1="; da1.display(cout); cout << endl;

    // now create a copy of this dynamic array using
    // copy constructor; this is same as da2(da1)
```

```
        DArray da2 = da1;
        da2[2] = 20;    // change a value in the copy
        cout << "da2="; da2.display(cout); cout << endl;

        // overwrite the existing da2 with the original da1
        da2 = da1;
        cout << "da2="; da2.display(cout); cout << endl;

        // wait until user is ready before terminating program
        // to allow the user to see the program results
        cout << "Press Enter to continue..." << endl;
        cin.ignore(10, '\n');
        cin.get();
        return 0;
}
```

The class *DArray* defines an integer array of variable length: You tell the class how big an array to create when you construct the object. It does this by wrapping the class around two data members: *nLength,* which contains the length of the array, and *pArray,* a pointer to an appropriately sized block of memory allocated off the heap.

The default constructor initializes *nLength* to the indicated length and then *pArray* to *nullptr.*

The *nullptr* keyword is new to the '11 standard. If your compiler doesn't recognize *nullptr,* you can add the following definition near the top of your program:

```
#define nullptr 0
```

If the length of the array is actually greater than 0, the constructor allocates an array of *int*'s of the appropriate size off the heap.

The copy constructor creates an array of the same size as the source object and then copies the contents of the source array into the current array using the protected method *copyDArray().* The destructor returns the memory allocated in the constructor to the heap using the *deleteDArray()* method. This method nulls out the pointer *pArray* once the memory has been deleted.

The assignment *operator=()* is a method of the class. It looks to all the world like a destructor immediately followed by a copy constructor. This is typical. Consider the assignment in the example *da2 = da1.* The object *da2* already has data associated with it. In the assignment, the original dynamic array must be returned to the heap by calling *deleteDArray(),* just like the *DArray* destructor. The assignment operator then invokes *copyDArray()* to copy the new information into the object, much like the copy constructor.

There are two more details about the assignment operator. First, the return type of *operator=()* is *DArray&,* and the returned value is always **this.* Expressions involving the assignment operator have a value and a type, both of which are taken from the final value of the left-hand argument. In the following example, the value of *operator=()* is *2.0,* and the type is *double.*

```
double d1, d2;
void fn(double);
d1 = 2.0;          // the type of this expression is double
                   // and the value is 2.0
```

This is what enables the programmer to write the following:

```
d2 = d1 = 2.0
fn(d2 = 3.0);      // performs the assignment and passes the
                   // resulting value to fn()
```

The value of the assignment *d1 = 2.0* (2.0) and the type *(double)* are passed to the assignment to *d2*. In the second example, the value of the assignment *d2 = 3.0* is passed to the function *fn()*, but the type of *operator=()* is matched to the declarations to find *fn(double)*.

A user-created assignment operator should support the same semantics as the intrinsic version:

```
fn(DArray&);       // given this declaration...
fn(da2 = da1);     // ...this should be legal
```

The second detail is that *operator=()* was written as a member function. The left-hand argument is taken to be the current object *(this)*. Unlike other operators, the assignment operator cannot be overloaded with a non-member function.

You can delete the default copy constructor and assignment operator if you don't want to define your own:

```
class NonCopyable
{
  public:
    NonCopyable(const NonCopyable&) = delete;
    NonCopyable& operator=(const NonCopyable&) = delete;
        };
```

An object of class *NonCopyable* cannot be copied via either construction or assignment:

```
void fn(NonCopyable& src)
{
    NonCopyable copy(src);    // not allowed
    copy = src;               // nor is this
}
```

If your compiler does not support the '11 extensions, you can declare the assignment operator protected:

```
class NonCopyable
{
  protected:
    NonCopyable(const NonCopyable&) {};
    NonCopyable& operator=(const NonCopyable&)
        {return *this};
};
```

If your class allocates resources such as memory off the heap, you *must* make the default assignment operator and copy constructors inaccessible, ideally by replacing them with your own version.

Overloading the Subscript Operator

The earlier *DemoAssignmentOperator* example program actually slipped in a third operator that is often overloaded for container classes: the subscript operator.

The following definition allows an object of class *DArray* to be manipulated like an intrinsic array:

```
int& operator[](int index)
{
    return pArray[index];
}
```

This makes an assignment like the following legal:

```
int n = da[0]; // becomes n = da.operator[](0);
```

Notice, however, that rather than return an integer value, the subscript operator returns a reference to the value within *pArray*. This allows the calling function to modify the value as demonstrated within the *DemoAssignmnentOperator* program:

```
da2[2] = 20;
```

You can see further examples of overloading the index operator for container classes in Chapter 27.

The Move Constructor and Move Operator

This entire subject is new to C++ '11.

Copy constructors and copy assignment operators are neat for retaining simple semantics for classes that you create. However, since their inception, C++ programmers have not been happy with the inefficiencies that they can create. Consider the following example:

```
MyContainer fn(int size)
{
    MyContainer localMC(size);
    return mc;
}

MyContainer mc(fn());
```

In this case, the function *fn()* creates a local *MyContainer* object *localMC* and then returns it to the caller by value. This simple call could result in the same *MyContainer* object being copied not once but twice:

1. As part of the return, C++ must make a temporary copy of the *localMC* object onto the return stack to return to the caller.

2. The subsequent call to the copy constructor copies the contents of this temporary object into the local *mc* object.

The second copy is unnecessary. Since the temporary object is about to be destructed anyway, the copy constructor could just "take" the assets away from the temporary object rather than go through the hassle of making a copy of something that's about to be put back on the heap anyway. This is the essence of the move constructor.

The move constructor looks like a copy constructor except for two things:

- ✔ A move constructor takes the resources from the source and gives them to the target rather than copying.

- ✔ The argument of the move constructor is of type *MyContainer&&,* the double ampersand meaning "only use for temporary values."

The following example program shows both the move constructor and move assignment operator in action:

```cpp
// DemoMoveOperator - demonstrate the move operator
#include <cstdio>
#include <cstdlib>
#include <iostream>
#include <cstring>

using namespace std;
class MyContainer
{
  public:
    MyContainer(int nS, const char* pS) : nSize(nS)
    {
        pString = new char[nSize];
        strcpy(pString, pS);
    }
    ~MyContainer()
    {
        delete pString;
        pString = nullptr;
    }

    //copy constructor
    MyContainer(const MyContainer& s)
    {
        copyIt(*this, s);
    }
    MyContainer& operator=(MyContainer& s)
    {
        delete pString;
        copyIt(*this, s);
        return *this;
    }

    // move constructor
    MyContainer(MyContainer&& s)
    {
        moveIt(*this, s);
    }
    MyContainer& operator=(MyContainer&& s)
    {
        delete pString;
        moveIt(*this, s);
        return *this;
    }

  protected:
    static void moveIt(MyContainer& tgt, MyContainer& src)
    {
        cout << "Moving " << src.pString << endl;
        tgt.nSize = src.nSize;
```

```
            tgt.pString = src.pString;
            src.nSize = 0;
            src.pString = nullptr;
        }
        static void copyIt(        MyContainer& tgt,
                            const MyContainer& src)
        {
            cout << "Copying " << src.pString << endl;
            delete tgt.pString;
            tgt.nSize = src.nSize;
            tgt.pString = new char[tgt.nSize];
            strncpy(tgt.pString, src.pString, tgt.nSize);
        }
        int nSize;
        char* pString;
};

MyContainer fn(int n, const char* pString)
{
    MyContainer b(n, pString);
    return b;
}

int main(int nNumberofArgs, char* pszArgs[])
{
    MyContainer mc(100, "Original");

    mc = fn(100, "Created in fn()");

    // wait until user is ready before terminating program
    // to allow the user to see the program results
    cout << "Press Enter to continue..." << endl;
    cin.ignore(10, '\n');
    cin.get();
    return 0;
}
```

The output from this program appears as follows:

```
Moving Created in fn()
Press Enter to continue...
```

The function *fn()* returns a temporary object that is moved over into the *mc* object using the move assignment operator, *operator=(MyContainer&&)*. The *moveIt()* function is a lot faster to execute than the *copyIt()* function would have been — it doesn't allocate memory off of the heap or copy anything. The *moveIt()* function simply takes the memory block from the *src* object which, in this case, is the temporary returned from *fn()*.

Make sure that you zero out the pointer in the *src* object; otherwise, the destructor will return the memory block to the heap, leaving the target object pointing to unallocated memory.

Chapter 23

Using Stream I/O

In This Chapter

▶ Performing input/output

▶ Rediscovering stream I/O as an overloaded operator

▶ Examining the other methods of the file class

▶ Using stream buffer I/O

*P*rograms appearing before this chapter read from the *cin* input object and output through the *cout* output object. Perhaps you haven't really thought about it much, but this input/output technique is a subset of what is known as *stream I/O*.

In this chapter, I describe stream I/O in more detail. I must warn you that stream I/O is too large a topic to be covered completely in a single chapter — entire books are devoted to this one topic. Fortunately for both of us, there isn't all that much that you need to know about stream I/O to write the vast majority of programs.

How Stream I/O Works

Stream I/O is based on overloaded versions of *operator>>()* and *operator<<()*. The declaration of these overloaded operators is found in the include file *iostream,* which are included in all the programs in this book beginning with Chapter 1. The code for these functions is included in the standard library, which your C++ program links with.

The following code shows just a few of the prototypes appearing in *iostream:*

```
//for input we have:
istream& operator>>(istream& source, char    *pDest);
istream& operator>>(istream& source, string &sDest);
istream& operator>>(istream& source, int     &dest);
istream& operator>>(istream& source, double &dest);
//...and so forth...
```

```
//for output we have:
ostream& operator<<(ostream& dest, char    *pSource);
ostream& operator<<(ostream& dest, string &sDest);
ostream& operator<<(ostream& dest, int     source);
ostream& operator<<(ostream& dest, double  source);
//...and so it goes...
```

When overloaded to perform I/O, *operator>>()* is called the *extractor* and *operator<<()* is called the *inserter.* The class *istream* is the basic class for input from a file or a device such as the keyboard. C++ opens the *istream* object *cin* when the program starts. Similarly, *ostream* is the basis for output. The prototypes above are for inserters and extractors for pointers to null terminated character strings (like "My name"), for *string* objects, for *ints*, and for *doubles*.

Default stream objects

C++ adds a chunk of code to the front of your program that executes before *main()* gets control. Among other things, this code creates the default input/output objects shown in Table 23-1.

Table 23-1		Standard Stream I/O Objects
Object	*Class*	*Purpose*
cin	*istream*	Standard *char* input
wcin	*wistream*	Standard *wchar_t* "wide char" input
cout	*ostream*	Standard char output
wcout	*wostream*	Standard *wchar_t* "wide char" output
cerr	*ostream*	Standard error output
wcerr	*wostream*	Standard error *wchar_t* "wide char" output
clog	*ostream*	Standard log
wclog	*ostream*	Standard *wchar_t* "wide char" log

You've seen *cin* and *cout* as they read input from the keyboard and output to the display, respectively. The user can reroute standard input and standard output to a file when he executes a program as follows:

```
C:>MyProgram <InputFile.txt >DefaultOut.txt
```

Here the operator is saying "Execute *MyProgram* but read standard input from *InputFile.txt* instead of the keyboard and send what would otherwise go to the standard output to the file *DefaultOut.txt.*"

Rerouting input and output works from the DOS prompt in Windows and under all versions of Unix and Linux. It's the easiest way to perform file input/output when you're trying to write something quick and dirty.

By default, the *cerr* object outputs to the display just like *cout,* except it is rerouted separately — rerouting *cout*-type default output to a file does not reroute *cerr* output. This allows a program to display error messages to the operator even if *cout* has been rerouted to a file.

Error messages should be sent to *cerr* rather than *cout* just in case the operator has rerouted standard output.

The *wcin, wcout,* and *wcerr* are wide version of standard input, output, and error, respectively. These are designed to handle Unicode symbols:

```
cout   << "This is narrow output" << endl;
wcout  << L"This is wide output"  << endl;
```

Stream Input/Output

The classes *ifstream* and *ofstream* defined in the include file *fstream* are sub-classes of *istream* and *ostream* designed to perform stream input and output to disk files. You can use the same extractors and inserters on *ifstream* and *ofstream* objects that you've been using on *cin* and *cout.*

The *ifstream* is actually an instantiation of the template class *basic_ifstream<T>* with *T* set to *char.* I discuss template classes in Chapter 26. The *basic_ifstream<T>* template class is instantiated with other types as well to provide different types of input classes. For example, the wide stream file class *wifstream* is based on the same *basic_ifstream<T>* with *T* set to *wchar_t.* The *ofstream* is the same as *basic_ofstream<char>*.

The classes *ifstream* and *ofstream* provide constructors used to open a file for input and output, respectively:

```
ifstream::ifstream(const char *pszFileName,
  ios_base::openmode mode = ios_base::in);
ofstream::ofstream(const char *pszFileName,
  ios_base::openmode mode = ios_base::out|ios_base::trunc);
```

The first argument is a pointer to the name of the file to open. The second argument specifies the mode. The type *openmode* is an integer type defined in *ios_base*. Also defined within *ios_base* are the possible values for *mode* listed in Table 23-2. These are bit fields that the programmer bitwise ORs together. (See Chapter 4 for an explanation of the ORing of bit fields.) The default mode for *ifstream* is to open the file for input with the pointer set to the beginning of the file (that's logical enough).

Table 23-2	Constants that Control How Files Are Opened
Flag	**Meaning**
ios_base::app	Seek to end-of-file before each write.
ios_base::ate	Seek to end-of-file immediately after opening the file, if it exists.
ios_base::binary	Open file in binary mode (alternative is text mode).
ios_base::in	Open file for input (implied for *istream*).
ios_base::out	Open file for output (implied for *ostream*).
ios_base::trunc	Truncate file, if it exists (default for *ostream*).

The default for *ofstream* is to open for output and to truncate the file if it exists already. The alternative to truncate is *ios_base::app,* which means append new output onto the end of the file if it exists already. Both options create a file if it doesn't already exist.

For example, the following *StreamOutput* program opens the file *MyName.txt* and then writes some important and absolutely true information to that file:

```
// StreamOutput - simple output to a file
#include <fstream>
using namespace std;

int main(int nNumberofArgs, char* pszArgs[])
{
    ofstream my("MyName.txt");
    my << "Stephen Davis is suave and handsome\n"
        << "and definitely not balding prematurely"
        << endl;
    return 0;
}
```

The destructor for the file stream classes automatically close the associated file. In my simple example, the *MyName.txt* file was closed when the *my* object went out of scope upon returning from *main()*. Global objects are closed as part of program termination.

Open modes

Table 23-2 shows the different modes that are possible when opening a file. However, you need to answer three basic questions every time you open a file:

✔ Do you want to read from the file or write to the file? Use *ifstream* to read and *ofstream* for writing. If you intend to both write to and read from the same file, use the *fstream* and set mode to *in | out,* but good luck — it's much better to write to a file completely and then close it and reopen it for reading as a separate object.

✔ If you are writing to the file and it already exists, do you want to add to the existing contents (in which case, open with *ate* set) or truncate the file and start over (in which case use *trunc*)?

✔ Are you reading or writing text or binary data? Both *ifstream* and *ofstream* default to text mode. Use *binary* mode if you are reading or writing raw, non-text data.

The primary difference between binary and text mode lies in the way that newlines are handled. The Unix operating system was written in the days when typewriters were still fashionable (when it was called "typing" instead of "keyboarding"). Unix ended sentences with a linefeed followed by a carriage return.

Subsequent operating systems saw no reason to continue using two characters to end a sentence, but they couldn't agree on which character to use. Some use the carriage return, others used the linefeed, now renamed newline. The C++ standard is the single newline.

When a file is opened in text mode, the C++ library converts the single newline character into what is appropriate for your operating system on output, whether it's a carriage return plus linefeed, a single carriage return, a linefeed, or something else entirely. It performs the opposite conversion while reading a file. The C++ library does no such conversions for a file opened in binary mode.

Always use binary mode when manipulating a file that's not in human-readable format. Otherwise, if a byte in the data stream just happens to be the same as a carriage return or a linefeed, the file I/O library will modify it.

Hey, file, what state are you in?

A constructed *fstream* object (including *ifstream* and *ofstream*) becomes a proxy for the file that it is associated with. For example, the stream object maintains state information about the I/O process. The member function *bad()* returns *true* if something "bad" happens. That nebulous term means that the file couldn't be opened, some internal object was messed up, or things are just generally hosed. A lesser error *fail()* indicates that either something *bad()* happened or the last read failed — for example, if you try to read an *int* and all the program can find is a character that rates a *fail()* but not a *bad()*. The member function *good()* returns *true* if both *bad()* and *fail()* are *false*.

Attempts to input from or output to a stream object that has an error set are ignored. The member function *clear()* zeros out the *fail* flag to give you another chance if the error is temporary — in general, *clear()* clears "failures" but not "bad" things. All attempts to output to an *ofstream* object that has an error have no effect.

This last paragraph is meant quite literally — no input or output is possible as long as the internal error state of the stream object you're using is non-zero. The program won't even try until you call *clear()* to clear the error flags if the error is temporary and you can clear it.

Can you show me an example?

The following example program demonstrates how to go about using the *ifstream* class to extract a series of integers:

```
// StreamInput - simple input from a file using fstream
#include <cstdio>
#include <cstdlib>
#include <fstream>
#include <iostream>
using namespace std;

ifstream& openFile()
{
    ifstream* pFileStream = 0;
    for(;;)
    {
        // open the file specified by the user
        string sFileName;
        cout << "Enter the name of a file with integers:";
        cin >> sFileName;

        //open file for reading
        pFileStream = new ifstream(sFileName.c_str());
```

```
        if (pFileStream->good())
        {
            pFileStream->seekg(0);
            cerr << "Successfully opened "
                 << sFileName << endl;
            break;
        }
        cerr << "Couldn't open " << sFileName << endl;
        delete pFileStream;
    }
    return *pFileStream;
}

int main(int nNumberofArgs, char* pszArgs[])
{
    // get a file stream
    ifstream& fileStream = openFile();

    // stop when no more data in file
    while (!fileStream.eof())
    {
        // read a value
        int nValue = 0;
        fileStream >> nValue;

        // stop if the file read failed (probably because
        // we ran upon something that's not an int or
        // because we found a newline with nothing after
        // it)
        if (fileStream.fail())
        {
            break;
        }

        // output the value just read
        cout << nValue << endl;
    }

    cout << "Press Enter to continue..." << endl;
    cin.ignore(10, '\n');
    cin.get();
    return 0;
}
```

The function *openFile()* prompts the user for the name of a file to open. The function creates an *ifstream()* object with the specified name. Creating an *ifstream* object automatically opens the file for input. If the file is opened properly, the function returns a reference to the *ifstream* object to use for reading. Otherwise, the program deletes the object and tries again. The only way to get out of the loop is to enter a valid filename or abort the program.

Don't forget to delete the *pFileStream* object if the open fails. These are the sneaky ways that memory leaks creep in.

The program reads integer values from the object referenced by *fileStream* until either *fail()* or the program reaches the end-of-file as indicated by the member function *eof()*.

Let me warn you one more time: Not only is nothing returned from reading an input stream that has an error, but also the buffer comes back unchanged. This program can easily come to the false conclusion that it has just read the same value it previously read. Furthermore, *eof()* will never return a *true* on an input stream that has an error.

Don't overflow that buffer!

If you look closely at the *openfile()* method in the StreamInput example program, you'll see yet another way to make sure that the operator doesn't overflow the character buffer. Let's review. I could have used something like the following:

```
char szFileName[80];   // any array size is possible
cin >> szFileName;     // input the name of the file to open
```

You can probably find code like this in the early chapters of this book (when you were still wearing your C++ training wheels). The problem with this approach is that nothing tells the extractor that the buffer is only 80 characters long — it will continue to read until it sees a newline, which might be thousands of characters later.

Well, 80 characters is a bit small. How about we increase the buffer size to 256 characters? That sort of misses the point; the implicit assumption you are making with this type of approach is that any buffer overflow is the result of an honest mistake (and a very long filename!). More and more this is not the case. Malicious users find ways to overflow these fixed size buffers all the time. Several major worms have been launched on the backs of buffer overflow attacks. (I will explain buffer overflows in detail in Chapter 28.)

One approach to avoiding buffer overflow that you have seen in earlier chapters is to use the *getline()* method to limit to the size of the buffer the number of characters that the program will read:

```
char szFileName[80];
cin.getline(szFileName, 80); // read not more than 80 chars
```

This code segment says read a line of input (up to the next newline character) but not more than 80 characters since that's the size of the buffer. Any characters not read are left for the next call to *getline()*.

Another approach is to make the buffer size fit the number of available characters. The extractor for the *string* class is smart enough to dynamically resize the buffer to fit the available data:

```
string sFileName;
cin >> sFileName; // string sizes buffer to fit amount of data
  input
```

The output from this program appears as follows (I added boldface to my input):

```
Enter the name of a file with integers:chicken
Couldn't open chicken
Enter the name of a file with integers:integers.txt
Successfully opened integers.txt
1
2
3
4
5
6
Press Enter to continue...
```

Code::Blocks for Windows opens the console application in the project directory so all you need to enter is the file name as shown. Code::Blocks for Macintosh opens the console window in your user directory so you need to enter the entire path to the file: `Desktop/CPP_Programs_from_Book/Chap23/StreamInput/integers.txt` (assuming that you installed the source files in the default location).

Other Methods of the Stream Classes

The *istream* and *ostream* classes provide a number of methods, as shown in Table 23-3 (this is not a complete list). The prototypes for these functions reside in the *fstream* include file. They are described in the remainder of this section.

Table 23-3 Major Methods of the I/O Stream Classes

Method	Meaning
`bool bad()`	Returns *true* if a serious error has occurred.
`void clear(iostate flags = ios_base::goodbit)`	Clears (or sets) the I/O state flags.
`void close()`	Closes the file associated with a stream object.
`bool eof()`	Returns *true* if no more characters are left in the file to be read.
`iostate exception()`	Returns the conditions that will cause an exception.

(continued)

Table 23-3 *(continued)*

Method	Meaning
`void exception(iostate)`	Sets the conditions that will cause an exception. Multiple conditions can be ORed together; e.g., *exception(ios_base::badbit|ios_base::failbit)*. See Chapter 24 for a discussion of exceptions.
`char fill()char fill` `(char newFill)`	Returns or sets the fill character.
`fmtflags flags()fmtflags` `flags(fmtflags f)`	Returns or sets format flags. (See the "Controlling format" section.)
`void flush()`	Flushes the output buffer to the disk.
`int gcount()`	Returns the number of bytes read during the last input.
`char get()`	Reads individual characters from the file.

`char getline(`
`   char* buffer,`
`   int count,`
`   char delimiter = '\n')`
	Reads multiple characters either until the end-of-file, until a delimiter is encountered, or until *count - 1* characters read. Tack a null onto the end of the line read. Do not store the delimiter read into the buffer.

`bool good()`	Returns *true* if no error conditions are set.

`void open( const char*`
`   filename, openmode`
`   mode = default)`
	Same arguments as the constructor. Performs the same file open on an existing object that the constructor performs when creating a new object.

`streamsize precision()`
`   streamsize precision(`
`   streamsize s)`
	Reads or sets the number of digits displayed for floating-point variables.

`ostream& put(char ch)`	Writes a single character to the stream.

`istream& read(`
`   char* buffer,`
`   streamsize num)`
	Reads a block of data. Reads either *num* bytes or until an end-of-file is encountered, whichever occurs first.

`istream& seekg(`
`   pos_type position)`
`istream& seekg(`
`   off_type offset,`
`   ios_base::seekdir)`
	Positions the read pointer either *position* bytes from the beginning of the file or *offset* bytes from the current position.

Method	Meaning

`istream& seekp(`
`  pos_type position)`
 	
`istream& seekp(`
`  off_type offset,`
`  ios_base::seekdir)`
	Positions the write pointer.

`fmtflags setf(fmtflags)`	Sets specific format flags. Returns old value.
`pos_type tellg()`	Returns the position of the read pointer.
`pos_type tellp()`	Returns the position of the write pointer.
`fmtflags unsetf(fmtflags)`	Clears specific format flags. Returns old value.
`int width()` `int width(int w)`	Reads or sets the number of characters to be displayed by the next formatted output statement.

`ostream& write(`
`  const char* buffer,`
`  streamsize num)`
	Writes a block of data to the output file.

Reading and writing streams directly

The inserter and extractor operators provide a convenient mechanism for reading formatted input. However, sometimes you just want to say, "Give it to me; I don't care what the format is." Several methods are useful in this context.

The simplest function, *get()*, just returns the next character in the input file. Its output equivalent is *put()*. The function *getline()* returns a string of characters up until some terminator — the default is a newline. *getline()* strips off the terminator but makes no other attempt to reformat or otherwise interpret the input.

The member function *read()* is even more basic. This function reads the number of characters that you specify, or less if the program encounters an end-of-file. The function *gcount()* always returns the actual number of characters read. The output equivalent is *write()*.

The following example program uses the *read()* and *write()* functions to create a backup of any file you give it by making a copy with the string ".backup" appended to the name:

```cpp
// FileCopy - make backup copies of the files passed
//            to the program
#include <cstdio>
#include <cstdlib>
#include <fstream>
#include <iostream>
using namespace std;

int main(int nNumberofArgs, char* pszArgs[])
{
    // repeat the process for every file passed
    for (int n = 1; n < nNumberofArgs; n++)
    {
        // create a filename and a ".backup" name
        string szSource(pszArgs[n]);
        string szTarget = szSource + ".backup";

        // now open the source for reading and the
        // target for writing
        ifstream input(szSource.c_str(),
                       ios_base::in|ios_base::binary);

        ofstream output(szTarget.c_str(),
          ios_base::out|ios_base::binary|ios_base::trunc);
        if (input.good() && output.good())
        {
            cout << "Backing up " << szSource << "...";

            // read and write 4k blocks until either an
            // error occurs or the file reaches EOF
            while(!input.eof() && input.good())
            {
                char buffer[4096];
                input.read(buffer, 4096);
                output.write(buffer, input.gcount());
            }
            cout << "finished" << endl;
        }
        else
        {
            cerr << "Couldn't copy " << szSource << endl;
        }
    }

    cout << "Press Enter to continue..." << endl;
    cin.ignore(10, '\n');
    cin.get();
    return 0;
}
```

The program iterates through the arguments passed to it, remembering that *pszArgs[0]* points to the name of the program itself. For every source file passed as an argument, the program creates the target filename by tacking ".backup" onto the end. It then opens the source file for binary input and the target for binary output, specifying to truncate the target file if it already exists.

If either the *input* or *output* object has an error set, the program outputs a "Couldn't copy" message without attempting to figure out what went wrong. If both objects are *good()*, however, the program enters a loop in which it reads 4K blocks from the *input* and writes them out to the *output*.

Notice that in the call to *write()*, the program uses the value returned from *gcount()* rather than hardcoding 4096. This is because, unless the source file just happens to be an integer multiple of 4096 bytes in length, the last call to *read()* will fetch less than the requested number of bytes before encountering end-of-file.

Controlling format

The *flags()*, *setf()*, and *unsetf()* methods are all used to set or retrieve a set of format flags maintained within the *istream* or *ostream* object. These format flags get set when the object is created to a default value that represents the most common format options. The options are shown in Table 23-4.

Table 23-4	The I/O Stream Format Flags
Flag	*If flag is true, then . . .*
boolalpha	Displays bool as either true or false rather than 1 or 0.
dec	Reads or writes integers in decimal format (default).
fixed	Displays floating point in fixed point as opposed to scientific (default).
hex	Reads or writes integers in hexadecimal.
left	Displays output left justified (i.e., pads on the right).
oct	Reads or writes integers in octal.
right	Displays output right justified (i.e., pads on the left).
scientific	Displays floating point in scientific format.
showbase	Displays a leading 0 for octal output and leading 0x for hexa-decimal output.

(continued)

Table 23-4 *(continued)*

Flag	If flag is true, then . . .
`showpoint`	Displays a decimal point for floating-point output even if the fractional portion is 0.
`skipws`	Skips over whitespace when reading using the extractor.
`unitbuf`	Flushes output after each output operation.
`uppercase`	Replaces lowercase letters with their uppercase equivalents on output.

The following code segment has been used in the past to display numbers in hexadecimal format (see the *BitTest* program in Chapter 4):

```
// read the current format flags
// (this is important when you need to restore the output
// format at a later time)
ios_base::fmtflags prevValue = cout.flags();

// clear the decimal flag
cout.unsetf(cout.dec);

// now set the hexadecimal flag
cout.setf(cout.hex);

// ...do stuff..

// call flags() to restore the format flags to their
// previous value
cout.flags(prevValue);
```

In this example, the program must both set the hexadecimal flags using *setf()* and unset (that is, clear) the decimal flag using *unsetf()* because the decimal, octal, and hexadecimal flags are mutually exclusive.

The final call to *flags()* restores the format flags to their previously read value. This is not necessary if the program is about to terminate anyway.

Further format control is provided by the *width()* method that sets the minimum width of the next output operation. In the event that the field does not take up the full width specified, the inserter adds the requisite number of fill characters. The default fill character is a space, but you can change this by calling *fill()*. Whether C++ adds the fill characters on the left or right is determined by whether the *left* or *right* format flag is set.

For example, the following segment

```
int i = 123;
cout.setf(cout.right);
cout.unsetf(cout.left);
cout.fill('+');
cout << "i = [";
cout.width(10);
cout << i;
cout << "]" << endl;
```

generates the following output:

```
i = [+++++++123]
```

Notice that the *width()* method applies only to the very next output statement. Unlike the other formatting flags, the *width()* must be reset after every value that you output.

What's up with endl?

Most programs in this book terminate an output stream by inserting the object *endl*. However, some programs include \n within the text to output a newline. What's the deal?

The \n is, in fact, the newline character. The expression *cout << "First line\ nSecond line;* outputs two lines. The *endl* object outputs a newline, but continues one step further.

Disks are slow devices. Writing to disk more often than necessary will slow down your program considerably. To avoid this, the *fstream* class collects output into an internal buffer known as a *cache* (pronounced like "cash"). The class writes the contents to disk when the buffer is full (this is known as *flushing the cache*). The *endl* object outputs a newline and then flushes the output cache. The member function *flush()* flushes the output cache without tacking a newline onto the end.

Note that the standard error object *cerr* does not buffer output.

Positioning the pointer within a file

The *istream* class maintains a read pointer that is the location within the file of the next byte to read. This is measured as "number of bytes from the beginning of the file." You can retrieve this using the *tellg()* method.

(Similarly, the *tellp()* returns a pointer to the next location to write in an *ostream* object.) Having saved off the location, you can later return to the same location by passing the value to *seekg()*.

An overloaded version of *seekg()* takes not an absolute position but an offset and a seek direction. The legal value for the seek direction is one of the following three constants:

- ✔ *ios_base::beg* (*beg* for *beginning of file*): The offset must be positive and is taken to be the number of bytes from the beginning of the file.

- ✔ *ios_base::end* (*end* for *end of file*): The offset must be negative and is taken to be the number of bytes from the end of the file.

- ✔ *ios_base::cur* (*cur* for *current position*): The offset can be either positive or negative and is the number of bytes to move the pointer (either forward or backward) from its current position.

Moving the read (or write) pointer around in a file can be very slow (in computer terms), so be judicious in the use of this feature.

Using the stringstream Subclasses

The stream classes give the programmer mechanisms for easily breaking input among *int, float,* and *char* array variables (among others). A set of so-called *stringstream* classes allow the program to read from an array of characters in memory as if it were reading from a file. The classes *istringstream* and *ostringstream* are defined in the include file *sstream*.

The older versions of these classes are *istrstream* and *ostrstream* defined in the include file *strstream*.

The *stringstream* classes have the same semantics as the corresponding file-based classes. This is demonstrated in the following *StringStream* program, which parses account information from a file:

```
// StringStream - read and parse the contents of a file
#include <cstdio>
#include <cstdlib>
#include <fstream>
#include <sstream>
#include <iostream>
using namespace std;
```

```
// parseAccountInfo - read a passed buffer as if it were
//                    an actual file - read the following
//                    format:
//                     name, account balance
//                    return true if all worked well
bool parseString(const char* pString,
                 char* pName, int arraySize,
                 long& accountNum, double& balance)
{
    // associate an istrstream object with the input
    // character string
    istringstream inp(pString);

    // read up to the comma separator
    inp.getline(pName, arraySize, ',');

    // now the account number
    inp >> accountNum;

    // and the balance
    inp >> balance;

    // return the error status
    return !inp.fail();
}

int main(int nNumberofArgs, char* pszArgs[])
{
    // must provide filename
    char szFileName[128];
    cout << "Input name of file to parse:";
    cin.getline(szFileName, 128);

    // get a file stream
    ifstream* pFileStream = new ifstream(szFileName);
    if (!pFileStream->good())
    {
        cerr << "Can't open " << pszArgs[1] << endl;
        return 0;
    }

    // read a line out of file, parse it and display
    // results
    for(int nLineNum = 1;;nLineNum++)
    {
        // read a buffer
        char buffer[256];
        pFileStream->getline(buffer, 256);
        if (pFileStream->fail())
        {
            break;
        }
```

```
        cout << nLineNum << ":" << buffer << endl;

        // parse the individual fields
        char name[80];
        long accountNum;
        double balance;
        bool result = parseString(buffer, name, 80,
                                  accountNum, balance);
        if (result == false)
        {
            cerr << "Error parsing string\n" << endl;
            continue;
        }

        // output the fields we parsed out
        cout << "Read the following fields:" << endl;
        cout << "   name = " << name << "\n"
             << "   account = " << accountNum << "\n"
             << "   balance = " << balance << endl;

        // put the fields back together in a different
        // order (inserting the 'ends' makes sure the
        // buffer is null terminated
        ostringstream out;
        out << name << ", "
            << balance << " "
            << accountNum << ends;

        string oString = out.str();
        cout << "Reordered fields: " << oString << endl;
    }

    cout << "Press Enter to continue..." << endl;
    cin.ignore(10, '\n');
    cin.get();
    return 0;
}
```

This program begins by opening a file called Accounts.txt containing account information in the format of *name, accountNumber, balance, \n*. Assuming that the file was opened successfully, the program enters a loop, reading lines until the contents of the file are exhausted. The call to *getline()* reads up to the default newline terminator. The program passes the line just read to the function *parseString()*.

parseString() associates an *istringstream* object with the character string. The program reads characters up to the '*,*' (or the end of the string buffer) using the *getline()* member function. The program then uses the conventional extractors to read *accountNum* and *balance*.

After the call to *parseString()*, *main()* outputs the buffer read from the file followed by the parsed values. It then uses the *ostringstream* class to reconstruct a *string* object with the same data but a different format (just for the fun of it).

The result from a sample execution appears as follows:

```
Input name of file to parse:Accounts.txt
1:Chester, 12345 56.60
Read the following fields:
   name = Chester
   account = 12345
   balance = 56.6
Reordered fields: Chester, 56.6 12345
2:Arthur,  34567 67.50
Read the following fields:
   name = Arthur
   account = 34567
   balance = 67.5
Reordered fields: Arthur, 67.5 34567
3:Trudie,  56x78 78.90
Error parsing string

4:Valerie, 78901 89.10
Read the following fields:
   name = Valerie
   account = 78901
   balance = 89.1
Reordered fields: Valerie, 89.1 78901
Press Enter to continue ...
```

Reflect a second before continuing. Notice how the program was able to resync itself after the error in the input file. Notice, also, the simplicity of the heart of the program, the *parseString()* function. Consider what this function would look like without the benefit of the *istringstream* class.

Manipulating Manipulators

You can use stream I/O to output numbers and character strings by using default formats. Usually the defaults are fine, but sometimes they don't cut it.

For example, I was less than tickled when the total from the result of a financial calculation from a recent program appeared as 249.600006 rather than 249.6 (or, better yet, 249.60). There must be a way to bend the defaults to my desires. True to form, C++ provides not one but two ways to control the format of output.

Depending on the default settings of your compiler, you may get 249.6 as your output. Nevertheless, you really want 249.60.

First, you can control the format by invoking a series of member functions on the stream object. For example, the number of significant digits to display is set by using the function *precision()* as follows (see Table 23-3):

```
#include <iostream>
void fn(double interest, double dollarAmount)
{
    cout << "Dollar amount = ";
    cout.precision(2);
    cout << dollarAmount;
    cout.precision(4);
    cout << interest << endl;
}
```

In this example, the function *precision()* sets the precision to *2* immediately before outputting the value *dollarAmount*. This gives you a number such as 249.60, the type of result you want. It then sets the precision to *4* before outputting the interest.

A second approach uses what are called manipulators. (Sounds like someone behind the scenes of the New York Stock Exchange, doesn't it?) *Manipulators* are objects defined in the include file *iomanip* to have the same effect as the member function calls. (You must include *iomanip* to have access to the manipulators.) The only advantage to manipulators is that the program can insert them directly into the stream rather than resort to a separate function call.

The most common manipulators and their corresponding meanings are shown in Table 23-5.

Table 23-5	Common Manipulators and Stream Format Control Functions	
Manipulator	*Member Function*	*Description*
dec	*setf(dec)*	Sets radix to 10
hex	*setf(hex)*	Sets radix to 16
oct	*setf(oct)*	Sets radix to 8
setfill(c)	*fill(c)*	Sets the fill character to *c*
setprecision(n)	*precision(n)*	Sets display precision to *n*
setw(n)	*width(n)*	Sets width of field to *n* characters*

* This returns to its default value after the next field is output.

If you rewrite the preceding example to use manipulators, the program appears as follows:

```
#include <iostream>
#include <iomanip>
void fn(double interest, double dollarAmount)
{
    cout << "Dollar amount = "
         << setprecision(2) << dollarAmount
         << setprecision(4) << interest << endl;
```

Chapter 24

Handling Errors — Exceptions

In This Chapter

▶ Introducing an exceptional way of handling program errors

▶ Finding what's wrong with good ol' error returns

▶ Examining throwing and catching exceptions

▶ Packing more heat into that throw

I know that it's hard to accept, but occasionally functions don't work properly — not even mine. The traditional means of reporting failure is to return some indication to the caller. C++ includes a mechanism for capturing and handling errors called *exceptions*. The handling of error conditions with exceptions is the subject of this chapter.

The exception mechanism is based on the keywords *try, catch,* and *throw* (that's right, more variable names that you can't use). In outline, it works like this: A function *trys* to get through a piece of code. If the code detects a problem, it *throws* an error indication that the calling function must *catch*.

The following code snippet demonstrates how that works in 1s and 0s:

```
//   FactorialException - demonstrate exceptions using
//                        a factorial function
//
#include <cstdio>
#include <cstdlib>
#include <iostream>
using namespace std;

// factorial - compute factorial
int factorial(int n)
{
    // you can't handle negative values of n;
    // better check for that condition first
    if (n < 0)
    {
        throw string("Argument for factorial negative");
    }
```

```
    // go ahead and calculate factorial
    int accum = 1;
    while(n > 0)
    {
        accum *= n;
        n--;
    }
    return accum;
}

int main(int nNumberofArgs, char* pszArgs[])
{
    try
    {
        // this will work
        cout << "Factorial of 3 is "
            << factorial(3) << endl;

        // this will generate an exception
        cout << "Factorial of -1 is "
            << factorial(-1) << endl;

        // control will never get here
        cout << "Factorial of 5 is "
            << factorial(5) << endl;
    }
    // control passes here
    catch(string error)
    {
        cout << "Error occurred: " << error << endl;
    }
    catch(...)
    {
        cout << "Default catch " << endl;
    }

    // wait until user is ready before terminating program
    // to allow the user to see the program results
    cout << "Press Enter to continue..." << endl;
    cin.ignore(10, '\n');
    cin.get();
    return 0;
}
```

main() starts out by creating a block outfitted with the *try* keyword. Within this block, it can proceed the way it would if the block were not present. In this case, *main()* attempts to calculate the factorial of a negative number. Not to be hoodwinked, the clever *factorial()* function detects the bogus request and throws an error indication using the *throw* keyword. Control passes to the *catch* phrase, which immediately follows the closing brace of the *try* block. The third call to *factorial()* is not performed.

Through a not-so-clever feature called an *exception specification,* you can add the type of objects that *factorial()* throws to its declaration. At one time, someone thought this would be a good idea, but times change. Exception specifications were never mandatory and have been deprecated in the 2011 standard. Exception specifications are not presented in this book.

Justifying a New Error Mechanism?

What's wrong with error returns like FORTRAN used to make? Factorials cannot be negative, so I could have said something like "Okay, if *factorial()* detects an error, it returns a negative number. The actual value indicates the source of the problem." What's wrong with that? That's how it was done for ages. ("If it was good enough for my grandpa. . .")

Unfortunately, several problems arise. First, although it's true that the result of a factorial can't be negative, other functions aren't so lucky. For example, you can't take the log of a negative number either, but logarithms can be either negative or positive. There's no value that a logarithm function can't return.

Second, there's just so much information that you can store in an integer. Maybe you can have –1 for "argument is negative" and –2 for "argument is too large." But, if the argument is too large, you want to know what the argument is because that information might help you debug the problem. There's no place to store that type of information.

Third, the processing of error returns is optional. Suppose someone writes *factorial()* so that it dutifully checks the argument and returns a negative number if the argument is out of range. If a function that calls *factorial()* doesn't check the error return, returning an error value doesn't do any good. Sure, you can make all kinds of menacing threats, such as "You will check your error returns or else," and the programmer may have the best of intentions, but you all know that people get lazy and return to their old, non-error-checking ways.

Even if you do check the error return from *factorial()* or any other function, what can the function do with the error? It can probably do nothing more than output an error message of its own and return another error indication to the caller, which probably does the same. Pretty soon, there's more error detection code than "real" code and it's all mixed together.

The exception mechanism addresses these problems by removing the error path from the normal code path. Furthermore, exceptions make error handling obligatory. If your function doesn't handle the thrown exception, control passes up the chain of called functions until C++ finds a function to handle the error. This also gives you the flexibility to ignore errors that you can't do anything about anyway. Only the functions that can actually handle the problem need to catch the exception.

Examining the Exception Mechanism

Take a closer look at the steps that the code goes through to handle an exception. When the throw occurs, C++ first copies the thrown object to some neutral place. It then begins looking for the end of the current *try* block.

If a *try* block is not found in the current function, control passes to the calling function. A search is then made of that function. If no *try* block is found there, control passes to the function that called it, and so on up the stack of calling functions. This process is called *unwinding the stack.*

An important feature of stack unwinding is that as each stack is unwound, objects that go out of scope are destructed just as though the function had executed a *return* statement. This keeps the program from losing assets or leaving objects dangling.

When the encasing *try* block is found, the code searches the first *catch* phrase immediately following the closing brace of the *catch* block. If the object thrown matches the type of argument specified in the *catch* statement, control passes to that *catch* phrase. If not, a check is made of the next *catch* phrase. If no matching *catch* phrases are found, the code searches for the next higher level *try* block in an ever-outward spiral until an appropriate *catch* can be found. If no *catch* phrase is found, the program is terminated.

Consider the following example:

```cpp
// CascadingException - the following program demonstrates
//                an example of stack unwinding
#include <cstdio>
#include <cstdlib>
#include <iostream>
using namespace std;

// prototypes of some functions that we will need later
void f1();
void f2();
void f3();

class Obj
{
  public:
    Obj(char c) : label(c)
    { cout << "Constructing object " << label << endl;}
    ~Obj()
    { cout << "Destructing object " << label << endl; }

  protected:
    char label;
};
```

```cpp
int main(int nNumberofArgs, char* pszArgs[])
{
    f1();

    // wait until user is ready before terminating program
    // to allow the user to see the program results
    cout << "Press Enter to continue..." << endl;
    cin.ignore(10, '\n');
    cin.get();
    return 0;
}

void f1()
{
    Obj a('a');
    try
    {
        Obj b('b');
        f2();
    }
    catch(float f)
    {
        cout << "Float catch" << endl;
    }
    catch(int i)
    {
        cout << "Int catch" << endl;
    }
    catch(...)
    {
        cout << string("Generic catch") << endl;
    }
}

void f2()
{
    try
    {
        Obj c('c');
        f3();
    }
    catch(string msg)
    {
        cout << "String catch" << endl;
    }
}

void f3()
{
    Obj d('d');
    throw 10;
}
```

The output from executing this program appears as follows:

```
Constructing object a
Constructing object b
Constructing object c
Constructing object d
Destructing object d
Destructing object c
Destructing object b
Int catch
Destructing object a
Press Enter to continue...
```

First, you see the four objects *a, b, c,* and *d* being constructed as *main()* calls *f1()* which calls *f2()* which calls *f3()*. Rather than return, however, *f3()* throws the integer 10. Because no *try* block is defined in *f3()*, C++ unwinds *f3()*'s stack, causing object *d* to be destructed. The next function up the chain, *f2()* defines a *try* block, but its only *catch* phrase is designed to handle a *string,* which doesn't match the *int* thrown. Therefore, C++ continues looking. This unwinds *f2()*'s stack, resulting in object *c* being destructed.

Back in *f1()*, C++ finds another *try* block. Exiting that block causes object *b* to go out of scope. C++ skips the first *catch* phrase for a *float.* The next *catch* phrase matches the *int* exactly, so C++ passes control to this phrase.

Control passes from the *catch(int)* phrase to the closing brace of the final *catch* phrase and from there back to *main()*. The final *catch(...)* phrase, which would catch any object thrown, is skipped because a matching *catch* phrase was already found.

What Kinds of Things Can I Throw?

The thing following the *throw* keyword is actually an expression that creates an object of some kind. In the examples so far, I've thrown an *int* and a *string* object, but *throw* can handle any type of object. This means you can throw almost as much information as you want. Consider the following update to the factorial program, *CustomExceptionClass*:

```
//
//  CustomExceptionClass - demonstrate the flexibility
//              of the exception mechanism by creating
//              a custom exception class
//
#include <cstdio>
#include <cstdlib>
#include <iostream>
#include <sstream>
using namespace std;
```

```cpp
// MyException - generic exception handling class
class MyException
{
  public:
    MyException(const char* pMsg, int n,
                const char* pFunc,
                const char* pFile, int nLine)
      : msg(pMsg), errorValue(n),
        funcName(pFunc), file(pFile), lineNum(nLine){}

    virtual string display()
    {
        ostringstream out;
        out << "Error <" << msg << ">"
            << " - value is " << errorValue << "\n"
            << "in function " << funcName << "()\n"
            << "in file " << file
            << " line #" << lineNum << ends;
        return out.str();
    }
  protected:
    // error message
    string msg;
    int    errorValue;

    // function name, file name and line number
    // where error occurred
    string funcName;
    string file;
    int lineNum;
};

// factorial - compute factorial
int factorial(int n) throw(MyException)
{
    // you can't handle negative values of n;
    // better check for that condition first
    if (n < 0)
    {
        throw MyException("Negative argument not allowed",
                          n, __func__, __FILE__, __LINE__);
    }

    // go ahead and calculate factorial
    int accum = 1;
    while(n > 0)
    {
        accum *= n;
        n--;
    }
    return accum;
}
```

```
int main(int nNumberofArgs, char* pszArgs[])
{
    try
    {
        // this will work
        cout << "Factorial of 3 is "
             << factorial(3) << endl;

        // this will generate an exception
        cout << "Factorial of -1 is "
             << factorial(-1) << endl;

        // control will never get here
        cout << "Factorial of 5 is "
             << factorial(5) << endl;
    }
    // control passes here
    catch(MyException e)
    {
        cout << e.display() << endl;
    }
    catch(...)
    {
        cout << "Default catch " << endl;
    }

    // wait until user is ready before terminating program
    // to allow the user to see the program results
    cout << "Press Enter to continue..." << endl;
    cin.ignore(10, '\n');
    cin.get();
    return 0;
}
```

This program appears much the same as the factorial program at the beginning of this chapter. The difference is the use of a user-defined *MyException* class that contains more information concerning the nature of the error than a simple string contains. The factorial program is able to throw the error message, the illegal value, and the exact location where the error occurred.

__FILE__, __LINE__, and __func__ are intrinsic #defines that are set to the name of the source file, the current line number in that file, and the name of the current function, respectively.

The catch snags the *MyException* object and then uses the built-in *display()* member function to display the error message. (See Chapter 23 for a review of how to use the *ostringstream* class to format an internal string.) The output from this program appears as follows:

```
Factorial of 3 is 6
Error <Negative argument not allowed> - value is -1
in function factorial()
in file C:\CPP_Programs_from_Book\Chap24\CustomExceptionClass\main.cpp line #52
Press Enter to continue...
```

Just Passing Through

A function that allocates resources locally may need to catch an exception, do some processing, and then rethrow it up the stack chain. Consider the following example:

```
void fileFunc()
{
    ofstream* pOut = new ofstream("File.txt");
    otherFunction();
    delete pOut;
}
```

As anyone who's read Chapter 8 knows, the memory allocated by *new* isn't returned to the heap automatically. If *otherFunction()* were to throw an exception, control would exit the program without invoking *delete,* and the memory allocated at the beginning of *fileFunc()* would be lost.

To avoid this problem, *fileFunc()* can include a *catch(...)* to catch any exception thrown:

```
void fileFunc()
{
    ofstream* pOut = new ofstream("File.txt");
    try
    {
        otherFunction();

        delete pOut;
    }
    catch(...)
    {
        delete pOut;
        throw;
    }
}
```

Within this phrase, *fileFunc()* returns the memory it allocated earlier to the heap. However, it is not in a position to process the remainder of the exception because it has no idea what could have gone wrong. It doesn't even know what type of object it just caught.

The *throw* keyword without any arguments rethrows the current exception object back up the chain to some function that can properly process the error.

Chapter 25

Inheriting Multiple Inheritance

In This Chapter

▶ Introducing multiple inheritance

▶ Avoiding ambiguities with multiple inheritance

▶ Avoiding ambiguities with virtual inheritance

▶ Figuring out the ordering rules for multiple constructors

▶ Getting a handle on problems with multiple inheritance

*I*n the class hierarchies discussed in other chapters, each class inherits from a single parent. Such single inheritance is sufficient to describe most real-world relationships. Some classes, however, represent the blending of multiple classes into one. (Sounds sort of romantic, doesn't it?)

An example of such a class is the sleeper sofa that creates the unbeatable combination of a harsh bed and an uncomfortable sofa. To adequately describe a sleeper sofa in C++, the sleeper sofa should be able to inherit both bed- and sofa-like properties. This is called *multiple inheritance.*

Describing the Multiple Inheritance Mechanism

Figure 25-1 shows the inheritance graph for class *SleeperSofa* that inherits both from class *Sofa* and from class *Bed.*

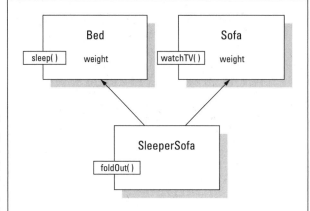

Figure 25-1:
Class hier-
archy of
a sleeper
sofa.

The code to implement class *SleeperSofa* looks like the following:

```cpp
//  MultipleInheritance - a single class can inherit from
//                        more than one base class
//
#include <cstdio>
#include <cstdlib>
#include <iostream>
using namespace std;

class Bed
{
  public:
    Bed(){}
    void sleep(){ cout << "Sleep" << endl; }
    int weight;
};

class Sofa
{
  public:
    Sofa(){}
    void watchTV(){ cout << "Watch TV" << endl; }
    int weight;
};

// SleeperSofa - is both a Bed and a Sofa
class SleeperSofa : public Bed, public Sofa
{
  public:
    SleeperSofa(){}
    void foldOut(){ cout << "Fold out" << endl; }

};
```

```
int main(int nNumberofArgs, char* pszArgs[])
{
    SleeperSofa ss;

    // you can watch TV on a sleeper sofa like a sofa...
    ss.watchTV();      // calls Sofa::watchTV()

    //...and then you can fold it out...
    ss.foldOut();      // calls SleeperSofa::foldOut()

    // ...and sleep on it
    ss.sleep();        // calls Bed::sleep()

    // wait until user is ready before terminating program
    // to allow the user to see the program results
    cout << "Press Enter to continue..." << endl;
    cin.ignore(10, '\n');
    cin.get();
    return 0;
}
```

Here the classes *Bed* and *Sofa* appear as conventional classes. Unlike in earlier examples, however, the class *SleeperSofa* inherits from both *Bed* and *Sofa*. This is apparent from the appearance of both classes in the class declaration. *SleeperSofa* inherits all the members of both base classes. Thus, both of the calls *ss.sleep()* and *ss.watchTV()* are legal. You can use a *SleeperSofa* as a *Bed* or a *Sofa*. Plus the class *SleeperSofa* can have members of its own, such as *foldOut()*. The output of this program appears as follows:

```
Watch TV
Fold out
Sleep
Press Enter to continue...
```

Is this a great country or what?

Straightening Out Inheritance Ambiguities

Although multiple inheritance is a powerful feature, it introduces several possible problems. One is apparent in the preceding example. Notice that both *Bed* and *Sofa* contain a member *weight*. This is logical because both have a measurable weight. The question is, "Which *weight* does *SleeperSofa* inherit?"

The answer is "both." *SleeperSofa* inherits a member *Bed::weight* and a separate member *Sofa::weight*. Because they have the same name, unqualified references to *weight* are now ambiguous. This is demonstrated in the following snippet, which generates a compile-time error:

```
#include <iostream>

void fn()
{
    SleeperSofa ss;
    cout << "weight = "
        << ss.weight    // illegal - which weight?
        << "\n";
}
```

The program must now indicate one of the two weights by specifying the desired base class. The following code snippet is correct:

```
#include <iostream>
void fn()
{
    SleeperSofa ss;
    cout << "sofa weight = "
        << ss.Sofa::weight  // specify which weight
        << "\n";
}
```

Although this solution corrects the problem, specifying the base class in the application function isn't desirable because it forces class information to leak outside the class into application code. In this case, *fn()* has to know that *SleeperSofa* inherits from *Sofa*. These types of so-called name collisions weren't possible with single inheritance but are a constant danger with multiple inheritance.

Adding Virtual Inheritance

In the case of *SleeperSofa,* the name collision on *weight* was more than a mere accident. A *SleeperSofa* doesn't have a bed weight separate from its sofa weight. The collision occurred because this class hierarchy doesn't completely describe the real world. Specifically, the classes have not been completely factored.

Thinking about it a little more, it becomes clear that both beds and sofas are special cases of a more fundamental concept: furniture. (I suppose I could get even more fundamental and use something like object with mass, but furniture is fundamental enough.) Weight is a property of all furniture. This relationship is shown in Figure 25-2.

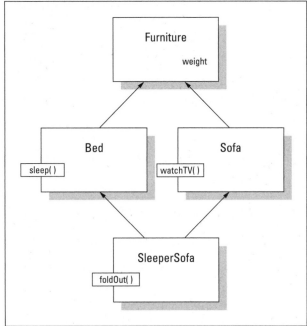

Figure 25-2:
Further
factoring of
beds and
sofas (by
weight).

Factoring out the class *Furniture* should relieve the name collision. With much
relief and great anticipation of success, I generate the C++ class hierarchy
shown in the following program, *MultipleInheritanceFactoring*:

```cpp
//  MultipleInheritanceFactoring - a single class can
//                   inherit from more than one base class
//
#include <cstdio>
#include <cstdlib>
#include <iostream>
#define TRYIT false
using namespace std;

// Furniture - more fundamental concept; this class
//             has "weight" as a property
class Furniture
{
  public:
    Furniture(int w) : weight(w) {}
    int weight;
};

class Bed : public Furniture
```

```
{
  public:
    Bed(int weight) : Furniture(weight) {}
    void sleep(){ cout << "Sleep" << endl; }
};

class Sofa : public Furniture
{
  public:
    Sofa(int weight) : Furniture(weight) {}
    void watchTV(){ cout << "Watch TV" << endl; }
};

// SleeperSofa - is both a Bed and a Sofa
class SleeperSofa : public Bed, public Sofa
{
  public:
    SleeperSofa(int weight) : Bed(weight), Sofa(weight) {}
    void foldOut(){ cout << "Fold out" << endl; }
};

int main(int nNumberofArgs, char* pszArgs[])
{
    SleeperSofa ss(10);

    // Section 1 -
    // the following is ambiguous; is this a
    // Furniture::Sofa or a Furniture::Bed?
#if TRYIT
    cout << "Weight = " << ss.weight << endl;
#endif

    // Section 2 -
    // the following specifies the inheritance path
    // unambiguously but it sort of ruins the effect
    SleeperSofa* pSS = &ss;
    Sofa* pSofa = (Sofa*)pSS;
    Furniture* pFurniture = (Furniture*)pSofa;
    cout << "Weight = " << pFurniture->weight << endl;

    // wait until user is ready before terminating program
    // to allow the user to see the program results
    cout << "Press Enter to continue..." << endl;
    cin.ignore(10, '\n');
    cin.get();
    return 0;
}
```

Imagine my dismay when I find that this doesn't help at all — the reference to *weight* in Section 1 of *main()* is still ambiguous. "Okay," I say (not really understanding why weight is still ambiguous), "I'll try casting *ss* to a *Furniture*."

```
#include <iostream.h>

void fn()
{
  SleeperSofa ss;
  Furniture* pF;
  pF = (Furniture*)&ss; // use a Furniture pointer...
  cout << "weight = "   // ...to get at the weight
       << pF->weight
       << "\n";
};
```

Casting *ss* to a *Furniture* doesn't work either. Now, I get some strange message that the cast of *SleeperSofa** to *Furniture** is ambiguous. What's going on?

The explanation is straightforward. *SleeperSofa* doesn't inherit from *Furniture* directly. Both *Bed* and *Sofa* inherit from *Furniture* and then *SleeperSofa* inherits from them. In memory, a *SleeperSofa* looks like Figure 25-3.

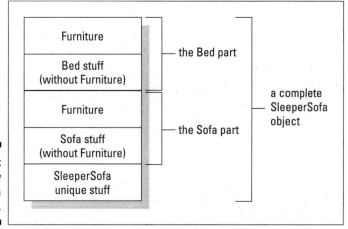

Figure 25-3:
Memory
layout of a
SleeperSofa.

You can see that a *SleeperSofa* consists of a complete *Bed* followed by a complete *Sofa* followed by some *SleeperSofa* unique stuff. Each of these sub-objects in *SleeperSofa* has its own *Furniture* part because each inherits from *Furniture*. Thus, a *SleeperSofa* contains two *Furniture* objects!

I haven't created the hierarchy shown in Figure 25-2 after all. The inheritance hierarchy I've actually created is the one shown in Figure 25-4.

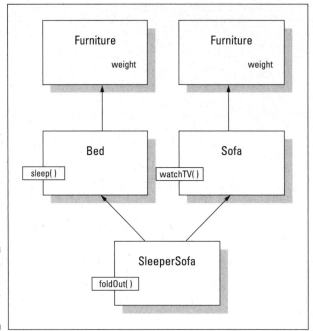

Figure 25-4:
Actual
result of my
first attempt.

The *MultipleInheritanceFactoring* program demonstrates this duplication of the base class. Section 2 specifies exactly which *weight* object by recasting the pointer *SleeperSofa* first to a *Sofa** and then to a *Furniture**.

But *SleeperSofa* containing two *Furniture* objects is nonsense. *SleeperSofa* needs only one copy of *Furniture*. I want *SleeperSofa* to inherit only one copy of *Furniture,* and I want *Bed* and *Sofa* to share that one copy. C++ calls this *virtual inheritance* because it uses the virtual keyword.

This is another unfortunate (in my opinion) overloading of a keyword.

Armed with this new knowledge, I return to class *SleeperSofa* and implement it as follows:

```
//  VirtualInheritance - using virtual inheritance the
//            Bed and Sofa classes can share a common base
//
#include <cstdio>
#include <cstdlib>
#include <iostream>
using namespace std;
```

```
// Furniture - more fundamental concept; this class
//             has "weight" as a property
class Furniture
{
  public:
    Furniture(int w) : weight(w) {}
    int weight;
};

class Bed : virtual public Furniture
{
  public:
    Bed(int w = 0) : Furniture(w) {}
    void sleep(){ cout << "Sleep" << endl; }
};

class Sofa : virtual public Furniture
{
  public:
    Sofa(int w = 0) : Furniture(w) {}
    void watchTV(){ cout << "Watch TV" << endl; }
};

// SleeperSofa - is both a Bed and a Sofa
class SleeperSofa : public Bed, public Sofa
{
  public:
    SleeperSofa(int w) : Furniture(w) {}
    void foldOut(){ cout << "Fold out" << endl; }
};

int main(int nNumberofArgs, char* pszArgs[])
{
    SleeperSofa ss(10);

    // the following is no longer ambiguous;
    // there's only one weight shared between Sofa and Bed
    // Furniture::Sofa or a Furniture::Bed?
    cout << "Weight = " << ss.weight << endl;

    // wait until user is ready before terminating program
    // to allow the user to see the program results
    cout << "Press Enter to continue..." << endl;
    cin.ignore(10, '\n');
    cin.get();
    return 0;
}
```

Notice the addition of the keyword *virtual* in the inheritance of *Furniture* in *Bed* and *Sofa*. This says, "Give me a copy of *Furniture* unless you already have one somehow, in which case I'll just use that one." A *SleeperSofa* ends up looking like Figure 25-5 in memory.

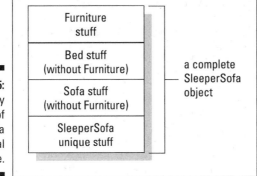

Figure 25-5:
Memory
layout of
SleeperSofa
with virtual
inheritance.

Furniture stuff

Bed stuff (without Furniture)

Sofa stuff (without Furniture)

SleeperSofa unique stuff

a complete SleeperSofa object

Here you can see that a *SleeperSofa* inherits *Furniture,* and then *Bed* minus the *Furniture* part, followed by *Sofa* minus the *Furniture* part. Bringing up the rear are the members unique to *SleeperSofa.* (Note that this may not be the order of the elements in memory, but that's not important for the purpose of this discussion.)

Now the reference in *fn()* to *weight* is not ambiguous because a *SleeperSofa* contains only one copy of *Furniture.* By inheriting *Furniture* virtually, you get the desired inheritance relationship as expressed in Figure 25-2.

If virtual inheritance solves this problem so nicely, why isn't it the norm? The first reason is that virtually inherited base classes are handled internally much differently than normally inherited base classes, and these differences involve extra overhead. The second reason is that sometimes you want two copies of the base class.

As an example of the latter, consider a *TeacherAssistant* who is both a *Student* and a *Teacher,* both of which are subclasses of *Academician.* If the university gives its teaching assistants two IDs — a student ID and a separate teacher ID — the class *TeacherAssistant* will need to contain two copies of class *Academician.*

Constructing the Objects of Multiple Inheritance

The rules for constructing objects need to be expanded to handle multiple inheritance. The constructors are invoked in the following order:

1. First, the constructor for any virtual base classes is called in the order in which the classes are inherited.

2. Then the constructor for all non-virtual base classes is called in the order in which the classes are inherited.

3. Next, the constructor for all member objects is called in the order in which the member objects appear in the class.

4. Finally, the constructor for the class itself is called.

Notice that base classes are constructed in the order in which they are inherited and not in the order in which they appear on the constructor line.

Voicing a Contrary Opinion

I should point out that not all object-oriented practitioners think that multiple inheritance is a good idea. In addition, many object-oriented languages don't support multiple inheritance.

Multiple inheritance is not an easy thing for the language to implement. This is mostly the compiler's problem (or the compiler writer's problem). But multiple inheritance adds overhead to the code when compared to single inheritance, and this overhead can become the programmer's problem.

More importantly, multiple inheritance opens the door to additional errors. First, ambiguities such as those mentioned in the section "Straightening Out Inheritance Ambiguities" pop up. Second, in the presence of multiple inheritance, casting a pointer from a subclass to a base class often involves changing the value of the pointer in sophisticated and mysterious ways. Let me leave the details to the language lawyers and compiler writers.

Third, the way in which constructors are invoked can be a little mysterious. Notice in the VirtualInheritance example that *SleeperSofa* must invoke the *Furniture* constructor directly. The *SleeperSofa* cannot initialize weight through either the *Bed* or the *Sofa* constructors.

I suggest that you avoid using multiple inheritance until you're comfortable with C++. Single inheritance provides enough expressive power to get used to.

One exception is that it's fairly safe to multiply inherit a class that contains only pure virtual methods and no data members. This is, in effect, C++'s implementation of what other languages such as Java and C# call an *interface*. The topic of interfaces is a bit beyond the scope of this book as it's not really a part of C++.

Chapter 26

Tempting C++ Templates

· ·

In This Chapter

▶ Examining how templates can be applied to functions

▶ Combining common functions into a single template definition

▶ Defining a template or class

▶ Implementing an initializer list for a user-defined class

· ·

*T*he standard C++ library provides a complete set of math, time, input/ output, and DOS operations, to name just a few. Many of the earlier programs in this book use the so-called character string functions defined in the include file *strings*. The argument types for many of these functions are fixed. For example, both arguments to *strcpy(char*, char*)* must be a pointer to a null-terminated character string — nothing else makes sense.

There are functions that are applicable to multiple types. Consider the example of the lowly *maximum()* function, which returns the maximum of two arguments. All of the following variations make sense:

```
int maximum(int n1, int n2); // return max of two integers
unsigned maximum (unsigned u1, unsigned u2);
double   maximum (double d1, double d2);
char     maximum (char c1, char c2);
```

I would like to implement *maximum()* for all four cases.

Of course, I could overload *maximum()* with all the possible versions:

```
double maximum(double d1, double d2)
{
    return (d1 > d2) ? d1:d2;
}
int maximum(int n1, int n2)
{
    return (n1 > n2) ? n1:n2;
}
```

```
char maximum(char c1, char c2)
{
    return (c1 > c2) ? c1:c2;
}

// ...repeat for all other numeric types...
```

This approach works. Now C++ selects the best match, *maximum(int, int)*, for a reference such as *maximum(1, 2)*. However, creating the same function for each type of variable is a gross waste of time.

The source code for all the *maximum(T, T)* functions follows the same pattern, where *T* is one of the numeric types. It would be so convenient if you could write the function once and let C++ supply the type *T* as needed when the function is used. In fact, C++ lets you do exactly this. These so-called *template definitions* are the subject of this chapter.

Generalizing a Function into a Template

A function template enables you to write something that looks like a function but uses one or more type holders that C++ converts into a true type at compile time.

The following MaxTemplate program defines a template for a generic *maximum()* function:

```
// MaxTemplate - create a template max() function
//               that returns the greater of two types
#include <cstdio>
#include <cstdlib>
#include <iostream>

using namespace std;

template <class T> T maximum(T t1, T t2)
{
    return (t1 > t2) ? t1 : t2;
}

int main(int argc, char* pArgs[])
{
    // find the maximum of two int's;
    // here C++ creates maximum(int, int)
    cout << "maximum(-1, 2) = "<<maximum(-1, 2) << endl;
```

```
    // repeat for two doubles;
    // in this case, we have to provide T explicitly since
    // the types of the arguments are different
    cout << "maximum(1, 2.5) = "<<maximum<double>(1, 2.5)
        << endl;

    cout << "Press Enter to continue..." << endl;
    cin.ignore(10, '\n');
    cin.get();
    return 0;
}
```

The keyword *template* is followed by angle brackets containing one or more type holders known as template parameters, each preceded by the keyword *class*, a constant, or both. In this case, the definition of *maximum<T>(T, T)* will call the "unknown type" *T*. Following the angle brackets is what looks like a normal function definition. In this case, the template function *T maximum<T>(T t1, T t2)* returns the larger of two objects *t1* and *t2*, each of which is of type *T*, where *T* is a class to be defined later.

A template function is useless until it is converted into a real function. C++ replaces *T* with an actual type known as a template argument. The *main()* function first invokes the template definition, passing two arguments of type *int*. In this case, C++ can instantiate the template providing *int* as the definition for *T*.

Creating a function from a template is called *instantiating* the template.

The second call is a problem — no single type can be provided for *T* in the template definition that matches both the *int* first argument and *double* second argument. Here the explicit reference instantiates the function *maximum(double, double)*. C++ promotes the *int* argument 1 to the *double* 1.0 before making the call.

The output from this program appears as follows:

```
maximum(-1, 2) = 2
maximum(1, 2.5) = 2.5
Press Enter to continue...
```

Be careful about terminology. For example, I used to be a hip, bad bicyclist, which is not the same thing as a bad hip bicyclist. Here's another example: A function template is not a function. The prototype for a function template is *maximum<T>(T, T)*. The function that this template creates when *T* is *int* is the function (not function template) *maximum(int, int)*. Your life will be easier if you remember to keep the terms straight.

Class Templates

C++ also allows the programmer to define class templates. A *class template* follows the same principle of using a conventional class definition with a placeholder for some unknown support classes. For example, the following *TemplateVector* program creates a vector for any class that the user provides. (A *vector* is a type of container in which the objects are stored in a row; an *array* is the classic vector example.)

I stored the *TemplateVector* class template definition in an include file called *templatevector.h* that appears as follows:

```cpp
// TemplateVector - a simple templatized vector class
template <class T>
class TemplateVector
{
  public:
    TemplateVector(int nArraySize)
    {
        // store off the number of elements
        nSize = nArraySize;
        array = new T[nArraySize];
        reset();
    }
    int size() { return nWriteIndex; }
    void reset() { nWriteIndex = 0; nReadIndex = 0; }
    void add(const T& object)
    {
        if (nWriteIndex < nSize)
        {
            array[nWriteIndex++] = object;
        }
    }
    T& get()
    {
        return array[nReadIndex++];
    }

  protected:
    int nSize;
    int nWriteIndex;
    int nReadIndex;
    T* array;
};
```

The following *TemplateVector* program includes and uses that template definition:

```cpp
// TemplateVector - implement a vector that uses a
//                  template type
#include <cstdlib>
#include <cstdio>
#include <iostream>
#include "templatevector.h"
using namespace std;

// intFn() - manipulate a collection of integers
void intFn()
{
    // create a vector of integers
    TemplateVector<int> integers(10);

    // add values to the vector
    cout << "Enter integer values to add to a vector\n"
         << "(Enter a negative number to terminate):"
         << endl;
    for(;;)
    {
        int n;
        cin  >> n;

        if (n < 0) { break; }
        integers.add(n);
    }

    cout << "\nHere are the numbers you entered:" << endl;
    for(int i = 0; i < integers.size(); i++)
    {
        cout << i << ":" << integers.get() << endl;
    }
}

// Names - create and manipulate a vector of names
class Name
{
  public:
    Name() = default;
    Name(string s) : name(s) {}
    const string& display() { return name; }
  protected:
    string name;
};
```

```
void nameFn()
{
    // create a vector of Name objects
    TemplateVector<Name> names(20);

    // add values to the vector
    cout << "Enter names to add to a second vector\n"
         << "(Enter an 'x' to quit):" << endl;
    for(;;)
    {
        string s;
        cin >> s;
        if (s == "x" || s == "X") { break; }
        names.add(Name(s));
    }

    cout << "\nHere are the names you entered" << endl;
    for(int i = 0; i < names.size(); i++)
    {
        Name& name = names.get();
        cout << i << ":" << name.display() << endl;
    }
}

int main(int argc, char* pArgs[])
{
    intFn();
    nameFn();

    cout << "Press Enter to continue..." << endl;
    cin.ignore(10, '\n');
    cin.get();
    return 0;
}
```

The class template *TemplateVector<T>* contains an array of objects of class *T*. The class template presents two member functions: *add()* and *get()*. The *add()* function adds an object of class *T* into the next empty spot in the array. The corresponding function *get()* returns the next object in the array. The *nWriteIndex* and *nReadIndex* members keep track of the next empty entry and the next entry to read, respectively.

The *intFn()* function creates a vector of integers with room for 10 with the declaration:

```
TemplateVector<int> integers(10);
```

The program reads integer values from the keyboard, saves them off, and then spits the values back out using the functions provided by *TemplateVector*.

The second function, *nameFn()*, creates a vector of *Name* objects. Again, the function reads in names and then displays them back to the user.

Notice that the *TemplateVector* handles both *int* values and *Name* objects with equal ease. Notice also the similarity between the *nameFn()* and *intFn()* functions, even though integers and names have nothing to do with each other.

A sample session appears as follows (I've bolded input from the keyboard):

```
Enter integer values to add to a vector
(Enter a negative number to terminate):
5
10
15
-1

Here are the numbers you entered:
0:5
1:10
2:15
Enter names to add to a second vector
(Enter an 'x' to quit):
Chester
Trude
Lollie
Bodie
x

Here are the names you entered
0:Chester
1:Trude
2:Lollie
3:Bodie
Press Enter to continue...
```

Tips for Using Templates

You should remember a few things when using templates. First, no code is generated for a template. (Code is generated after the template is converted into a concrete class or function.) This implies that a *.cpp* source file is almost never associated with a class template. The entire class template definition, including all the member functions, are usually contained in an include file so that it can be available for the compiler to expand.

Second, a class template does not consume memory. Therefore, there is no penalty for creating class templates if they are never instanced. On the other hand, a class template uses memory every time it is instanced (except as noted in the next section). Thus, the code for *Array<Student>* consumes memory even if *Array<int>* already exists.

Finally, a class template cannot be compiled and checked for errors until it is converted into a real class. Thus, a program that references the class template *Array<T>* might compile even though *Array<T>* contains obvious syntax errors. The errors won't appear until a class such as *Array<int>* or *Array<Student>* is created.

External Template Instantiations

The *TemplateVector* example program instanced *TemplateVector* twice: once for integers and once for *Name* objects. Once instanced, other functions within *main.cpp* could refer to *TemplateVector<int>* without incurring any further penalty. However, suppose my program included a second source module; say, *secondModule.cpp*. Now suppose that *secondModule.cpp* also made use of *TemplateVector<int>*. This second module would instantiate its own copy of *TemplateVector<int>*. For large programs, consisting of dozens of separate modules, this could mean recompiling dozens of copies of the same code. This can mean a lot of overhead both in compile time and in the size of the resulting code.

The 2011 standard adds the keyword *extern* to avoid this overhead. In this example, the programmer would include the following declaration somewhere near the beginning of *secondModule.cpp:*

```
extern template class TemplateVector<int>;
```

This says, "don't instantiate another copy of *TemplateVector<int>* because some other module has already instantiated one that you can use."

Implementing an Initializer List

Simple arrays can be initialized with an initializer list as shown here:

```
int myArray[] = {10, 20, 30, 40, 50};
```

The 2011 standard implements a class template known as *initializer_list<T>* that provides the same capability to user-defined containers.

The Macintosh version of Code::Blocks does not support initializer lists as of this writing.

C++ 2011 converts a list of objects contained within braces into a vector of class *initializer_list<T>*. The programmer can use this list to initialize a user-defined object. For example, the *TemplateVector* class in the *MyVector* program adds the following constructor:

```
class TemplateVector
{
  public:
    TemplateVector(const std::initializer_list<T> il) :
        TemplateVector(il.size())
    {
        // copy the contents of il into the vector
        for(const T* p = il.begin(); p < il.end(); p++)
        {
            add(*p);
        }
    }
    // ...the rest of the class is the same...
};
```

This allows the programmer to write the following:

```
// MyVector - demonstrate the use of initializer list
#include <cstdlib>
#include <cstdio>
#include <iostream>
#include "templatevector.h"
using namespace std;

int main(int argc, char* pArgs[])
{
    // the following two are equivalent
    // TemplateVector<int> myVector{10, 20, 30, 40, 50};
    TemplateVector<int> myVector = {10, 20, 30, 40, 50};

    for(int i = 0; i < myVector.size(); i++)
    {
        cout << i << " : " << myVector.get() << "\n";
    }

    cout << "Press Enter to continue..." << endl;
    cin.ignore(10, '\n');
    cin.get();
    return 0;
}
```

The list *{10, 20, 30, 40, 50}* is passed to the *TemplateVector(initializer_list<int>)* constructor. That constructor first allocates a vector of length 5 and then copies the contents of the initializer list into the vector. The output of this program appears as follows:

```
0 : 10
1 : 20
2 : 30
3 : 40
4 : 50
Press Enter to continue...
```

Chapter 27

Standardizing on the Standard Template Library

. . . .

In This Chapter

▶ Using the string class

▶ Maintaining entries in a Standard Template Library list

▶ Accessing container elements from an iterator

. . . .

Some programs can deal with data as it arrives and dispense with it. Most programs, however, must store data for later processing. A structure that is used to store data is known generically as a *container* or a *collection*. (I use the terms interchangeably.) This book has relied heavily on the array for data storage so far. The array container has a couple of nice properties: It stores and retrieves things quickly. In addition, the array can be declared to hold any type of object in a type-safe way. Weighed against these advantages, however, are two large negatives.

First, you must know the size of the array at the time it is created. This requirement is generally not achievable, although you will sometimes know that the number of elements cannot exceed some "large value." Viruses, however, commonly exploit this type of "it can't be larger than this" assumption, which turns out to be incorrect. There is no real way to "grow" an array except to declare a new array and copy the contents of the old array into the newer, larger version.

Second, inserting or removing elements anywhere within the array involves copying elements within the array. This is costly in terms of both memory and computing time. Sorting the elements within an array is even more expensive.

C++ now comes with the Standard Template Library, or STL, which includes many different types of containers, each with its own set of advantages (and disadvantages).

> The C++ Standard Template Library is a very large library of sometimes-complex containers. This session is considered just an overview of the power of the STL.

The string Container

The most common form of array is the null-terminated character string used to display text, which clearly shows both the advantages and disadvantages of the array. Consider how easy the following appears:

```
cout << "This is a string";
```

But things go sour quickly when you try to perform an operation even as simple as concatenating two of these null-terminated strings:

```
char* concatCharString(const char* s1, const char* s2)
{
    int length = strlen(s1) + strlen(s2) + 1;
    char* s = new char[length];
    strcpy(s, s1);
    strcat(s, s2);
    return s;
}
```

The STL provides a *string* container to handle display strings. The *string* class provides a number of operations (including overloaded operators) to simplify the manipulation of character strings (see Table 27-1). The same *concat()* operation can be performed as follows using *string* objects:

```
string concat(const string& s1, const string& s2)
{
    return s1 + s2;
}
```

Table 27-1	Major Methods of the *string* Class
Method	*Meaning*
string()	Creates an empty string object.
string(const char)*	Creates a string object from a null-terminated character array.
string(const string& s)	Creates a new string object as a copy of an existing string object *s*.
~string()	Destructor returns internal memory to the heap.

Method	Meaning
`string& operator=(const string& s)`	Overwrites the current object with a copy of the string *s*.
`istream& operator>>()`	Extracts a string from the input file. Stops when after *istream::width()* characters read, error occurs, EOF encountered, or white space encountered. Guaranteed to not overflow the internal buffer.
`ostream& operator<<()`	Inserts string to the output file.

`string operator+(const string& s1,`
`    const string& s2)`
`string operator+(const sring& s1,`
`    const char* pszS2)`
	Creates a new string that is the concatenation of two existing strings.

`string& operator+=(`
`    const string& s);`
`string& Operator+=(`
`    const char* pszS)`
	Appends a string to the end of the current string.

`char& operator[](size_ type index)`	Returns the *index*'th character of the current string.
`bool operator==(const string& s1,` `    const string& s2)`	Returns *true* if the two strings are lexicographically equivalent.
`bool operator<(const string& s1,` `    const string& s2)`	Returns *true* if *s1* is lexicographically less than *s2* (i.e., if *s1* occurs before *s2* in the dictionary).
`bool operator>(const string& s1,` `    const string& s2)`	Returns *true* if *s1* is lexicographically greater than *s2* (i.e., if *s1* occurs after *s2* in the dictionary).
`string& append(const string& s)` `string& append(const char* pszS)`	Appends a string to the end of the current string.
`char at(size_type index)`	Returns a reference to the *index*'th character in the current string.
`size_t capacity()`	Returns the number of characters the current string object can accommodate without allocating more space from the heap.
`int compare(const string& s)`	Returns < 0 if the current object is lexicographically less than *s*, 0 if the current object is equal to *s*, and > 0 if the current object is greater than *s*.

(continued)

Table 27-1 *(continued)*

Method	Meaning
`const char* c_str()` `const char* data()`	Returns a pointer to the null-terminated character array string within the current object.
`bool empty()`	Returns *true* if the current object is empty.

`size_t find(const`
`string& s,`
`    size_t index = 0);`
	Searches for the substring *s* within the current string starting at the *index*'th character. Returns the index of the substring. Return *string::npos* if the substring is not found.

`string& insert(size_t`
`index,`
`    const string& s)`
`string& insert(size_t`
`index,`
`    const char* pszS)`
	Inserts a string into the current string starting at offset *index*.

`size_t max_size()`	Returns the maximum number of objects that a string object can hold, ever.

`string& replace(size_t`
`index,`
`    size_t num,`
`    const string& s)`
`string& replace(size_t`
`index,`
`    size_t num,`
`    const char* pszS)`
	Replaces *num* characters in the current string starting at offset *index*. Enlarges the size of the current string if necessary.

`void resize(size_t size)`	Resizes the internal buffer to the specified length.
`size_t size()` `size_t length()`	Returns the length of the current string.

`string substr(size_t`
`index,`
`    size_t length)`
	Returns a string consisting of the current string starting at offset index and continuing for length characters.

The C++ '11 standard says that functions such as *max_size()* return a number of type *size_type*. I have listed the argument types in Table 27-1 as *size_t* because that's the way they are declared in the gcc compiler that comes with this book. Currently they are both synonyms for *unsigned long int*. Be forewarned that at some future date these two types might diverge and the argument types in Table 27-1 might change from *size_t* to *size_type*.

The following *STLString* program demonstrates just a few of the capabilities of the *string* class:

```
// STLString - demonstrates just a few of the features
//             of the string class which is part of the
//             Standard Template Library
#include <cstdlib>
#include <cstdio>
#include <iostream>
using namespace std;

// removeSpaces - remove any spaces within a string
string removeSpaces(const string& source)
{
    // make a copy of the source string so that we don't
    // modify it
    string s = source;

    // find the offset of the first space;
    // search the string until no more spaces found
    size_t offset;
    while((offset = s.find(" ")) != string::npos)
    {
        // remove the space just discovered
        s.erase(offset, 1);
    }
    return s;
}

// insertPhrase - insert a phrase in the position of
//                <ip> for insertion point
string insertPhrase(const string& source)
{
    string s = source;
    size_t offset = s.find("<ip>");
    if (offset != string::npos)
    {
        s.erase(offset, 4);
        s.insert(offset, "Randall");
    }
    return s;
}


int main(int argc, char* pArgs[])
{
    // create a string that is the sum of two strings
    cout << "string1 + string2 = "
         << (string("string 1") + string("string 2"))
         << endl;
```

```
// create a test string and then remove all spaces
// from it using simple string methods
string s2("This is a test string");
cout << "<" << s2 << "> minus spaces = <"
     << removeSpaces(s2) << ">" << endl;

// insert a phrase within the middle of an existing
// sentence (at the location of "<ip>")
string s3 = "Stephen <ip> Davis";
cout << s3 + " -> " + insertPhrase(s3) << endl;

cout << "Press Enter to continue..." << endl;
cin.ignore(10, '\n');
cin.get();
return 0;
}
```

The *main()* function begins by using *operator+()* to append two strings together. *main()* then calls the *removeSpaces()* method to remove any spaces found in the string provided. It does this by using the *string.find()* operation to return the offset of the first " " that it finds. Once found, *removeSpaces()* uses the *erase()* method to remove the space. The function picks up where it left off, searching for spaces and erasing them until *find()* returns *npos,* indicating that it didn't find what it was looking for.

The constant *npos* is a constant of type *size_t* that is the largest unsigned value possible. It is numerically equal to −1. This is used for the "not found position" just like '\0' is the "non-character."

The *insertPhrase()* method uses the *find()* method to find the insertion point flagged by the substring *"<ip>"*. The function then calls *erase* to remove the *"<ip>"* flag and *string.insert()* to insert a new string in the middle of an existing string.

The resulting output is as follows:

```
string1 + string2 = string1string2
<this is a test string> minus spaces = <thisisateststring>
Stephen <ip> Davis -> Stephen Randall Davis
Press Enter to continue...
```

At its core, a *string* is still an array. The operations provided by the STL make it easier to manipulate *string* objects but not that much faster. Inserting into the middle of a *string* still involves moving the contents of arrays around.

The *string* class is actually an instantiation of the class template *basic_class<T>* with *T* set to *char.* The *wstring* class is another name for *basic_class<wchar_t>*. This class provides the same character manipulations shown here for wide strings. The C++ '11 definition adds *u16string* and *u32string,* which extends the string manipulation methods to UTF-16 and UTF-32 character strings. All comparisons between two string objects are performed lexicographically — that is, which of the two strings would appear first in the dictionary of the current language.

Iterating through Lists

The Standard Template Library provides a large number of containers — many more than I can describe in a single chapter. However, I provide here a description of one of the more useful families of containers.

The STL *list* container retains objects by linking them like Lego blocks. (Chapter 13 shows a simplistic implementation of a linked list.) Objects can be snapped apart and snapped back together in any order. This makes the *list* ideal for inserting objects and sorting, merging, and otherwise rearranging objects. Table 27-2 shows some of the methods of the *list* containers.

Table 27-2	Major Methods of the *list* Template Class
Method	**Meaning**
`list<T>()`	Creates an empty list of objects of class *T*.
`~list<T>()`	Destructs the list, including invoking the destructor on any *T* objects remaining in the list.
`list operator=(const list<T>& l)`	Replaces the contents of the current list with copies of the objects in list *l*.
`bool operator==(const list<T>& l1, const list<T>& l2)`	Performs a lexicographic comparison between each element in the two lists.
`list<T>::iterator begin()`	Returns an iterator that points to the first element in the current list.
`void clear()`	Removes and destructs every object in the current list.
`bool empty()`	Returns *true* if the current list is empty.
`list<T>::iterator end()`	Returns an iterator that points to the next entry beyond the end of the current list.
`list<T>::iterator insert( list<T>::iterator loc, const T& object)`	Adds *object* to the list at the position pointed at by the iterator *loc*. Returns an iterator that points to the added object.
`void pop_back() void pop_front()`	Removes the last or first object from the current list.

(continued)

Table 27-2 (continued)

Method	Meaning
`void push_back(const T& object)` `void push_front(const T& object)`	Adds an object to the end or front of the current list.
`list<T>::reverse_ iterator rbegin()`	Returns an iterator that points to the last entry in the list (useful when iterating backward through the list, starting at the end and working toward the beginning).
`list<T>::reverse_ iterator rend()`	Returns an iterator that points to the entry before the first entry in the list (useful when iterating backwards through the list).
`void remove(const T& object)`	Removes all objects from the current list that are the same as *object* (as determined by *operator==(T&, T&)*).
`size_t size()`	Returns the number of entries in the current list.
`void sort()`	Sorts the current list such that each object in the list is less than the next object as determined by *operator<(T&, T&)*.
`void splice(list<T>::iterator pos, list<T>& source)`	Removes the objects from the *source* list and adds them to the current list in front of the object referenced by *pos*.
`void unique()`	Removes any subsequent equal objects (as determined by *operator==(T&, T&)*).

The constructor for *list<T>* creates an empty list. Objects can be added either to the front or end of the list using *push_front()* or *push_back()*. For example, the following code snippet creates an empty list of *Student* objects and adds two students to the list:

```
list<Student> students;
students.push_back(Student("Dewie Cheatum"));
students.push_back(Student("Marion Haste"));
```

Making your way through a list

The programmer iterates through an array by providing the index of each element. However, this technique doesn't work for containers like *list* that don't allow for random access. One could imagine a solution based in methods such as *getFirst()* and *getNext();* however, the designers of the Standard Template Library wanted to provide a common method for traversing any type of container. For this, the Standard Template Library defines the iterator.

An *iterator* is an object that points to the members of a container. In general, every iterator supports the following functions:

- ✔ A class can return an iterator that points to the first member of the collection.
- ✔ The iterator can be moved from one member to the next.
- ✔ The iterator returns an indication when it reaches the end of the list.
- ✔ The program can retrieve the element pointed to by the iterator.

The Standard Template Library also provides reverse iterators for moving backward through lists. Everything I say about iterators applies equally for reverse iterators.

The code necessary to iterate through a *list* is different from that necessary to traverse a *vector* (to name just two examples). However, the iterator hides these details.

The method *begin()* returns an iterator that points to the first element of a list. The indirection *operator*()* retrieves a reference to the object pointed at by the iterator. The ++ operator moves the iterator to the next element in the list. A program continues to increment its way through the list until the iterator is equal to the value returned by *end()*. The following code snippet starts at the beginning of a list of students and displays each of their names:

```
void displayStudents(list<Student>& students)
{
    // allocate an iterator that points to the first
    // element in the list
    list<Student>::iterator iter = students.begin();

    // continue to loop through the list until the
    // iterator hits the end of the list
    while(iter != students.end())
    {
        // retrieve the Student the iterator points at
        Student& s = *iter;
        cout << s.sName << endl;

        // now move the iterator over to the next element
        // in the list
        iter++;
    }
}
```

Declarations for iterators can get very complex. This is probably the best justification for the *auto* declaration introduced with the '11 standard:

```
for(auto iter = students.begin(); iter != students.end(); iter++)
{
    cout << iter->sName << endl;
}
```

This declares *iter* to be an iterator of whatever type is returned by the method *list<Student>::begin()*, avoiding the tortured declarations shown in the earlier code snippet. How cool is that!

Operations on an entire list

The STL library defines certain operations on the entire list. For example, the *list<T&>::sort()* method says "I'll sort the list for you if you'll just tell me which objects go first." You do this by defining *operator<(const T&, const T&)*. This operator is already defined for the intrinsic types and many library classes such as *string*. For example, you don't have to do anything to sort a list of integers:

```
list<int> scores;
scores.push_back(10);
scores.push_back(1);
scores.push_back(5);
scores.sort();
```

The programmer must define her own comparison operator for her own classes if she wants C++ to sort them. For example, the following comparison sorts *Student* objects by their student ID:

```
bool operator<(const Student& s1, const Student& s2)
{
    return s1.ssID < s2.ssID;
}
```

Can you show me an example?

The following *STLListStudents* program demonstrates several functions you've seen in this section. It creates a list of user-defined *Student* objects, iterates the list, and sorts the list.

The program appears as follows:

```
// STLListStudents - use a list to contain and sort a
//                   user defined class
#include <cstdio>
#include <cstdlib>
#include <iostream>
#include <list>

using namespace std;

// Student - some example user defined class
class Student
{
  public:
    Student(const char* pszS, int id)
      : sName(pszS), ssID(id) {}
    string sName;
    int ssID;
};

// the following function is required to support the
// sort operation
bool operator<(const Student& s1, const Student& s2)
{
    return s1.ssID < s2.ssID;
}

// displayStudents - iterate through the list displaying
//                   each element
void displayStudents(list<Student>& students)
{
    // allocate an iterator that points to the first
    // element in the list
    // list<Student>::iterator iter = students.begin();
    auto iter = students.begin();

    // continue to loop through the list until the
    // iterator hits the end of the list
    while(iter != students.end())
    {
        // retrieve the Student the iterator points at
        Student& s = *iter;
        cout << s.ssID << " - " << s.sName << endl;

        // now move the iterator over to the next element
        // in the list
        iter++;
    }
}
```

```
int main(int argc, char* pArgs[])
{
    // define a collection of students
    list<Student> students;

    // add three student objects to the list
    students.push_back(Student("Marion Haste", 10));
    students.push_back(Student("Dewie Cheatum", 5));
    students.push_back(Student("Stew Dent", 15));

    // display the list
    cout << "The original list:" << endl;
    displayStudents(students);

    // now sort the list and redisplay
    students.sort();
    cout << "\nThe sorted list:" << endl;
    displayStudents(students);

    cout << "Press Enter to continue..." << endl;
    cin.ignore(10, '\n');
    cin.get();
    return 0;
}
```

This program defines a list of user-defined *Student* objects. Three calls to *push_back()* add elements to the list (hard-coding these calls keeps the program smaller). The program then calls *displayStudents()* to display the contents of the list both before and after the list has been sorted using the template library *sort()* function.

The output of this program appears as follows:

```
The original list:
10 - Marion Haste
5 - Dewie Cheatum
15 - Stew Dent

The sorted list:
5 - Dewie Cheatum
10 - Marion Haste
15 - Stew Dent
Press Enter to continue...
```

The iterator *iter* is declared twice in this program. Use the *auto* version if your compiler is compliant with the 2011 standard. Comment out that line and uncomment the more complicated declaration before it, if not.

Chapter 28

Writing Hacker-Proof Code

• •

In This Chapter

▶ How to avoid becoming a soldier in someone's botnet army

▶ Getting a handle on SQL injection

▶ Understanding buffer overflow hacks

▶ Defensive programming against buffer overflows

▶ Getting a little help from the operating system

• •

*I*n the interest of full disclosure, I should admit right now: I'm not sure that it's possible to write hacker-proof code. Those slippery devils always seem to find a way. But by knowing some of their tricks and how to counter them, you can write programs that are very hacker resistant.

There is more to hacker-proofing that just writing code. Program protection takes a multitude of forms which I describe in Chapter 30. However, since this book is about writing programs, after all, and since code writing is probably the most important component to hacker-proofing, let's start there.

Understanding the Hacker's Motives

Why would a hacker want to break into one of the lowly C++ console programs presented in this book? The short answer is, "He wouldn't." The programs in this book are all written to be executed from the keyboard at normal user privileges. If the user can get to the keyboard to execute one of these programs, then he can execute any other command that he wants. He doesn't need to resort to hacks.

Think a little further into the future, however. After you've finished this book and sharpened your C++ skills, you land that really sweet job that you were looking for at the, hmmm, at the bank. Yeah, that's the ticket. You're a big-time programmer at the bank, and you've just finished writing the back-end code for some awesome ledger application that customers use to balance their accounts. Performance is great because it's C++, and the customers love it. You're looking forward to that big bonus that's surely coming your way.

Then you get called to the Department Vice President's office. Seems that hackers have found a way to get into your program from its interface to the Internet and transferred money from other peoples' accounts into their own. Millions have been lost. Disaster! No bonus. No promotion. Nobody will sit with you in the cafeteria. Your kids get bullied on the playground. You'll be lucky to keep your now greatly reduced job.

The point of this story is that real world programs often have multiple interfaces unlike the simple programs in this book. For example, any program that reads a port or connects to a database is susceptible to being hacked.

What is the hacker after:

- If you're lucky, the hacker is doing nothing more than exploiting some flaw in your program's logic to cause it to crash. As long as the program is crashed, no one else can use it. This is called a *Denial of Service (DoS)* attack because it denies the service provided by your program to everyone else.

 DoS attacks can be expensive because they can cost your company lost revenue from business that doesn't get conducted or customers who give up in frustration because your program is not taking calls right now. And this doesn't even include the cost of someone going into the code to find and fix the susceptibility.

- Some hackers are trying to get access to information that your program has access to but to which the user has no right. A good example of this would be *identify theft*.

 The loss of information is more than embarrassing as a good hacker may be able to use this information to turn around and steal. For example, armed with the proper credentials, the hacker can then call up a bank teller on the phone and order sums of money be transferred from our hacked customers' accounts to his own where he can subsequently withdraw the funds. This is commonly the case with SQL injection attacks, which I describe in the following section.

- Finally, some hackers are after remote control of your computer. If your program opens a connection to the Internet and a hacker can get your program to execute the proper system calls, that hacker can turn your program into a remote terminal into your system. From there, the hacker can download his own program onto your machine, and from then on you are said to be *owned*.

 Perhaps the hacker wants access to your accounts, where he can steal money, or maybe he just wants your computer itself. This is the case with groups of owned computers that make up what is known as a *botnet*.

 But how does this work? Your bank program has a very limited interface. It asks the user for his account number, his name, and the amount of his deposit. Nowhere does it say, "Would you like to take over this computer?" or "What extra code would you like this computer to execute?"

A bot-what?

The term *botnet* is a contract of "robot network," meaning a network of roboted (also called *zombie*) computers. A zombied computer runs along like normal as long as it's not needed. It can run spreadsheets and Code::Blocks and whatever else, but sitting deep in the background is a backdoor that's open to the person with the proper program and the passwords — the botnet master.

When the botnet master decides he needs the zombie computer, he sends commands to his slave, and it dutifully starts carrying out the master's instructions. The owner of the zombied computer may not even notice that there's anything wrong, other than the fact that his computer runs kind of slow sometimes.

Botnets can do lots of things, but one of their best tricks is to swamp legitimate Web sites with bogus requests in another form of Denial of Service attack. Suppose, for example, that you don't like the Brotherhood of Aryan Goatherders, and you want to bring down their BAG site so that no one can read their lies. You try to swamp the site with requests from your computer, but you can't because the BAG's computer is just as fast as yours. So you buy four or five computers and have all of them hit their Web site at once. That works for a few minutes, but it doesn't take long to figure out that all these requests are coming from just a few source IP addresses, so the system administrator for the Brotherhood (very unfairly) blocks requests from your PCs!

But what if you could rent the services of a botnet army consisting of thousands of PCs all over the world? Each computer has to generate only a few requests per second in order to bring the BAG site completely to its knees. And what can the system administrator do about it? He can't block every PC he sees without blocking legitimate users of the site. The BAG might as well just give up and close the site down.

The two most common hacker tricks that you must deal with in your code are code injection and buffer overflow.

Understanding Code Injection

Code injection occurs when the user entices your program to execute some piece of user-created code. "What? My program would never do that!" you say. Consider the most common and, fortunately for us, easiest to understand variant of this little scam: SQL injection.

Examining an example SQL injection

Let me start with a few facts about SQL:

- ✔ *SQL* (often pronounced "sequel") stands for Structured Query Language.
- ✔ SQL is the most common language for accessing databases.

    ✔ SQL is used almost universally in accessing relational databases.

    ✔ SQL is not the subject of this book.

This last bullet is important because I have no intent of teaching you SQL just so you can follow the examples presented here. If you don't already know SQL, it's sufficient to say that SQL is often interpreted at runtime. Very often, C++ statements will send an SQL query to a separate database server and then process and display whatever the server sends back. A typical SQL query within a C++ program might look like the following:

```
char* query = "SELECT * FROM transactions WHERE
          accountID='123456789';"
results = submit(query);
```

This code says, "*SELECT* all of the fields *FROM* the transactions table *WHERE* the *accountID* (presumably one of the fields in the transaction table) is equal to 123456789 (the user's account id)." The *submit()* library function might send this query off to the database server. The database server would respond with all of the data it has on every transaction that the user has ever made on this account, which would get stored into the collection *results.* The program would then iterate through *results,* probably displaying the transactions in a table with each transaction on a separate row.

The user probably doesn't need that much data. Maybe just those transactions between *startDate* and *endDate,* two variables that the program reads from the user's query page. This more selective C++ program might contain a statement like the following:

```
char* query = "SELECT * FROM transactions WHERE
          accountID='123456789'"
      " AND date > '" + startDate + "' AND date < '" +
          endDate + "';";
```

If the user enters **2013/10/1** for a *startDate* and **2013/11/1** for *endDate,* then the resulting query that gets sent to the database is the following:

```
SELECT * FROM transactions WHERE accountID='123456789' AND
          date > '2013/10/1' AND date < '2013/11/1';
```

In other words, show all the transactions made in the month of October 2013. That makes sense. What's the problem?

The problem arises if the program just accepts whatever the user enters as start and end dates and plugs them into the query. It doesn't do any checking to make sure that the user is entering just a date and nothing but a date. This program is far too trusting.

What if a hacker were to enter **2013/10/1** for the *startDate,* but for the *end-Date* he were to enter something like **2013/11/1' OR accountID='234567890**. (Notice the unbalanced single quotes.) Now the combined SQL query that gets sent to the database server would look like

```
SELECT * FROM transactions WHERE accountID='123456789' AND
       date > '2013/10/1' AND date < '2013/11/1' OR
       accountID='234567890';
```

This says, "Show me all the transactions for the account 123456789 for the month of October 2013, plus all the transactions for some other account 234567890 that I don't own for any date."

This little example may raise a few questions in the reader's mind: "How did the hacker know that he could enter SQL statements in place of dates?" He doesn't know — he just tries entering bogus SQL into every field that accepts character text and sees what happens. If the program complains, "That's not a legal date," then the hacker knows that the program checks to make sure that input dates are valid and SQL injection won't work here. If, on the other hand, the program displays an error message like *Illegal SQL statement,* then the hacker knows that the program accepted the bogus input and shipped it off to the database server which then kicked it back. Success! Now all he has to do is formulate the query just right.

So how did the hacker know that the account ID was called *accountID?* He didn't know that either, but how long would it take to guess that one? Hackers are very persistent.

Finally, how did the hacker know that *234567890* was a valid account number? Again, he didn't — but do you really think that the hacker's going to stop there? Heck no. He's going to try every combination of digits he can think of until he finds some really big accounts with really big balances that are worth stealing from.

Let me assure you of three things:

✔ SQL injection was very common years ago.

✔ It was just this simple.

✔ With a better knowledge of SQL and some really tortured syntax, a good hacker can do almost anything he wants with an SQL injection like this.

So how can the programmer avoid this hack?

Avoiding code injection

The first rule of avoiding code inject is never, *ever,* allow user input to be processed by a general-purpose language interpreter. The error with the SQL-injection example was that the program accepted user input as if it were always a date and inserted it into an SQL query that it then shipped off to the database engine for processing.

The safest and most user-friendly approach would have been to provide the user a calendar graphic from which he could select the start and end dates. The program would then create a date based on what the user clicked. If this is not possible, then the program should have carefully checked the input to make sure that the input was in the proper format for a date, in this case **yyyy/mm/dd** — in other words, four digits followed by a slash followed by two digits and a slash and finally two more digits. Nothing else should be considered acceptable input.

Sometimes you can't be that specific about the format. If you must allow the user to enter flexible text, then you can at least avoid special characters. For example, it's pretty much impossible to do SQL code injection without using either a single or double quote. You can't insert HTML tags without using a less than (<) and greater than (>) sign. Or you could just take the approach that anything other than ASCII text will not be tolerated:

```
// check some string 's' to make sure it's straight ASCII
size_type off = s.find_first_not_of(
    "abcdefghijklmnopqrstuvwxyzABCDEFGHIJKLMNOPQRSTUVWXYZ01234567890_");
if (off != string::npos)
{
    cerr << "Error\n";
}
```

This code searches the string *s* for a character that's not one of the characters A through Z, a through z, 0 through 9, or underscore. If it finds such a character, then the program rejects the input.

If you allow only the Latin characters shown here, your application will not be useable in many foreign markets such as those that don't use English character sets (such as Arabic, Chinese, Hebrew, or Russian, to name just a few). You may have to take the opposite approach and just look for the bad characters.

Overflowing Buffers for Fun and Profit

The second common hacker method that I present is the dreaded buffer overflow. First you'll see a very small program with a very big vulnerability. You'll see how this vulnerability comes about and how it can be exploited by a hacker. Then you'll see a number of different ways to mitigate the vulnerability.

Can I see an example?

Consider the smallest, simplest hackable program that I could devise:

```cpp
// BufferOverflow - this program demonstrates how a
//                  program that reads data into a fixed
//                  length buffer without checking can be
//                  hacked
#include <cstdio>
#include <cstdlib>
#include <fstream>
#include <iostream>
#include <cstring>
#include <string>

using namespace std;

// getString - read a string of input from the user prompt
//             and return it to the caller
char* getString(istream& cin)
{
    char buffer[64];

    // now input a string from the file
    char* pB;
    for(pB = buffer;*pB = cin.get(); pB++)
    {
        if (cin.eof())
        {
            break;
        }
    }
    *pB = '\0';

    // return a copy of the string to the caller
    pB = new char[strlen(buffer) + 1];
    strcpy(pB, buffer);
    return pB;
}

int main(int argc, char* pArgv[])
{
    // get the name of the file to read
    cout <<"This program reads input from an input file\n"
           "Enter the name of the file:";
    string sName;
    cin >> sName;

    // open the file
    ifstream c(sName.c_str());
```

```
    if (!c)
    {
        cout << "\nError opening input file" << endl;
        exit(-1);
    }

    // read the file's content into a string
    char* pB = getString(c);

    // output what we got
    cout << "\nWe successfully read in:\n" << pB << endl;

    cout << "Press Enter to continue..." << endl;
    cin.ignore(10, '\n');
    cin.get();
    printf("Done!");
    exit(0);
    return 0;
}
```

This program starts by prompting the user for the name of a file. The program then opens that file and passes the open file handle to the function *getString()*. This function does nothing more than read the contents of the file into a buffer, create a copy of that buffer in a memory block that it allocates off of the heap, and then returns that chunk of heap memory to the caller.

The output from a sample run of this program appears as follows:

```
This program reads input from an input file
Enter the name of the file:OK_File.txt

We successfully read in:
This is benign input.
Press Enter to continue...
```

Here the user told the program to read the file *OK_File.txt* and display the results, which it did.

Code::Blocks for Windows opens the console application in the project directory so all you need to enter is the file name *OK_File.txt* as shown. Code::Blocks for Macintosh opens the console window in your user directory so you need to enter the entire path to the file: *Desktop/CPP_Programs_from_Book/Chap28/ BufferOverflow/OK_File.txt* (assuming that you installed the source files in the default location). This same tip is applicable to every file in this chapter.

The problem with this program lies in *getString()*. The programmer was told that each input file contains a short string of not more than 20 characters. Not wanting to be stingy, she allocated a 64-character buffer just to make sure that there was enough room to hold the file contents. The file *OK_File.txt* contains the string *This is benign input.* which may have been a little longer than the promised 20 characters but fits comfortably within the 64-character buffer. But let's try the program again with the file *Big_File.txt;* the output of this run is shown in Figure 28-1.

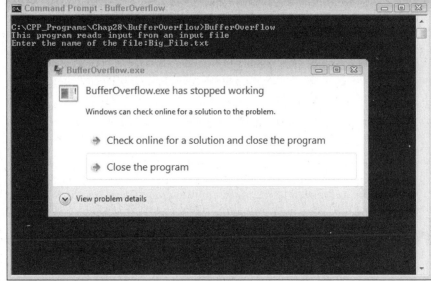

Figure 28-1:
The result
of executing
the *Buffer-
Overflow*
program on
Big_File.txt.

When presented this new file, the *BufferOverflow* program crashed rather than generating any reasonable output.

What you don't know is that the file *Big_File.txt* contains the following:

```
ABCDEFGHIJKLMNOPQRSTUVWXYZ0123456789
abcdefghijklmnopqrstuvwxyz0123456789
ABCDEFGHIJKLMNOPQRSTUVWXYZ0123456789
abcdefghijklmnopqrstuvwxyz0123456789
ABCDEFGHIJKLMNOPQRSTUVWXYZ0123456789
abcdefghijklmnopqrstuvwxyz0123456789
ABCDEFGHIJKLMNOPQRSTUVWXYZ0123456789
abcdefghijklmnopqrstuvwxyz0123456789
```

"Wait a minute!" you say. "That's not fair. That file contains more than 20 characters." True. And it contains more than 64 characters, and for some reason that caused the program to crash. Hackers don't play fair.

How does a call stack up?

This entire section is fairly technical. You can skip it if you're not into the details of computer memory.

Consider how computer memory is laid out: There are variables known as global variables that are accessible to all functions. These variables reside at fixed memory locations so that everyone can find them. But most variables are declared within the scope of a single function. The memory for these variables is allocated when the function is called and is deallocated when the function returns. Computers do this through a mechanism known as the stack.

The stack pointer (which in assembly language parlance normally carries the name ESP) points to the next available location on the stack. A function can invoke a *PUSH* instruction to save a value in a register to the stack. This automatically decrements the ESP so that the memory isn't used for something else. A corresponding *POP* instruction restores the value to the register and increments the ESP back to its original pre-*PUSH* location.

Another value that gets pushed onto the stack is the return address whenever a function is called. The 80x86's instruction *CALL getString* pushes the next address onto the stack and then jumps to the address of the *getString()* function. This is shown graphically as a busy but interesting capture from the Code::Blocks debugger in Figure 28-2.

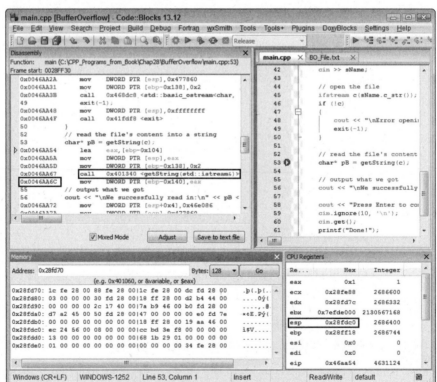

Figure 28-2:
The ESP and the stack memory immediately before the call to *getString()*.

The program is stopped at the beginning of the call to *getString()* (which you can tell by the yellow arrows in Figure 28-2, both in the right source view that shows only the C++ source and in the left mixed disassembly view that shows the C++ source and the 80x86 assembly language that was generated.) Notice on the left that the instruction after the *CALL* to *getString()* is *0x0046AA6C*. The CPU Registers window shows that the value of the ESP is *0x0028FDC0*.

Figure 28-3 shows the same windows immediately after the call to *getString()*. Notice that the ESP has been decremented by 4 bytes (the size of a return address) to *0x0028FDBC* and that the ESP now points to the value *0x0046AA6C*, the address of the next instruction after the *CALL*. This is called the *return address*.

What you actually see on the stack in Figure 28-3 is *6C-AA-46-00*. This is because the 80x86 processor stores all values with the least significant byte at the smallest address. This is called *Little Endian*.

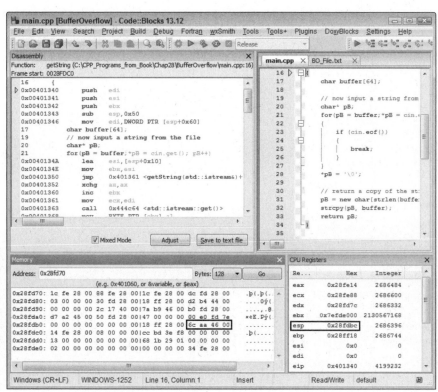

Figure 28-3:
The ESP and the stack memory immediately after the call to *getString()*.

Figure 28-4 shows the situation immediately after a successful return from *getString()*. The small yellow arrow in the disassembly window shows that the instruction pointer is indeed pointing to the instruction immediately after the *CALL* and the ESP has returned to its former value of *0x0028FDC0*.

That's all very nice, but so what? Well, C++ also stores locally defined variables on the stack. For example, the 64-byte *buffer* in *getString()* is stored on the stack. As long as the program writes only 64 bytes (or less) into this buffer, everything is fine; but if the program tries to write more data into *buffer* than *buffer* can hold, the remaining data spills over and starts overwriting other data. If the program writes far enough, it will eventually overwrite the return address. This is exactly what happened when *getString()* read the oversized *Big_File.txt*. This is shown in Figure 28-5.

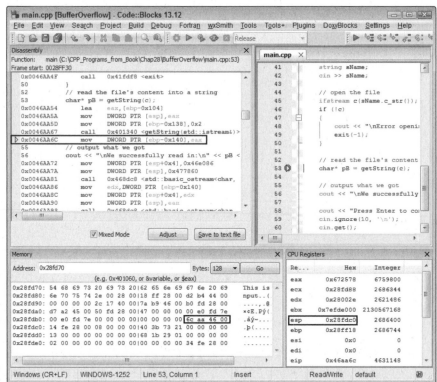

Figure 28-4: The ESP and the stack memory immediately after the return from *getString()*.

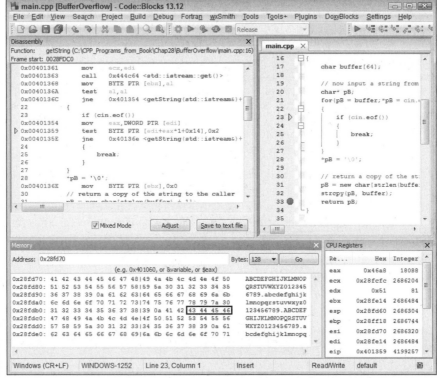

Figure 28-5:
The return address on the stack are overwritten when *getString()* tries to read *Big_File.txt.*

You can see that the location *0x0028FDC0* no longer contains the return address, but rather the value *0x46454443*, which happens to be the ASCII characters *"FEDC"*, which you can also see along with many of the other characters from *Big_File.txt* on the right of Figure 28-5.

Remember to read the bytes from right to left since the 80x86 is Little Endian.

This doesn't cause a problem as long as the program is processing through *getString(),* but when the program tries to return, the return address that's on the stack is not a return address at all. Instead, it points to some illegal address, and the program crashes as soon as it executes the *RET* statement at the end of *getString().*

Hacking BufferOverflow

The *BufferOverflow* program crashed because the contents of *Big_File.txt* overflowed *buffer* and overwrote the return address within the function *get-String().* When the function attempted to execute a return instruction, control passed to some garbage address, and the program crashed.

But what if you could engineer the text file so that it overwrote the return address not with crazy ASCII characters, but with the address of some code that you wanted to force the program to execute? When *getString()* executed a *RET*, it wouldn't crash, it would go off and execute the code you want it to.

But where could you put this extra code? What better place than within the text that's already been read into *buffer?* So the hack goes like this:

1. Create a machine language program that does whatever you want the program to do and insert it into the input file first.

2. Make sure that the input overflows the buffer just far enough that the return address gets overwritten with the address of *buffer* itself.

3. When the program reads the text into the buffer, it will in effect load the hacker code into *buffer* and then overwrite the return address.

4. When *getString()* tries to return to where it was called in *main()*, control will pass to the beginning of *buffer,* where the hacker code gets executed.

This sounds pretty tricky, and actually, it is. But remember that the hacker can execute your program as often as he wants. When executed with a good debugger, he can figure out how big to make the buffer and what address to use for *buffer.*

Just to show you that such a thing is possible, check out the following run:

```
C:\CPP_Programs\Chap28\BufferOverflow>BufferOverflow
This program reads input from an input file
Enter the name of the file:BO_File.txt
You've been hacked!
C:\CPP_Programs\Chap28\BufferOverflow>
```

Here the program starts out like normal by prompting the user for an input file. This time the user entered the file name *BO_File.txt.* In response, the program didn't output the contents of the file as you might expect, nor did it crash. Instead, in response to this file, the program output the ominous message "You've been hacked!" and exited. Notice in particular that the program didn't output the normal "Press Enter to continue. . .". This program went directly to Jail, didn't pass Go, and didn't collect $200! Control never returned from *getString()* back to *main().*

How did this hack work?

Let me start off by saying that the point of this chapter is not to teach you how to hack other people's programs — the point is to keep you from being hacked yourself. Let me also say that the details of this hack have nothing to do with learning C++ programming, so feel free to skip this sidebar if you want. However, it seems only fair that you get to see how this hack worked in detail. If you are familiar with 80x86 assembly language, you will probably be able to follow this small program. If not, then you may want to just accept my assurances that it works and kick the can on down the road.

The Hex Editor that comes with Code::Blocks displays the contents of the *BO_Text.txt* file as follows:

```
0000: 90 90 55 89 E5 31 C0 B0 F8 29 C4 90 90 EB 24 31   U   1   )   $1
0010: C0 8B 1C E4 36 88 43 13 B8 45 AA 47 01 WD 01 01      6   C  U  G  -
0020: 01 01 FF D0 31 C0 50 B8 F9 FE 42 01 2D 01 01 01      1 P      B -
0030: 01 FF D0 E8 D7 FF FF FF 59 6F 72 27 76 65 20 62    You've b
0040: 65 65 6E 20 68 61 63 6B 65 64 21 90 70 FD 28 00  een hacked! p (
```

That's not very enlightening. Other than the string *You've been hacked!,* the remainder of the file appears to be garbage. Let's try an 80x86 disassembler.

```
; set up a stack frame to protect our code from being
; overwritten when we make a function call below
; we do this by subtracting a big number like F8 from ESP
entryPoint:
  NOP                    ; 90
  NOP                    ; 90
  PUSH EBP               ; 55
  MOV ESP,EBP            ; 89 E5
  XOR EAX,EAX            ; 31 C0
  MOV F8,AL              ; B0 F8
  SUB EAX,ESP            ; 29 C4


; the following can be replaced by an INT 3 (0xCC) during debug and test
  NOP                    ; 90
  NOP                    ; 90


; put the address of the output message on the stack by jumping to a call
  JMP label2             ; EB 24
label1:

; null terminate the string by writing a 0 to *ESP + 13
  XOR EAX,EAX            ; 31 C0
  MOV [ESP],EBX          ; 8B 1C E4
  MOV AL,SS:[BX+13]      ; 36 88 43 13


; now call print (but can't have any zeros in the address)
; this value changes every time you rebuild the program!
  MOV print+01010101,EAX ; B8 45 AA 47 01
  SUB 01010101,EAX       ; 2D 01 01 01 01
  CALL EAX               ; FF D0 (calls 0047AA45)
```

(continued)

(continued)

```
; and then call exit passing a 0 (this call doesn't return)
   XOR EAX,EAX          ; 31 C0
   PUSH EAX             ; 50
   MOV exit+01010101,EAX ; B8 F9 FE 42 01
   SUB 01010101,EAX     ; 2D 01 01 01 01
   CALL EAX             ; FF D0 (calls 0041FDF8)

label2:
   CALL label1          ; E8 D7 FF FF FF
   "You've been hacked!"
   90                   ; this will be overwritten the terminating null
   address of entryPoint ; B0 FD 28 00
                        ; this will overwrite the return address
```

Of course, the disassembler didn't create the comments — I've added those to help you out a bit.

The most important part of this program is the last 4 bytes. These overwrite the return address with the address *0x0028FDB0*, which is the address of *buffer* on the stack. How did I know that? I had to single-step the program with an assembly language debugger and note the address of *buffer* myself.

The *getString()* function copies this file into the fixed length *buffer*, dutifully overwriting its own return address before encountering the terminating *NULL*. It goes on to make a copy of this string out of heap memory, a process that we care nothing about. When *getString()* tries to return to *main()*, control passes to the label *entryPoint*.

The first couple of instructions do nothing — *NOP* stands for No Op or No Operation. These are there in case the hack misses the address by a few bytes.

The next few instructions are very important. After *getString()* executes a return, *buffer* is no longer in scope. This means that all of your code is vulnerable to being overwritten if an interrupt occurs or the next time a function is called. This small section of code moves the ESP around the small program so that it is not overwritten by the upcoming function calls.

The next small section of code is where I hard-coded breakpoint instructions (*INT3* or *0xCC*) when I was debugging this code. They appear as *NOP*s in the production version that you are seeing.

The next *JMP* instruction jumps down to the label *label2*. The *CALL* instruction located here first pushes the address of the following instruction, which is actually the address of the string *You've been hacked!*, and then jumps back to *label1*. This sleight of hand is the hacker's way of pushing the address of the string onto the stack. That done, the program then makes sure that the string is null terminated by writing a 0 at the location 13 bytes deep into the string. (The *XOR EAX,EAX*, which means EXCLUSIVE OR the contents of the *EAX* register with itself, puts a zero in the *EAX* register.)

The next block of code actually does nothing more than call the *print()*, which is located at *0x0046A944*. Unfortunately, the program can't call this function directly since its address contains a null byte. This null byte would cause the copying of the block to terminate before overwriting the return address. To avoid this, I added a 1 to each byte of the address stored in memory, and then I subtract this one back out before I use the address. The program copies *0x0147AA45* into the *EAX* register and then subtracts *0x01010101* to calculate the desired address. The *CALL EAX* calls the resulting address contained in the *EAX* register. This outputs the "You've been hacked!" message.

How did I know that *print()* was located at *0x0046A944*? By examining the call to *print()* in *main()*.

The final block calls the *exit()* function using the same trick to terminate the program. Control does not return from *exit()*.

In fact, the file *BO_File.txt* (which stands for Buffer Overflow File, by the way) contains a small machine language program that outputs the message "You've been hacked!" and then calls *exit(0)* to exit normally. In addition, it's crafted in just such a way that it overwrites the return address with the beginning of the buffer to cause this program to be executed when *getString()* attempts to return, just as described earlier.

The details of a hack like this are very specific to exactly how the executable file is laid out in memory. This particular version of *BO_File.txt* works on only versions of *BufferOverflow* built for Windows with a particular version of gcc. This is not a limitation of the overflow hack itself — I could create a version of *BO_File.txt* for Linux or Macintosh and for a different version of gcc. Since you may not be using the same version of gcc that I am, I have included the *.exe* executable in the BufferOverflow directory right next to the source code. To execute this version, you will need to open a console in Windows, navigate to the proper directory (in my case, *C:\CPP_Programs_from_Book\Chap28\ BufferOverflow*), and enter the command **BufferOverflow**.

Avoiding buffer overflow — first attempt

You can look at the hackable error in *getString()* as a combination of two problems: The programmer used a fixed-length buffer, and she assumed that the input would not overflow that buffer. This error can be fixed by addressing either one of these assumptions.

The following *NoBufferOverflow1* program addresses the second assumption by making sure that the input does not exceed the size allocated to the fixed-size buffer:

```cpp
// NoBufferOverflow1 - this program avoids being hacked by
//           limiting the amount of input into a fixed buffer
#include <cstdio>
#include <cstdlib>
#include <fstream>
#include <iostream>
#include <cstring>
#include <string>

using namespace std;

// getString - read a string of input from the user prompt
//             and return it to the caller
char* getString(istream& cin)
{
    char buffer[64];

    // now input a string from the file
    // (but not more than our buffer will hold)
    int i;
    for(i = 0; i < 63; i++)
    {
        // read the next character into the buffer
        buffer[i] = cin.get();

        // exit the loop if we read a NULL or EOF
        if ((buffer[i] == 0) || cin.eof())
        {
            break;
        }
    }
    // make sure that the buffer is null terminated
    buffer[i] = '\0';

    // return a copy of the string to the caller
    char* pB = new char[strlen(buffer) + 1];
    if (pB != nullptr)
    {
        strcpy(pB, buffer);
    }
    return pB;
}
```

This version of *getString()* reads input from the file until either one of three things happen: the function reads a null, the function reads an End of File, or the function reads 63 bytes.

Remember to leave 1 extra byte for the terminating null.

The output of this program to all three files is as you would expect. The *OK_File.txt* outputs a benign message:

```
This program reads input from an input file
Enter the name of the file:OK_File.txt

We successfully read in:
This is benign input.
Press any key to continue...
```

The program outputs only the first 63 bytes of *Big_File.txt* but, hey, it doesn't crash:

```
This program reads input from an input file
Enter the name of the file:Big_File.txt

We successfully read in:
ABCDEFGHIJKLMNOPQRSTUVWXYZ0123456789
abcdefghijklmnopqrstuvwxyz
Press any key to continue...
```

The program also reads in the first 63 bytes of our hack program contained in *BO_File.txt,* but since it doesn't exceed the limits of *buffer* and therefore doesn't overwrite the return address, no harm is done and there is no hack.

```
This program reads input from an input file
Enter the name of the file:BO_File.txt

We successfully read in:
ÉÉUëo1 ╚┊°)—ÉÉδ$1 └ïL Σ6êC‼┐ U¬G☺-☺☺☺☺ ╨1 └P┐ ·■B☺-☺☺☺☺ ╨Φ╫
            You've
Press Enter to continue...
```

This is the normal way to avoid buffer overflow: Make sure that you don't copy more data into the buffer than the buffer can hold, no matter what kind of garbage is contained in the buffer.

Avoiding buffer overflow — second attempt

An alternative approach to available buffer overflow is to make sure that the buffer can grow to accommodate the size of the input. There are several flexible-size containers in the Standard Template Library. The most common is the *vector* class. (See Chapter 27 for details.)

```
// NoBufferOverflow2 - this program avoids being hacked by
//                     using a variable-size buffer
#include <cstdio>
#include <cstdlib>
#include <fstream>
#include <iostream>
#include <cstring>
#include <string>
#include <vector>

using namespace std;

// getString - read a string of input from the user prompt
//             and return it to the caller
char* getString(istream& cin)
{
    // create a variable-size buffer with an initial
    // length of 64 characters; however, this buffer can
    // grow if there are more than 64 characters in the
    // input file
    vector<char> buffer;
    buffer.reserve(64);

    // now input a string from the file
    for(;;)
    {
        // read the next character
        char c = cin.get();

        // exit the loop if we read a NULL or EOF
        if ((c == 0) || cin.eof())
        {
            break;
        }

        // add the character to the buffer and grow the
        // buffer if necessary to accommodate
        buffer.push_back(c);
    }
    // make sure that the buffer is null terminated
    buffer.push_back('\0');

    // return a copy of the string to the caller
    char* pB = new char[buffer.size()];
    if (pB != nullptr)
    {
        strcpy(pB, buffer.data());
    }
    return pB;
}
```

This version of *getString()* creates a variable-size *vector* of *char* objects. The function sets the initial size of the vector to 64 characters, but *buffer* will grow automatically if necessary. Once in the loop, the function uses the function *push_back()* to push each character onto the end of the vector.

The *vector* class overloads the bracket operator, so I could have said *buffer [index] = c;* however, in order to improve performance, the bracket operator does not check for buffer overflow. The *push_back()* method first checks that there is enough room in the buffer to handle the character being added. If not, *push_back()* allocates another buffer, twice as big as the first, and copies the contents of the smaller buffer into the larger. It repeats this process every time it needs more room in the input buffer.

The output of *NoBufferOverflow2* is indistinguishable from the fixed buffer version when reading small files:

```
This program reads input from an input file
Enter the name of the file:OK_File.txt

We successfully read in:
This is benign input.
Press Enter to continue...
```

However, the output differs from the fixed buffer version when reading really large files:

```
This program reads input from an input file
Enter the name of the file:Big_File.txt

We successfully read in:
ABCDEFGHIJKLMNOPQRSTUVWXYZ0123456789
abcdefghijklmnopqrstuvwxyz0123456789
ABCDEFGHIJKLMNOPQRSTUVWXYZ0123456789
abcdefghijklmnopqrstuvwxyz0123456789
ABCDEFGHIJKLMNOPQRSTUVWXYZ0123456789
abcdefghijklmnopqrstuvwxyz0123456789
ABCDEFGHIJKLMNOPQRSTUVWXYZ0123456789
abcdefghijklmnopqrstuvwxyz0123456789
Press Enter to continue...
```

You can see that this version of *getString()* reads the entire input file rather than chopping off input at 63 bytes.

Similarly, *NoBufferOverflow2* has no problem reading the buffer overflow hack file:

```
This program reads input from an input file
Enter the name of the file:BO_file.txt

We successfully read in:
ÉÉÜ̃ëo1╠¦°)–ÉÉδ$1╚ïL∑6êC╟┤U¬G⊖-⊖⊖⊖⊖ ╨1╙P┐ ·∎B⊖-⊖⊖⊖⊖ ╨ᵠ╫   You've been hacked!Ép²(
Press Enter to continue...
```

A lot of garbage gets printed out, but no hack occurs.

Another argument for the string class

In a way, all of the buffer overflow examples in this chapter are a bit contrived. In actual practice, the safest approach would have been to read input into an object of class *string*. Most of the functions associated with *string* are designed to vary the size of the internal buffer to accommodate the amount of input.

```cpp
// NoBufferOverflow3 - this program avoids being hacked by
//                     using the string class
#include <cstdio>
#include <cstdlib>
#include <fstream>
#include <iostream>
#include <string>

using namespace std;

// getString - read a string of input from the user prompt
//             and return it to the caller. Terminate the
//             string at a null or the end-of-file
string getString(istream& cin)
{
    string s;
    getline(cin, s, '\0');
    return s;
}
```

The call to *getline()* says read from *cin* into the string *s* until either a null or an end-of-file is encountered (the EOF is implied in every call to *getline()*). The size of the buffer in *s* is not fixed but expands to hold whatever is thrown at it.

Just as before, the output of this version is indistinguishable from the others when reading a benign file:

```
This program reads input from an input file
Enter the name of the file:OK_File.txt

We successfully read in:
This is benign input.
Press Enter to continue...
```

This output of this version is also identical to *NoBufferOverflow2* for the over-sized cases such as *Big_File.txt:*

```
This program reads input from an input file
Enter the name of the file:Big_File.txt

We successfully read in:
ABCDEFGHIJKLMNOPQRSTUVWXYZ0123456789
abcdefghijklmnopqrstuvwxyz0123456789
ABCDEFGHIJKLMNOPQRSTUVWXYZ0123456789
abcdefghijklmnopqrstuvwxyz0123456789
ABCDEFGHIJKLMNOPQRSTUVWXYZ0123456789
abcdefghijklmnopqrstuvwxyz0123456789
ABCDEFGHIJKLMNOPQRSTUVWXYZ0123456789
abcdefghijklmnopqrstuvwxyz0123456789
Press Enter to continue...
```

And for the buffer overflow *BO_File.txt* case:

```
This program reads input from an input file
Enter the name of the file:BO_file.txt

We successfully read in:
ÉÉÛèσ1 ⁴¦¦º)−ÉÉδ$1 ᴸïLΣ6êC‼┐U¬GΘ-ΘΘΘΘ ⁴ᴸ1ᴸP┐ ·■BΘ-ΘΘΘΘ ⁴ᴸΦ╫   You've been hacked!Ép²(
Press Enter to continue...
```

Again, garbage but no hack.

Why not always use string functions?

Given the relative simplicity of the *NoBufferOverflow3* program compared with the other two, why wouldn't a programmer always use the *string* class and its associated functions? In a way, the answer is, "You should." But you need to keep in mind that internally this program is every bit as complicated as the vector-based *NoBufferOverflow2* version. The *getline()* function is calling a variable-size container such as *vector* for you. Even though you may not be making all these extra calls, the calls are being made, and the performance of the function reflects that fact. The versions of *getString()* that rely on fixed-size buffers are considerably faster than those that use variable-size structures.

This difference is not noticeable if the program calls *getString()* only once or even only a thousand times, but it can be considerable if this function were being called in the middle of a very time critical loop.

Thus, the *string* or *vector* versions of *getString()* are the way to go for general use, but there may be conditions that justify the use of fixed-size buffers.

There is no measurable difference in performance between the version of *getString()* that does not check for buffer overflow and the one that does. There is no justification for leaving yourself exposed to hacking by buffer overflow even if you're trying to shave a few instructions off of the execution time.

Let the operating system help

CPU manufacturers and operating system vendors have combined to devise ways to help avoid buffer overflow hacks. Two of the most common are Address Space Layout Randomization (ASLR) and Data Execution Prevention (DEP).

One of the Achilles heels of the preceding hack is that I had to hard code the address of *buffer* on the stack. I could do this because my version of Windows always loads that particular program, *BufferOverflow.exe,* the same way. But what if it were to vary things a bit every time it executed the program? For example, what if the operating system added some small constant to the stack pointer before executing the program each time? It wouldn't make any difference to the program, but it would make it impossible for the hacker to know what value to overwrite the return address with since the address of *buffer* would be slightly different every time the program executed. This moving memory around is known as Address Space Layout Randomization (ASLR).

Another vulnerability of this hack is the fact that at least for a small period of time the processor was being asked to execute machine instructions that were stored in an area reserved for data (namely the machine code that got loaded into *buffer*). Most 80x86 processors have the ability known as Data Execution Prevention (DEP) to mark code segments as either executable or not executable (using a flag known as the *Nx* flag). Operating systems that support DEP mark memory segments where code is stored as executable while marking areas intended only for data, such as the stack where *buffer* is stored as not executable. This buffer overflow hack would have been trapped by the processor as soon as control passed to the beginning of *buffer.* The CPU would have thrown an exception that someone was trying to execute instructions stored in non-executable memory — a no-no of the first order. The operating system would catch the exception and immediately throw the miscreant program out of memory before any hacker harm could be done.

In Windows Vista and later, DEP is enabled for most Windows kernel processes and many applications to avoid hackers from gaining administrator privileges but is often not enabled for user code. The Task Manager will show you which processes have DEP enabled and which do not (you have to enable this column — by default, this column is not displayed). This figure shows the output of the Task Manager on my Windows 7 machine while *BufferOverflow* is executing. Notice that the process created is called *BufferOverflow.exe*32,* indicating that this is a 32-bit process. Also notice that DEP is disabled for this process. There doesn't appear to be a way to tell gcc to generate code that enables DEP on Windows.

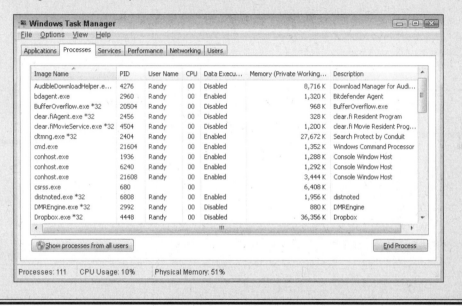

Part VI
The Part of Tens

the
part of
tens

In this part...

- ✔ Avoiding bugs
- ✔ Preventing hacking
- ✔ Visit `www.dummies.com` for great Dummies content online.

Chapter 29

Ten Ways to Avoid Adding Bugs to Your Program

In This Chapter

▶ Enabling all warnings and error messages

▶ Using a clear and consistent coding style

▶ Limiting the visibility

▶ Adding comments to your code while you write it

▶ Single-stepping every path at least once

▶ Avoiding overloaded operators

▶ Heap handling

▶ Using exceptions to handle errors

▶ Declaring destructors to be virtual

▶ Avoiding multiple inheritance

*I*n this chapter, I look at several ways to minimize errors, as well as ways to make debugging the errors that are introduced easier.

Enable All Warnings and Error Messages

The syntax of C++ allows for a lot of error checking. When the compiler encounters a construct that it can't decipher, it has no choice but to generate an error message. Although the compiler attempts to sync back up with the next statement, it does not attempt to generate an executable program.

Disabling warning and error messages is a bit like unplugging the Check Engine light on your car dashboard because it bothers you: Ignoring the problem doesn't make it go away. If your compiler has a Syntax Check from Hell mode, enable it.

Don't start debugging your code until you remove or at least understand all warnings generated during compilation. Enabling all warning messages if you then ignore them does you no good. If you don't understand the warning, look it up. What you don't know *will* hurt you.

Adopt a Clear and Consistent Coding Style

Coding in a clear and consistent style not only enhances the readability of your program but also results in fewer coding mistakes. Remember, the less brain power you have to spend deciphering C++ syntax, the more you have left over for thinking about the logic of the program at hand. A good coding style enables you to do the following with ease:

- ✔ Differentiate class names, object names, and function names.
- ✔ Know something about the object based on its name.
- ✔ Differentiate preprocessor symbols from C++ symbols (that is, *#defined* objects should stand out).
- ✔ Identify blocks of C++ code at the same level (this is the result of consistent indentation).

In addition, you need to establish a standard module header that provides information about the functions or classes in the module, the author (presumably, that's you), the date, the version of the compiler you're using, and a modification history.

Finally, all programmers involved in a single project should use the same style. Trying to decipher a program with a patchwork of different coding styles is confusing.

You can let Code::Blocks maintain your source code style for you. Select Settings➪Editor and then select Source Formatter on the left. From the menu on the right, you can select your preferred source code style. Now select Pluggins➪Source Code Formatter to completely reformat your modules.

Limit the Visibility

Limiting the visibility of class internals to the outside world is a cornerstone of object-oriented programming. The class is responsible for its own internals; the application is responsible for using the class to solve the problem at hand.

Specifically, limited visibility means that data members should not be accessible outside the class — that is, they should be marked as *protected*. (Another storage class, *private*, is not discussed in this book.) In addition, member functions that the application software does not need to know about should also be marked *protected*. Don't expose any more of the class internals than necessary.

A related rule is that public member functions should trust application code as little as possible. Any argument passed to a public member function should be treated as though it might cause bugs until it has been proven safe. A function such as the following is an accident waiting to happen:

```cpp
class Array
{
  public:
    explicit Array(int s)
    {
        size = 0;
        // new throws exception if memory not available
        pData = new int[s];
        size = s;
    }
    ~Array()
    {
        delete[] pData;
        size = 0;
        pData = nullptr;
    }
    //either return or set the array data
    int data(int index)
    {
        return pData[index];
    }
    int data(int index, int newValue)
    {
        int oldValue = pData[index];
        pData[index] = newValue;
        return oldValue;
    }
  protected:
    int size;
    int *pData;
};
```

The function *data(int)* allows the application software to read data out of *Array*. This function is too trusting; it assumes that the *index* provided is within the data range. What if the *index* is not? The function *data(int, int)* is even worse because it overwrites an unknown location.

What's needed is a check to make sure that the *index* is in range. In the following, only the *data(int)* function is shown for brevity:

```
int data(unsigned int index)
{
    if (index >= size)
    {
        throw Exception("Array index out of range");
    }
    return pData[index];
}
```

Now an out-of-range *index* will be caught by the check. (Making *index* unsigned precludes the necessity of adding a check for negative *index* values.)

Comment Your Code While You Write It

You can avoid errors if you comment your code while you write it rather than wait until everything works and then go back and add comments. I can understand not taking the time to write voluminous headers and function descriptions until later, but you always have time to add short comments while writing the code.

Short comments should be enlightening. If they're not, they aren't worth much. You need all the enlightenment you can get while you're trying to make your program work. When you look at a piece of code you wrote a few days ago, comments that are short, descriptive, and to the point can make a dramatic contribution to helping you figure out exactly what it was you were trying to do.

In addition, consistent code indentation and naming conventions make the code easier to understand. It's all very nice when the code is easy to read after you're finished with it, but it's just as important that the code be easy to read while you're writing it. That's when you need the help.

Single-Step Every Path at Least Once

It may seem like an obvious statement, but I'll say it anyway: As a programmer, it's important for you to understand what your program is doing. Nothing gives you a better feel for what's going on under the hood than single-stepping the program with a good debugger. (Code::Blocks contains an integrated debugger.)

Beyond that, as you write a program, you sometimes need raw material to figure out some bizarre behavior. Nothing gives you that material better than single-stepping new functions as they come into service.

Finally, when a function is finished and ready to be added to the program, every logical path needs to be traveled at least once. Bugs are much easier to find when the function is examined by itself rather than after it has been thrown into the pot with the rest of the functions — and your attention has gone on to new programming challenges.

Avoid Overloading Operators

Other than using the assignment operator *operator=()*, you should hold off overloading operators until you feel comfortable with C++. Overloading operators other than assignment is almost never necessary and can significantly add to your debugging woes as a new programmer. You can get the same effect by defining and using the proper public member functions instead.

After you've been C-plus-plussing for a few months, feel free to return and start overloading operators to your heart's content.

Manage the Heap Systematically

As a general rule, programmers should allocate and release heap memory at the same "level." If a member function *MyClass::create()* allocates a block of heap memory and returns it to the caller, there should be a member function *MyClass::release()* that returns the memory to the heap. Specifically, *MyClass::create()* should not require the parent function to release the memory. This certainly doesn't avoid all memory problems — the parent function may forget to call *MyClass::release()* — but it does reduce the possibility somewhat.

Use Exceptions to Handle Errors

The exception mechanism in C++ is designed to handle errors conveniently and efficiently. In general, you should throw an error indicator rather than return an error flag. The resulting code is easier to write, read, and maintain. Besides, other programmers have come to expect it — you wouldn't want to disappoint them, would you?

It is not necessary to throw an exception from a function that returns a "didn't work" indicator if this is a part of everyday life for that function. Consider a function *lcd()* that returns the least common denominators of a number passed to it as an argument. That function will not return any values when presented a prime number (a prime number cannot be evenly divided by any other number). This is not an error — the *lcd()* function has nothing to say when given a prime.

Declare Destructors Virtual

Don't forget to create a destructor for your class if the constructor allocates resources (such as heap memory) that need to be returned when the object reaches its demise. Having created a destructor, don't forget to declare it virtual (almost) every time especially if you know that your class is likely to be inherited and extended by subclasses. The problem is demonstrated in the following code snippet:

```cpp
#include <iostream>

using namespace std;
class Person
{
  public:
    Person(const char* pszName)
    {
        psName = new string(pszName);
    }
    ~Person()
    {
        delete psName; psName = nullptr;
    }

  protected:
    string* psName;
};
class Student : public Person
```

```
{
  public:
    Student(const char* pszName, unsigned ID,
            const char* pszMajor)
        : Person(pszName), mID(ID)
    {
        psMajor = new string(pszMajor);
    }
    ~Student()
    {
        delete psMajor; psMajor = nullptr;
    }
  protected:
    unsigned mID;
    string* psMajor;
};

void fn()
{
    Person* p = new Student("Stew Dent", 1234, "Physics");
    delete p;
}
```

The function *fn()* creates a *Student* object. The *Student* class extends a class *Person* that allocates heap memory to hold the person's name in the constructor and returns it in the destructor. In addition, the *Student* constructor allocates memory that it returns in its own destructor.

The problem occurs when *fn()* stores the returned pointer to a *Student* in a variable declared *Person**. This is allowed because a Student IS_A Person (see Chapter 11 if this doesn't make sense). The problem is that the *delete p* invokes the *Person* destructor but not the *Student* destructor, resulting in a memory leak.

Making the following change to the class solves the problem:

```
class Person
{
  public:
    Person(char* pszName) { psName = new string(pszName);}
    virtual ~Person() { delete psName; / nullptr; }

  protected:
    string* psName;
};
```

This causes C++ to invoke the destructor based on the pointer's actual type (in this case *Student**) and not its declared type (*Person**).

Okay, so when should I not declare the destructor virtual? Declaring any member in a class virtual means that C++ must add an extra pointer or two to each object of that class to keep track of its virtual members. Thus, if you were to declare a lot of *Person* objects, an extra few pointers per object might be a big deal.

As a general rule, if you expect someone to inherit your class then declare its destructor virtual. And if you are about to inherit from an existing base class, make sure that its destructor is declared virtual as well.

Avoid Multiple Inheritance

Multiple inheritance, like operator overloading, adds another level of complexity that you don't need to deal with when you're just starting out. Fortunately, most real-world relationships can be described with single inheritance.

After you feel comfortable with your level of understanding of C++, experiment with setting up some multiple inheritance hierarchies. That way, you'll be ready when the unusual situation that requires multiple inheritance to describe it accurately arises.

Chapter 30

Ten Ways to Protect Your Programs from Hackers

In This Chapter

▶ Protecting yourself from user input

▶ Handling failures in your code

▶ Maintaining a program log

▶ Following good development process

▶ Practicing good version control

▶ Authenticating users securely

▶ Managing your sessions

▶ Obfuscating your code

▶ Signing your code

▶ Using encryption securely

Chapter 28 describes things you should do in your code to avoid writing programs that are vulnerable to hackers. It also describes features that you can enable if your operating system supports them, such as Address Space Layout Randomization (ASLR) and Data Execution Prevention (DEP). This chapter describes further steps you can take as part of the software development process to defend yourself from the "hackerata."

Don't Make Assumptions about User Input

The programmer has a frame of mind when writing a program. She's thinking about the problem that she's trying to solve. Given that a person can keep only so many things in her mind at one time, she's probably not thinking much beyond the immediate problem.

Programmer's tunnel vision is okay during the early development phase. At some point, however, the programmer (or, better yet, some other programmer who had nothing to do with the development of the code) needs to sit back and forget about the immediate problem. She needs to ask herself, "How will this program react to illegal input?"

For example, in the field for the username, suppose someone enters several thousand garbage characters. How will the program react? Ideally, you want the program to respond with an error message like, "What the heck are these several thousand characters doing in the place where I expected a name?" Barring that, a simple "I don't understand what you mean" is fine.

In fact, anything short of crashing or corrupting data is acceptable. This is because a crash indicates a possible intrusion vector that a hacker can exploit to get your program to do something that you don't want it to do.

Not every crash is exploitable, but many crashes are. In fact, throwing lots of garbage input at a program and looking for the crashes is called *fuzzing the program* and is often the first step to finding exploits in deployed applications.

Here are some of the rules for checking input:

- ✔ Make no assumptions about the length of the input.
- ✔ Don't accept more input than you have room for in your fixed-length buffers (or used variable-size buffers).
- ✔ Check the range of every numerical value to make sure that it makes sense.
- ✔ Check for and filter out special characters that may be used by a hacker to inject code.
- ✔ Don't pass raw input onto another service, such as a database server.

And perform all of the same checks on the values returned from remote services. The hacker may not be on the input side, he may be on the response side.

Handle Failures Gracefully

By this, I don't mean "Don't be a sore loser." What I mean is that your program should respond reasonably to failures that occur within the program. For example, if your call to a library function returns a *nullptr,* the program should detect this and do something reasonable.

Reasonable here is to be understood fairly liberally. I don't necessarily mean that the program needs to sniff around to figure out exactly why the function didn't return a reasonable address. It could be that the request was for way too much memory due to unreasonable input. Or it could be that the constructor detected some type of illegal input. It doesn't matter. The point is that the program should restore its state as best it can and set up for the next bit of input without crashing or corrupting existing data structures such as the heap.

In general this means the following:

- ✔ Check for illegal input to interface functions and throw an exception when you detect it.
- ✔ Catch and handle exceptions at the proper points.

 Some programmers are good at checking for illegal input and throwing exceptions when problems occur, but they're not so good at catching exceptions and handling them properly. I would give this type of programmer a B–. At least their programs are hard to exploit, but they're easy to crash, making them vulnerable to the relatively less dangerous Denial of Service attacks.

Another rule of thumb is to fail secure. For example, if you are trying to check someone's password and the user inputs 2,000 characters replete with embedded SQL statements, not only is it necessary to reject this garbage, but you must also not approve this nonsense as if it were a valid password. Whenever you catch an exception, you should not assume things about the state of the system (like the fact that the user has been properly identified and credentialed) that may not be true. It is far better to require the user to reenter his credentials after a major failure than it would be to assume that an invalid user has already been approved.

Maintain a Program Log

Create and maintain runtime logs that allow someone to reconstruct what happened in the event of a security failure. (Actually, this is just as true in the event of any type of failure.) For example, you probably want to log every time someone signs into or out of your system. You'll definitely want to know who was logged into your system when a security event occurred — this is the group that's most at risk of a security loss and who are most suspicious when looking for culprits. In addition, you'll want to log any system errors which would include most exceptions.

A real-world production program contains a large number of calls that look something like the following:

```
log(DEBUG, "User %s entered legal password", sUser);
```

This is just an example. Every program will need some type of log function. Whether or not it's actually called *log()* is immaterial.

This call writes the string *User* xxx *entered legal password,* where *xxx* is replaced by the name contained in the variable *sUser* to the program log file when the system is in Debug mode. When the program is not in Debug mode, this call does nothing — this is to avoid paying a performance penalty for logging too much information when everything is going smoothly.

System log functions usually support anywhere from two to five levels of severity that dictate whether log messages get written out or not. There are some failures that are always written to the log file:

```
if (validate(sUser, sPassword) == true)
{
    log(DEBUG, "User %s entered legal password", sUser);
}
else
{
    log(ALWAYS, "User %s entered illegal password",
        sUser);
}
```

Here, the program logs a valid user password only when the system is in Debug mode, but it always logs an invalid user password just in case this represents an attempt by someone to break into the system by guessing passwords.

Log files must be maintained. Generally, that means running a job automatically at midnight or some other time of decreased use that closes the current log file, moves it into a separate directory along with the day's date, and opens a new log file. This keeps a single log file from getting too big and unwieldy. It also makes it a lot easier to go back to past log files to find a particular event.

In addition, reviewing log files is a boring, thankless, and therefore error-prone job. This makes it a job best performed by computers. Most large systems have special programs that scan the log file looking for anomalies that may indicate a problem. For example, one or two invalid passwords per hour is probably nothing to worry about — people fat-finger their passwords all the time. But a few thousand invalid passwords in an hour is probably worth getting excited about. This may indicate an attempt at forced entry by brute-force guessing a password.

An entire *For Dummies* book could be written on log file maintenance. There is way more to this topic than I can cover here. Log files must be backed up daily and cleaned out periodically lest they grow forever. In addition, someone or some program needs to monitor these log files to detect problems such as repeated attempts to guess someone's password.

Maintaining a system log gives the system administrator the raw material that she needs to reconstruct what happened in the event that the unthinkable happens and a hacker makes it into the system.

Follow a Good Development Process

Every program should follow a well thought out, formal development process. This process should include at least the following steps:

- ✔ Collect and document requirements, including security requirements.
- ✔ Review design.
- ✔ Adhere to a coding standard.
- ✔ Undergo unit test.
- ✔ Conduct formal acceptance tests that are based on the original requirements.

In addition, peer reviews should be conducted at key points to verify that the requirements, design, code, and test procedures are high quality and meet company standards.

I am not against New Age development techniques such as recursive and agile development. But *agile* is not a synonym for *sloppy* — just because you are using an agile development process does not mean that you can skip any of the preceding development steps.

I am also not a Process Nazi. The preceding steps do not need to be as formal or as drawn out for a small program involving one or two developers as they would be for a project that employs dozens of systems analysts, developers, and testers. However, even small programs can contain hackable security flaws, and it takes only one for your computer to become somebody's bot.

Implement Good Version Control

Version control is a strange thing. It's natural not to worry about version 1.1 when you're under the gun to get version 1.0 out the door and into the waiting users' outstretched hands. However, version control is an important topic that must be addressed early because it must be built into the program's initial design and not bolted on later.

One almost trivial aspect of version control is knowing which version of the program a user is using. Now this sounds kind of stupid, but believe me, it's not. When a user calls up and says, "It does this when I click on that," the help desk really needs to know which version of the program the user is using. He could be describing a problem in his version that's already been fixed in the current version.

A program should have an overall version number that either gets displayed when the program starts or is easily retrievable by the user (or both). Usually the version number is displayed as part of the help system. In the code, this can be as simple as maintaining a global variable with the version number that gets displayed when the user selects Help⇨About. The programmer is responsible for updating this version number whenever a new version gets pushed out to production. This Help window should also display the version number of any Web services that the program uses, if possible.

A more pernicious aspect of version control is how to roll new versions of the application out to users. This includes both the code itself and changes to the data structures, such as database tables, that the application may access.

The code roll-out problem is trivial with browser-based Web applications — you simply load a new version onto the server, and the next time the user clicks on your page, he gets the new version. However, this problem is much more difficult for applications that install onto the user's computer. The problem is that this is a great opportunity for hackers to exploit your application.

Suppose for example that you have devised a really cool update feature in your application. The user clicks on Update Now, and the application goes back to the server and checks for a new version. If a new version is available, the application automatically downloads the update and installs it.

If a hacker figures out the protocol that your application uses for downloading updates and if that protocol is not sufficiently secured, a hacker can convince your application on other people's computers to download a specially modified version that she's created, complete with malware of her own creation. Pretty soon your entire user base is infected with some type of malware that you know nothing about.

I'm not saying that automatic updates can't be done securely — obviously they can, or companies like Microsoft and Apple wouldn't do them. I'm just saying that if you do choose the automatic-update route, you need to be very careful about how you implement security.

Even if you go the old fashioned route and have the user download a new *MyApplication_Setup.exe* that installs the new application, you need to worry about whether some hacker may have uploaded a version of your program laced with malware. Most download Web sites are pretty careful about checking applications for malware. Another approach is to calculate a secure checksum and include it with the download file. The user can then recalculate that checksum on the file that he downloads. If the number he calculates doesn't match the number that you uploaded, then the executable file may have been tampered with and the user shouldn't install the program. Although this approach is pretty secure, very few users bother.

Authenticate Users Securely

User authentication should be straightforward: The user provides an account name and a password, and your program looks the account name up in a table and compares the passwords. If the passwords match, the user is authenticated. But when it comes to antihacking, nothing is that simple.

First, never store the passwords themselves in the database. This is called storing them *in the clear* and is considered very bad form. It's far too easy for a hacker to get his hands on the password file. Instead, save off a secure transform of the password.

This is known as a *secure hash,* and there are several such algorithms defined; the most common are MD5, SHA1, and SHA256. All of these hash functions share several common properties: It is very unlikely that two passwords will generate the same hash value, it is virtually impossible to figure out the original password from the hashed value, and even a small change in the password results in a wildly different hashed value.

Unfortunately no secure hash function is included in the standard C++ library, but there are standard implementations of the most common algorithms in many open source libraries. In addition, the algorithms, along with sample code for each of these, is available on Wikipedia.

In practice, these hash functions work as follows:

1. The user creates a password when he registers with the application.

2. The application appends a random string (known as a *salt*) to either the front or the end of the password the user enters.

3. The application runs the resulting string through one of the secure hash algorithms.

   For example, the SHA256 algorithm generates a 64-digit hexadecimal-number (256-bit) result. The application stores this result and the salt string in a database table along with the user's name.

Why salt? It's bad for the heart

The salt value adds security to the process by making it difficult for a hacker to deduce the password, even if he intercepts the hashed value by sniffing the line. It does this in two ways:

✔ One successful technique at guessing passwords is to construct a table of pre-hashed common passwords. This is known as a *password dictionary.*

When the hashed password comes over the line, the hacker looks up the hashed value in the dictionary — this is a very quick operation. If it is found, then the hacker knows the user's password. However, this technique will not work, even if the user picks a common password, if a random long salt value has been added.

✔ A salt can help make up for passwords that are too short.

For example, a hacker who knows that a user is lazy and doesn't use passwords with more than six characters has no trouble trying all possible six-letter combinations to reconstruct a password from its hash. But a 6-letter password combined with a random 30-letter hash cannot be calculated in advance. Lastly, a random salt value gives two different users with the same password a different hash value.

However, salts aren't magic. The salt value is transmitted in the clear. If the user chooses a sufficiently short password (say, four characters) and the hacker knows this, the hacker can still generate the hashes of all possible four-letter passwords combined with the salt string and break the lazy user's password.

Remember that for a salt to be effective it needs to have three properties:

✔ It must be generated separately for each user — using the same salt value over and over doesn't add any security.

✔ It must be sufficiently long (say 20 or 30 characters).

✔ It must be random.

When the user logs in, the application goes through the following steps to verify the user's password:

1. Uses the username to look up the salt values and the hashed password in the user table.

2. Adds the salt string to the user's password and calculates the secure hash.

3. Compares this newly calculated value to the value stored in the table. If it matches the value stored in the table, then the user is authenticated.

This algorithm has the advantage that if a hacker were to get hold of the password table, it would still be difficult for him to create a password that would match one of the existing hashes.

It may be difficult but it is not impossible to find a password that matches a given hash value, however — the MD5 algorithm, though popular, is particularly susceptible to this type of attack. If you suspect that the password table has been compromised, you must invalidate all of the user accounts and force people to securely reregister with the application.

Once you've authenticated a user, your application should assign that user a role that specifies the types of things that he is allowed to do in the application. Consider a weekly status report application. A normal user should only be able to edit entries that he creates. He may or may not be able to read other users' entries. A person assigned the role of supervisor may be able to edit other users' entries. Only the few users assigned the role of administrator should be able to edit the tables, register new users, or change the roles of other users.

By keeping the number of administrators to a minimum, you reduce the number of vulnerabilities that your application exposes. For example, if a hacker breaks into a normal user's account, he can do little more than edit that user's status information. Bad but certainly not a disaster.

And, finally, your application should keep statistics on user log-ins. You should consider deactivating the accounts of users that haven't used the system in a long time. In addition, the application should react automatically to repeated attempts to log in with the wrong password by either permanently, or at least temporarily, locking out the account. This will make it much more difficult for a computer on the other end of a connection to run through thousands or millions of possible passwords attempting to brute-force guess one.

Manage Remote Sessions

You can make certain assumptions when all of your application runs on a single computer. For one thing, once the user has authenticated himself, you don't need to worry about him being transformed into a different person (unless your application is intended to run at Hogwarts Academy of Witchcraft and Wizardry). Applications that communicate with a remote server can't make this assumption — a hacker who is listening on the line can wait until the user authenticates himself and then hijack the session.

What can the security-minded programmer do to avoid this situation? You don't want to repeatedly ask the user for his password just to make sure that the connection hasn't been hijacked. The alternative solution is to establish and manage a *session*. You do this by having the server send the remote application a session cookie once the user has successfully authenticated himself.

The term *cookie* is not very descriptive. It is actually a string of digits or characters. A cookie can be in a file on the hard disk, or it can be held in RAM. Session cookies are generally held in RAM for extra security. All modern browsers include support for cookies.

A cookie may include information such as a hash of the user's password and the time that the session started. Throughout the session, the server periodically challenges the remote application for a copy of the cookie. As long as the remote application presents a valid cookie, the server can be reasonably certain that the person on the other end of the connection is the same person who entered the correct password in the first place.

If at any time the remote application cannot produce a cookie that matches the cookie provided to it at the beginning of the session, the server application automatically logs the user off and refuses to listen to the remote application until it can log in again with valid username and password. If the connection between the server and the application is lost, the server invalidates the cookie, thereby forcing the application to reauthenticate. When the user logs out, the session cookie is also invalidated.

In this way the server can be reasonably certain than some nefarious application hasn't managed to hijack the user's session. But what about in the other direction? How does the application know whether it can trust the server? A way to solve this problem is for the remote application to generate a cookie back to the server that uniquely identifies it as a legitimate server.

A second approach, one that is much more secure, is to establish a secure session using a standard protocol like Secure Socket Layer (SSL) or Transport Layer Security (TLS). While the details are well beyond the scope of this book, these protocols allow the server and the remote application to exchange passwords in a secure fashion. These passwords are then used to encrypt all communication between the two for the remainder of the session. This encryption precludes a hacker from intercepting the session — without the password, the hacker can't understand what the server is saying nor trick the server into accepting its output. Further, since the messages are encrypted with keys that are exchanged securely, a hacker can't even understand what information is being exchanged between the server and the remote app if she happens to be listening on the line.

Obfuscate Your Code

Code obfuscation is the act of making the executable as difficult for a hacker to understand as possible.

To *obfuscate* means to make obscure or unclear.

The logic is simple. The easier it is for a hacker to understand how your code works, the easier it will be for the hacker to figure out vulnerabilities.

The single easiest step you can take is to make sure that you only ever distribute a Release version of your program that does not include debug symbol information. When you first create the project file, be sure to select that both a Debug and a Release version should be created, as shown in Figure 30-1. The only real difference between these two is the compiler switches: The Debug version includes the *-g* switch, which tells the compiler to include symbol table information in the executable file. This symbol information tells the debugger where each line of code is located within the executable and where each variable is stored. This information is necessary in order to set break points and display the value of variables. But if this information is available in the version distributed to customers, then the hacker will be given a blue print to each line of your source code.

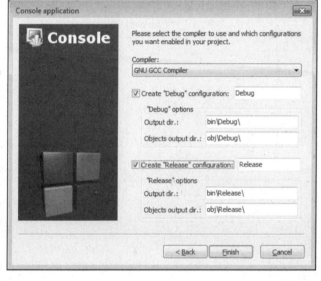

Figure 30-1:
The wizard
used to
create
programs
allows you
to create
both a
Debug and
a Release
version of
the project.

The Release version of Code::Blocks does not include the gcc *-g* switch, so no symbol information is included in its executable.

The Release version may also include enhanced code optimizations to generate faster or smaller executable files via one of the various gcc *-O* switches.

You can add a Release version to an existing project in Code::Blocks by selecting Project➪Properties and then selecting the Build Targets tab to reveal a dialog box like that shown in Figure 30-2. Select Add and fill in the name of the new target. Make sure that the settings in this top-level dialog box match the Debug settings (for example, make sure that the type is Console Application and that the target executable and object directories are filled in). Then select Build options and make sure that the Release target does not have the *-g* compiler switch set.

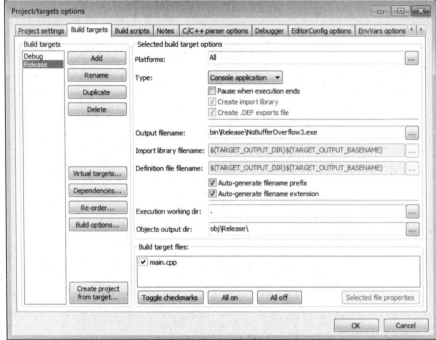

Figure 30-2:
You can
add a new
build target
from the
Project⇨
Properties
window.

You will need to build the Debug version during Unit Test and Debug; but before final test and release, you should tell Code::Blocks to generate the Release version of the program by selecting Build⇨Select Target⇨Release⇨Build⇨Rebuild. To keep things straight, Code::Blocks puts the Release executable in a separate target directory.

Never, ever, distribute versions of your application with symbol information included.

You should always endeavor to make your source code as simple, clean, and clear as you possibly can. However, you can purchase a commercial code obfuscator that mangles your program to make it more difficult to reverse engineer. Some obfuscators work on the machine code, and some work at the source level, generating a C++ program from your C++ that even you would be hard pressed to follow. The critical thing about any obfuscator is that while it makes the code more difficult for a human to follow, it does not change the meaning of the code in any way.

Don't put too much faith in code obfuscators. It may make the code harder to reverse engineer, but it's still not impossible. Given enough time, a determined hacker can reverse engineer any program.

Sign Your Code With a Digital Certificate

Code signing works by generating a secure hash of the executable code and combining it with a certificate issued by a valid certificate authority. The process works like this: The company creating the program must first register itself with one of the certificate authorities. Let's use the example of my great retirement hope, My Company, Inc. I must first convince one of the commercially available certificate authorities that My Company, Inc., is in fact a real company and not just some den of thieves or figment of my imagination. I do this by revealing its address, its phone numbers, the names and addresses of its officers, the URL of its Web site, and so on. I may also be asked to produce My Company's tax filings for the past few years to prove that this isn't some bogus claim.

Once the certificate authority is convinced that My Company is a valid software entity, it issues a certificate. This is a long number that anyone can use to verify that the holder of this certificate is the famous My Company of San Antonio.

Executables generated by My Company can then be signed with this certificate. Signing an executable does two things:

- ✔ It creates a secure hash that would make it very difficult (as close to impossible as possible) for a hacker to modify the executable without being detected by the user's computer.

- ✔ It insures the user that this program was created by a legitimate software development company.

When a user runs my program for the first time, the application presents its certificate and secure hash combination to the operating system. The OS first calculates a hash of the executable and compares it to the hash presented. If these match, then the OS is reasonably certain that the executable is the same one that My Company shipped out of its doors. The OS then validates the certificate to make sure that it is valid and hasn't been revoked. If that matches, the OS presents a dialog box to the user that states this application is a valid executable from My Company, Inc., and asks whether it should continue executing it.

Use Secure Encryption Wherever Necessary

Like any good warning, this admonition has several parts. First, "Use encryption wherever necessary." This tends to bring to mind thoughts of communicating bank account information over the Internet, but you should think more general than that. Data that's being communicated, whether over the Internet or over some smaller range, is known generally as *Data in Motion.* Data in Motion should be encrypted unless it would be of no use to a hacker.

Data stored on the disk is known as *Data at Rest.* This data should also be encrypted if there is a chance of the disk being lost, stolen, or copied. Businesses routinely encrypt the hard disks on their company laptops in case a laptop gets stolen at the security scanner in the airport or left in a taxi somewhere. Small portable storage devices such as thumb drives are especially susceptible to being lost — data on these devices should be encrypted.

Encryption is not limited to data — the entire communication session should be encrypted if a hacker could coax your application into revealing secrets by spoofing either the remote application or the server.

But this section's title says "Use Secure Encryption." Don't make up your own encryption scheme or try to improve upon existing schemes because the results won't be secure. Encryption algorithms go through years of testing and evaluation by experts before they are adopted by the public. Don't think that you are going to improve on them on your own. You are more likely to just mess them up.

A good example of this lies in the Wi-Fi in your phone, tablet, or laptop. The original definition for Wi-Fi (known as 802.11b) used a reasonably secure published algorithm for securing the packets of information sent over the airwaves. It called this standard WEP (Wired Equivalent Privacy, sometimes erroneously labeled Wireless Encryption Protocol). Unfortunately, the designers of 802.11b didn't implement the protocol correctly, which left 802.11b hopelessly vulnerable to hacking. By 2004, programs were available on the Web that could break a WEP-encrypted data stream in three minutes or less. This flaw was recognized fairly quickly, and subsequent standards replaced WEP with the more secure WPA2 (Wi-Fi Protected Access).

When the holes in WEP were first discovered, the Wi-Fi Alliance, keepers of the 802.11 standard, knew they had a problem. The replacement encryption standard that they wanted could not be implemented on many of the existing Wi-Fi Access Points that were built to support WEP. Therefore, the Wi-Fi Alliance decided to release an intermediate standard known as WPA1. This protocol implemented the original encryption algorithm the way it should have been implemented in the first place. Since it was so similar to WEP, WPA1 could be implemented on existing hardware with relatively minor changes to the firmware. Nevertheless, the fixes resulted in a significant increase in security over the flawed WEP implementation. However, WPA1 was never intended to be anything more than a stop-gap. The completely new WPA2 standard was introduced in 2004 and required on all devices built after 2006. Secure applications no longer allow the use of WEP. For example, the Payment Card Industry outlawed its use in 2008. Though I saw support for WPA1 as late as 2010, WPA2 is the state of the art as of this writing.

Index

• *Symbols and Numerics* •

- - (decrement) unary operator
  defined, 50–51
  looping statements, 74–75
  order of precedence, 48
  prefix and postfix versions, 51, 74–75
- (negative) unary operator
  defined, 50
  order of precedence, 48
- (subtraction) binary operator, 48, 136
! (NOT) logical operator, 54
! = (inequality) logical operator, 54
symbol, 154, 158
% (modulus) binary operator, 304
  defined, 48
  order of precedence, 48
& (AND) bitwise operator
  defined, 62
  test program using, 65–67
  using, 64
  values, 63
& (unary) pointer operator, 123–124
&& (AND) logical operator
  defined, 54–55
  general discussion, 53
  short-circuit evaluation, 58–59
( ) parenthesis, order of precedence
  and, 50
* (multiplication) binary operator,
  48, 137
* (unary) pointer operator, 123, 125–126,
  193–194
* . * wildcards, 150
. (dot) operator, 304
/ (division) binary operator, 48
/ / (double slash) comment
  characters, 28

/* */ comment characters, 28
: : (scope resolution) operator, 183–184,
  304, 375
; (semicolons), 28
? : (ternary) operator, 304
\ \ (backslash) character, 42–43
^ (XOR) bitwise operator
  defined, 62
  test program using, 65–67
  values, 64
| (OR) bitwise operator
  defined, 62
  test program using, 65–67
  values, 63
| | (OR) logical operator
  defined, 54–55
  short-circuit evaluation, 58
~ (NOT) bitwise operator
  defined, 62
  destructors, 221
  using, 64
  values, 63
+ (addition) binary operator, 48, 136
+ (positive) unary operator
  defined, 50
  order of precedence, 48
++ (increment) unary operator
  defined, 50–51
  iterators, 377
  looping statements, 74
  order of precedence, 48
  prefix and postfix versions, 51
  reasons for creating, 51
< (less than) logical operator, 54–55, 371
<< (insertion) operator, 304, 315–316, 371
<= (less than or equal to) logical
operator, 54–55
= (assignment operator), 30, 51–52, 54,
  371, 375

== (equality) logical operator
  assignment operator versus, 54
  defined, 54
  `list` class, 375
  `string` class, 371
-> (arrow) operator, 194, 304
> (greater than) logical operator, 54–55, 371
>= (greater than or equal to) logical
    operator, 54–55
>> (extraction) operator, 304, 315–316, 371
\0 (null character), 42–43, 114–115
\0nn (octal character), 42–43

• A •

abstract classes
  concept of, 295–297
  passing, 298
  subclasses of, 298
`accumulator` value, 81, 84, 109
addition (+) binary operator, 48, 136
Address Space Layout Randomization
    (ASLR), 404
AND (&) bitwise operator
  defined, 62
  test program using, 65–67
  using, 64
  values, 63
AND (&&) logical operator
  defined, 54–55
  general discussion, 53
  short-circuit evaluation, 58–59
app flag, 318
`append( )` function, 371
arguments
  default values for, 101–102
  defined, 93
  functions with, 95–97
  functions with multiple, 97
  optional nature of, 94
  passing by reference, 102–103
  passing by value, 102–103
ArrayDemo sample program
  `displayArray( )` function, 108–109
  `inputValues[ ]` array, 109
  overview, 107–108

`readArray( )` function, 108–109
`sumArray( )` function, 108–109
ArrayOfStudents sample program, 191–192
arrays
  accessing individual elements of, 106
  applying operators to addresses,
      138–139
  arrays of, 112
  of characters
    concatenating strings, 115–117
    creating, 112–113
    creating strings of characters, 114–115
    utilizing, 146–147
  constructing, 244
  contrasted with pointers, 142–144
  declaring, 106
  defined, 105
  deleting, 224
  disadvantages of, 369
  example of, 107–109
  initializing, 110
  of objects
    allocating off heap, 200
    constructing, 218–219
    declaring, 191–192
  of pointers, 145–146
  range-based loops, 111–112
  relationship to pointers, 136–138
  size of, 106, 109
  string-handling functions, 117–118
  wide string-handling functions, 118–120
  writing beyond range of, 110–111
arrow (->) operator, 194, 304
ASLR (Address Space Layout
    Randomization), 404
`assert( )` function, 165
assignment operator (=), 30, 51–52, 54,
    371, 375
assignment operators
  copy constructors versus, 305–306
  deleting, 310
  move constructor and, 312–314
  order of precedence, 48
  overloading, 305, 306–311
  overview, 51–52
  return type and value, 310

at( ) function, 371
ate flag, 318, 319
auto keyword, 45, 46
automatic variables, 110

• *B* •

backslash character (\\), 42–43
bad( ) function, 320, 323
base 2 (binary) number system, 60
base 8 (octal) number system, 60–61
base 10 (decimal) number system, 59–60
base 16 (hexadecimal) number system,
    61–62
beg flag, 330
begin( ) function, 375, 377–378
binary (base 2) number system, 60
binary flag, 318, 319
binary operators
    defined, 47
    order of precedence, 48
bits, defined, 60
BitTest sample program, 57, 65–66, 328
bitwise logical operators
    defined, 62
    general discussion, 53
    test of, 65–67
    using, 64
    values, 63–64
bool (Boolean) variables
    defined, 39, 44
    list class, 375
    logical operations, 55–56
    string class, 371–372
boolalpha flag, 327
Boolean constants, 40
BoolTest sample program, 55–56
botnets, 382–383
branch statements, 69–71
BranchDemo sample program, 70–71
break command, 80–82, 85
BreakDemo sample program, 80–81
Budget sample programs, 3, 299
buffer overflow
    avoiding, 322, 397–402
    call stack, 389–393
    example of, 387–389

general discussion, 386
hacking, 394–397
operating system helps, 405–406
string class, 402–404
BufferOverflow sample program, 387–389,
    394, 397
bug avoidance
    avoiding multiple inheritance, 416
    avoiding overloading operators, 413
    clear and consistent coding style, 410
    commenting, 412
    declaring destructors virtual, 414–416
    enabling all warning and error messages,
        409–410
    limiting visibility of class internals,
        411–412
    managing heap memory systematically, 413
    single-stepping programs, 413
    using exceptions to handle errors, 414
building, defined, 10
bytes, defined, 60

• *C* •

C++
    basic concepts, 9–11
    comments, 27–28
    declarations, 29
    defined, 2
    expressions
        defined, 30
        storing results of, 30–31
    framework, 27
    I/O statements, 30
    as low-level standard programming
        language, 2
    as object-oriented language, 2
    as portable language, 2
    programs
        building, 24–25
        creating projects, 19–21
        downloading and installing project
            files, 23–24
        entering code, 21–23
        executing, 25–26
    statements, 28–29
    as strongly typed language, 34

C++ 2011 standard
  0x standard, 12
  automatic declarations, 45
  const expressions, 160
  constructing members with initializers, 237–238
  default constructor, 232–233
  delegating constructors, 230–231
  deleting assignment operator, 310
  deleting copy constructor, 258, 310
  for each loops, 79
  explicit keyword, 245
  external template instantiations, 366
  final keyword, 287
  gcc compiler, 10
  inheritance of constructors by subclasses, 279
  initializer lists, 367
  invoking constructors other than default, 244
  iterators, 378, 380
  move constructor, 247, 258, 312–314
  nullptr constant, 145, 202, 309
  override descriptor, 286–287
  range-based loops, 111–112, 144
  size of arrays, 106
  size_type type, 372
  static member functions, 267
  static_assert( ) function, 165
  wchar_t variables, 43
C++ 2014 standard
  binary numbers, 62
  const expressions, 161
  constant expressions, 85
  defining constants of separate, user-defined types, 161–162
  gcc compiler, 10
  size of arrays, 106
cache flushing, 329
CALL instruction, 390–392, 396–397
CallMemberFunction sample program, 179–182
CallStaticMember sample program, 265–267
capacity( ) function, 371
CascadingException sample program, 340–342

case sensitivity
  general discussion, 2, 22
  statements, 29
  variables, 29
catch keyword, 337–338, 340, 342, 345
cerr object, 316–317
char (character) variables
  char string variables versus, 40
  character sets, 43
  defined, 39, 44
  naming conventions, 45
char string (character string) variables
  char variables versus, 40
  defined, 39
  naming conventions, 45
char_16t (UTF-16 character) variables, 43
char_32t (UTF-32 character) variables, 43
CharDisplay sample program, 113
cin input device, 30, 316
class keyword, 176
class members, 262. *See also* static members
classes
  abstract
    concept of, 295–297
    passing, 298
    subclasses of, 298
  accessing members of, 177
  creating objects from, 176
  defined, 171, 175, 215
  format of, 176
  member functions
    accessing other members from, 182
    calling, 180–182
    defining, 177, 179–180
    defining in classes, 185–186
    defining separately from classes, 187–188
    identifying current object, 183
    overloading, 188–189
    reasons for using, 177
  naming conventions, 176
  objects versus, 215
  protected members
    function of, 208–209
    general discussion, 207

giving nonmember functions access to, 211–213

need for, 208

protecting internal state of classes, 210

using classes with limited interfaces, 211

scope resolution, 183–184

clear( ) function, 320, 323, 375

clog object, 316

close( ) function, 323

code obfuscation, 426–428

Code::Blocks environment

32-bit program, 26

creating projects, 19–21

defined, 10

downloading, 5

installing

for Macintosh, 15–19

for Ubuntu Linux, 13–15

for Windows, 11–14

Management window, 21–22

windowed programs, 11, 26

Command Line Tools (Mac), installing, 16–17

comments

creating while coding, 412

defined, 27

length of, 28

compare( ) function, 371

comparison operators, defined, 54

compilers, defined, 10

compiling, defined, 10

computer language (machine language), 9

concat( ) function, 370

Concatenate sample program

original version of, 115–117

wide character version of, 119–120

concrete classes, 296

concrete functions, 296

conditional clause, 75

conditional compilation, 163

const keyword, 40, 129–130, 143, 160–161, 165

constants

Boolean, 40

floating-point, 37

integer, 40

long integer, 40

variables declared as, 40–41

constexpr constant, 160–161

ConstructArray sample program, 218–219

ConstructDataMembers sample program, 236–237

ConstructingMembers sample program, 233–235

ConstructMembers sample program, 219–221

ConstructMembersWithInitializers sample program, 237–239

constructors

cannot be virtual, 288

combining, 230–231

constructing arrays, 244

constructing complex data members, 233–237

constructing constant data members, 239

constructing duplexes, 219–221

constructing members with initializers, 237–239

constructing multiple objects, 218–219

constructing single objects, 217–218

constructing subclasses, 278–279

copy

assignment operator versus, 305–306

automatic, 250–251

example of, 248–250

overview, 247

reasons for using, 248

shallow versus deep copies, 252–255

temporary objects, 256–258

default, 231–233, 235

defined, 216

defining with arguments, 225–227

delegating, 230–231

inheritance of by subclasses, 279

move, 258–260, 312–314

multiple inheritance, 356–357

open files for input and output, 317–318

overloading, 228–231

rules for order of construction

global objects, 241–243

local objects, 240

order of declaration, 243

overview, 239–240

static objects, 240–241

type conversion, 245

ConstructorsCallingEachOther sample program, 230–231
ConstructorWArg sample program, 226
ConstructorWDefaults sample program, 229–230
ConstructSeparateID sample program, 235–236
ConstructStatic sample program, 240–241
continue command, 82
ContinueDemo sample program, 82
Conversion sample program
  building, 24–25
  comments, 27–28
  creating project, 19–21
  declarations, 29
  downloading and installing project files, 23–24
  entering code, 21–23
  executing, 25–26
  expressions
    defined, 30
    storing results of, 30–31
  framework of, 27
  I/O statements, 30
  statements, 28–29
cookies, 425–426
copy constructors (X::X(const X&))
  automatic, 250–251
  example of, 248–250
  overview, 247
  reasons for using, 248
  shallow versus deep copies, 252–255
  temporary objects, 256–258
CopyConstructor sample program, 248–250
cout output device, 30, 316
__cplusplus__ constant, 164
.CPP extension, 9
create( ) function, 413
cur flag, 330
CustomExceptionClass sample program, 342–345

• D •

data( ) function, 412
Data Execution Prevention (DEP), 404–405
__DATE__ constant, 164

Debian Linux, 14–15
dec flag, 327, 334
decimal (base 10) number system, 59–60
declarations
  automatic, 45
  defined, 29
  function, 92
  prototype, 99–100
decltype( ) keyword, 45, 46
decrement (--) unary operator
  defined, 50–51
  looping statements, 74–75
  order of precedence, 48
  prefix and postfix versions, 51, 74–75
DeepCopy sample program, 254–255
default keyword, 232
DefaultCopyConstructor sample program, 250–251
#define command
  defined, 154
  defining constants to be used throughout program, 157–158
  defining function-like macros with arguments, 158–159
  inline functions, 160
delete keyword, 133–134, 222, 224, 233, 253
DemoAssignmentOperator sample program, 306–311
DemoMoveOperator, 313–314
demotion, defined, 45
denial of service (DoS) attacks, 382–383
DEP (Data Execution Prevention), 404–405
DestructMembers sample program, 222–224
destructors
  closing files for input and output, 319
  declaring virtual, 288–289, 414–416
  destructing subclasses, 279
  reasons for using, 221
  using, 221–224
digital certificates, 429
display( ) function, 344
DisplayMonths sample program, 147
DisplayString sample program, 114, 140
division (/) binary operator, 48
do . . . while loops, 73
DoS (denial of service) attacks, 382–383

dot (.) operator, 304
double (double precision) variables
  accuracy, 38, 41
  defined, 39
  naming conventions, 45
  range, 38, 41
  size, 41
double slash (//) comment characters, 28

• E •

editors, defined, 10
#else command, 163
empty( ) function, 372, 375
encryption, 429–430
end( ) function, 375, 377
end flag, 330
#endif command, 163
endl value, 55–56, 329
environments, defined, 10
eof( ) function, 322, 323
equality (==) logical operator
  assignment operator versus, 54
  defined, 54
  list class, 375
  string class, 371
#error command, 164–165
error messages. *See also* exception
    handling mechanism
  creating compiler errors, 164
  enabling all, 409–410
  error: expected primary-
    expression before '>' token, 25
  file state, 320
  illegal SQL statement, 385
  overview, 24–25
  sent to cerr, 317
ESP (stack pointer), 390–392, 396
exception( ) function, 324
exception handling mechanism
  example of, 337–338
  exception specification, 339
  overview, 414
  process for, 340–341
  reasons for using, 339
  rethrowing exceptions up the chain,
    345–346
  throwing objects, 342–345

executable files (.exe), 10, 154
explicit keyword, 245
expressions
  calculation, 30
  defined, 30
  mathematical operations, 48–49
  mixed-mode, 44–45
  storing results of, 30–31
extended names (signatures), 98
extern keyword, 366
extraction (>>) operator, 304, 315–316, 371

• F •

factorial( ) function, 337–339
FactorialException sample program,
    337–338
factoring
  abstract classes
    concept of, 295–297
    passing, 298
    subclasses of, 298
  culling common properties from similar
    classes, 294–295
  defined, 291
  direct inheritance versus, 292–294
fail( ) function, 320, 322
__FILE__ constant, 164, 344
FileCopy sample program, 326–327
fileFunc( ) function, 345–346
fill( ) function, 324, 328, 334
final keyword, 286–287
find( ) function, 372, 374
fixed flag, 327
flags( ) function, 324, 327–328
float (floating-point) variables
  accuracy, 38, 41
  calculation speed, 37
  counting, 37
  defined, 36, 39
  logical operations, 57–58
  naming conventions, 45
  overflow, 42
  overview, 36–37
  range, 38, 41
  size, 41
FloatAverage sample program, 37–38
floating-point constants, 37

flow-control statements
  branch statements, 69–71
  looping statements
    autoincrement/autodecrement
      feature, 74–75
    avoiding infinite loops, 78
    break command, 80–82
    continue command, 82
    general discussion, 71
    for loops, 75–78
    nesting, 82–84
    range-based loops, 79
    while loops, 72–73
  overview, 69
  switch statements, 84–85
flush( ) function, 324, 329
for each loops (range-based loops), 79,
    111–112, 144
for loops
  conditional clause, 75
  empty sections, 76
  examples of, 76–78
  format of, 75
  initialization clause, 75
ForDemo sample programs, 76–78
ForEachDemo sample program, 79
forward declarations, 212
friend keyword, 211–213
  __func__ constant, 164, 344
function declarations, 92
functional programming
  abstraction, 170–171
  classification, 172
  member functions, 178–179
FunctionDemo sample program
  calling sumSequence( ), 92–93
  defining displayExplanation( ), 92
  defining sumSequence( ), 92
  overview, 89–92
  splitting loops into multiple
    functions, 93
functions. *See also* member functions
  arguments
    default values for, 101–102
    defined, 93
    functions with, 95–97
    functions with multiple, 97

optional nature of, 94
passing by reference, 102–103
passing by value, 102–103
defined, 89, 93
example of
  calling sumSequence( ), 92–93
  defining displayExplanation( ), 92
  defining sumSequence( ), 92
  overview, 89–92
  splitting loops into multiple functions, 93
main( ), 97
name collision, 156–157
overloading names of, 98–99
passing objects to
  calling functions with object pointers,
    196–197
  calling functions with object values,
    195–196
  calling functions with reference
    operator, 198–199
  memory consumption and copying
    objects, 199
passing pointers to
  as arguments, 127–128
  by reference, 128–129
  by value, 127, 129
prototype declarations, 99–100
return values, 93–94
simple, 94
variable storage types, 104
fuzzing the program, 418

• *G* •

-g switch, 427
gcc compiler
  defined, 10
  downloading, 5
  installing
    for Macintosh, 16–19
    for Ubuntu Linux, 14–15
    for Windows, 11–13
gcount( ) function, 324, 325, 327
get( ) function, 324, 325
getline( ) function, 324, 325, 332,
    402–403

getString( ) function, 388, 390–394,
    396–398, 401–404
global objects
  defined, 216, 240
  going out of scope, 222
  rules for order of construction, 239,
    241–243
good( ) function, 320, 324, 327
GraduateStudent sample program, 278–279
greater than (>) logical operator, 54–55, 371
greater than or equal to (>=) logical
    operator, 54–55

• *H* •

.h extension, 157
hacker-proof code
  avoiding user input assumptions, 417–418
  botnets, 382–383
  buffer overflow
    avoiding, 397–402
    call stack, 389–393
    example of, 387–389
    general discussion, 386
    hacking, 394–397
    operating system helps, 405–406
    string class, 402–404
  checking for illegal input, 418–419
  code obfuscation, 426–428
  denial of service attacks, 382–383
  development process, 421
  digital certificates, 429
  encryption, 429–430
  exception handling, 418–419
  fuzzing the program, 418
  general discussion, 381
  hackers' motives, 381–382
  program logs, 419–421
  remote session management, 425–426
  secure user authentication, 423–425
  SQL injection
    avoiding, 386
    example of, 383–385
  version control, 421–423
HAS_A relationships, 280
head pointers, 202, 265

heap memory
  allocating arrays of objects off, 200
  allocating objects off, 199–200
  assignment operator, 306
  classes that automatically
    allocate, 201
  constructors and destructors, 217,
    221–223, 227, 252–254
  exception handling mechanism,
    345–346
  limited scope, 131–133
  managing systematically, 413
  overview, 130–131
  solving scope issues using, 133–134
hex flag, 327, 334
hexadecimal (base 16) number system,
    61–62
hexidecimal character (\xnn), 42–43

• *I* •

identity theft, 382
#if command, 154, 162–163
if statements, 70–71
#ifdef command, 163
#ifndef command, 163
ifstream class, 317, 319, 320–321
in flag, 318, 319
#include command, 157
  defined, 154
  enclosing file in quotes versus
    brackets, 155
  include files, 155, 157, 186
increment (++) unary operator
  defined, 50–51
  iterators, 377
  looping statements, 74
  order of precedence, 48
  prefix and postfix versions, 51
  reasons for creating, 51
indentation, 22, 71
inequality (!=) logical operator, 54
infinite loops, 78
inheritance
  defined, 171, 273–274
  example of, 275–277

inheritance *(continued)*
  factoring
    abstract classes, 295–298
    culling common properties from similar
      classes, 294–295
    defined, 291
    direct inheritance versus, 292–294
  HAS_A relationships, 280
  IS_A relationships, 274–275, 291
  multiple inheritance mechanism
    avoiding, 416
    disadvantages of, 357
    general discussion, 347
    name collision, 349–351
    object construction, 356–357
    overview, 348–349
    virtual inheritance, 350–356
  need for, 274–275
  polymorphism (late binding)
    constructors, 288
    declaring functions as not
      overrideable, 287
    declaring functions virtual, 285–286
    defined, 284
    destructors, 288–289
    need for, 284
    overriding base class functions,
      281–284, 286–287
    static member functions, 287
  subclasses
    constructing, 278–279
    destructing, 279
    inheriting constructors, 279
    overview, 277
  transitive nature of, 275
InheritanceExample sample program,
  275–277
initialization clause, 75
initializer lists
  arrays, 110
  defined, 244
  invoking constructors other than
    default, 244
  range-based loops, 79
  templates, 366–368
inline functions, 160
  advantages of, 186
  defining member functions in classes,
    185–186

inline keyword, 160
insert ( ) function, 372, 374, 375
insertion (<<) operator, 304, 315–316, 371
instances, defined, 171, 176
int (integer) variables
  accuracy, 41
  defined, 34, 38
  logical operations, 57
  naming conventions, 45
  overflow, 42
  range, 36, 41
  size, 41
  truncation, 35–36
IntAverage sample program, 37, 154
integer constants, 40
integers, defined, 34
intrinsic constants, 164–165
I/O statements, 30
IS_A relationships, 274–275, 291
isLegal sample program, 101
istream class, 316, 323, 329–330, 371
istringstream class, 330, 332–333
istrstream class, 330
iteration, defined, 110
iterators, 376–378

• J •

JMP instruction, 396

• L •

late binding. *See* polymorphism
Layout sample program, 123–124
lcd ( ) function, 414
left flag, 327
length ( ) function, 372
less than (<) logical operator,
  54–55, 371
less than or equal to (<=) logical
  operator, 54–55
level of abstraction, 170
__LINE__ constant, 164, 344
linked lists
  adding objects to head of, 202
  advantages of, 201
  declaring linkable classes, 202
  defined, 201

example of, 203–206
head pointers, 202
moving through elements in, 203
LinkedListClass sample program, 268
LinkedListData sample program,
203–206
linker, 154
linking, defined, 10
list class
example of, 378–380
iterators, 376–378
methods of, 375–376
operations on entire lists, 378
overview, 375
lists
initializer
arrays, 110
defined, 244
invoking constructors other than
default, 244
range-based loops, 79
templates, 366–368
linked
adding objects to head of, 202
advantages of, 201
declaring linkable classes, 202
defined, 201
example of, 203–206
head pointers, 202
moving through elements in, 203
Little Endian, 391, 393
local objects
defined, 216
going out of scope, 222
rules for order of construction,
239–240
logical operations
bitwise logical operators
defined, 62
general discussion, 53
test of, 65–67
using, 64
values, 63–64
reasons for using, 53–54
short-circuit evaluation, 58–59

simple logical operators, 53, 54
storing logical values
Boolean variables, 55–56
floating-point variables, 57–58
integer variables, 57
long double variables
accuracy, 41
defined, 39
range, 41
size, 41
long int (long integer) variables
accuracy, 41
defined, 38
naming conventions, 45
range, 41
size, 41
long integer constants, 40
long long int (long long integer)
variables
accuracy, 41
defined, 39
range, 41
size, 41
looping statements
autoincrement/autodecrement feature,
74–75
avoiding infinite loops, 78
break command, 80–82
continue command, 82
general discussion, 71
for loops, 75–78
nesting, 82–84
range-based loops, 79
while loops, 72–73

• M •

machine language (computer
language), 9
Macintosh
installing Code::Blocks environment,
17–19
installing Command Line Tools, 16–17
installing Xcode, 16
MacroConfusion sample program, 158

main( ) function
  accessing arguments to, 148–149
    from Code::Blocks, 150
    from command prompt, 149–150
    from Windows, 150–151
  overview, 97
  rules for order of construction, 241–242
manipulators, 333–335
mathematical operations
  applying to pointer variables, 135–136
  assignment operators, 51–52
  binary operators, 47–48
  expressions, 48–49
  general discussion, 47
  order of precedence, 49–50
  unary operators, 50–51
max_size( ) function, 372
maximum( ) function, 359–361
MaxTemplate sample program, 360–361
MD5 algorithm, 423–424
member functions
  accessing other members from, 182
  calling, 180–182
  constructors
    cannot be virtual, 288
    combining, 230–231
    constructing arrays, 244
    constructing complex data members,
      233–237
    constructing constant data members, 239
    constructing duplexes, 219–221
    constructing members with initializers,
      237–239
    constructing multiple objects, 218–219
    constructing single objects, 217–218
    copy, 247–258
    default, 231–233, 235
    defined, 216
    defining with arguments, 225–227
    delegating, 230–231
    move, 258–260, 312–314
    multiple inheritance, 356–357
    open files for input and output, 317–318
    overloading, 228–231
    rules for order of construction, 239–243
    type conversion, 245
  defining, 177, 179–180
  defining in classes, 185–186

defining separately from classes, 187–188
destructors
  declaring virtual, 288–289
  reasons for using, 221
  using, 221–224
identifying current object, 183
overloading, 188–189
overriding base class functions, 281–284
reasons for using, 177
static, 265–267, 287
virtual
  constructors, 288
  declaring, 285–286
  declaring functions as not
    overrideable, 287
  destructors, 288–289
  overriding base class functions, 286–287
  pure, 296
  static, 287
methods, 180. *See also* member functions
Microsoft Windows, installing Code::Blocks
    environment, 11–14
MinGW Compiler Suite, 12
mixed-mode expressions, 44–45
modules
  defined, 99
  headers, 410
modulus (%) binary operator
  defined, 48
  order of precedence, 48
  syntax changes, 304
move constructors (X::X(X&&)), 258–260,
    312–314
MoveCopy sample program, 258–260
multiple inheritance mechanism
  avoiding, 416
  disadvantages of, 357
  general discussion, 347
  name collision, 349–351
  object construction, 356–357
  overview, 348–349
  virtual inheritance, 350–356
MultipleInheritance sample program,
    348–349
MultipleInheritanceFactoring sample
    program, 351–354
multiplication (*) binary operator, 48, 137

• *N* •

\n (newline character), 28, 42, 154, 319, 329
name collision, 156–157, 349–350
NameDataSet sample program, 268–269
namespaces, 156–157
negative (-) unary operator
  defined, 50
  order of precedence, 48
nested loops, 82–84
NestedDemo sample program, 83–84, 90
new keyword, 133–134
newline character (\n), 28, 42, 154, 319, 329
No Operation (NOP) instruction, 396
NoBufferOverflow sample programs,
    398–403
nonmember functions
  defined, 180
  giving access to protected members,
    211–213
NOP (No Operation) instruction, 396
NOT (!) logical operator, 54
NOT (~) bitwise operator
  defined, 62
  destructors, 221
  using, 64
  values, 63
NTBS (null-terminated byte strings),
    114–115
null character (\0), 42–43, 114–115
nullptr constant, 144–145, 149, 202,
    309, 418
null-terminated byte strings (NTBS),
    114–115
number systems
  binary (base 2), 60
  decimal (base 10), 59–60
  hexadecimal (base 16), 61–62
  octal (base 8), 60–61
Nx flag, 404

• *O* •

object files (.o), 154
object-oriented programming (OOP)
  abstraction, 169–170
  classification, 171–172
  functional programming versus, 170–172
objects
  allocating off heap memory, 199–200
  arrays of
    allocating off heap memory, 200
    declaring, 191–192
  classes versus, 215
  creating from classes, 176
  defined, 215
  global
    defined, 216, 240
    going out of scope, 222
    rules for order of construction, 239,
      241–243
  local
    defined, 216
    going out of scope, 222
    rules for order of construction, 239–240
  naming conventions, 176
  object pointers
    arrow pointers, 194
    declaring, 192–193
    dereferencing, 193–194
  passing to functions
    calling functions with object pointers,
      196–197
    calling functions with object values,
      195–196
    calling functions with reference
      operator, 198–199
    memory consumption and copying
      objects, 199
  static
    defined, 240
    rules for order of construction, 239–241
ObjPtr sample program, 192–193
oct flag, 327, 334
octal (base 8) number system, 60–61
octal character (\0nn), 42–43
ofstream class, 317–318, 319
online resources
  Budget sample program source code, 3
  Cheat Sheet (companion to book), 4
  Code::Blocks environment, 5
  Command Line Tools (Mac), 16–17
  Frequently Asked Questions (FAQ), 5
  gcc compiler, 5
  source code (companion to book), 4
  Xcode development package, 16

OOP. *See* object-oriented programming
open( ) function, 324
openFile( ) function, 321–322
operators
  assignment, 30
  defined, 30
  functions versus, 303–304
  overloading, 304, 413
OR (|) bitwise operator
  defined, 62
  test program using, 65–67
  values, 63
OR (| |) logical operator
  defined, 54–55
  short-circuit evaluation, 58
ostream class, 316, 323, 371
ostringstream class, 330, 333
ostrstream class, 330
out flag, 318, 319
outline functions, 187–188
OverloadConstructor sample program,
    228–229
overloading
  assignment operators, 305, 306–311
  constructors, 228–231
  functions, 98–99
  member functions, 188–189
  operators, 304, 413
  subscript operator, 311
OverloadOverride sample program,
    282–283, 285
override descriptor, 286–287

• P •

parameters, 148
parseString( ) function, 332–333
PassObjPtr sample program, 196–197
PassObjRef sample program, 198–199
PassObjVal sample program, 195–196
pointer variables
  accessing arguments to main( )
    from Code::Blocks, 150
    from command prompt, 149–150
    overview, 148–149
    from Windows, 150–151

addresses, 122–123
applying operators to, 135–136, 142
arrays
  applying operators to addresses,
    138–139
  of character strings, 146–147
  contrasted with pointers, 142–144
  of pointers, 145–146
  relationship to pointers, 136–138
const keyword, 129–130
defined, 121
head pointers, 202
heap memory block
  limited scope, 131–133
  overview, 130–131
  solving scope issues using, 133–134
link pointers, initializing, 202, 205
nullptr constant, 144–145
object pointers
  arrow pointers, 194
  declaring, 192–193
  dereferencing, 193–194
operators, 123–124
passing to functions
  as arguments, 127–128
  by reference, 128–129
  by value, 127, 129
positioning within files, 329–330
string manipulation
  with character pointers, 139–141
  improving efficiency with, 141
using, 125–126
variable size, 121–122
polymorphism (late binding)
  constructors, 288
  declaring functions as not
    overrideable, 287
  declaring functions virtual, 285–286
  defined, 284
  destructors, 288–289
  need for, 284
  overriding base class functions, 281–284,
    286–287
  static member functions, 287
pop_back( ) function, 375
pop_front( ) function, 375

positive (+) unary operator
  defined, 50
  order of precedence, 48
precision( ) function, 324, 334
preprocessor
  commands
    #define command, 154, 157–162
    #if command, 154, 162–163
    #include command, 154–155, 157
  defined, 153–154
  intrinsic constants, 164–165
  typedef keyword, 166
PrintArgs sample program, 148–151
private keyword, 209, 411
program logs (system logs)
  maintaining, 420–421
  overview, 419–421
  reviewing, 420
projects
  creating, 19–21
  defined, 19
  naming, 21
promotion, defined, 45
protected keyword. See protected
    members
protected members
  declaring constructors as, 257
  function of, 208–209
  general discussion, 207
  giving nonmember functions access to,
    211–213
  limiting visibility of class internals, 411
  need for, 208
  protecting internal state of classes, 210
  using classes with limited interfaces, 211
public keyword, 176, 208, 277
push_back( ) function, 376
push_front( ) function, 376
put( ) function, 324, 325

● R ●

range-based loops (for each loops), 79,
    111–112, 144
rbegin( ) function, 376
read( ) function, 324, 325–327
Red Hat Linux, 14–15

release( ) function, 413
remove( ) function, 376
removeSpaces( ) function, 374
rend( ) function, 376
replace( ) function, 372
resize( ) function, 372
resolving calls, 189
return 0 statement, 31
right flag, 327

● S ●

salt value, 423–424
SavingsClassOutline sample program,
    187–188
scientific flag, 327
scope
  defined, 131
  limited, 131–134
scope resolution (::) operator, 183–184,
    304, 375
secure hash, 423–424
Secure Socket Layer (SSL), 426
security
  avoiding user input assumptions, 417–418
  checking for illegal input, 418–419
  code obfuscation, 426–428
  development process, 421
  digital certificates, 429
  encryption, 429–430
  exception handling mechanism
    example of, 337–338
    exception specification, 339
    overview, 418–419
    process for, 340–341
    reasons for using, 339
    rethrowing exceptions up the chain,
      345–346
    throwing objects, 342–345
  fuzzing the program, 418
  hacker-proof code
    botnets, 382–383
    buffer overflow, 386–406
    denial of service attacks, 382–383
    general discussion, 381
    hackers' motives, 381–382
    SQL injection, 383–385, 386

security *(continued)*
  multiple inheritance mechanism
    avoiding, 416
    disadvantages of, 357
    general discussion, 347
    name collision, 349–351
    object construction, 356–357
    overview, 348–349
    virtual inheritance, 350–356
  operators
    functions versus, 303–304
    insertion and extraction, 304
    move constructor and operator, 312–314
    overloading assignment operator, 306–311
    overloading subscript operator, 311
    shallow copies, 305–306
  program logs, 419–421
  remote session management, 425–426
  secure user authentication, 423–425
  Standard Template Library
    general discussion, 369–370
    list class, 375–380
    string class, 370–375
  stream I/O
    default stream objects, 316–317
    endl object, 329
    example of, 320–321
    file state, 320
    format control, 327–329
    function of, 315–316
    manipulators, 333–335
    open file modes, 319
    opening and closing files, 317–319
    positioning pointers within files, 329–330
    reading and writing directly to streams, 325–327
    reading from files, 319
    stringstream subclasses, 330–333
    writing to files, 319
  templates
    class template templates, 362–365
    code generation, 365
    compilation and error checking, 366
    external instantiations, 366
    general discussion, 359–360
    generalizing functions into, 360–361
    initializer lists, 366–368
    instantiating, 361
    memory consumption, 366
    string class, 374–375
  version control, 421–423
seekg( ) function, 324, 330
seekp( ) function, 325
segment violation errors, 143
semicolons (;), 28
set manipulator, 334
setf( ) function, 325, 327
setw( ) function, 334
SHA256 algorithm, 423–424
ShallowCopy sample program, 252–253
short int (short integer) variables
  accuracy, 41
  defined, 38
  range, 41
  size, 41
short-circuit evaluation, 58–59
showbase flag, 327
showpoint flag, 328
signatures (extended names), 98
simple logical operators, 53, 54
size( ) function, 372, 376
sizeof keyword, 121
skipws flag, 328
sort( ) function, 376, 378, 380
source files, defined, 9
splice( ) function, 376
SQL (Structured Query Language) injection
  avoiding, 386
  checking for illegal input, 418–419
  example of, 383–385
SquareDemo sample program, 95–97
SSL (Secure Socket Layer), 426
stack pointer (ESP), 390–392, 396
Standard Template Library (STL)
  general discussion, 369–370
  list class
    example of, 378–380
    iterators, 376–378
    methods of, 375–376
    operations on entire lists, 378
    overview, 375

`string` class
  capabilities of, 373–374
  methods of, 370–372
  overview, 370
  template, 374–375
statements
  branch, 69–71
  case sensitivity, 29
  declaration, 29
  defined, 28
  expressions, 30–31
  I/O, 30
  looping
    autoincrement/autodecrement feature,
      74–75
    avoiding infinite loops, 78
    `break` command, 80–82
    `continue` command, 82
    general discussion, 71
    `for` loops, 75–78
    nesting, 82–84
    range-based loops, 79
    `while` loops, 72–73
  switch, 84–85, 146
  whitespace, 28
`static` keyword, 104, 261
static members
  defined, 261
  static data members
    counting objects, 264–265
    flagging actions, 265
    need for, 261–262
    providing space for head pointer, 265
    referencing, 263–264
    using, 262–263
  static member functions, 265–267, 287
  `this` keyword, 268–269
static objects
  defined, 240
  rules for order of construction, 239–241
`static_assert( )` function, 165
`__STDC__` constant, 164
STL. *See* Standard Template Library
STLListStudents sample program, 378–380
STLString sample program, 373–374
`strcat( )` function, 118
`strcmp( )` function, 118

`strcpy( )` function, 118, 143, 359
stream I/O
  default stream objects, 316–317
  `endl` object, 329
  example of, 320–321
  file state, 320
  format control, 327–329
  function of, 315–316
  manipulators, 333–335
  open file modes, 319
  opening and closing files, 317–319
  positioning pointers within files, 329–330
  reading and writing directly to streams,
    325–327
  reading from files, 319
  `stringstream` subclasses, 330–333
  writing to files, 319
StreamInput sample program, 320–323
StreamOutput sample program, 318
`string` class
  capabilities of, 373–374
  methods of, 370–372
  overview, 370
  template, 374–375
string manipulation
  with character pointers, 139–141
  functions for, 117–118
  wide functions for, 118–120
`string` variable, 120
StringStream sample program, 330–333
`strlen( )` function, 118
`strncat( )` function, 118
`strncmp( )` function, 118
`strncpy( )` function, 118
`strstr( )` function, 118
`struct` keyword, 176
Structured Query Language. *See* SQL
    injection
subclasses
  of abstract classes, 298
  constructing, 278–279
  defined, 171
  destructing, 279
  inheriting constructors, 279
  overview, 277
`submit( )` function, 384
subscript operator, overloading, 311

substr( ) function, 372
subtraction (-) binary operator, 48, 136
switch statements, 84–85, 146
system logs. *See* program logs
sz prefix, 115

• T •

\t (tab character), 42–43
tellg( ) function, 325, 329
tellp( ) function, 325, 330
template keyword, 361
Template sample program, 27
templates
  class template templates, 362–365
  code generation, 365
  compilation and error checking, 366
  external instantiations, 366
  general discussion, 359–360
  generalizing functions into, 360–361
  initializer lists, 366–368
  instantiating, 361
  memory consumption, 366
  Standard Template Library
    general discussion, 369–370
    list class, 375–380
    string class, 370–375
  stream I/O, 317
  string class, 374–375
TemplateVector sample program, 362–365,
  367–368
ternary (? :) operator, 304
this keyword, 268–269
throw keyword, 337–338, 342–346
__TIME__ constant, 164
__TIMESTAMP__ constant, 164
Transport Layer Security (TLS), 426
trunc flag, 318, 319
truncation
  avoiding with floating-point variables,
    36–37
  defined, 35
  logical operations, 57–58
  overview, 35–36
try keyword, 337–338, 340, 342
typedef keyword, 166

• U •

Ubuntu Linux
  installing Code::Blocks environment, 15
  installing gcc compiler, 14–15
unary operators, order of precedence, 48
Unicode Transformation Format (UTF),
  43–44
unique( ) function, 376
unitbuf flag, 328
unsetf( ) function, 325, 327
unsigned keyword, 39
unsigned variables, 39
unwinding the stack, 340
uppercase flag, 328
user authentication, 423–425
UTF (Unicode Transformation Format),
  43–44
UTF-16 character (char_16t) variables, 43
UTF-32 character (char_32t) variables, 43

• V •

variables. *See also* pointer variables
  automatic, 110
  Boolean
    defined, 39, 44
    list class, 375
    logical operations, 55–56
    string class, 371–372
  character
    char string variables versus, 40
    character sets, 43
    defined, 39, 44
    naming conventions, 45
  character string
    char variables versus, 40
    defined, 39
    naming conventions, 45
  common types, 38–40
  declaring
    automatically, 45
    constant, 40–41
    overview, 33–34
  defined, 29, 33

double precision
  accuracy, 38, 41
  defined, 39
  naming conventions, 45
  range, 38, 41
  size, 41
floating-point
  accuracy, 38, 41
  calculation speed, 37
  counting, 37
  defined, 36, 39
  logical operations, 57–58
  naming conventions, 45
  overflow, 42
  overview, 36–37
  range, 38, 41
  size, 41
integer
  accuracy, 41
  defined, 34, 38
  logical operations, 57
  naming conventions, 45
  overflow, 42
  range, 36, 41
  size, 41
  truncation, 35–36
long double
  accuracy, 41
  defined, 39
  range, 41
  size, 41
long double precision
  accuracy, 41
  defined, 39
  range, 41
  size, 41
long integer
  accuracy, 41
  defined, 38
  naming conventions, 45
  range, 41
  size, 41
long long integer
  accuracy, 41
  defined, 39
  range, 41
  size, 41

mixed-mode expressions, 44–45
naming, 29
nonprintable characters, 42–43
overflow, 42
range, 41
short integer
  accuracy, 41
  defined, 38
  range, 41
  size, 41
signed and unsigned versions, 39
syntax, 29
unsigned, 39
UTF-16 character, 43
UTF-32 character, 43
wide character, 39, 43–44
VariableSize sample program, 121–122
vectors, 362–365
version control, 421–423
virtual inheritance, 350–356
virtual keyword, 285, 354–355
virtual member functions
  constructors, 288
  declaring, 285–286
  declaring functions as not
    overrideable, 287
  destructors, 288–289
  overriding base class functions, 286–287
  pure, 296
  static, 287
VirtualInheritance sample program,
  354–356
Visual Studio, 5
Visual Studio Express, 5
void keyword, 94, 372, 375–376

• **W** •

warning messages, enabling all, 409–410
wcerr object, 316–317
wchar_t (wide character) variables, 39,
  43–44
wcin object, 316–317
wclog object, 316
wcout object, 316–317
wcscat( ) function, 119
wcscmp( ) function, 119

wcscpy( ) function, 119
wcslen( ) function, 119
wcsncat( ) function, 119
wcsncmp( ) function, 119
wcsncpy( ) function, 119
wcsstr( ) function, 119
WEP (Wired Equivalent Privacy), 430
while loops
    autodecrement feature, 74–75
    overview, 72–73
WhileDemo sample program, 72–74
whitespace, 2
    defined, 28
    enforcing, 71
wide character (wchar_t) variables, 39,
    43–44
wide string-handling functions, 118–120
width( ) function, 325, 328–329
Wi-Fi Alliance, 430
Wi-Fi Protected Access (WPA1 and WPA2)
    standards, 430
wifstream class, 317
Wired Equivalent Privacy (WEP), 430

wistream class, 316
workspaces, defined, 24
wostream class, 316
WPA1 and WPA2 (Wi-Fi Protected Access)
    standards, 430
write( ) function, 325–327
wstring class, 374

• *X* •

Xcode development package,
    installing, 16
\xnn (hexidecimal character), 42–43
XOR (^) bitwise operator
    defined, 62
    test program using, 65–67
    values, 64
XOR instruction, 397

• *Z* •

zombies, 383

Notes

Notes

Notes

Notes

Notes

Notes

About the Author

Stephen R. Davis, CISSP (who goes by the name "Randy") lives with his wife and two dogs in Corpus Christi, Texas. Randy has three kids and two grandkids with more on the way (grandkids, not kids). Randy develops browser-based applications for Agency Consulting Group.

Dedication

To Janet, the love of my life.

Author's Acknowledgments

I find it very strange that only a single name appears on the cover of any book, but especially a book like this. In reality, many people contribute to the creation of a *For Dummies* book. From the beginning, acquisitions editor Constance Santisteban, project editor Pat O'Brien, and my agent, Claudette Moore, were involved in guiding and molding the book's content. During the development of the seven editions of this book, I found myself hip-deep in edits, corrections, and suggestions from a group of project editors, copy-editors, and technical reviewers — this book would have been a poorer work but for their involvement. And nothing would have made it into print without the aid of Suzanne Thomas, who coordinated the first and second editions of the book, Susan Pink, who worked on the third and sixth editions, Katie Feltman who worked on the sixth edition, and Danny Kalev, who did the technical review of the sixth and seventh editions. Nevertheless, one name does appear on the cover and that name must take responsibility for any inaccuracies in the text.

Finally, a summary of the animal activity around my house. For those of you who have not read any of my other books, I should warn you that this has become a regular feature of my *For Dummies* books.

I moved to the "big city" in 2005, which meant giving away our dogs Chester and Sadie. I tried to keep our two Great Danes, Monty and Bonnie, but they were just too much for the backyard. We were forced to give them away as well. I married my high school sweetheart in 2011 and moved from Dallas back to my home town of Corpus Christi which meant adopting a new pair of dogs (more like, they adopted me). Jack is a stubborn, black dog of an unidentifiable breed. Scruffy is said to be a wire haired dachshund but you couldn't tell by his appearance as he stays shaved most of the time.

If you are having problems getting started, I maintain a FAQ of common problems at www.stephendavis.com. You can e-mail me questions from there if you don't see your problem. I can't write your program (you don't know how often I get asked to do people's homework assignments), but I try to answer most questions.

Publisher's Acknowledgments

Acquisitions Editor: Connie Santisteban

Project Editor: Pat O'Brien

Copy Editor: Laura K. Miller

Technical Editor: Danny Kalev

Editorial Assistant: Anne Sullivan

Sr. Editorial Assistant: Cherie Case

Project Coordinator: Melissa Cossell

Cover Image: © iStockphoto.com/gavni

Apple & Mac

iPad For Dummies,
5th Edition
978-1-118-72306-7

iPhone For Dummies,
7th Edition
978-1-118-69083-3

Macs All-in-One
For Dummies, 4th Edition
978-1-118-82210-4

OS X Mavericks
For Dummies
978-1-118-69188-5

Blogging & Social Media

Facebook For Dummies,
5th Edition
978-1-118-63312-0

Social Media Engagement
For Dummies
978-1-118-53019-1

WordPress For Dummies,
6th Edition
978-1-118-79161-5

Business

Stock Investing
For Dummies, 4th Edition
978-1-118-37678-2

Investing For Dummies,
6th Edition
978-0-470-90545-6

Personal Finance
For Dummies, 7th Edition
978-1-118-11785-9

QuickBooks 2014
For Dummies
978-1-118-72005-9

Small Business Marketing
Kit For Dummies,
3rd Edition
978-1-118-31183-7

Careers

Job Interviews
For Dummies, 4th Edition
978-1-118-11290-8

Job Searching with Social
Media For Dummies,
2nd Edition
978-1-118-67856-5

Personal Branding
For Dummies
978-1-118-11792-7

Resumes For Dummies,
6th Edition
978-0-470-87361-8

Starting an Etsy Business
For Dummies, 2nd Edition
978-1-118-59024-9

Diet & Nutrition

Belly Fat Diet For Dummies
978-1-118-34585-6

Mediterranean Diet
For Dummies
978-1-118-71525-3

Nutrition For Dummies,
5th Edition
978-0-470-93231-5

Digital Photography

Digital SLR Photography
All-in-One For Dummies,
2nd Edition
978-1-118-59082-9

Digital SLR Video &
Filmmaking For Dummies
978-1-118-36598-4

Photoshop Elements 12
For Dummies
978-1-118-72714-0

Gardening

Herb Gardening
For Dummies, 2nd Edition
978-0-470-61778-6

Gardening with Free-Range
Chickens For Dummies
978-1-118-54754-0

Health

Boosting Your Immunity
For Dummies
978-1-118-40200-9

Diabetes For Dummies,
4th Edition
978-1-118-29447-5

Living Paleo For Dummies
978-1-118-29405-5

Big Data

Big Data For Dummies
978-1-118-50422-2

Data Visualization
For Dummies
978-1-118-50289-1

Hadoop For Dummies
978-1-118-60755-8

Language &
Foreign Language

500 Spanish Verbs
For Dummies
978-1-118-02382-2

English Grammar
For Dummies, 2nd Edition
978-0-470-54664-2

French All-in-One
For Dummies
978-1-118-22815-9

German Essentials
For Dummies
978-1-118-18422-6

Italian For Dummies,
2nd Edition
978-1-118-00465-4

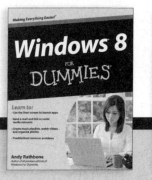 **Available in print and e-book formats.**

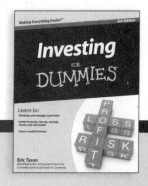 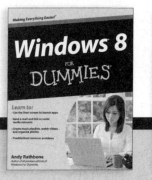  

Available wherever books are sold. **For more information or to order direct visit www.dummies.com**

Math & Science

Algebra I For Dummies,
2nd Edition
978-0-470-55964-2

Anatomy and Physiology
For Dummies, 2nd Edition
978-0-470-92326-9

Astronomy For Dummies,
3rd Edition
978-1-118-37697-3

Biology For Dummies,
2nd Edition
978-0-470-59875-7

Chemistry For Dummies,
2nd Edition
978-1-118-00730-3

1001 Algebra II Practice
Problems For Dummies
978-1-118-44662-1

Microsoft Office

Excel 2013 For Dummies
978-1-118-51012-4

Office 2013 All-in-One
For Dummies
978-1-118-51636-2

PowerPoint 2013
For Dummies
978-1-118-50253-2

Word 2013 For Dummies
978-1-118-49123-2

Music

Blues Harmonica
For Dummies
978-1-118-25269-7

Guitar For Dummies,
3rd Edition
978-1-118-11554-1

iPod & iTunes
For Dummies, 10th Edition
978-1-118-50864-0

Programming

Beginning Programming
with C For Dummies
978-1-118-73763-7

Excel VBA Programming
For Dummies, 3rd Edition
978-1-118-49037-2

Java For Dummies,
6th Edition
978-1-118-40780-6

Religion & Inspiration

The Bible For Dummies
978-0-7645-5296-0

Buddhism For Dummies,
2nd Edition
978-1-118-02379-2

Catholicism For Dummies,
2nd Edition
978-1-118-07778-8

Self-Help & Relationships

Beating Sugar Addiction
For Dummies
978-1-118-54645-1

Meditation For Dummies,
3rd Edition
978-1-118-29144-3

Seniors

Laptops For Seniors
For Dummies, 3rd Edition
978-1-118-71105-7

Computers For Seniors
For Dummies, 3rd Edition
978-1-118-11553-4

iPad For Seniors
For Dummies, 6th Edition
978-1-118-72826-0

Social Security
For Dummies
978-1-118-20573-0

Smartphones & Tablets

Android Phones
For Dummies, 2nd Edition
978-1-118-72030-1

Nexus Tablets
For Dummies
978-1-118-77243-0

Samsung Galaxy S 4
For Dummies
978-1-118-64222-1

Samsung Galaxy Tabs
For Dummies
978-1-118-77294-2

Test Prep

ACT For Dummies,
5th Edition
978-1-118-01259-8

ASVAB For Dummies,
3rd Edition
978-0-470-63760-9

GRE For Dummies,
7th Edition
978-0-470-88921-3

Officer Candidate Tests
For Dummies
978-0-470-59876-4

Physician's Assistant Exam
For Dummies
978-1-118-11556-5

Series 7 Exam For Dummie
978-0-470-09932-2

Windows 8

Windows 8.1 All-in-One
For Dummies
978-1-118-82087-2

Windows 8.1 For Dummies
978-1-118-82121-3

Windows 8.1 For Dummies
Book + DVD Bundle
978-1-118-82107-7

 **Available in print and e-book formats.**

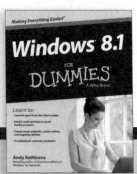

Available wherever books are sold. **For more information or to order direct visit www.dummies.com**

Take Dummies with you everywhere you go!

Whether you are excited about e-books, want more from the web, must have your mobile apps, or are swept up in social media, Dummies makes everything easier.

For Dummies is the global leader in the reference category and one of the most trusted and highly regarded brands in the world. No longer just focused on books, customers now have access to the For Dummies content they need in the format they want. Let us help you develop a solution that will fit your brand and help you connect with your customers.

Advertising & Sponsorships

Connect with an engaged audience on a powerful multimedia site, and position your message alongside expert how-to content.

Targeted ads • Video • Email marketing • Microsites • Sweepstakes sponsorship

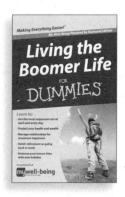

Dummies products make life easier!

- DIY
- Consumer Electronics
- Crafts
- Software
- Cookware
- Hobbies
- Videos
- Music
- Games
- and More!

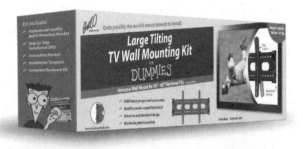

For more information, go to **Dummies.com** and search the store by category.